V. L. PARRINGTON

V. L. Parrington

Through the Avenue of Art

~

H. LARK HALL

The Kent State University Press
Kent, Ohio, and London, England

For my teachers

© 1994 by The Kent State University Press, Kent, Ohio 44242
All rights reserved
Library of Congress Catalog Card Number 93-9201
ISBN 0-87338-480-6
Manufactured in the United States of America

Library of Congress Cataloging-in-Publication Data

Hall, H. Lark, 1949–
    V. L. Parrington : through the avenue of art / H. Lark Hall.
    p.   cm.
    Based on the author's thesis (doctoral)—Case Western Reserve
University, 1979.
    Includes bibliographical references and index.
    ISBN 0-87338-480-6 (alk. paper) ∞
    1. Parrington, Vernon Louis, 1871–1929.   2. American literature—
History and criticism—Theory, etc.   3. English literature—History
and criticism—Theory, etc.   4.   United States—Intellectual life—
Historiography.   5. Great Britain—Intellectual life—
Historiography.   6. Literary historians—United States—Biography.
7. College teachers—United States—Biography.   I. Title.
PS29.P3H24 1994
810.9—dc20   93-9201
                                                                              CIP

British Library Cataloging-in-Publication data are available.

Contents

Preface

"It is with a certain feeling of temerity that I offer the present study of a field of American letters which has been pretty largely neglected," wrote Vernon Louis Parrington on the opening page of *Main Currents in American Thought: An Interpretation of American Literature from the Beginnings to 1920.*[1] It is with a certain feeling of historical justice that I now offer, nearly three-quarters of a century after his death, this first full study of Parrington's life.

Parrington, born in Illinois in 1871 and dying in England in 1929, was a man in search of a personal myth. Successively he found his self-image mirrored in Victorian novels, painting, poetry, Populism, religion, the arts and crafts movement, American literature, and American history. Through it all ran the thread of teaching—at the College of Emporia, the University of Oklahoma, and the University of Washington. His only major books appeared at the end of his life, the three volumes of *Main Currents in American Thought: The Colonial Mind, 1620–1800,* and *The Romantic Revolution in America, 1800–1860,* in 1927 and *The Beginnings of Critical Realism in America, 1860–1920,* in 1930, posthumously, in fragmentary form. *Main Currents,* a rebellious work for a rebellious generation searching for intellectual moorings in a time of political and economic upheaval, was received with near acclaim.

For the next few decades, it was one of the most influential and highly regarded texts in literature, history, and American Studies. But in each of these fields—with the entrenchment of the New Criticism in the 1940s, the rise of consensus history in the 1950s, and the incorporation of social scientific perspectives in the 1960s, respectively—*Main Currents* began to appear as "a noble ruin," its pioneering role discredited and its author "pretty largely neglected." Yet in the 1980s trends in both historical and literary studies helped prepare the way for a fresh look at Parrington and his work: the rapprochement between social history and intellectual history, a self-consciousness of methodology particularly as reflected in efforts to reconstruct the American literary canon, a multidisciplinary interest in critical theory, and the revival of interest in historicism among literary scholars.[2] One can argue that *Main Currents* is the culmination of Parrington's search for a personal myth. If so, a reconsideration of the man will entail a rereading of the text.

I believe that Parrington was a more complex person than we have realized and that his complexities affected the genesis, design, and composition of *Main Currents*. Although his most sympathetic treatments have come from those critics who have considered him as a historian of ideas, none have considered him as an intellectual himself or as a member of the group of intellectuals who came to maturity at the turn of the century and sought to forge a synthesis between culture and politics. This context not only illuminates Parrington's personality; it highlights what I think is the fundamental concern in *Main Currents:* the drama of the life of the mind. Concern with the conditions and prospects of intellectual life in American culture gives a unity to the many biographical portraits in *Main Currents* that is obscured by an explanation based primarily on the function of the liberal tradition in American politics.

The first nine chapters of this book are biographical; the last three chapters offer some directions for new interpretations of *Main Currents*. My intention is not to engage directly in the continuing controversy over the volumes' merits; rather, it is to illumine Parrington's methods in writing them. My primary interest is in biography, not critical debate, although critical debate could scarcely be avoided in portraying a person who practiced it so assiduously.

Parrington's extant personal papers—including correspondence, published and unpublished manuscripts, teaching materials, diaries, architectural drawings, and mementos ranging from photographs snapped on his Brownie camera to hunting rifles—have been privately held since his death and are now in the care of a grandson, Stevens Parrington Tucker, of Pacific Grove, California. The present status of the papers presents several obstacles to conventional documentation procedures. Since the papers are privately held, it is not possible for the reader to consult or to study the original sources, large blocks of which constitute my research materials. Further, if and when the papers or a portion of them are donated to an archive and/or published, very likely they will be organized differently from their current arrangement. Materials not subject to these problems—such as readily available references and accessible archival sources—are conventionally placed in endnotes. However, for Parrington's personal papers, sources difficult to locate, or other privately held materials, I have most often identified the source in the text. The Bibliography provides a checklist of Parrington's writings and should be consulted as an adjunct to the endnotes.

Most of Parrington's remaining effects tightly fill a four-drawer filing cabinet. These documents helped structure the framework and proportions of this biography as well as determined some of its research problems. Parrington saved almost all of his course work from his two years at Harvard, but with the exception of his brief "Autobiographical Sketch," his papers include little information about his family or his own childhood and youth.[3] He saved notes made for class preparation, but many were lost during a disastrous fire at the University of Oklahoma in 1907, and virtually none exist from his University of Washington years after he gave up the lecture method. He kept diaries in pocket-sized notebooks from the time he was nineteen, but after 1905 they became "garden books" containing almost no explicit personal or intellectual information, and a gap exists for the crucial years 1908–17.[4] He saved the typed manuscripts of the poems that occupied so much of his energy in his late twenties and early thirties, but the nearly completed manuscript of a novel, "Stuart Forbes: Stoic," written primarily during his fourteen-month grand tour of England and France, in page after page of his tiny backhand script, remains in disarray.

Parrington preserved many materials documenting the formation of *Main Currents,* including notes and trial chapters dating from the early 1900s as well as the complete manuscripts of two unpublished predecessors: "The Democratic Spirit in American Letters, 1620–1870" (ca. 1914–16) and "The Democratic Spirit in Early American Letters, 1620–1800" (ca. 1923). But most of the books and papers housed in his office at the University of Washington, where he spent the last twenty-one years of his career, disappeared in the weeks following his untimely death. Perhaps they became the treasured souvenirs of devoted students and colleagues. Consequently, gaps appear in the depiction of Parrington's later teaching and idea formulation, at a crucial point when documentation might have been enlightening. For example, his copies of fellow historian Charles A. Beard's works as well as most studies in social criticism used in his classes are missing from the remains of his personal library.

Parrington's correspondence files are nearly bare until 1927, the time of the April publication of the first two volumes of *Main Currents.* For the decade's closing years, they reveal a scholarly network that helps place him in the midst of contemporary academic and critical thinking. (Fortunately, Parrington kept carbon copies of his replies.) After that, there is nearly silence again, except for condolences to his wife, sales records from his publishers, a few notes upon the posthumous publication of the third volume of *Main Currents* in November 1930.

Prior to my work, the Parrington collection had been consulted by only a few other persons. Eric F. Goldman gained permission from Parrington's widow, Julia, to quote from letters and to read other documents, including his unpublished "Autobiographical Sketch," when Goldman prepared "J. Allen Smith: The Reformer and His Dilemma" during the summer of 1942 while guest teaching at the University of Washington; this research was later incorporated in *Rendezvous with Destiny: A History of Modern American Reform* (1953). In the mid-1950s, Parrington's son Vernon L.

Parrington, Jr., used them more extensively in writing a 225-page biographical portrait of his father, which did not reach publication. The papers were in the care of Parrington's son when Richard Hofstadter was given access to them in late 1967 while writing *The Progressive Historians: Turner, Beard, Parrington* (1968). Hofstadter spent four days in late November 1967 in Seattle and tapped this rich resource for his eighty-five-page discussion of Parrington, which has been the longest published study available. Parrington's papers and effects were then stored informally, and the extent of their contents was not fully known until Stevens Parrington Tucker removed them from Seattle after his uncle's death in 1974 and undertook the job of organizing, collating, and in some cases—such as the diaries—transcribing.[5]

The omissions in *The Progressive Historians* aroused my curiosity. In the Bibliographical Essay, Hofstadter stated flatly, "There is no adequate biographical account of Parrington"; "no account of Parrington at the University of Washington"; "Information about intellectual influences on Parrington is fragmentary"; and observed, "I do not know whether his radicalism, undoubtedly raised to a new pitch by the war period and its aftermath, actually waned somewhat by the time *Main Currents* was published." The text raised further issues. There was the underlying paradox of a lifelong professor of English being treated as a historian: could he have been so blind to aesthetics and so ill-prepared in interpreting the past? There was the notation regarding Parrington's "early desire to become a Presbyterian minister" but no effort to trace the impact of religion in his life. (In fact, Parrington was a member of the Methodist Episcopal Church.) There was the claim that Parrington's Harvard experience was "a provocative disaster," yet Parrington's preserved Harvard course work yielded a fascinating commentary on his intellectual development. It became clear that Hofstadter had seen only part of Parrington's papers, for he also did not know about the existence of the diaries, the manuscript of "Stuart Forbes: Stoic," or the typescript of "The Democratic Spirit in American Letters, 1620–1870."[6]

In addition to the debt I owe Richard Hofstadter, both for his provocative questions and his incisive analysis, several other people have been important in shaping my thinking and showing me gaps in the existing portrait of Parrington. Gene Wise's description in *American Historical Explanations* (1973; 2d ed. 1980) of the Progressive and Counter-Progressive historiographical models was influential in developing the view of Parrington as a premodernist rather than a postrealist figure, as a forerunner to, for example, R. W. B. Lewis and Reinhold Niebuhr instead of as a coda to Moses Coit Tyler and Frederick Jackson Turner. Robert A. Skotheim and Kermit Vanderbilt's article "Vernon Louis Parrington: The Mind and Art of a Historian of Ideas" (1962) offered a model for evaluating historical interpretation through literary style. Skotheim's chapter on Parrington in

American Intellectual Histories and Historians (1966) suggested placing him in the context of late nineteenth- and early twentieth-century intellectual life, as an addition to the figures treated by Christopher Lasch in *The New Radicalism in America, 1889–1963: The Intellectual as a Social Type* (1965).

Vanderbilt's classic, *American Literature and the Academy* (1986), is a special case of warm mutual interests in Parrington and in literary history leading to independent undertakings. His chapter on Parrington draws upon my dissertation and was published while I was completing the first draft of this biography. Although I stress that Parrington's primary allegiance and fundamental contribution were to the broad terrain of the history of ideas, we have both made "a new case for Parrington as a literary historian and critic who appreciated . . . aesthetic criteria." We attribute many of the characteristics of the treatment of writers in *Main Currents* to the demands of writing intellectual history rather than strictly literary history, while affirming that Parrington "was able to set aside his ideological bias in favor of liberal writers when he established through his many judgments of aesthetic excellence a canon of sorts for American literature and a miniature pantheon of authors chosen solely on artistic grounds."[7]

A few additional comments on Parrington criticism will help clarify my contribution to it. James L. Colwell's "Populist Image of Vernon Louis Parrington" (1962), which examined the Emporia context of Parrington's intellectual development, inspired my trips to Gorham, Maine, and to the Universities of Oklahoma and Washington as well as back to Kansas. I essentially support Richard Reinitz's explanation of *Main Currents*'s historical outlook in "Vernon Louis Parrington as Historical Ironist" (1977), later incorporated in *Irony and Consciousness: American Historiography and Reinhold Niebuhr's Vision* (1980). I agree, however, with Arthur Ekirch's view, proposed much earlier in "Parrington and the Decline of American Liberalism" (1951) and restated in *The Decline of American Liberalism* (1955), that Parrington's pessimism about the course of American history is clearly manifested in his first volume.

David Noble's interpretation of the Progressive mind influenced me at an early juncture. His chapter on Parrington in *Historians Against History: The Frontier Thesis and the National Covenant in American Historical Writing Since 1830* (1965) persuasively discusses *Main Currents* in the tradition of the jeremiad. Noble's argument is flawed, however, by a common misreading created by the physical distortion of the unfinished Volume 3. The Addenda, the materials collected at the end of *The Beginnings of Critical Realism in America* and supplied by the editor, is not Parrington's text. The final item in the Addenda, "A Chapter in American Liberalism," does not contain Parrington's last words on contemporary culture, for Volume 3 was actually designed to conclude with a positive rating of literary innovations in the 1920s.[8]

Russell J. Reising's *American Quarterly* essay "Reconstructing Parrington" (1989) concurs with my view of Parrington as an inaugurator of trends in modern American literary criticism. Reising is acute in questioning whether Lionel Trilling ever seriously read *Main Currents* before he launched what proved to be the most devastating critical attack on Parrington's sensibility in the essay revised as "Reality in America" for inclusion in *The Liberal Imagination* (1950). In a related vein, Gregory S. Jay's "Hegel and the Dialectics of American Literary Historiography: From Parrington to Trilling and Beyond" (1991) offers detailed substantiation for my argument that Parrington's Marxism is evidenced in his dialectical portrayal of the historical development of American thought.[9]

Much of my interpretation of Parrington's personality can be read as a refutation of Trilling's implication that he was one-dimensional and failed to carry on the cultural dialectic within himself or to recognize it in others. I argue for a reading of *Main Currents*, partly as a reflection of Parrington's internal debate, partly as Parrington envisioning the history of American thought as variations of his own intellectual conflicts, especially the tension between art and politics. Indeed, it is because he could not resolve this tension that *Main Currents* exists in the form it does.

This brings me to the significance of my subtitle. The phrase "through the avenue of art" appears in the approximately fifty-page "Autobiographical Sketch" that Parrington wrote in early 1918. Toward the end of the sketch, he explains how after the turn of the century his interests shifted from art to politics, from belles lettres to social thought, from English literature and culture to American literature and culture:

> Consciously I was neither radical nor conservative, and yet my reading was drawing me inevitably out of the narrower field of polite literature into the new world of social thought that was rising about me. Carlyle, Ruskin, Morris became increasingly my teachers—above all others Morris. I have always been a rebel, I think, but with the bias of my training in art and letters I must enter the field of radicalism through such an avenue if at all. My economics must be sugar-coated for me. Shelley ought to have aroused me, or William Blake; but they did not. And it was not till William Morris came with the charm of his prose style that I was shaken out of the lethargy of the cultural. *To enter the field of modern social thought through the avenue of art,* may seem strange to a younger generation; but it was a common experience in days when Ruskin and Morris were prophets to a world content with its smug Manchesterism. (Emphasis added)

Parrington's description of the process of entering "the field of modern social thought through the avenue of art" provides a conceptual map of his intellectual development and forms the conceptual core of my book. Parrington's uniqueness as a historian—his chosen entryway to the field of modern social thought—comes from growth achieved through an artist's sensibility.

Main Currents in American Thought remains the only attempt by a single author to write "a comprehensive history of national letters from the Puritans to the most recent past."[10] Its cousins in literary history are all multiedited and multiauthored, from *The Cambridge History of American Literature* (1917–21), in which Parrington's essay "The Puritan Divines, 1620–1720," appeared, to *The Literary History of the United States* (1948), to *The Columbia Literary History of the United States* (1988). Such analogues in intellectual history as Charles and Mary Beard's *Rise of American Civilization* (1927) and Merle Curti's *Growth of American Thought* (1943) are written from unified viewpoints but place limited emphasis on the role of creative writers in the shaping of culture.

Ironically, although one persistent theme in Parrington criticism has been his neglect or even dismissal of aesthetic values, the considerable attention *Main Currents* does pay to literature, its bountiful selections from a rich array of primary texts, distinguishes it from more purely historical works, even those of less expansive time sweep as Ralph H. Gabriel's *Course of American Democratic Thought* (1940), Henry Steele Commager's *American Mind* (1950), even Henry May's *End of American Innocence* (1958). Yet Parrington's very desire "to enter the field of modern social thought" caused him to moderate his enthusiasm for particular writers and his personal pleasure in belles lettres in *Main Currents,* the scope of which was broader than the subjects he daily pursued in his literature courses.

Richard Hofstadter has suggested that Parrington's early efforts at self-cultivation in an uninspiring, parochial prairie environment may have helped produce a "sense of the *separateness* of art from the social and physical world."[11] Parrington's intention in *Main Currents* is to yoke social thought and art, history and literature, politics and poetry, yet his judgments are not marked by a reconciling tone or synthesizing ideological strategies but rather by his identification with the autonomous figure of the rebellious artist. As a result, he empathizes with detached outsiders and criticizes ensconced insiders, no matter what their vocational, disciplinary, or political affiliation may be. How this identification was further reinforced by the personal, professional, and pedagogical expectations of early twentieth-century higher education is an underlying theme of this biography. Through the conflicts and paradoxes in his own life, he saw the intellectual and cultural development of the nation writ large.

Despite my desire to vivify Parrington's life, in the following pages the personal Parrington may seem subsumed by the published history of *Main Currents.* For many reasons, Parrington remains an intensely private man. I have rarely exerted my biographer's prerogative to omit details; rather, I have incorporated almost all relevant personal information gathered in my research. A handful of revealing reminiscences by his daughter Louise may serve to set the tone for the portrait to follow. She remembers Parrington (called "Father") playfully keeping candy in his pockets or around his study to be found by his three fond children. She does not recall Parrington raising his voice in anger. The most severe reprimand he ever administered was, "Louise, that does not become you." She treasures the memory of the two broadcasting foxglove seeds in the wooded area surrounding "Camp," the faculty outing club property located across Puget Sound. Later, when she was an English major at the University of Washington, father and daughter would walk to classes from their University District home to the nearby campus, practicing French. Although the family did not attend church, Louise followed Parrington's recommendation to take a course in the Bible as literature, although the professor's class was not nearly as exciting as her father's.[12]

These collective memories—of a calm, cherishing father who loved nature and maintained traditional ideals of culture—do not dovetail with one persistent image of Parrington, that of the fiery Populist committed to social reform and touting the merits of realistic fiction. The disjunction between who Parrington may have been and who we might like him to be is among the paradoxes that mark his career.

He was a lifelong professor of English, who continued to teach nineteenth-century British poetry while developing courses in twentieth-century American literature, but he won a Pulitzer Prize in history. His journey "through the avenue of art" was not without unanticipated costs, but it bore the reward of a sharpened sense of the intellectual's role. He found resonant expression of his own experience in Matthew Arnold's lines from "Stanzas from the Grande Chartreuse":

> Wandering between two worlds, one dead,
> The other powerless to be born,
> With nowhere yet to rest my head,
> Like these, on earth I wait forlorn.[13]

Yet he produced an eloquent testimony to the power of ideas in American life.

Acknowledgments

This book could not have reached completion without the gracious and generous cooperation of the Parrington family. Since I was allowed access to Parrington's papers, I have been extended warm hospitality and the chance to participate in a mutually loved subject. My sense of Parrington's personality was illuminated during an extensive interview with his surviving daughter, Mrs. W. Stevens Tucker (Louise Wrathal Parrington). To her son, Stevens Parrington Tucker, I want to express my deep gratitude for permission to study, consult, and quote Parrington's papers as well as for many personal kindnesses and continued support of a long-term project. Both Professor Tucker and his mother read the final version of my manuscript and assisted in many invaluable tasks in preparation for publication. Professor Tucker also provided all the photographs for this biography, a task for which I owe him special thanks.

The origins of my study can be traced to a fall 1974 seminar at Case Western Reserve University, where I completed a dissertation on Parrington in 1979. A draft of this manuscript was begun in 1981 and finished by 1987. Revisions have proceeded since then, between the claims of family and teaching. My review of recent commentary on Parrington has affirmed rather than altered my views of his significance. I apologize in advance for possible discontinuities in tone and emphasis resulting from the delay between the original formation of my arguments and the current state of literary history and criticism. Some of my early work on Parrington cannot now be duplicated. For example, many of the persons I interviewed in the late 1970s who had known Parrington personally have died, and the house he designed and helped build in Norman, Oklahoma, has been torn down.

Three important errors made in my dissertation can now be corrected. Parrington's mother outlived both her sons and died in 1930, not in 1916, as his children once believed. My photograph of Mary Louise McClellan Parrington's gravestone in the Maplewood Cemetery in Emporia revealed this fact and illuminated a puzzling rift in family history and relations. Parrington's English Department colleague at the University of Oklahoma, Wilbur R. Humphreys, was not fired along with his chairman in 1908 but resigned in protest of the political machinations of the Board of Regents. Yet another photograph taken on a pilgrimage by some persistent travelers confirmed that Parrington is buried in the village cemetery in Winchcombe, England, not in the garden of the George Inn, his lodging when he suffered a massive heart attack on June 16, 1929.

My primary sources and contacts have been supplemented by research in all the major Parrington locales, except for his birthplace in Aurora, Illinois, and the stops on his European travels. Moving from east to west, I would like to acknowledge the help and contributions of the Gorham Historical Society and Cecilia Vaughan; The Way College of Emporia, Victor Paul Wierwille, president, the Emporia Library, the Americus town clerk's office, and several citizens who spoke frankly to a stranger by telephone; John Ezell, former director, and the staff of the Western History Collections, University of Oklahoma Libraries; Gary Lundell of the University of Washington Archives and Records Center, the University of Washington Libraries, and the former Parrington students who corresponded with me, and those who kindly agreed to be interviewed: W. Stull Holt, E. H. Eby, Gladys Savage, Garland Ethel, Robert Burke, Robert Heilman, and Egbert O. Oliver.

For additional assistance, I would also like to acknowledge the National Endowment for the Humanities, for a summer stipend; Colby-Sawyer College, New London, New Hampshire, for a summer study grant; Western Reserve Historical Society, Cleveland, Ohio, for genealogical information; Baker Library, Dartmouth College, the Free Library of Philadelphia, and Van Pelt Library, University of Pennsylvania, for interlibrary loan and other services; and James L. Colwell, for the loan of his personal research materials.

Chapters 4, 5, and 6 include material from "V. L. Parrington's Oklahoma Years, 1897–1908: 'Few Highlights and Much Monotone'?" *Pacific Northwest Quarterly* 72 (January 1981): 20–28. I am grateful for permission to incorporate the essay into this study. Portions of Chapter 3 were included in "A Geography of V. L. Parrington," a paper given at the Pacific Northwest American Studies Association annual meeting in Moscow, Idaho, April 17, 1981, and the second part of Chapter 8 was delivered, with some changes, as "V. L. Parrington: A Literary Refugee Among the Drilled Hosts of the Historians" at the Organization of American Historians annual meeting in Philadelphia, April 3, 1982.

Morrell Heald, Linda K. Kirby, Roger B. Salomon, David D. Van Tassel, and Gene Wise read all or portions of early versions of this manuscript. Robert A. Skotheim and Kermit Vanderbilt graciously took time from other commitments to read and comment on the entire new first draft. Each then performed this invaluable service again as readers for The Kent State University Press. They have been both ideal critics and scholarly models. Russell J. Reising's informative critique guided a midstage revision. My father, Myron M. Hall, and mother, Flora B. Hall, assisted at early stages of research and preparation, and my mother shared the proofreading with me. Carolyn Longo transformed my typescript with her word-processing skills. The staff at The Kent State University Press—especially John Hubbell, Director; Julia Morton, Senior Editor; and Linda Cuckovich, Assistant Editor—and Trudie Calvert, who performed the herculean role of copyeditor, have made the entire publishing process cheerful and instructive. My husband, Thomas R. Quinn, has always made it possible for me to work; and my children, Amity (born during Chapter 8) and Kieran (born just after the notes were compiled), have happily taught me about patience and priorities.

A book so centrally concerned with a teacher and his teaching offers a place to acknowledge, all too belatedly, a debt to Gene Wise (1939–83). Like many who knew him, I came to appreciate the particular meaning Gene gave to the phrase "style of mind." His passion might be summarized as charting changes in ideas, under a variety of cultural influences, over time. As a teacher, he had ample opportunity to witness this phenomenon in his students as we argued our way through the journals kept for his classes. As students, we came to understand it through his example of engagement with the life of learning. Much like Parrington, Gene followed his own scholarly path, published one influential book, and died tragically before his career fulfilled its promise.

V. L. Parrington

1
~

God in History
The Early Years, 1871–1891

The Figure on the Stage

On the night of January 20, 1891, Vernon Parrington stood on the stage of the College of Emporia's Austin Chapel and began to deliver an eighteen-minute oration entitled "God in History." The occasion was one of the highlights of the academic year, the annual oratorical contest. Parrington was nineteen and a half years old, a junior at the small institution founded less than a decade earlier by the Presbyterian Synod of Kansas. The day before the contest, he had practiced his oration, as he had done all fall, before his elocution teacher, Agnes Law. Then he had gone downtown to pick up his clothes, which were being pressed, and to purchase a new shirt and tie. Now, occupying the conspicuous first place on the program, he was conscious of his appearance and mindful of his well-drilled gestures and inflections.

"Across the gulf of centuries," Parrington intoned, "uniting the present and remote past, History throws its mighty span. Keeping pace with the ever-widening sphere of human activity, the record forms an infallible witness to the progress of human development. On it are imprinted the marks of peoples and of ages, and the completed whole will show the struggle of existence." Having painted this panoramic scene, the young orator rhetorically observed: "As successive generations come and go, upon each presses the same thought: What rules in the affairs of men? Is there a higher, a controlling power; or is man thrown upon existence, the plaything of chance?" To answer the question, Parrington brought in an authoritative illustration: "It is said that Gibbon, as he sat among the ruins of Rome and gazed upon their majesty, confessed in his heart, cold skeptic though he was, intervention of a superior destiny." Then, moving from the general to the particular, he queried: "May not we, seated among the vaster ruins of humanity, discern amidst the outward chaos and confusion, the existence of an omnipotent purpose unfolding through the centuries? Shall we not acknowledge the intervention of a supreme power; of one who holds in his hand the destiny of time, and whose purpose shall move on irresistible—the God of History?" Having given his listeners no chance to consider anything but

I

Gibbon's perspective, Parrington answered confidently in the affirmative: "Yes, there is a God in History. A living principle, emanating from a divine origin, actuates the movements of humanity. The source may be veiled in mystery but the living stream flows on, winding through and around society, turning the desert of disorder into a luxuriant ever-blooming garden of design."[1]

With his thesis stated, he applied the requisite flourishes to his argument, one with which the audience could sympathize, for most attended Sunday services—mainly Protestant—and depended for their livelihoods on ever-bearing fields if not ever-blooming gardens. Those imbued with Calvinistic doctrines of grace were in accord with Parrington's explanation of God's method in history—"to effect great results by unexpected means." The parents who had established farms and commercial enterprises in Kansas after the Civil War and were now sending their sons and daughters to college had surely also been motivated by the speaker's explanation of the purpose in history: "What is it that through all the changes of the ages has been calling to struggling man—look up! look up! What is it that has led him out of the darkness and strife of the past into the light and peace of the present, if it not be that unfaltering, divine purpose? If History teaches anything it teaches this—God works for good."

The oration neared conclusion in millennial overtones. Though "theories, practices, institutions spring up, flourish for a time, then fall," nevertheless, "as time draws nearer its completion, the shaping hand of the Divine Architect will become more manifest." Yet Parrington's vision of the millennium was shaped by the spirit of the Sermon on the Mount rather than by the apocalyptic imagery of Revelation: "War and revolution will cease, and peace will work her lasting victories. . . . Naught shall have been in vain, . . . all shall merge in perfect harmony in that final consummation."

With that optimistic profession of faith in the eventual establishment of a peaceful kingdom of God on this earth, Parrington stepped away from the podium. He was followed by his friend Vern Byers, who chose a less lofty theme but one no doubt more pertinent to the daily lives of Emporia citizens, contraction of currency. Next, his closest chum, Vern Cook, spoke on Jewish renationalization, a topic made current by the new Zionist movement. Tom Marshall delivered the fourth and last oration, which treated "men not measures," evidently as the starting point for social reform.

The four contestants were all members of the same fraternity and literary society and constituted almost the entire junior class. Though Parrington had felt somewhat embarrassed throughout his performance, when the points were totaled, all three judges awarded him first on delivery. On thought and composition, two judges rated him second, but one rated him first. Thus "God in History" carried the day, netting the proud winner $25 and the honor of competing in the state tournament. That evening Parrington modestly confided in his diary, "The contest was a decided success."[2]

The figure on the stage of Austin Chapel, professing his faith in a Divine Architect guiding humanity ever onward until His plan is ultimately revealed and History culminates in the establishment of His harmonious kingdom, might be indistinguishable from many another young college student, especially at a denominational school in the early 1890s, who had not yet been exposed to the ideas of Darwin, Marx, and Freud. Certainly that figure bears little resemblance to the author of *Main Currents in American Thought,* known for adapting the economic interpretation of history to literature and for portraying the development of American ideas as a debate between liberal and conservative political traditions.

One wonders whether Parrington would have won first prize if he had offered his audience an alternative to Gibbon's conclusion, if to the question, "Is there a higher, a controlling power?" he had answered "No," man is indeed "thrown upon existence, the plaything of chance." Although the nineteen-year-old did believe in a Divine utopia and did answer affirmatively, "Yes, there is a God in History," a second, contradictory theme can be clearly discerned in his oration. This theme was not audible to his listeners then and would not become audible to many sophisticated critics for a quarter of a century. For to support his belief in the handiwork of a Divine Architect, Parrington made the claim that "the immutable law of progress is dominant" in history. "With an ever-widening sweep humanity moves onward," he perorated, "and each cycle of activity leaves the floodmark of advancement higher." Such a claim may be justified by faith, but it was not justified by human experience when the idea of progress began to clash with twentieth-century reality. By the late 1920s, Parrington joined other liberals and intellectuals, who despaired over the promises of democracy and the viability of traditional cultural values in the wake of World War I, and flatly stated, "It is a misfortune that America has never subjected the abstract idea of progress to critical examination."[3]

In his oration Parrington conjoined his faith in God with a belief in progress as beneficent when he attempted to define the purpose of history. And this search for historical purpose, with its attendant consideration of the role of progress, marks a link between the thinking of the younger and the older man. Similarly, in the oration's discussion of historical development, another such link can be abstracted from its Christian context. To support his claim that God's method is "to effect great results by unexpected means," Parrington did not simply give examples of the mysterious workings of Providence. He described those workings in terms that reflect an implicitly dialectical, if not implicitly ironical, mode of thinking as well as an interest in distinctly political, characteristically Progressive ideas. "Take whatever revolution you please," Parrington urged his audience,

and you will find that each one which has effected a final advance, has been preceded by a distinguishable line of causation. It may differ as to the phenomena, but the essential principle remains the same. Today, above the degradation of the masses, sits despotic power. To maintain, to extend authority, is its only ambition. Will is law, and to it the rights of the individual, the rights of society must conform. Tomorrow, comes the inevitable result. First a low murmur of discontent, and thought is awakened. Thought begets thought; it grows and permeates all classes. It discloses to society the knowledge of its condition, and the next day, with almost startling suddenness, comes revolution.

Parrington might have been echoing rhetoric drawn from the Social Gospel movement or simply from the blend of Populist politics and grass-roots Protestantism that helped nominate William Jennings Bryan for the presidency five years later, yet talk of revolution jars with the oration's final vision of truth reigning through "an eternity of peace." Several paragraphs later he returned to his description of historical development, writing that "out of conflict comes a purer society, from each revolution springs advancement." This he illustrated with an example from American history:

Intolerance and persecution drove to a new continent an earnest people. Through trial and hardship they grew into a nation. On American soil the forces of the past had concentrated to produce a sublime idea of freedom. But the consummation was not yet. Themselves freed from persecution they became oppressors. The ensign of liberty floated over a people half free, half slave. The purification must come through conflict, the nation tried by the test of war.

This passage—particularly telling in view of John Brown's antislavery role in Kansas—closes with the conviction that liberty and justice have now triumphed, but through the work of God, not by the efforts of men. At this point, Parrington did not see a problem in reconciling his faith in God's purposes and methods with his belief in progress and view of history as the record of conflict. When illumination came and he began wrestling with the essential dilemma of late nineteenth-century culture, it was profoundly disturbing and issued in the religious crisis so characteristic of his generation. And like other members of that generation—Jane Addams, for example—Parrington resolved the crisis by focusing on the secular side of the argument and by redefining his faith in cultural and political terms.

When Parrington delivered "God in History" the second time, in the Kansas State Inter-Collegiate Oratorical Contest held in the Emporia Opera House on February 20, 1891, it was one of the most memorable days of his life. Many years later he could "hear yet that pandemonium of enthusiasm, that mad uproar of noise; . . . see the confused mass of swaying bodies and waving arms, the flutter of colors and the brandishing of canes."[4]

This time he was scheduled to appear sixth in a field of seven. Parrington was confident he had won the contest, and he did score the highest number of points for thought and composition. But he was rated down on delivery by one judge, and J. I. Games of Baker University was awarded first for

"Civilization of the Anglo-Saxon." The College of Emporia's delegate took second in a very close decision. Parrington got up the next day "feeling pretty blue" but went back down to the Opera House to participate in electing the next year's officers for the Inter-Collegiate Oratorical Association and then picked up his $20 prize. By evening he was in good enough spirits to spend "a very pleasant time dancing at the 'Home,' " as the women's dormitory at the College of Emporia was called. On Sunday he went to church, as usual, and at the campus on Monday he received a good many congratulations, which helped assuage his disappointment in the opinion of the sixth judge.

Second-place winners in the state contest were automatically named as delegates to the interstate contest, to be held in Des Moines in early May. On his way to the convention in Des Moines, Parrington stopped in Chicago. It was his first visit to that, or any other, city. In retrospect, the trip assumed the dimensions of the classic pilgrimage made by many another young midwesterner who participated in the intellectual migration from small towns and farms to Chicago in the late nineteenth century. In an autobiographical sketch written nearly three decades later, Parrington wrote, in accents foreshadowing the works and experience of such authors as Carl Sandburg, Floyd Dell, and Sherwood Anderson:

> Although I have since come to dislike Chicago as the ugly and vulgar home of a cut-throat capitalism, I was then young enough to come under its spell. The pall of smoke which hung above it, the rattle and roar of the traffic in the streets, the thronged sidewalks, the fascinating shop-windows, all seemed to my simple country soul compact of romance; and I recall how my pulse quickened and my imagination stirred as I stood at Wabash and Michigan Avenues under the elevated track and felt the rumble and heard the roar of a train passing over my head, a living thing winding its way through the heart of this marvelous city of trade. The roaring noises were the evidence that great things were being done, the soot-laden air was proof that great furnaces were blazing—Chicago was a young giant that could laugh at fate because her hands were strong.[5]

But in May 1891, Parrington recorded much less dramatically in his diary how he was met on Friday by an uncle at the train station, toured several fourteen- and fifteen-story buildings, was impressed by the beauty of Lake Michigan, shopped in Marshall Field's, attended a baseball game, visited the site of the World's Fair in Jackson Park, attended a Baptist church, then on Monday had his photograph taken at Brand's Studio and observed the activities at the Board of Trade. Bidding farewell to the relatives with whom he had stayed, Parrington boarded the westbound train for Aurora, where he had been born and spent his early childhood. After visiting more cousins, aunts, and uncles in Aurora and in Batavia—where he availed himself of the opportunity to go sightseeing with a pretty girl—he finally arrived in Des Moines on May 7.

He found the interstate contest less exciting than talking politics with other delegates. First place was awarded to Frank Felter of Indiana University, who was to become a well-known economist and called his oration "The Heir Apparent." The other contestants, all males, representing Illinois, Minnesota, Iowa, Colorado, Nebraska, Wisconsin, and Missouri, as well as Kansas, gave orations titled "Loyalty to Principle—the Nucleus of Reform," "Charles Sumner as a Philanthropist," "The Evolution of Democracy," "The Brazilian Revolution," "A Lost Citizenship," "The Value of Emotion," and "The Message of the New World to the Old." Parrington sat through his second hearing of "Civilization of the Anglo-Saxon" but had regained his sense of perspective sufficiently to observe that J. I. Games "did well." He was happy to arrive back home on May 9, after an overnight stop in Kansas City, where he had a souvenir tintype made and visited the *Times* building.

Following this exposure to the world beyond Emporia, Parrington was occupied with playing baseball and tennis, helping edit the school newspaper, taking his final exams, and spending pleasant evenings dancing and "joshing" with coeds. He wrote an essay, "The Grounds of Theistic Belief," and finished a painting titled "Venus." He said good-bye to his classmates the day after commencement, presuming that his school days at Emporia had ended, for he planned to fulfill his senior requirements at Harvard. In preparation for this second journey, he independently resumed his college French studies, but his plans and efforts appeared in vain when word was received on June 20 that he had been refused financial aid. Then on July 5 another letter came from Cambridge announcing that he had been awarded $150 from the Price Greenleaf Fund.[6]

The certainty of attending Harvard set Parrington on a diligent program of almost daily study in the town library. He continued reading French, began working through Whitney's larger German grammar, and read several novels: Thackeray's *Vanity Fair* and *The Newcomes*, Amelia Rives's *Witness of the Sun*, Dinah M. Craik's *Brave Lady*, and for an introduction to New England character, Henry James's *Bostonians*. By August this schedule had to be cut down slightly, for he was often needed at the family farm, about ten miles away in nearby Americus, to help with such harvesting chores as threshing wheat, canning strawberries, and picking apples.

When the College of Emporia's term began in early September, Parrington occasionally attended classes, partly for the stimulation and partly to resume his social life. At last, on September 26, came "the day," as he described it in his diary, "of my first great step for myself." In the afternoon he went with his mother to the depot, where a group of his friends had gathered to see him off. He boarded the train that would take him to Cambridge, feeling that the ties that had bound him to Emporia for over six years were "irrevocably broken." Reflecting upon the significance of his departure, later that day Parrington recorded in his diary: "There is a great deal of sadness about it—to leave parents, friends, and all the associations of the past and start out anew, depending and calculating on a very uncertain future. Yet it is what we all must do, and so I can but reiterate 'Deo et humanitate' and go on, God helping me. I must—nay I will—work out a faithful, if not brilliant, work."

In the next two years, Parrington's future sometimes seemed even more uncertain than it did at this moment. And there were occasions, in Cambridge and during the years beyond, when he needed to call upon this resolute sense of purpose to continue his work. He had decided to begin that work at Harvard primarily because both his parents were New Englanders. The forces that brought them to Kansas influenced the thinking of the figure on the stage in Austin Chapel, delivering his oration, "God in History." In many respects a self-made man, Parrington later seemed content to remain vague about his antecedents. Although he took a small measure of pride in his New England ancestry, it was the larger significance of his ancestors' migration to and within this country that interested him and influenced his conception of American social and economic development.

Patterns of Migration

Vernon's paternal grandparents, John and Ann Wrathal Parrington, were born in Yorkshire, England. Nothing about Ann Wrathal's heritage was passed on to her descendants. The only information that survives regarding John Parrington's family is that his father was known as "the greatest wit in Yorkshire." The couple lived in Barnsley, in the wool-producing region between Sheffield on the south and Leeds to the north. John Parrington was a weaver, though it is not clear whether he was self-employed or worked in one of the new mills. In the late 1820s, just before the first Reform Bill was passed, he made the decision to emigrate in hopes of improving his family's economic condition. With his wife and two young children, William and Mary, he first settled in Portsmouth, New Hampshire. There, in 1830, a second son, John William, was born. Shortly thereafter, the family moved to what is now Gorham, Maine, about twelve miles west of Portland, a settlement begun a century earlier when participants in King Philip's War were rewarded with tracts of land in this heavily forested area, part of the ancestral lands of the Narragansett Indians.

In 1832, John Parrington bought a Gorham carpet-weaving factory from Hugh Gilroy. Gilroy had emigrated from the north of Ireland in about 1827 and began the first ingrain carpet-weaving in the state of Maine, but he was unable to keep abreast of technological advances. The Yorkshire weaver made some improvements in the machinery, then his health began failing, and in 1835 he sold out to General James Irish. Irish installed new machinery, hired a foreman trained in the Lowell mills who subsequently purchased the original factory, then in 1844 the establishment was destroyed by fire.[7]

The year after selling the factory to Irish, John Parrington died at the age of thirty-seven, leaving a widow and four children. A second daughter, Sarah, had been born in Gorham in July 1833. The family's fortunes at first seemed destined to follow those of the carpet-weaving business. In January 1838, sixteen-year-old William died of consumption; in March, a fifth child, a year-old baby, also died.[8] Unable to care for her surviving children, Ann Wrathal found temporary homes for them. Eventually, as in the cases of so many other immigrants, these children fulfilled the hopes of their parents.

In July 1846, Mary Parrington, born in Yorkshire, was wed to James Warren. He was the grandson and namesake of a James Warren who had come to Gorham from nearby Saco in about 1770 and settled on a prospering farm on Flaggy Meadow Road. In 1773, James of Saco married Martha McLellan, the youngest child of Hugh and Elizabeth McLellan. Scotch-Irish émigrés, the McLellans were among Gorham's first settlers, having arrived in Maine in 1733 and bought land from Colonel Shubael Gorham in 1739. A highly successful farmer and lumberman, Hugh McLellan paid in 1763 and for many years thereafter the highest provincial tax recorded in the town. Hugh's relatives and descendants intermarried, built themselves a solid financial base, and became leading citizens in southern Maine.

About the time of Martha McLellan and James Warren's marriage, her father completed construction on the first brick house in Cumberland County. The two-story dwelling was symbolic of the family's social and economic status. Still standing, the house is located on the campus of the Gorham branch of the University of Maine-Portland and is listed on the National Register of Historic Places. The union of the McLellans and Parringtons, of the histories of two contrasting sets of immigrants, was not as durable as the life of the brick house, for Mary Parrington and James Warren had no children. In the decade before her death, Mary's nephew Vernon came to Gorham and stayed in the old farmhouse on Flaggy Meadow Road during his Christmas and summer vacations while he was a student at Harvard.[9]

During those vacations, Vernon also became acquainted with his cousin Warren Dunnell of Portland, the son of his aunt Sarah, John and Ann Parrington's younger daughter. Sarah A. Parrington had married Mark Hill Dunnell from nearby Buxton shortly after he graduated from Waterville College (now Colby College) in Waterville, Maine. Dunnell pursued a brief career in education and Republican state politics before beginning a law practice in Portland. After a year's Civil War duty and a stint as consul at Vera Cruz, in 1865 Dunnell moved to Minnesota, where he served as state superintendent of public instruction, in the Minnesota legislature, and for six terms as a Republican member of Congress (1871–83, 1889–91).[10]

Ann Wrathal's other surviving child, John William, lived as a boy in the home of James Mann, then a partner in the Gorham trading firm of Lord and Mann. The Manns had resided in Gorham for several generations and were prominent in military and political affairs. In 1848, James Mann began a career in politics, serving as state representative and state senator before moving to Louisiana, where he was elected to Congress after the Civil War. By that time, John William Parrington had graduated from a local academy, where his brother-in-law, Mark Dunnell, was the principal. Dunnell helped prepare the aspiring student, only seven years his junior, to attend his alma mater. John Parrington was twenty-six when he received his diploma from Waterville in 1856, an act that seemed to justify the Yorkshire weaver's faith in America. As his son later reflected,

> Could one fancy the orphaned son of a weaver in England going up to Oxford or to any other school? Except for that matter of emigration my father would have become an English factory hand, on a wage of a few shillings a week, without hope of betterment. The old world would have killed what was best in him, in reducing him to a wage slave; the new world was kinder—

After Waterville, John Parrington planned to enter the law but first taught several years in the Boys' Latin High School in Portland. Then the principalship of the West Side High School in Aurora, Illinois, a town about thirty miles west of Chicago, became available, and Parrington took the opportunity to leave New England and go west. One of the students at Aurora's West Side High School was Mary Louise McClellan. In 1861, when she was eighteen and he was thirty-one, the principal married Mary Louise. Only in its last phases did the path that brought the new Mrs. Parrington to Illinois share features with the one that brought her husband. Though both Mary Louise McClellan's family and the McLellans who settled in Maine were Scotch-Irish and originated in County Argyle, the difference in orthography, observed in the earliest records, apparently indicates a divergent ancestry.[11]

In 1718, a company of Scotch Presbyterians emigrated from Londonderry to Worcester, Massachusetts. They came partly to escape religious persecution but met with it again in Worcester, where the partially constructed meetinghouse was torn down by a mob. Some of the original band then left to settle in more tolerant towns, but among those who stayed and adapted to Worcester's ways was James McClellan. In December 1722, he married Elizabeth Hall from nearby Sutton, the daughter of Deacon Percival Hall, one of Sutton's original proprietors, long prominent in town affairs and a representative to the provincial legislature.[12]

All the succeeding generations of McClellans had sons named James, and Vernon Parrington's mother's lineage can be directly traced through them.

One of James and Elizabeth's grandsons, known as Deacon James, was good-natured, financially successful, and a leader in the Baptist church—an indication of how well the McClellans had conformed to Sutton's anti-Presbyterian ways. His oldest son, James, as a youth served briefly (eleven days) as a private in Captain Arthur Daggett's company of Sutton minutemen, part of Colonel Ebenezer Larned's regiment, which "marched in the alarm of April 19th, 1775." The regiment viewed, but did not participate in, the Battle of Bunker Hill, joining the right wing of the army that formed a protective line stretching from Boston to Roxbury.[13]

He returned home and also became prominent in the Baptist church structure before moving with his wife and six surviving children to Chautauqua County, New York, in the early 1830s. In 1836 they moved further west to the new settlement of Bristol, in what is now Kendall County, Illinois. One of their daughters, Martha, married John M. Van Osdel, the first important architect in Chicago. Although most of his buildings were destroyed in the 1871 fire, he designed the Tremont House and the first and third Palmer Houses; did the finishing work on the first ships built in Chicago; and designed homes for Chicago's first mayor, William Ogburn, and other wealthy families. Van Osdel also is credited with the first City Hall and Courthouse Building and the five-story buildings with iron fronts built before the mid-1860s. This uncle provided Vernon Parrington with a family model when his own interests turned to architecture during his early thirties.

In Bristol, James McClellan carried on the tradition of Sutton solidity, building the town's first frame house and, as one local history puts it, "having capital, was a leader in every worthy enterprise until his death." What led this James McClellan from a prosperous Massachusetts farm to Chautauqua and on to the wilderness conditions of Bristol is not known. Evidently pioneering agreed with him, for he lived until his late seventies, just after the Civil War. These conditions did not agree as well with his son James or with his son's family. James's first wife died after less than two years of marriage, but shortly afterward he married Eunice Clark Sherman, who was raised in western New York. Their five children were all born in Illinois. Among them was yet another James; a daughter Medora, who became the mother of Wesley Mitchell, the influential Columbia University economist; and Mary Louise, born on June 16, 1843.[14]

James McClellan, Jr., as he was known, had entered the Baptist ministry, in the tradition of the James McClellans before him, but left because of ill health, then led a roving life, which included teaching school and writing for early Chicago newspapers. An ardent supporter of the Liberty party, the anti-Garrisonian wing of the American Anti-Slavery Society, James McClellan, Jr., contributed in 1847 a series of letters about that party's origins and aims to the *Western Citizen*, a short-lived Chicago newspaper. Vernon grew up hearing the story that his house was a link in the underground railway and as an adult was proud to count both his grandfathers as radicals. The census of 1850 shows the family living in Chicago's third ward and lists James's occupation as printer. That same year, his second wife died, evidently in childbirth. James remarried in 1851 and had two more daughters. The series of family tragedies took their toll, for he died four years later at the age of forty-two. After their parents' deaths, the children were scattered among relatives—similar to the fate of the Yorkshire weaver's children in Gorham—and Mary Louise went to live with a Sherman uncle near Chautauqua. She returned to the little village of Bristol briefly before going to school in nearby Aurora and marrying John Parrington.[15]

The couple's early married life was interrupted by the Civil War. On September 7, 1863, John Parrington entered the Union army with the commission of captain and was assigned to Company A of the Fourth Colored Infantry, one of the Union regiments composed of black soldiers. He was wounded in the hand during the second attack on Petersburg, the battle in which Captain Vernon King, for whom he named a son, was cut in two by a shell. At the close of the war, he was stationed for a period of garrison duty at Fort Totten, near New York City. In May 1866, he was breveted a lieutenant colonel (an honorary promotion) and returned to Aurora. Louise—she was called by her middle name as an adult—and her husband immediately began planning a family, for on December 7 she gave birth to twin girls, Louise and Florence. Evidently premature, they died the same day.

Instead of resuming his high school principalship, John Parrington began practicing law—as he had wanted to do in Waterville—then went into politics, a natural step for a Civil War veteran who grew up in the political atmosphere of James Mann's household. He was elected clerk of courts of Kane County; to hold office he had to move a few miles away to Geneva, the county seat. There on January 25, 1869, a son, John McClellan, was born. Upon the expiration of the clerkship's term, John Parrington returned with his family to Aurora and the practice of law. In Aurora, on August 3, 1871, a second son, Vernon Louis, was born. Vernon's recollections of his Aurora childhood are fragmentary but vivid:

> There I lived for six years—blank for the most part, but with odd little bits quite unrelated emerging from the blankness: my straw hat with streamers suddenly flying from my head as I was crossing the bridge over the Fox River with my mother, and sailing off down the stream; a horrible face looking in at me through a window as I sat on the kitchen floor playing—which turned out to be a neighbor boy with a mask on; the queer talk of some Scotch neighbors whom I liked greatly.[16]

By the early 1870s, the fever of westward migration that followed the close of the Civil War touched John Parrington, by then in his middle forties. Finding his law office confining, he traveled to Texas, bought a herd of sheep, and drove them to market, realizing very little profit. The next year he tried his fortune elsewhere. Traveling to Lyon County, Kansas, then at the edge of the line of settlement, he secured several pieces of land near Americus, the county seat. In the spring of 1877, the family left Illinois and moved to Americus, at first living in a house in town.

On the outskirts of present-day Americus stands a sign bearing the legend "Welcome to Americus—The City of Progress." At the city park in the center of town, the remnant of a New England common, stands another which reads "Lyon County, Kansas—A Good Place to Live." A century ago, young Vernon did find it a good place to live, with its dozen business places—including the blacksmith shop, a favorite loafing spot "where treasures were to be picked out of piles of iron scraps and excitement attended the shoeing of a refractory horse"—clustered on and near Main Street. There "on Saturday afternoons the farmers' wagons and saddle horses were as thick as they could tie to the hitching posts" and hospitable "lean-to wooden porches covered the plank sidewalks in front of the shops."[17]

Yet progress bypassed Americus during his boyhood. After surveying the site in the early 1850s, the founders built confidently along the west side of the square, certain that the railroads being constructed across the state to carry livestock and grain from the Southwest to Chicago would make the town flourish. The first warning note was sounded in 1860, when enterprising citizens in newly founded (1859) Emporia, about ten miles to the southeast, swung a vote that switched the county seat there from Americus. Then in 1869 the east-west main branch of the Atchison-Topeka-Santa Fe Railroad was run through Emporia, making a major junction with the north-south main line of the Missouri-Kansas-Tennessee. Between 1870 and 1880, Emporia's population doubled, reaching well over four thousand—and nearly doubled again by 1890—while that of Americus was cut in half, down to a little over four hundred. Thus when John Parrington moved his family out to the new four-room farmhouse located on the quarter-section he had homesteaded two miles north of town, Americus was the dwindling nucleus of a farming community, and all major trading was conducted in bustling Emporia, two hours' drive away by team and buggy.[18]

The stretches of prairie grass on the Parringtons' almost level 160 acres were punctuated by a single cottonwood tree. Their small white house with its queer hipped roof stood exposed to the winds with little landscaping to screen or beautify it. Twelve acres were devoted to apples, a rare crop in Kansas, which achieved the desired effect of transplanting a bit of New England to the Midwest. The rest of the cultivated land was given over to corn, the staple crop of the region, which provided food for all the livestock and fuel for the kitchen stove. Vernon's older brother did most of the heavy field work, and he helped with such household chores as washing dishes, churning, scrubbing, laundering, and carrying the swill bucket out to the pigs, picking his way through a pasture that was miry in winter and the source of irritating insect bites in summer.

During the winter months the two boys went to school a mile up the road in a building—"a frankly utilitarian affair dedicated to the three R's and not at all to culture"—picturesquely known as Pumpkin Ridge, though no one raised pumpkins and no ridge was in sight. At school, they made a passionate acquaintance with baseball and first came in contact with German and Bohemian immigrants. For recreation, they hunted jackrabbits and squirrels with homemade weapons, then prairie chickens, quail, ducks, and geese after growing old enough to handle shotguns. The life was not without its joys, but it was hard, as it was for their neighbors. Louise made ends meet by selling butter and eggs, for John Parrington soon found himself ill suited to farm life. A lifelong Republican, he had "an incorrigible love of political dickering" and shortly after coming to Americus involved himself in county and local party affairs. Finally determining to run for county office again, he was nominated for probate judge at the 1884 convention and won the office in the same election that saw the defeat of the presidential aspirations of another adopted son of Maine, James G. Blaine.[19]

This change in occupation entailed moving to Emporia, now the county seat. The following spring, the household goods were piled on a wagon and the family left the farm, living for a year in the southeast part of town, then settling in the northwest section, on the corner of Tenth and Rural streets. Although he retained ownership of the farm and lived there periodically during harvest time and after retiring from the bench in 1888, the move into Emporia was the last step in the series of transitions that had carried John Parrington and his wife away from their New England roots.

These transitions made Vernon Parrington more rather than less typical of other members of his generation, the sons and grandsons of immigrants, born in the Middle West. In their moves from the eastern seaboard, his grandfather McClellan and his father contributed to the demographic shift that pushed American settlement from behind the Appalachian line in 1815 to the point in 1890, saliently observed by Frederick Jackson Turner, when no contiguous north-south demarcation could be drawn between the Appalachians and the Pacific Coast.[20] James McClellan's and John Parrington's many shifts in occupation and residence illustrate the restlessness and rootlessness that contributed to the reality of romantic conceptions of individualism that so profoundly influenced nineteenth-century economic and political trends. Both the parallel hardships these shifts wrought in his parents' childhoods and the role education played in mitigating those hardships contributed to the psychosocial dynamics and cultural values that shaped young Vernon's development.

Emporia, 1885–1891

The 1884 election that produced John Parrington's change of status from a farmer to a judge had corresponding effects on his sons. At first those effects were symbolic and highly visual. "Our outward transformation was magical. Never did boys put off country ways and put on town ways more speedily," Parrington later wrote. It was the kind of transformation that built the Sears and Roebuck empire, and it contributed to Parrington's life-long fascination with fashion:

> For years our summer dress had been a pair of overalls that came halfway between the knee and the ankle, a pair of suspenders, a blue gingham shirt and a straw hat—nothing else, no underclothes, no shoes, no coat. In winter we wore the old-fashioned boots, well-smeared with tallow, into the tops of which we stuck our "pants" legs. The boots with their bright leather fronts were about the first sacrifice on the altar of progress. They were the very hallmark of the countrified and we hastened to enjoy the feeling of sophistication which came from putting our feet in town shoes. Soon we became connoisseurs in scarves and neckties. For a few fleeting months we were seduced by the unwonted spell of celluloid collars; but that was while we were still victims of lingering country prejudices. Our eyes were soon opened and a celluloid collar became henceforth the sign of a country jake, and aroused our mirth when it appeared . . . encircling the neck of some clod-hopper. It could not have been much more than a year before we had risen to the dignity of custom made suits, and after that it was a nice question of cuts and styles.[21]

In the spring of 1885, Vernon briefly attended the public school. But in September he and his brother—then aged fourteen and sixteen—entered the Preparatory Department of the College of Emporia. In addition to the public high school, a state normal school had been created in Emporia by legislative act in 1863. Yet John Parrington chose to send his sons to a private institution where they could repeat his own pattern of New England schooling: training in an academy followed by a collegiate curriculum emphasizing classical subjects. Louise Parrington, coming from a long line of Baptist deacons, may also have influenced the decision to send the boys to a church-related institution. "As this college was planted by men of clear and pronounced convictions on the subject of evangelical Christianity," an early catalog explains, "it is presumed that the entire trend of instruction here given will be toward Christ, and not away from him." Moreover, it was the "cherished hope of the Trustees and friends of this college that it may become a training school for the gospel ministry." Of those graduating between 1889 and 1898, a full 52 percent did enter the ministry, although this proportion was cut in half for those graduating in the following decade and was reduced to less than 1 percent during the 1919–28 period.[22]

Chartered in 1882, the College of Emporia formally opened in November 1883, holding classes in an ill-equipped suite of rooms in a downtown office building. In addition to the president, Reverend John F. Hendy, who taught courses in mental and moral science as well as the required Bible study classes, the faculty consisted of three members: Robert Cruikshank, who was in charge of English grammar, Greek, Latin, and algebra; E. N. Graves, a lawyer who also substituted in local pulpits, as part-time assistant in mathematics; and Albertine Wetter from St. Louis, who gave instruction in art and modern languages. The student body numbered seventeen, all at the preparatory level. By the next year enrollment increased to 73, and a proper building—a limestone Gothic edifice to be called Stuart Hall after a philanthropic New Yorker who donated $10,000 for the purpose—was being erected west of downtown on thirty-eight acres of land donated by the city. In the fall of 1885, when the Parrington boys arrived, the faculty had increased to six, the total enrollment numbered 125, and there were 9 collegiate-level students. Vernon entered the junior, or beginning, preparatory class, and John entered the senior "prep" class, along with a certain Will A. White from El Dorado, Kansas, who lengthened his name to William Allen White and became the nationally known editor of the *Emporia Gazette.*[23]

That first year Vernon completed the prescribed courses in beginning French, Latin, arithmetic, and English. Curiously, perhaps because there was no designated English instructor and duties in this area were divided among the faculty, this last course was actually a survey of United States history. Latin was his favorite subject, primarily because of the personality of the professor, Hugh Macmaster Kingery. Kingery took an active interest in the college's extracurricular life, becoming adviser to a short-lived secret fraternity (forced to disband after a few years as inimical to religious purposes) and editing an early campus newspaper, the *Semi-Weekly Miniature,* which existed briefly during the spring of 1887.

One issue of the *Miniature*—it was only four pages long and measured five by seven inches—reports that V. Parrington held the highest rank in the middle preparatory class. This is one of the few indications of his scholastic achievement, for a disastrous fire gutted Stuart Hall in 1915 and destroyed all student grades and records. Following the pattern of late nineteenth-century curricula, the College of Emporia had ambitiously outlined three alternative courses of study, the classical, the philosophical, and the literary. But in both the upper preparatory grades and at the collegiate level the differences between the courses were reflected only in the choice of language, with the literary and philosophical students taking French and German instead of Greek and Latin. Vernon was enrolled in the classical course throughout his Emporia years, thus his middle preparatory classes consisted of Latin (reading Caesar), first-year Greek, mathematics (algebra), and English (standard grammar instead of history). He also took freehand drawing in the modest Art Department, established two years earlier. This exposure to art was to have far-reaching effects on Vernon. It was art, not literature, that captured his imagination during his teens. No literature course was offered during his preparatory years. Indeed, during his entire six years of study at the College of Emporia, no one was ever hired specifically to teach English language and literature; the duties continued to be divided among the faculty.[24]

By the time he was sixteen, during his senior prep year, Parrington had determined to become a painter. An announcement for a reception and exhibition of drawings and paintings given by the art students held in June of that year shows him with no entries in the oil painting category. But he was represented by five drawings of subjects appropriate for one enrolled in the classical course: "Apollo Belvedere from Cast," "Foot from Cast," "Demosthenes from Cast," "Michael Angelo's Hand," and an unidentified "Group of Objects." All the other exhibitors were females, including his cousin Gertrude Titsworth, and this may well provide another clue to his attraction to art classes. Vernon combined classical subjects with feminine socializing that spring in at least two other activities, dramatic productions put on for the benefit of the college "Home." In one, tableaux representing various national groups were presented, including ones on Indians (Pocahontas) and America (Priscilla and John Alden). Vernon appeared as Gracchi in the Roman tableau, "Cornelia and Her Jewels." In another, a Greek feast featuring sketches from the *Iliad* and the *Odyssey*, he took the role of Eurymachus in "Ulysses' Return."[25]

During his last preparatory year, Vernon continued his studies in Latin, Greek, and mathematics as well as completing a required course in Biblical Studies. His English course again did not focus on language or literature but studied "Universal History," similar to the way U.S. History had been studied in his beginning English class. How these courses were organized and whether historical documents were also read for their literary value is not known. But one wonders what influence this disciplinary mixture had on Vernon's later perceptions of what ought—or could—be taught in an English course once he himself became an English professor. He pursued his interest in drawing and painting as a special student in the Art Department and enrolled in a botany course. The study of botany was an expression of his earlier interests. Since childhood he had loved flowers, bringing home bouquets from the garden of the mother of his Americus chum Vern Cook and planting lilacs to soften the rawness of the Parringtons' boxlike farmhouse. He collected wildflowers and species of prairie grass in a herbarium designed for the purpose, valuing the effort enough to preserve the collection his entire life.[26]

Parrington and the College of Emporia grew up together. Though the curriculum was old-fashioned and the teaching probably unexceptional, he and his brother felt that "it was a God-send to us, for it picked us up, crude and untaught and carried us forward till the world of ideas and exact knowledge lay open to us." It was a small world, but it offered a nonthreatening environment of manageable proportions to a newcomer to town ways who had a spotty educational background. The student body was drawn almost entirely from Emporia and nearby Kansas towns, ensuring a fairly homogeneous milieu. The college also grew up with the town, and the sense of building something new pervaded the institution's early years just as it dominated the outlook of local farmers and businessmen. Pioneering in its many senses marked every stage of Parrington's life, as it marked the lives of his forebears. The resiliency he exhibited in his professional career in constructing innovative curricula and coping with recalcitrant administrations and institutional changes was partly a product of his early Emporia experiences.[27]

By the fall term of 1888, the enrollment reached 116, including the 15 members of Parrington's freshman class, and the faculty had increased to ten. Vernon's courses were identical in title to those of his senior prep year. He advanced in Latin (Horace, Livy, Ovid, prose composition), Greek (Lysias, the *Iliad,* composition), and mathematics (geometry); in his required biblical course, he studied Old Testament history; in natural science, physiology and zoology; and at last in his third term of English read a Shakespearian play. During the three terms of his sophomore year (1889–90), the same six courses were required, with the significant addition of a history sequence. A local judge, Charles B. Graves, was hired to teach U.S. constitutional history during the fall term; and during the winter and spring terms English history was offered when the college expanded to include a Department of History and Political Science, yet no trained instructor was hired, and the course was at first taught by the professor of mathematics and astronomy.[28]

Though the curriculum showed little change that year, Parrington began to change, growing introspective enough to start keeping a diary. The initial entry, made on January 1, 1890, when he was eighteen and a half, is disappointingly unreflective: "A pleasant day. Spent the afternoon playing tennis with Bart Jay. In the evening I escorted Fannie Jay to a party at Walt's and had a very enjoyable time. Today does not seem like 'New Year's' it is so warm and pleasant." The final entry for 1890, made on December 31, illustrates that Parrington had undertaken the recording of his daily activities with a serious object in mind:

> Well, a year has sped away since I began to keep this little diary, a year full of work and action; but as to results, are they proportional to the opportunities? With all the privileges encompassing me I fear very much I am not accomplishing what I ought and might. A year has gone by, and I am no better spiritually than last Jan. It will not do. Nor am I any nearer to a solution to the problem of a life's work. Am nearly 20 and it is getting of vital importance. Will it be solved a year hence? . . .

This was my first attempt at keeping a diary, and while I am not completely satisfied yet, the record of the year, such as it is, is unbroken. The coming year I hope to improve on it, making a larger, fuller, one.

This passage is the only one of its kind in the 1890 diary. If Parrington was not yet using the diary as a means of confession or meditation, he was employing it to measure the congruity between work and action, opportunities, and privileges. In this respect, Parrington was beginning to exhibit one of the characteristic traits that David Riesman observed in inner-directed personalities: "Inner-directed person[s] . . . tend to feel throughout life that their characters are something to be worked on. The diary-keeping that is so significant a symptom of the new type of character may be viewed as a kind of inner time-and-motion study by which the individual records and judges his output day by day. It is evidence of the separation between the behaving and scrutinizing self." Riesman's observation becomes increasingly relevant as one reads Parrington's diaries over the years. In later life Parrington commented that "the trick of being close-mouthed seems to be a Parrington characteristic."[29] But even the 1890 diary's disjunction between entries containing prosaic details (the weather, baseball scores, buying clothes, completing household chores) and the single reflective entry made as the year departed illustrates "the separation between the behaving and scrutinizing self." The existence of this separation helps explain much of the pattern of Parrington's personal and professional life.

The diaries' emphasis on "the behaving self" furnishes important facts regarding Parrington's last year and a half as a student at the College of Emporia. For example, we learn that in his last two sophomore terms, he achieved academic averages of 96.6 and 96 and ranked second in his class, a fraction behind those outscoring him in geology, the required natural science course. During the middle term of his junior year (grades for the other terms are omitted), though, Parrington ranked first with a 96.4 average. His overall Emporia collegiate average was 94.9; the improvement over his freshman year indicates a change in academic performance occurring with the onset of his diary keeping.

Despite creditable grades in sophomore trigonometry, Parrington elected to take French rather than calculus. He also appears to have obtained permission to substitute an art course for third-year Greek. These were two early manifestations of the literary and aesthetic interests that shaped his future pursuits. Two other junior courses are worth noting: a term and a half of political economy (which employed Walker's standard text) and two terms of psychology (studying cognitive powers and motive powers) that he enjoyed immensely.

In addition, the topics of various class assignments and of orations prepared for the literary society are indicative of historical themes that long concerned Parrington. For sophomore English, his debate was titled "Is

Monarchy Superior to Democracy?" but he found it difficult to locate supporting materials in the library. For this course, which was taught by Hugh
Kingery, the Latin professor, he also wrote an Emersonian essay called "Experience as a Teacher" and one that critically analyzed the course text, the
widely used *Art of Discourse* by Henry Noble Day. Although apparently
no essays were required during Parrington's junior English course, which
was devoted to studying Anglo-Saxon, or junior political science course, for
his sophomore history class he wrote a two-thousand-word paper discussing Puritan and Cavalier in England. Finally, early in 1890 he delivered his
first oration, vaguely titled "The American Nobility," and early in 1891
he delivered another, "Gustavus Adolphus and the Advance of Protestant
Toleration."

The diaries also provide an index to Parrington's independent reading.
As a boy in Americus, he thrilled to *Robinson Crusoe* and pored over the
stories of Indian fights and frontier adventures in *St. Nicholas' Magazine,* to
which he subscribed, trading issues with his inseparable friend Vern Cook,
who subscribed to *Youth's Companion.* As an adolescent, his "favorite
field" became the Victorian novel. "Dickens, Thackeray, George Eliot, Trol-
lope, Reade, I consumed eagerly, together with a host of other books of miscellaneous nature," Parrington later recalled. His 1890–91 fare included
Edward Bulwer Lytton's *Lucile,* George Eliot's *Mill on the Floss,* Georg
Moritz Eber's *Uarda* and *Joshua,* Charles Kingsley's *Hypatia,* H. Rider
Haggard's *Allan Quartermain,* Jules Verne's *Texar's Revenge,* and William
Makepeace Thackeray's *Pendennis.* Because the college's library was so
small, most of his books were drawn from the Emporia city library. This
practice had far-reaching effects on Parrington, who "instinctively dissoci-
ated books and reading from college work—they belonged to the freer
world beyond the academic walls."[30]

The early diary entries clearly show that young Vernon was as interested
in extracurricular activities, especially sports, as in the volumes—or lack of
them—in either library. In the summers, the Parrington boys played on the
city baseball team, the Browns. John was the first manager and captain of
the College of Emporia's baseball team, and in the spring of 1890 the brothers helped organize its first baseball club. Vernon initially pitched and
played shortstop, then moved behind the plate to become the team's star
catcher. Louise Parrington was drafted to help sew the first uniforms, made
from heavy white flannel and worn with white caps, red belts, and red
stockings to carry out the school colors of crimson and white. Thus the fortunes of baseball became a family affair, no doubt providing much animated dinner table conversation, particularly when Louise's sons returned
home on weekends from usually victorious games played against neighboring teams from Salina, Wichita, and the Haskell Indian Institute.

John graduated from the college in June 1890, giving a commencement oration titled "Philosophy and Religion." He began working for the

Emporia Gazette, following the example of his grandfather McClellan, who had worked as a printer and journalist in Chicago. Without the aid of his brother, that fall Vernon organized the college's first tennis association and was fittingly elected president. In the absence of football and basketball, tennis became a major fall and winter sport, and the College of Emporia's players won most of their matches, ably aided by Vernon's new Sears and Roebuck racquet.

Parrington retained enthusiasm for outdoor activities throughout his life, although after turning thirty he stopped participating in field sports. But he also pursued the college's indoor activities and took leadership roles in them. In the spring of his freshman year, Vernon was a ringleader in a splinter group that withdrew from the college's single literary society for men, the Philologic (there was also a female society, the "WWW"), and began a second society, the Adelphi. The existence of two groups encouraged the competitive spirit as the members debated each other on campus and participated in oratorical contests. As evidenced by his athletic participation, Vernon relished team combat and looked for opportunities to put his organizational skills to work. He was elected president of the Adelphis and helped draw up their constitution. The preamble illustrates that he did not neglect individualistic and idealistic goals for social and competitive ones: "The capacity of the mind for an ever progressive development, the importance of literary culture in the practical pursuits of life, as well as the duty of self-development: being imperative in all, are considerations which should be realized in their fullest sense."[31]

He also combined literary culture with leadership roles by working on the school newspaper, *College Life,* founded in the fall of 1889. He was elected associate editor in his junior year with the responsibility for canvassing for subscriptions and mailing out the weekly issues, though he apparently contributed at least one poem and an article on fraternities in college. Moreover, his sphere was extended beyond the campus borders not only by his baseball reputation but by his election as president of the Kansas State Oratorical Association for the year beginning in February 1890.

In addition to participating in these formal activities, Vernon maintained close friendships with Vern Byers and Vern Cook, his Americus pal who also left a farm to attend school in Emporia. The trio, familiarly known on campus as "the three V's," shared a healthy adolescent interest in mixed social life, availing themselves of opportunities to attend dances, parties, and taffy pulls at the college "Home" as well as to accompany girls to the local Kandy Kitchen after various school events and back to the dorm after church services.

In a small midwestern town like Emporia, churchgoing provided a primary social outlet for collegians and other members of the community. Although it is not clear whether Louise Parrington initially maintained her Baptist relationship or whether Judge Parrington had a religious preference, when their sons entered the College of Emporia in 1884 they indicated membership in the Methodist Episcopal Church in their own handwriting in the official enrollment ledger. That church attendance was a regular part of Vernon's weekly schedule is vividly attested to by his diaries. Each Sunday he spent in Emporia he recorded an almost unvarying pattern of morning and evening attendance. When he was unable to attend services, as in the case of illness, he inscribed the omission, as if to square his conscience with his Maker. The college required Sabbath observance in local churches of the students' choice, yet this injunction could have been enforced only for those who lived in campus housing, and Vernon lived at home.

Interest in religion was another concern that the three V's shared, in addition to first names, ages, oratory, hunting, and women. By October of his junior year, Vern Byers had decided to become a minister. The news surprised Parrington very much, which suggests that these otherwise close friends did not confide all their nearest thoughts. After graduating from the college, Byers attended McCormick Theological Seminary in Chicago, and after receiving his master's degree from Princeton's theological school, he became the pastor of a Presbyterian church in Peckville, Pennsylvania. By the end of his senior year, Vern Cook had also decided to attend seminary, though Parrington was not as surprised at this decision as he was troubled by the announcement of Cook's engagement to Agnes Law, the three friends' former elocution teacher at the College of Emporia. Cook graduated from Northwestern University's Garrett School of Theology in 1895 and served briefly as pastor of a Methodist church in West McHenry, Illinois. When his always delicate health began to fail, he first returned to Americus, then moved to Colorado Springs, where he died of tuberculosis in 1899.[32]

Parrington's response to religion during his College of Emporia years did not issue, like his friends', in a decision to attend seminary. Nor was he committed to a denominational creed, despite his Methodist membership. He visited whichever Emporia church offered the best preaching and thus was often attracted to addresses at the Congregational church, as well as occasionally dropping in on the Presbyterians and at least once, out of curiosity, on the Roman Catholics. Parrington was drawn, not by emotionalism or piety, but by intellectual vigor, freshness of ideas, the force of the preacher's personality, and—perhaps above all—by his mode of expression. In brief, he was drawn by the style of ideas and of their delivery, two features that an aspiring young orator might well profit from, much as he would profit from a college lecture or a speech delivered in a secular forum. When he attended Sunday evening services, church-sponsored musical events, or meetings of the Epworth League, the choice of destination appears, however, to have been determined by which young woman might be seated in the row ahead of him. The closest he came to being affected by a demonstration of faith was describing the ordination of Methodist elders as "interesting." Parrington's churchgoing helped fulfill his intellectual and social needs; at least these are the facets of his Sunday experiences that he most often recorded in his diaries.

Yet if Parrington was not highly concerned about personal faith in his late teens, he was soon to enter a stage where thinking and religion would separate into very different orders of experience. Emporia was not bereft of other sources of ideas. Vernon was aware of the meetings of the Farmers' Alliance, once accompanied his mother to a discussion of women's suffrage, attended several temperance gatherings, and discussed politics with his brother and college friends. But as in the case of religion, his experience of growing up on a farm may have prevented him from abstracting political ideas—thinking—from issues of family and community concern—farming. Despite his father's service on the bench, the family continued to operate the farm and experienced the same problems that made their Americus neighbors responsive to Populist arguments. As Lyon County probate judge, John Parrington knew very well that high interest rates were forcing foreclosures. One might have profitably eavesdropped on the dinner table conversations in the household on Emporia's Rural Street as the Panic of 1893 drew closer.

In neither politics nor religion did Parrington's courses during his three years at the College of Emporia provide the intellectual leverage that might have caused him to turn aside from his pleasant round of extracurricular activities and gain perspective on the social ills that the official institutional and cultural spokesmen were inadequately addressing. While Parrington's initial 1890 diary entry may be taken as a typical example of his daily concerns, the ideas he tried to formulate in his 1891 oration "God in History" were what he packed in his intellectual luggage when he boarded the train for Cambridge.

2

~

Evolution
Harvard, 1891–1893

"I Propose to Make Myself"

Parrington's journey to Cambridge took him through Chicago, where he revisited his McClellan relatives. He had his photograph taken again at Brand's Studio. At Detroit, the train was ferried across Lake Michigan into Ontario, and he was outside the United States for the first time. On September 30, he reached Boston and spent several hours wandering among its "narrow, crazy streets, with small poor buildings," finding only Beacon Street "notable." Then he took the cars for Harvard and located his room ("very pleasant, tho' not elegant") at 13 Mt. Auburn Street. That evening he inscribed in his diary: "Well, I am here in Cambridge, the place of which I have heard since I was old enough to know aught of it. How I will like it I can't tell, but I propose to make myself."

In the passage in *The Lonely Crowd* discussing the significance of diary keeping, David Riesman observed that inner-directed persons "even when they have left home . . . continue to bring themselves up."[1] Parrington's initial Harvard diary entry illustrates the duty-bound conscience—striving to fulfill his parents' wishes and to continue his own closely monitored program of self-development—that lies at the center of Riesman's concept of the inner-directed personality. But is Parrington proposing to make himself like Cambridge, an interpretation that certainly reflects a duty-bound conscience and describes his early Harvard experiences? Or is Parrington proposing to make himself, in the sense of self-construction? Whether the two readings are ambiguous and complementary or whether one is more accurate than the other, self-making in its varied interpretations became the hallmark of his first year at Harvard.

The process began the next day when Parrington registered for his courses. His three years' work at the College of Emporia was not all accepted as transfer credit so he was required to enter as a junior. The 304 members of the class of 1893 included Billings Learned Hand, later an eminent federal jurist; William Vaughn Moody, whose promising poetic career was cut short by death in 1910; David Saville Muzzey, later an author of high school U.S. history texts; and Oswald Garrison Villard, who served as one of the influential editors of the *Nation*. George Cram Cook, the architect and Greek revival exponent, joined the class the following year. That fall, Edwin Arlington Robinson was on campus as a special student; Henry Adams's nephew Charles Francis Adams was in his third year of law school; Norman Hapgood was a second-year law student, a classmate of Parrington's roommate; Hutchins Hapgood and Robert Morss Lovett were seniors.[2]

Charles W. Eliot was midway in his forty-year term (1869–1909) as Harvard's president. Under his leadership the elective system had been developed, requiring only two half-year lecture courses in chemistry and physics and a freshman language course (German or French) in addition to three English courses: Freshman Rhetoric and Composition, Sophomore Themes, and Junior Forensics. Parrington's prior record satisfied all but the last requirement, and he enrolled in a Forensics (English C) section taught by Jefferson B. Fletcher. As a Harvard upperclassman he could choose from a broad and rich range of courses and professors, but he selected very narrowly, concentrating on English and language courses. Whether he was unaware of what Harvard had to offer—in the era when William James, George Santayana, Josiah Royce, and Hugo Münsterberg taught philosophy and psychology and A. B. Hart and Edward Channing American history—or was intellectually unadventurous, or perhaps was following the dictates of his father, is unknown.

Nevertheless, that first year he enrolled in several courses directed by illustrious professors: English 12, an elective composition course, with Barrett Wendell; Philosophy 4, Ethics, with George Herbert Palmer; Fine Arts 1, Principles of Delineation, Color and Chiaroscuro, with Charles Herbert Moore. Four courses fulfilled the required junior load, but Parrington ambitiously took two extra electives: French 1b, Reading at Sight of French Prose, with R. L. Sanderson, and History 11, European History during the Seventeenth Century and the First Half of the Eighteenth, with George Bendelari. He had taken six courses at Emporia, but Harvard demanded more, even though none were advanced courses and Forensics was a half course (extending over two semesters but with half the work of a full course).[3]

Of these new courses, Wendell's composition class had the greatest effect on Parrington's development as a writer and on his preparation for his own teaching career. The major work for the course comprised short daily themes, which provide a running commentary on his impressions and activities, and longer fortnightly themes. The first fortnightly was an autobiographical sketch. Written in early October, this handwritten three-and-a-half-page theme exhibits the good-natured spirit and confident outlook he had earlier manifested. Of his boyhood on the Americus farm, he wrote: "Those were happy days, I doubt if at any time since I have enjoyed life so spontaneously and unrestrictedly. Very existence was a pleasure . . . in that free country life." After describing his prior college studies, Parrington commented modestly:

This work I did with varying degrees of excellence, never remarkably well and never especially poorly. . . .

During this period the average number of College honors fell to my share, some of real value, others of less, but all received with down right pleasure and satisfaction.

My college life thus far, on the whole, I have thoroughly enjoyed, both because I really enjoy a moderate amount of study and also because the social life of the College was of the pleasantest. Viewing the twenty years of my life in all aspects, I count myself greatly blessed. I have always had a pleasant home and my parents, tho' not wealthy have been able to add to their love the practical benefits following from the necessities and comforts of life. I have never had to experience any of the great sorrows or trials of life and above all I have, due both to inheritance and early life, a strong body and sound constitution.

He then defined himself as "a Westerner, both in sympathies and education," and concluded by stating, "My life's work is not yet decided upon. I propose to devote a few years to teaching; after that—I know not what."

The equanimity the theme illustrates—the word "pleasure" appears two times and forms of "enjoy" and "pleasant" (this last also being the most characteristic adjective in Parrington's earlier diaries) occur twice—was soon disturbed. Away from his familiar small-town environment and loving family, here he had a more than moderate amount of study, very little social life, and fewer opportunities for physical exercise. Notes at discord with the autobiographical theme began sounding in his earliest Harvard diary entries. On October 3, after his first visit to Mt. Auburn Cemetery, Parrington wrote, "Am feeling rather sad today. It may be homesickness, for I looked rather wistfully on the hills to westward." On October 8, he was more certain of his feelings: "Am feeling rather sad and homesick. It is hard for one raised in a pleasant home to go to an absolutely strange place and start life there. I shall be able to sympathize with others after my experience." Those others, of course, might well include his own parents. On October 16, he reflected, after watching the football team practice:

Am not reconciled to the change entirely. Altho' in the morning I feel confident and contented, towards even. almost invariably the sadness and discouragement comes back, especially if anything goes wrong. It helped me today to look on the statue of the old puritan who left all his old ties and associations and went forth bravely into the wilderness and did his duty. What discouragement must have been his.[4]

At the end of the month, the diary illuminates the progression from unusual emotional intensity to regaining a sense of self-control. On October 22, having done his duty by turning in a theme to Wendell and receiving "a fearful mark," Parrington confessed: "Am feeling worse tonight than ever before. Two years of this damnable humiliation before I am free. Oh! How I wish it past." The day after this agonized and rare outburst he wrote: "Am feeling somewhat better but only slowly recovering my equilibrium. I am going to exercise my will power after this. I haven't sufficient assurance— any little discouragement knocks my feelings way down below par. I must get over it, know I am right and go ahead." The following evening, after attending French class, working in the fine arts studio, reading Edmund Spenser, and attending a speech by Congressman Roger Q. Mills of Texas, Parrington resolved: "I propose to henceforth to tell everybody metaphorically to go to the devil. I am as good as anybody and am going to do as I please." Yet three days later he suffered a relapse of self-doubt:

Am feeling fairly well, only not natural, not myself. I am either homesick or lack confidence in myself. I rather think it is the latter. Am I homesick? That is a question. Every day comes the thought of the sad seriousness of my move, cutting off all associations and customs and starting entirely anew. I feel fearfully discouraged at times. I am trying to do my duty, tho' God knows.

The following day he called on Wendell and received a more favorable report on his themes than expected, and consequently felt better, though he found the cause "trivial." In these passages Parrington internalized his doubts, ascribing their origin to his own deficiencies in character (lacking self-confidence) instead of to external forces such as grades or homesickness. Concomitantly, he assumed all responsibility for the successful re-establishment of his equilibrium, believing that the performance of duty must alleviate discouragement. It was not study alone, however, that turned the tide for Parrington but the resumption of his social life. On Halloween he visited a Miss Frost at Wellesley: on November 3 he rode into Boston with his roommate to watch the election returns; on November 4 he went to a meeting organizing an Oxford League at Harvard and played whist with a Miss Burgess; on November 10 he received an A on a Forensics assignment and felt better after exercising at the gym; on November 12 he had "a delicious day" receiving letters from home, playing cards again with Miss Burgess, and receiving an invitation from Miss Frost to a concert at Wellesley. By November 13 the critical first wave had safely passed. After studying for ten hours, Parrington could write: "Am feeling quite well and quite at home. Am liking Harvard better the more I get accustomed to it."

Following this significant juncture, he experienced brief but expected pangs of homesickness on Thanksgiving; then on the last day of November, after getting a C on a history exam, he wrote: "It seems to me I'm in a chronic state of discouragement. I can't seem to come up to what I ought to have. Well, I'm not going to fuss but take my dose like a man." But after the first two difficult months, the discouragement appears to be subsiding; at least he stopped recording it in his diary, although depriving himself of this outlet may point to another effort in self-control. The next important step in maturation came when Parrington ceased to feel that he was "taking his dose" and began to enjoy his work. But this took longer than his attempts at mastering his personal insecurities.[5]

In addition to providing an internal counterpoint to his autobiographical fortnightly theme, Parrington's daily diary entries provided him with material for the daily themes required in Wendells' composition course. The themes and diaries bear a series of interesting relations to each other. By objectifying the diary entries, Parrington gained another mode of keeping a "time and motion study," yet the distance between the two modes also illustrates a further separation between "the behaving and the scrutinizing self." Perhaps the necessity of achieving this distance helped Parrington overcome his discouragement and attain a sense of making his days at Harvard count. Moreover, it was a necessity imposed by a professor, and one whom he at first disliked, two facts that no doubt clarified the process of winnowing the inviolately private from that which could be bartered in public. Finally, the need to produce a theme five days a week forced Parrington to observe the life, activities, and environment around him. In this way, the act of writing became a method of gaining control over the adjustment to a new place.

The majority of the first semester's themes were descriptive, forcing students to achieve precision in using words. Parrington's attention was drawn to such new scenes as Faneuil Hall, hearing Phillips Brooks preach, Cambridge weather, a newsboy delivering the *Herald,* an organ-grinder on a Boston street. The statue of the "old puritan" in whom Parrington saw a kindred spirit became the subject of one theme, but the feelings it evoked were masked by formal classroom prose. Several themes concern the familiar Kansas landscape and past, an acceptable avenue to channel his thoughts of home: a lone cottonwood tree, perhaps the one on the Americus farm, day breaking over the prairie. A description of a hunting expedition is an exercise in dialect: "Bring in some more o' that wood Bill, and pile the brush a little higher agin the winder. Dye hear how the geese are flying south? and see the pesky wolves skulking yonder in the edge of the forest. There's goin'ter to be a reg'lar blizzard tonight." Another establishes a link between home and Harvard, contrasting John Brown's neglected wilderness grave and the well-tended resting place of Charles Sumner in the peaceful beauty of Mt. Auburn.

Wendell was generally satisfied with Parrington's descriptive efforts in the short daily themes but was more severe with the fortnightly themes. Parrington saved every daily theme but destroyed most of the fortnightlies, although he preserved several of the title sheets with Wendell's comments. Parrington revised his Emporia oration "Gustavus Adolphus and the Advance of Protestant Toleration" for an assignment to write a piece of journalism. It was deemed "not suitable for a newspaper," though Wendell did add that it was "in all respects a better theme" than the two preceding ones. An assignment of literary criticism met with the judgment, "Certainly it has not that preciseness of outline which should mark effective criticism." And a sonnet, titled "An Old Time Friend," received a grade of C and the observation that only four lines scanned properly, but "unless your ear is seriously defective, you should be able to do much towards curing an elementary fault so incessant."[6]

It was not the relative difficulty of these assigned topics and approaches that bothered Parrington but having to meet more rigorous expectations after the lack of direction—but concomitant freedom to follow his bent— he had experienced at Emporia. It was not that Parrington was unresponsive to discipline, but he was already exhibiting the trait that characterized his later teaching and scholarship: chafing under externally imposed restraints while finding his primary motivation in internal discipline.

Wendell was, of course, the first trained English professor Parrington had encountered. In Emporia, literature and writing had been generally private pursuits, containing their own private discoveries. There he also excelled in the highly public mode of oratory and happily participated in the external system of oratorical contest rules. These experiences proved an asset in his Forensics class at Harvard. That Harvard of 1891 required a course in debating whereas Harvard of 1991 does not is a way to measure the cultural value once placed on spoken and written discourse that has, in the twentieth century, been supplanted by an emphasis on visual and emotional responsiveness. Neither speaking well nor writing well—nor a college degree—in a diverse technological society with access to the varied forms of mass communications now bears such a direct relation to the future social and economic status of the undergraduate.[7]

In the long run, Parrington's training in oratory and forensics contributed to the argumentative organization of *Main Currents in American Thought,* which Howard Mumford Jones described as "a lawyer's brief."[8] He gained immediate satisfaction from Forensics by doing very well in a course, achieving academic status. For Parrington's intellectual development, the course was highly significant because it enabled him to link his independent reading in literature with his penchant for argumentation, a penchant that may be traced to his father's profession as a lawyer and judge. Professor Fletcher required four forensics, preceded by the writing of detailed briefs (essentially outlines of the points to be considered in the corresponding essays). Two sets of these briefs and forensics consider the proposition, "Can the historical novel truthfully represent the life of the past?" The first set, completed in November, received a B grade and argued the negative case. Fletcher commented on the brief, "Your case is delightfully clear in presentation but perhaps a little one-sided in interpretation." In the forensic, Parrington maintained that the historical novelist was hampered by difficulty in understanding the past because of changed circumstances and by difficulty in portraying the past because of lack of specific knowledge of the time in which the work was set. He also emphasized the problem of "fancy" glamorizing the past when the writer lacked a sufficient grasp of social life to achieve verisimilitude of context and character. Unfortunately, he gave no examples to illustrate his points. When the positive case was developed in December, Parrington did add a few references to *Robinson Crusoe, The Merchant of Venice, David Copperfield, Adam Bede,* and *Silas Marner.* The brief received a B +, but Fletcher was obliged to observe: "I fear only that you will suffer yourself to be misled by abstractions. Try as far as possible to stick to the concrete and specific." The advice was not followed; the forensic received a B and the comment:

> It is neat, clear, and interesting; it is tantalisingly abstract and in the air. As an advocate, it must be owned that you damn by faint praise. . . . I do object to your tendency to play with abstractions. Perhaps the question of blank possibility raised by your subject justifies you; but justification will not remove for yourself the literary and logical evils of this metaphysical vice.

Parrington might have forestalled later critics of *Main Currents* if he had more closely followed Fletcher's advice. Yet the promises and the limitations of the positive side of the proposition, upon which the development of realism depended, were even then perceived by the youthful student. They provide grounds to refute the view that the mature Parrington was insensitive to the relation between form and content, slighting the role of aesthetics while emphasizing that of ideology. "What, then, in our proposition is meant by 'truthfully represent the life of the past'?" he queried.

> Simply this, to represent life of a former time approximately; in its general relations only, as relatively true as can be done of contemporary times by the same medium. We must remember however that from the nature of the medium the representation will be only generally correct. . . . It would be manifestly unfair and unreasonable to task the novel beyond its possibilities and demand of it a slavishly exact representation.

The essay then considers the problem of character portrayal, letting the weight of the solution fall on the psychological acumen of the author. Less conventional is his point regarding how authors may gain knowledge of past manners and customs. Indeed, on this point Parrington could not be faulted—allowing for advances in research techniques during the last century—by contemporary social historians:

There are within reach various sources whence the student may gain knowledge of past customs and manners. First, histories and contemporary literature, presenting the main facts and manners of thinking of the age; as well as minor tendencies and peculiarities. Again—portraits, pictures, statuary, relics, etc; legends, anecdotes, etc.—preserved; contemporary language, revealing a significant internal picture of the real life and heart of the people. Upon these an age cannot help but imprint its peculiarities and temper . . . little unimportant things tho' some of them may be.

During the second semester, when the briefs and forensics turned to purely artistic matters, Parrington overcame his "vice" of making metaphysical abstractions and consequently received A marks. Parrington's assurance in handling the topic, "Does Rembrandt gain or lose by his system of chiaroscuro?" was not only the result of a semester of practice under Fletcher's tutelage but also of his years drawing and painting at the College of Emporia and of his recent experience in Charles Herbert Moore's fine arts course, "Principles of Delination, Color, and Chiaroscuro."

Harvard's Fine Arts Department was, of course, distinguished by the presence of Charles Eliot Norton, but Parrington either did not know of Norton's reputation or chose Moore simply on the basis of interest. Norton's courses (primarily for upper-division and graduate students) were lecture courses while Moore's (primarily for undergraduates) included practice in drawing and watercolors. Parrington spent regular weekly hours in the well-equipped studio, an outlet he enjoyed and would profit from in later life. Moore's lectures were heavily based on collateral reading that included a fair selection from John Ruskin. This exposure bore fruit in Parrington's Forensics course as well as in the classes in nineteenth-century British literature he developed soon after leaving Harvard. Moore introduced him to concepts regarding the relation between art and nature, the role of the imagination in transforming reality, the problem of portraying emotions and moods in portraits (not just achieving accuracy of physical detail), and what Moore termed "Preraphaelism"—a movement whose implicit social principles, as developed by William Morris, would markedly shape Parrington's ideas concerning the function of art and the artist in society.[9]

Of Parrington's three other courses, his French studies seem to have been a pleasure but his history class was a source of irritation. For a time in the fall, he sat in on an elementary course giving practice in writing and speaking French, in addition to his readings in French prose with Robert L. Sanderson (French 1b). A clue concerning John Parrington's influence in this area is provided by an early November diary entry which notes that Vernon "wrote a letter in French to Father." Parrington was not as fortunate in his choice of history instructors. George Bendelari was known on campus as "the Man of Many Languages," teaching Italian (he was a Neapolitan by birth) and Spanish in addition to European history. Described as "a devoted but not successful teacher," Bendelari left Harvard in 1894 to work in the literary department of the *New York Sun.*[10]

As in his choice of fine arts courses, Parrington appears to have selected Bendelari's survey of seventeenth- and early eighteenth-century European history on the basis of interest: the 1600s and 1700s corresponded to the periods in literature—from the later Shakespearean canon through the development of journalism by Joseph Addison and Richard Steele and the beginnings of the novel—with which he was familiar from Emporia and studied in both Wendell's and Fletcher's courses. The choice was misguided, however, both because of Bendelari's focus and the quality of his instruction. Considering Parrington's later interests, one can only speculate about the effects on the composition and conception of *Main Currents* if he had enrolled in Channing's colonial American history course or History of American Institutions, or Hart's Constitutional and Political History of the United States (1783–1865), his Government and Administration in the United States (which treated national, state, and municipal levels), or his historical and comparative study of the federal government. The author of "God in History" also passed by Ephraim Emerton's religious history courses, as well as such offerings in the Political Economy Department as Economic Theory and Principles of Sociology.

Finally, in selecting Palmer's Ethics course from the philosophy offerings, Parrington bypassed William James's psychology courses, Santayana's courses in the history of European ideas, Royce's course in metaphysics (including a seminar which in 1891–92 focused on the development of the Hegelian system), and Charles Carroll Everett's courses in religious ideas (including "The Psychological Basis of Religious Faith," perhaps avoided after an improperly administered dose of biblical studies at Emporia). He also bypassed F. G. Peabody's "Ethics of the Social Questions," which considered "the questions of Charity, Divorce, the Indians, Temperance, and the various phases of the Labor Question (Socialism, Communism, Arbitration, Cooperation, etc.) as problems of practical Ethics."

The senior member of the department, Palmer was a figure in his own right and had deep interests in educational theory and literature. His wife, Alice Freeman Palmer, who served as the second president of Wellesley College (1882–87) was a champion of women's education. Several of her essays appeared jointly with his well-known treatise "Self-cultivation in English" and contributions to the debate over the elective system in the volume *The Teacher.* He edited the works of the English metaphysical poet George Herbert, wrote on Shakespeare's sonnets, and translated Sophocles and Homer. These interests must certainly have carried over into the classroom. According to Ralph Barton Perry, Palmer's Philosophy 4 course, which he taught from 1884 until his retirement in 1913, was "one of the most famous and popular courses in Harvard College."[11]

Commenting on his Harvard years in his mid-forties, Parrington described Palmer as "the only first-rate teacher I came under," testimony to his role in broadening Parrington's mind. At first taught historically, beginning in 1899 Philosophy 4 (The Theory of Ethics) was taught systematically, with the introductory lectures devoted first to distinguishing philosophy's subject of inquiry (consciousness) from that of the physical sciences (matters that can be verified), then to distinguishing ethics from such related areas as history, aesthetics, and religion. Palmer then successively considered ten ethical issues: goodness, obligation or duty, virtue, conscience, egoism (including pessimism), altruism, relativism, freedom, sanctions, and redemption. These were subjects that Parrington had previously heard debated in his Sunday morning rounds of Emporia's churches. Readings included selections from Kant, Schopenhauer, and Plato, and four theses were required. The first thesis topic is of special significance: a critique of Herbert Spencer's *Data of Ethics*.[12]

Published in 1879, *Data of Ethics* is the first of the three-volume *Principles of Ethics*, which together with corresponding volumes on the principles of psychology, biology, and sociology comprise Spencer's *Synthetic Philosophy. Data of Ethics* provides an alternative, utilitarian outline to the field of ethics as developed by Palmer and was one of the initial course readings. Parrington's critique was divided in two parts, the first summarizing Spencer's argument and the second analyzing it, focusing on the issues of goodness and obligation (the opening topics in the course). Along with Parrington's diary entries on adjusting to Harvard, this analysis is the most important source for documenting the shaking of his once secure foundations. At the beginning he appended a troubled but thoughtful note:

> I do not feel satisfied with the position into which I am forced in the following remarks. It seems presumptuous for me to say that I believe Mr. Spencer wrong when I am unable to refute his arguments or offer substitute hypotheses. Yet, while I confess the plausibility of his arguments, his conclusions do not satisfy me, and I cannot believe his position the true one. I have tried rather in my remarks to outline my difficulties than to refute Mr. Spencer's arguments. My remarks will undoubtless seem crude and ill-advised yet they express my belief in so far as I have crystalised my thoughts into beliefs.

Parrington's immediate difficulty is made clear in the last sentence: the issue in the critique and the course is not one of crystallizing beliefs but of clarifying ideas, an elementary confusion that might be attributed to the College of Emporia's parochialism. Parrington's chief expressed difficulty was with Spencer's "utilitarian hypothesis that all actions are primarily influenced by the amount of pleasure or pain derivable therefrom." He found this formulation "both inadequate and demeaning" but was undecided whether goodness and badness were absolute or relative terms. "Yet ought there not be something, somewhere which we may consider good. . . . A something definite from which to measure?" Yearning for such a standard, Parrington then maintained, as we might expect after having glimpsed some of the motive forces of his character, "Whether there be an absolute goodness or not, there is a universal sense of duty, of obligation, to do right and avoid wrong." In the next paragraph he confessed that he was perplexed by the evident relativism of moral judgment. Then he wrote this revealing illustrative dialogue:

> Ask a man why he does one thing and not another. "Why," he will say, "the one is right and the other wrong." Yes, but why right or wrong? In nine cases out of ten he will be at a loss for an answer. Custom, the mandates of Deity or the law—In fact he will be uncertain; he thinks as his fathers have thought before him and never questioned their beliefs. I have been hitherto in about that condition. . . . What then is the final standard of goodness, I must leave unanswered. I do not know.

Such doubts contain the beginnings of knowledge. Unfortunately, the two theses required during the spring semester, on the freedom of the will and conscience, no longer survive, so we cannot see Parrington wrestling with these issues under Palmer's guidance. He received a C on the Spencer critique and a B in the course, grades less significant as academic measures than as marks on the road to intellectual independence. The hesitations in his Ethics essay came just nine months after the certainties of "God in History." In Palmer's course, then, Parrington began experiencing the crucial separation between thinking and religion. Yet this did not in the beginning affect his habit of church attendance or of recording it in his diary. Indeed, the Boston area offered a quality of preaching as different from Emporia's as Phil 4 was from President Hendy's Old Testament history.

On his first Sunday (October 4) in Cambridge, he went into Boston with his roommate to Fremont Temple and heard George Claude Lorimer, then in the evening heard Episcopalian Phillips Brooks at Harvard. "He had a fine sermon," Parrington observed, "but most peculiar delivery, talking very rapidly, or rather reading." On Tuesday he went to the regularly held but not required campus chapel services, led by Brooke Hereford of the Boston Unitarian church, and "enjoyed it very much." On Saturday, after studying in the library, he went into Boston again and bought a Bible, the Sunday School Teacher's edition published by Oxford. The next morning he chose to stay home and read and in the evening attended but did not enjoy services at a Methodist church.

His diaries reveal that the demands of study intruded increasingly on his church attendance; they also began to include comments on the message as well as the delivery of the preacher. For example, when he first heard Lyman Abbott (editor of the *Outlook*) at a Congregational church, he noted: "He preached on 'God is love,' and it was grand. I never head a sermon which so beautifully and clearly disclosed the character of God. It helped me more than all the sermons I have heard for months." When Abbott later preached at Harvard's chapel on wisdom, Parrington described it as "a magnificent sermon, strong, clear, and to the point." There he also heard Henry Van Dyke, who "preached a good sermon." Once he attended Boston's historic King's Chapel, where the major attraction was not the preaching but catching sight of Dr. Oliver Wendell Holmes, who looked "just like his picture, round, full, boyish-faced and with a pleasant appearance." The first time he heard Edward Everett Hale, another Boston attraction, the young former orator found his sermon "just fair," noting that "I was not at all carried away with him." The second and third times, Hale rated the same average mark, and after he delivered the baccalaureate address, Parrington flatly stated, "I really don't care much for Hale."

As in Emporia, these Sunday outings occasionally provided a stroll with a young woman, though he was usually accompanied by his roommate or a Harvard acquaintance. But during the first fall, Parrington's Sunday socializing most often took the form of writing letters home to his friends and family. His diary shows his regular correspondence with half a dozen Emporians, his disappointment when the return letters arrived slowly, his pleasure in receiving copies of *College Life* (now edited by Vern Cook), and efforts to keep abreast of the fortunes of the college's oratorical contestants and events.

In these entries Parrington's relationship with his parents begins to come into focus. Although it may have been a Harvard affectation, at this time Parrington started referring to his father as "the Judge" and made a distinction between writing letters "home" and "to the Judge." "Home" was his usual designation for his mother (when writing to his brother, John is called by name), who continued to play the nurturant role by sending Vernon thoughtful gifts of handkerchiefs and collar buttons and directions for buying an overcoat and proper dress clothes. Significantly, the next Christmas, when he received a short letter from the Judge and his only present was a box of a dozen kerchiefs from Louise, Parrington wrote in his diary, "She always remembers me, anyway. There's no getting around it, a fellow's best friend is his mother."

These divisions in affective response and appellations provide support for interpreting the Parrington household dynamics in terms of the classic description of the Victorian home. The Victorian father is stern, authoritarian ("the Judge"), absent at work in the external world. The Victorian mother is warm, understanding, near, close by the hearth fire ("home"). The father metes out discipline and order; the mother nurtures the inner life of the child as well as satisfying its physical needs. John Parrington, it should be stressed, had also occupied the commanding roles of school principal and army officer (though Vernon did not call him "Captain" as many

Emporians did), while in Kansas his wife was "the best farmer in the family," assuming a large share in raising stock, crops, and flowers. Moreover, John Parrington was fourteen years older than Louise. Forty-two when Vernon was born, in his early sixties during Vernon's Harvard years, he was old enough to be his son's grandfather. Calling his father "the Judge" emphasizes Vernon's consciousness about his father's public role, but it also may indicate a growing awareness of the distance between the aging parent and the maturing son. These disparities in ages and parental relationship patterns later affected Vernon's attitude toward his own marriage and family life.

Parrington's feelings regarding his family were further heightened when he spent Christmas vacation in Maine and met his father's relatives for the first time. (His mother's immediate family all lived in Illinois, and when residing in Cambridge he never became acquainted with his more distant McClellan relatives in nearby Sutton.) Departing on December 22 for Portland, he was seasick on this first boat voyage and the next morning took a local train to Gorham. Vernon was met at the station by his uncle James Warren ("My what a queer looking old man he is— . . . long, lank, dressed in loose, vile-fitting clothes he is the typical down-easter"), and they drove out two miles in the family carriage to the century-old farmhouse built for Martha McLellan on Flaggy Meadow Road. Parrington found his Aunt Mary (his father's sister) to be "a little mite of a woman, weighing only about 95 pounds . . . very kind and pleasant with her quick puttering ways." With the childless old couple lived James's spinster sister Rebecca, "rather a grim old maid with some quaint, queer expressions and manners." One wonders how these impressions contributed to his conception of his father.

Christmas Eve was rainy and dreary, and he received no letters from home; but he did see Hugh McLellan's brick house and other spots— Tommy Brook and Fort Hill—that had figured in his father's past. On Christmas Day he delved further into the past, reading Elisha Kellogg's *Good Old Times,* a fictionalized account aimed at juveniles of Hugh McLellan's arrival and settlement in Gorham. Yet his thoughts kept turning westward. His mother and brother remained in Emporia, but his father had traveled to the Pacific Coast to investigate timber holdings acquired on Whidby Island, near Seattle. Though Parrington enjoyed the Gorham neighbors he met during his ten-day stay, his mood is best measured by his New Year's Eve diary entry, which gives a rare glimpse of his sense of familial connections:

> Well, another year is gone, and a new one lies stretching downward into the unknown before us. The year that has gone has brought the beginning of manhood and the leaving behind of boyhood, for to me my change in life seems to be that. And it has brought changes, temporary they may be, to the family. Father

is out on the Pacific Coast, I on this Atlantic Seaboard here, while Mother and John are at home in Emporia. When we shall all be together again I cannot tell, yet I believe it will be granted. For the past year I have much to be thankful for, and on the whole I have been successful. My development I feel has been rapid, and I feel this last evening of '91 nearer to man's estate, with all its responsibilities but privileges. Well, well, the year is past, completed and gone, and so I will lay this little record aside and take up a fresh one, looking not back into the past but forward into the future, hopefully, calmly, and prepare to take my share in the universal struggle. Only now a little prayer for the failures of the past and an earnest one for aid in what shall come.

Lest we think Parrington's diary keeping and prayer were pro forma exercises, derived from nineteenth-century models and not genuine expressions of his character, his inscription on New Year's Day is instructive: "Again I begin afresh a new book to keep the record of a year. May my life be, as it were, begun afresh and all its impurities be left behind. God help me this year." He began freshly taking his share in the universal struggle a few days later after his return to Cambridge by attending church in the morning and vespers in the evening, preparatory to facing another semester at Harvard.

This semester included not only the work in his six courses but the completion of senior year requirements at the College of Emporia, which would award him a B.A. in June along with hometown classmates. His major task was writing a thesis for an ethics course, History of Free Thought. The course text was Adam Storey Farrar's *Critical History of Free Thought in Reference to the Christian Religion,* originally delivered as Oxford's distinguished Bampton Lectures in 1862. The lectures' content, in juxtaposition with the secular emphasis of Palmer's ethics course and Parrington's religious habits of mind, could not have been more fortuitous. Farrar's intent was to present a historical analysis of "the forms of doubt or unbelief in reference mainly to the intellectual element which has entered them, and the discovery of the intellectual causes which have produced or modified them. Thus the history," he planned, "while not ceasing to belong to church history, becomes also a chapter in the history of philosophy, a page in the history of the human mind." Although in his eight lectures Farrar treated the spirit of critical inquiry that had challenged traditional Christian doctrine, in the past he had focused on the contemporary crisis of faith precipitated by the appeal of scientific method in the early nineteenth century. As one might expect from a text used at Emporia, the burden of the lectures was to educate clergymen to defend intelligently their viewpoint in encounters with current forms of doubt and to press the lesson "that in all ages of peril, earnest men have found the truth by the method of study united to prayer."[13]

Despite their practical application, the lectures did provide Parrington with an example of someone within the church grappling with questions that increasingly troubled him. When those questions came, however, they were not assuaged by Emporia's religious environment but exacerbated by Harvard's secular one.

In January Parrington added something new to his social life: the theater. Sarah Bernhardt was appearing in Boston. "She is grand. The finest actor I ever saw. Although decidedly French I like it. How her words rippled out! As smooth and sweet as anything I ever heard," he rhapsodized after seeing her in Victorien Sardou's *Cléopâtre*. Two days later he returned to see her in *Leah*, which impressed him even more. "The audience went wild. What a sweet, strange, passionate, seductive voice and personality the Bernhardt has! I believe she could do anything she wished with any man. . . . She lacks just a touch of the nobler, purer. Ah, I enjoyed it tho'." The following week, after cutting a class (history) for the first time and attending a Yale-Harvard debate ("My first hearing of Eastern college speakers, and I will say they can't compare with some Western ones I know"), he heard the coloratura soprano Adelina Patti at the Music Hall. He found her "rather nice looking altho' one can see the wrinkles" and her highly cultivated voice satisfying, but his final judgment was "Give me Sarah Bernhardt anytime."

In the next few months he also saw Julia Marlowe ("A fascinatingly beautiful woman and while not so passionate as Sarah Bernhardt, still an entrancing actress!") in *Romeo and Juliet* and Fanny Davenport in *Cleopatra* ("Simply magnificent. Fanny, while not, of course, quite up to the Bernhardt, yet is fine"). Parrington's extracurricular calender also included concerts at Wellesley, where the talk and feminine companionship were more enjoyable than the music. And when spring came, he began spending happy but wistful afternoons watching the Harvard baseball team practice. These outings lifted his spirits above the doldrums of the fall. His early 1892 diary reveals a more positive and relaxed frame of mind toward both his studies and his Harvard environment.

Parrington's Christmas in Gorham had the unexpected result of providing material for his second semester's work in Wendell's composition course. Instead of fortnightly themes on different topics, the students were to outline and develop a longer project, turning in successive chapters every two weeks. Parrington decided to try his hand at fiction, thinking he would enjoy "the change to a lighter, freer style" because so much of his other writing was "philosophical and argumentative." He conceived a short story in six chapters, titled "The House of Memoire." The setting is the southern Maine coast. In a house built on a slight rise in a grove of trees overlooking the sea lives the aging Giles Memoire, who as a youth had left England against his father's will, an act the father punished by cursing Giles and his descendants with misfortune and a never-to-be-fulfilled desire to return to England. One by one Giles's children die, and as the story opens he is a moody, silent man dreaming impotent dreams of leaving Maine, cared for by an eighteen-year-old granddaughter, Margaret. The first-person narrator of the story is Ralph Fordham, a stranger to the area spending the summer in a nearby village. Margaret discovers the family curse in a packet of yellowed letters and falls in love with Ralph, who vainly entreats her to break the curse and leave the house. She refuses; he goes away; she dies after a life of seclusion, and the House of Memoire becomes extinct.

Wendell "amused himself for [a] half-hour" reading the first two chapters aloud to the class but after those uncomfortable moments relieved the author by saying, "On the whole few men in the course could surpass it for that kind of work." That the remark was tongue-in-cheek may be proved by Wendell's written comment on the third chapter: "Romantically connotative. And on the whole less overdone than I should have expected. . . . On the other hand you are a third through your story & nothing whatever has happened: a curious fault in what purports to be a narrative." After the fifth installment, focusing on the love affair between Margaret and Ralph, Wendell recommended that Parrington read the closing pages of the chapter on force in his composition text, then observed, "Your style is strained, fantastic, pseudo-passionate to a point which is not apparently warranted by the underlying emotion." Despite Wendell's criticism of his approach and style, Parrington had intentionally chosen them, believing that "the weird and unusual—if not carried to the extreme—is the quality best fitted to raise an imperfect work above the commonplace and conventional." Perhaps he erred in the judgment, but he wrote about something he knew. For, of course, Ralph is Parrington; the house is modeled on Hugh McLellan's; Giles and Margaret are partly inspired by Hugh and Martha McLellan Warren and other Gorham relatives and residents.[14]

But outside of the setting, the story's greatest debts are to Edgar Allan Poe and Nathaniel Hawthorne, figures whose treatments in *Main Currents* would consistently be criticized for lack of attention to aesthetic criteria. Ironically, Poe and Hawthorne were two of the authors who delighted Parrington in the collateral reading for Wendell's course. Though he did not (or need not) name his major influence in the required outline for "The House of Memoire," in late January his diary stated explicitly that the story's basis is to be "somewhat weird, rather on the style of Hawthorne." Then in late February, he recorded: "Read several of Poe's tales. What weird and strange creations they are! And yet I like them." This encounter inspired Parrington independently to write what he termed "a short tale of 'mystery'." His taste for the exotic and gothic had, however, first been expressed in a January short story titled "The Princess Mini—An Egyptian Fragment." Obviously, he had read his share of popular romantic novels with foreign settings and pseudo-historical plots such as *Uarda: A Romance of Ancient Egypt* and *Joshua: A Tale from Biblical Times* by the German author Georg Moritz Ebers. On "The Princess Mini" Wendell commented, with masterful restraint: "A subject so eccentric demands an eccentric style. Your style suits it. . . . This is . . . work of a kind not to be often practiced."

"The Fall of the House of Usher" also left its mark on "The House of Memoire." Though Poe is not mentioned again in Parrington's diary, he became the subject of a daily theme (which Wendell termed "Appreciative"), quoted here in its entirety:

> I have just been reading some of Poe's tales. What strange, weird, fantastic, yet marvelously fascinating creations they are! One reads them wonderingly, admiringly, recognising their weirdness—and in some cases morbidness—yet held the more by this very element of strangeness.
>
> The striking success of his works—poetical as well as prose—is due, it seems to me, to the fact that he knew exactly what he wished to accomplish. "The effect which one wishes to produce," says he himself, "is what must be held clearly in mind and everything must subserve that." Whatever is irrelevant is cut out unsparingly and as a result, we have his tales, short and free, very marvels of clearness and elegance. A better exemplification of the rules which should govern literary work, I have never seen, than these same weird tales.
>
> Would there were more Poe's among our geniuses.[15]

Hawthorne, however, proved most inspiring to Parrington. By early April he was enjoying portions of *Mosses from the Old Manse* and rereading *The Scarlet Letter.* "I do think it one of the most remarkable books I have ever read. How I have longed to see Hawthorne!" his diary exclaimed. "He is my ideal of a writer. Quiet, gentle, lovable." A month later he completed *The Marble Faun* but did not like it as well as *The Scarlet Letter.* This response was elaborated in another daily theme, in which Parrington questioned Hawthorne's own opinion, cited in a recent biography, that *The Faun* was his greatest work. "The 'Faun' is highly finished and strongly romantic," he observed, "but lacks concentration and is not sustained. The 'Scarlet Letter' on the other hand is, in every sense, a remarkable production. Sustained, strongly conceited, keenly analytic and highly finished, it is marked by the perfection of that half-weird romantic flavor, heightened here by a deep sadness, which is Hawthorne's most exquisite quality." Wendell's note on this late May theme asked Parrington to consider *The House of the Seven Gables,* another obvious model for "The House of Memoire." When Parrington read *Seven Gables* the first time is not known, but he reread the novel during the summer of 1892, finishing it one Sunday morning instead of going to church. "I fairly love Hawthorne," he exclaimed in his diary. "He is my favorite, par excellence, of all writers. Quaint, subtle, chaste, elegant—his style is nearly perfect."

Parrington's positive response to Hawthorne and Poe is almost ironic because he found the work of William Dean Howells—the dean of the American realist tradition which *Main Currents* supposedly champions—in every way inferior. After reading *Shadow of a Dream* in May, he recorded in his diary: "I am doing my best to understand Howells' qualities, but am not able to yet. I must admit I don't like his bald, crude, realism." Subsequently, Howells became the subject of three consecutive daily themes. In the first, which Wendell called "judicial," Parrington wrote, with a certainty whose sources were in the genteel tradition he later severely criticized:

> While I have little sympathy with realism generally, I admit it has done literature a good in doing away somewhat with the more or less melodramatic style of handling which had hitherto prevailed. Howells, however, I think goes too far. Literature his novels are not. His style is bald, insipid, commonplace. What a difference between his "isnts" and "arents," his careless sentences and colloquialisms savoring of slang, and Hawthorne's finished luminous style! As psychological or social studies I consider his works inferior to both the English and French modern schools.
>
> In short I do not see how Mr. Howells influence can survive his death, except, perhaps as the most decided exponent of realism, he may be read as a sort of curiosity by students of American literature.

The following day, in a theme Wendell judged "good criticism," he caustically observed: "One might as well read a phonographic reproduction of an average after dinner chat, as to read one of Howells society novels. It would doubtless do one as much good and its substance prove as edifying." On the third day his theme contrasted *The Rise of Silas Lapham* ("the work of a blunt, matter of fact, everyday man, who acts rather than feels") with Henry Wadsworth Longfellow's *Hyperion* ("the work of a poet who feels and longs rather than acts"). Parrington's choice of contrasts and Wendell's judgment of the theme as "smooth" should be evaluated in light of the altered perspective on romanticism and realism that the newly emerging naturalistic school would contribute to literary history. On this development, the student and professor would part company. For now, they were in agreement.[16]

Whether this concord was owing to Wendell's critical influence, Wendell's gradebook, or Parrington's natural inclinations, it was paralleled by a reversal of Parrington's initial impression of his professor as arrogant and overbearing. At the end of the academic year he wrote in his diary: "Great boy old Barrett, after all. I don't like him and yet I can't say I dislike him. Bright, worldly, shallow. Eng 12, however, while a source of an abundance of worry, work, and anger, has been of great help." For Wendell's eyes, earlier that day he had modified his evaluation of his experience in his last daily theme:

> The course has been a benefit to me. I feel now that I am in a position to go on and intelligently follow out the lines sketched by the year's work. Whether I ever do or not I shall at least have acquired a deeper appreciation of the beauties of true literary art and a keener enjoyment, as well, in the variant, fleeting pictures which life . . . sketches, erases, and resketches continually.
>
> As such I shall always remember old Eng 12 kindly, almost lovingly.

This stance measures the degree of Parrington's adjustment to Wendell, the only professor to be the subject of several diary entries. It also measures the degree of Parrington's adjustment to Harvard, when contrasted with his fall confessions of self-doubt, loneliness, and lack of confidence. His final grades, though not on par with those received at Emporia, were respectable. With the exception of a C in Bendelari's history course, which he thought should have been a B, he was generally satisfied with his marks: two A's, in French and Forensics, and B's in Palmer's ethics course, Moore's fine arts course, and—despite his diligence—in "old Eng 12."

Although much of his reading had been of English authors—Charlotte Brontë, Charles Dickens, Oliver Goldsmith, Rudyard Kipling—Parrington had initiated an acquaintance with American literature, as his exposure to Hawthorne, Poe, Longfellow, and Howells illustrates. American history he imbibed from the Boston environment: in an early fall diary entry he had observed, "It is hard to realize how close I am to the very centre and heart of American history." But neither American history nor literature was yet at the center of his focus of interest and study. He did keep abreast of political events, but his attitudes were still indistinguishable from the Republican partisanship of his father. For example, in February 1892 the founding of the national People's party at the St. Louis convention that nominated veteran Greenbacker James B. Weaver for president became the subject of a daily theme:

> And so a new party has stepped forth into this chilly world. I hope at least it will live to get out of its swaddling clothes, but I fear it won't. What a strange mixture its platform is! With its wild schemes to do away with National Banks and float a mass of fiat money; its free coinage of silver and subtreasury scheme with other unheard of ideas, it shows its fantastical element pretty plainly.
>
> The American people however are far too sensible on the whole to be caught by any such schemes, and after all the number of fanatics is not dangerously large. So we may be confident that this new party will speedily pass away and be forgotten except by searchers for political curios.

This judgment might have been retracted more quickly than it was—by 1896 he was a firm supporter of the "fantastical" free silver scheme—if Parrington had gone home to Emporia after the semester's close and witnessed the economic situation on the Middle Border that eventuated in the crises of 1893. But the family finances were too limited to include the price of a train ticket, and so he returned to Gorham to spend the summer months with his aunt and uncle.

"The Past Year Has Been Unsettling"

When Parrington boarded the boat for Maine after successfully completing his junior exams and attending Harvard's baccalaureate and commencement exercises, he was in the curious position of already possessing a bachelor's degree. He had been awarded his A.B. in absentia from the College of Emporia, and thus the three V's technically graduated together, forming three-fifths of the class of 1892. These events appear to have stiffened his resolve "to make myself." On his first day in Gorham, he wrote in his diary: "Well! I am out here again and for a time probably. It won't be stupid, as I'm going to work. Yes, I am. I've made up my mind, and when I say I will—well, I will."

But Parrington did not allow for the unexpected. The Warrens' hay crop had to be harvested the first three weeks in July so the summer began just as his Emporia ones had. And there were regular farm chores to help with, including the pleasant tasks of picking strawberries, blueberries, and blackberries as they came in season. There were obligatory visits to meet relatives and friends of his Aunt Mary's. There was a trip to the cemetery to see the graves of his grandparents—John Parrington, the Yorkshire weaver, and his wife, Ann Wrathal—and the graves of his Uncle William and the baby who died in infancy. He met the wife of James Mann, who had raised his father. He attended the village church all but four Sundays with his aunt, duly recording the omissions in his diary. And there was regular socializing with Gorham residents of his own age, also in town for college vacations.

Most exciting were excursions beyond Gorham. Parrington spent a day rowing among the islands off Portland, another enviously watching the bathers at Old Orchard Beach, and one in New Hampshire. At the end of August, he spent six days at Prout's Neck, Maine, unchaperoned with several young Gorham men and women. Here Parrington found a good deal to take his mind away from work—clam-digging, fishing, bathing in the sea for the first time ("it was immense. I simply love it"), playing tennis, dancing, singing, telling stories, participating in candy pulls. The company of several lively, attractive girls was especially appealing, as the diary entry made after returning to Gorham makes clear: "Well, I had a bully good time and one which I will remember. For one thing, I got in more hugging—and more varied—than ever before in so short a time."

Parrington sorely needed the rest and recreation such activities afforded. He was occasionally troubled by headaches and before leaving for Prout's Neck was ill periodically, events that contradicted his image of himself as "possessing a sound body and constitution."[17] But he had promised himself a studious summer, and his conscience bothered him when he was unfaithful to his planned regimen. "Fooled around greater part of the day without doing much," "Lay around all afternoon," "Did little studying, but not much," "Accomplished little except to chore around," "Loafed around at Osborne's—must quit it," are sample reproofs in his summer diary.

In between his farm chores, outings, and bouts of conscience, Parrington spent the greater portion of his "work" time studying German so he would not have to enroll in a beginning course in the fall. In addition to rereading *The House of the Seven Gables*, he read Hawthorne's *Fanshawe* ("a simple tale and quite pleasant . . . but not comparable to *Scarlet Letter*"), Kipling's "Life's Handicap" (intoned aloud to his aunt), "Hiawatha" ("I like it"), and selections from Tennyson ("*Idylls of the King* . . . are really wonderful"). Parrington wrote another short story, an Indian legend titled "Dividing Rock," probably inspired by Hugh McLellan's struggles with the Narragansetts, and sent it off (with unsuccessful results) to the *Portland Transcript*. Finally, he attended several political meetings with his uncle. The 1892 campaign was under way, but the ardent supporter of William McKinley was disappointed when the candidate was unable to appear at an August rally.

Parrington quietly celebrated his twenty-first birthday on August 3, staying at home and writing. The occasion prompted this reflection: "Je suis un homme parce que j'ai vingt et un ans aujourd' hui. Will not feel, however, that I am a man till another year, when I strike out for myself. 21, 42, 63 . . . a third of life is gone already." Here Parrington—always interested in tabulating and categorizing, as evidenced by the regular inclusion of grades, baseball scores, oratory results, and his current height and weight in his diary—was projecting his inner-directed "time and motion study" into the future. He had a definite sense of what he should accomplish and the stages through which his life should progress. When these ideals were not achieved, it was a source of tension. But now and in later life, that tension produced a redoubled effort to work harder.

When Parrington returned to Cambridge in late September, he was quickly immersed in course work and thus found an immediate counter to any lingering feelings of having dissipated his vacation. In contrast to the previous fall, when melancholic introspection characterized his diary, the burdens of studying became a constant theme. "Lots and lots of work," "In room all day studying and working," "A hard day, on the jump continually," "Filled the day just full of work. Have little leisure to loaf," "Hard at work and put in a thoroughly good day," "Bully for Columbus. If it hadn't been for him we would have had to grind today," "Put in the day grinding like the deuce. . . . Well, one month of college '92–'93 done for. How time passes!" run successive entries in October. These certainly bore out his exclamation upon arriving back on campus, "My! but things seem different from last year!" He also had a new room, at 65 Oxford Street; a new roommate, J. W. Eichinger, another senior; and a new place to takes his meals, at Memorial Hall, the University Commons, where the food and company were more substantial and warming than his previous dining arrangements.

The necessity for "grinding" was the result of registering for seven courses, all in languages and literature. After his disappointment with Bendelari, he ventured no further in the History Department; and despite his pleasure in Palmer's teaching, he did not pursue offerings by other members of the philosophy faculty. Perhaps because of timidity, perhaps of clarifying professional goals, Parrington narrowed and concentrated rather than broadened and diversified his academic choices. He continued with French, taking a half course (French 4), Practice in Writing and Speaking French, from Alphonse Brun in tandem with Professor Sanderson's French Prose and Poetry (French 2), which included reading La Fontaine, Corneille, Racine, Molière, Beaumarchais, Alfred de Musset, and Balzac as well as historical grammar and composition. Following up on his studies at Gorham, he enrolled in two German classes: German C, an intermediate course including grammar, composition, translation, sight-reading, and selections from eighteenth- and nineteenth-century writers; and German E, a half course in grammar and practice in writing. He did venture further in Romance languages by enrolling in the beginning Italian course (grammar, reading selections, and elementary compositions) taught by the chairman of the Germanic and Romance Philology Department, Edward S. Sheldon.[18] Sheldon impressed him as "a queer, little man," and though the pronunciation struck him as odd, he thought the course would prove easy. Finally, he took two English electives, Anglo-Saxon under George Lyman Kittredge and Eighteenth-Century British Literature with Lewis Gates.

This load was simply too heavy. A few weeks into the semester, he transferred from German C to German 1a, a less advanced course taught by Hans C. G. von Jagemann, who served as chairman of the Modern Language Association six years later, in 1899. In early November he was totally unprepared for an exam in German E and flunked outright, turning in a blank paper. "The fact is," he explained in his diary, "I have more work on my hands than I can do." The next day he dropped the course, hoping to improve his performance in his six remaining classes. Yet in the middle of the month he recorded, "Nothing but grind, grind, and it seems to be about as much advantage as the fairy mill on the bottom of the sea." And on Thanksgiving, after reading Alexander Pope in the morning and enjoying an elegant dinner at Memorial, he wanted to go to the theater but could not spare the time. But a comment indicates that social activities were decreasing in his priorities: "Am getting to grudge every moment which is not put in reading or writing." That he was not merely nurturing a martyr complex, forcing himself to spend a holiday studying, is illustrated by a diary entry made only two weeks later: "Pleasant. Put in a hard day's work. Work, work, plenty of it. I only wish that the days were longer or that I didn't have to spend so great a proportion of them asleep. Am getting every day to believe more in the genius of work." A week later, as the Christmas holidays approached, he modified this zeal: "I continue to work hard and get low marks. Never, no never, had such luck before. May I never have such again."

Though German dragged down his grades, his two English classes, both half courses, were also demanding. In retrospect, Parrington's choices might be viewed as determining the direction of his future literary studies. Now knowledgeable of at least the lights of Harvard's English faculty, he had wisely enrolled in a course with Kittredge and no doubt was advised that Anglo-Saxon provided a firm foundation for further study. The disciple and successor to Francis J. Child, who had presided over the development of English as an independent scholarly field in the 1860s and 1870s from its status of providing rhetoric and oratory as an adjunct to entering the ministry (as it was still at Emporia in Parrington's day), Kittredge was making his reputation as a Shakespeare scholar as well as teaching Chaucer and folkloric courses. But he handed Parrington's class over to his assistant, Alfred C. Garrett, "a young instructor who failed hopelessly." Whether the fault lay with the instructor or the student—he received an ignominious C for the year—and though Parrington later claimed he would have "hated Kittredge for the petty tyrant that he was," one wonders what might have happened if he had been more thoroughly captured by philological studies or by Kittredge's interests and influential instruction.[19]

Eighteenth-Century British Literature was the only upper-division course Parrington took at Harvard. Lewis Gates did not cut as commanding a figure as did either Wendell or Kittredge, nor did he publish prolifically. In addition to the three volumes edited for Henry Holt's Men of Letters series—selections from the prose writings of Cardinal Newman, Matthew Arnold, and the less well-known Francis Jeffrey with lengthy introductions—his other significant work is a collection of ten essays, *Studies and Appreciations* (1900), most of which had previously appeared in periodicals. As in the cases of the Holt introductions, these essays emphasize the writers' style and ideas in relation to their times and primarily consider nineteenth- rather than eighteenth-century figures such as Tennyson, Charlotte Brontë, Hawthorne, Poe, Elizabeth Barret Browning, Thomas Carlyle, and Matthew Arnold.

How far Gates's literary approaches, as indicated by the thrust of his published work, entered into his Harvard classroom may be measured by their similarity to the critical standards employed by Parrington in his own teaching and writing. In this regard, one essay in *Studies and Appreciations* is of particular importance: "Taine's Influence as a Critic." Gates sensibly devotes most of the piece to criticisms, such as those made by Charles Augustin Sainte-Beuve, of Hippolyte Taine's application of scientific principles to art, the method made most familiar through his *History of English Literature*. Yet Gates's personal evaluation is revealed in the essay's conclusion:

[P]erhaps we are not so apt to realize how much he has done to redeem literary criticism from being a paltry juggling with fine phrases and to give it seriousness of purpose, dignity, and a recognized standing. He was charged with thoroughgoing materialism; but in an age of *decadence*, when the descendants of the Romanticists and idealists are for the most part engaged in dilettante experiments on their senses and emotions, such materialism as Taine's is as healthy as sea air.[20]

The essay was published in the *Nation* on the occasion of Taine's death on March 5, 1893, during the spring Parrington was enrolled in Gates's course. (Indeed, Parrington's first mention of Taine is in a February 1893 diary entry, so we may conclude that he was introduced to the French critic by Gates.) That Gates contributed to the *Nation* may provide an indication of his political attitudes; it certainly further underscores the independence of mind evidenced in his other writings. He was clearly an apostle of the cultural attitudes expressed by Matthew Arnold, which sought a rapprochement between the promises of romanticism and the realities of the late nineteenth century's scientism; he was just as clearly not an adherent of rigid aesthetic standards or literary canons.

How these intellectual traits were manifested in Gates's treatment of students is illuminated by a noteworthy footnote in American literary history. Shortly after Parrington left Cambridge, Frank Norris enrolled as a special student at Harvard during the 1894–95 academic year and took a composition course from Gates. Norris had graduated from the University of California in 1894 and had begun writing his early novel, *McTeague,* in 1892 or 1893 but desired some direction from graduate study and perhaps the distinction of Harvard training. Gates encouraged Norris, and the manuscript was completed to the point of Trina's murder. When *McTeague* was finally published in 1899, Norris dedicated it to "L. E. Gates of Harvard University." The defender of Taine must have recognized more than sheer expressive power in Norris's exploration of the naturalistic principles derived from his assiduous reading of Émile Zola.[21]

Though in his 1918 autobiographical sketch Parrington, who had read Norris and could not have failed to observe the dedication, credits Gates with giving him valuable instruction in composition, his Harvard diaries do not remark upon Gates or his course except to record Parrington's allied reading and the progress on his papers. During the fall term, four short (three to four pages) themes were required. The first discussed Daniel Defoe's humor, which Parrington observed was not humor in the usual sense but grave and matter-of-fact. The second considered Defoe's imagination, which impressed Parrington for its "remarkable definiteness" and vivid detail but also as lacking in spiritual and mysterious qualities—the traits he so admired in Hawthorne. The third theme described three reasons for the *Tatler*'s success, yet Parrington found that although single numbers were highly readable, on the whole this famous periodical was disappointing. The fourth, comparing Addison's and Hawthorne's styles, shifted beyond the eighteenth century and into an American subject. Parrington argued that Hawthorne's vital, light and free, subtle style was superior to and more in keeping with present ideas than Addison's stately, heavy, and objective one. Here are echoes of the antirealistic bias that marked his criticism of Howells and his preference for the more imaginatively romantic.

During the spring term, Gates required two long theses. The first, turned in in mid-January, built upon the fall's prose investigations and treated the development of the novel before Richardson. The thesis also built upon the arguments Parrington had honed the previous year in his briefs and forensics written for Jefferson B. Fletcher that considered whether the historical novel could truly represent the past. His work in Forensics had been abstract and criticized for lacking examples, whereas this thesis shows Parrington working much more closely with the literary material at hand. It also shows him discussing literature in the context of the economic, political, and social factors that informed its conception, style, emphasis, and reception. This was the method he would pursue in *Main Currents* in treating literature and creative writers.

For those who have known Parrington only as an Americanist, it should be pointed out that one of his most popular courses at the University of Washington was in eighteenth-century British literature. Much of the foundation for this course was laid in his work for Gates. The similarity between the themes, emphases, and style in Parrington's fifty-one-page English 7 thesis, for which he received an A, and his mature publications is striking. For example, on the opening page he dissents from the attribution of the novel's origin to Henry Fielding (by Sir Walter Scott) and to Defoe (by Sir Leslie Stephen) because "they assume that an individual created the novel, and they take no notice of the forces which had created this individual." He then argues that "the fact is that the novel, like every other complicated form of literature, was the product of development," and cites for substantiation Thomas Sergeant Perry's *English Literature of the 18th Century,* published just a decade earlier. "In other words," Parrington explains,

> to use the popular phrase, it has been evolved, along with and because of the evolution of society. As the old age of feudalism and chivalry passed away, the old fiction gradually died out. As the new civilization—the civilization which we term modern—gradually arose, a new phase of fiction was developed, to meet the new conditions. The difference between the two fictions, roughly speaking, is the difference in the spirit of feudalism and of modern democracy.

Parrington attributes the literary and political displacement of the knight by the common man to the rise of the middle class during the 1750–1850 period. This new reading public was less interested in "romance," in the episodic narration of uncommon events, than in the portrayal of bourgeois manners and character. Both the newspaper, as pioneered by Addison and Steele in the *Tatler* and the *Spectator,* and the novel, with its antecedents in the Spanish picaresque, Parrington emphasizes, were developed primarily as responses to changes in life-style and political power rather than as inventions of individual authors. The impact of evolutionary thinking as it affected late nineteenth-century literary criticism is markedly apparent in the outline of Parrington's argument and in the diction of the passage quoted above.[22]

Of further significance are the interpretative method and imagery in the thesis's sketch of Defoe. Parrington sees Defoe's career, beginning in journalism and including the writing of novels and biographies, as exemplifying the stages in the novel's development and "advancing along lines not simply the result of individual selection but . . . controlled largely by the spirit of the age." The thrust of the sketch, however, is at variance with this "environmental" interpretation. If the nationality and dates of the author in the following passage were changed, it could fit any number of writers described in *Main Currents,* who, though innovative, squandered their talents:

> Defoe is a unique figure in the literature of Queen Anne's time. Compared with the dignity and classical elegance of Addison and his school, *he seems to have fallen upon the wrong age.* He belongs rather to the 19th than to the 18th century. He has all the push and restless energy of a modern journalist. . . . He was blessed with shrewd common sense and just enough education to enable him to use his native abilities to the best advantage, without having them warped by classic affectations. He was a master of the "plain homely" vigorous English, which would suit the taste of the people, far more than the "elegant" style of the litterateur. But . . . *He veered with every wind. . . .* He thought far more of present profit, than his reputation with later generations. He believed in serving up a dish as it came piping hot from the oven; what this dish consisted of, whether scandal or biography, or fiction under the verisimilitude of truth—it mattered little to him, so it suited the public taste. (Emphasis added)

Professor Fletcher might have judged this portrait as another instance of damning by faint praise, but the passage and the argument of the thesis as a whole show Parrington shifting away from the critical principles manifested during his year with Barrett Wendell. If Parrington was not yet an exponent of realism, under Gates he began learning to make connections between literary romance and political and social elitism.

Parrington's second thesis for Gates, "Nature in the Poetry of Thompson, Young, Gray, Collins and Wordsworth," was not so much a retreat from the implications of the first one as expressive of his deep-seated attraction to art and beauty. That may be one reason he received "an easy A" on the fifty-seven-page effort completed in early May. Another is that he again drew upon material from a first-year Harvard class, Fine Arts with Professor Moore. The thesis evaluated these five English romantic poets in light of Ruskin's discussion, in the third volume of *Modern Painters,* of Greek classicism and its ideals of symmetry and proportion and its conception of nature as subordinate to man. Parrington argued that the romantic movement was a spiritual protest against the revival of classicism in the seventeenth and eighteenth centuries, itself a result of the desire to order the extravagances of the Renaissance.

The two theses illustrate succinctly the two major and apparently contradictory claims on Parrington's taste in and treatment of literature that thereafter characterized his criticism and thinking. On one hand, Parrington was committed to art that portrays the political and social realities of common life; on the other, he was committed to the free play of artistic imagination with its expression of spiritual aspiration. The former case helps explain his championing of such American writers as Hamlin Garland and Sinclair Lewis; the latter helps explain his attraction to such writers as James Branch Cabell (as well as to Poe's and Hawthorne's gothicism). These dual facets are so thoroughly ingrained and Parrington's habit of analyzing according to these categories—with the attendant multiple and shifting definitions of forms of the terms "realism" and "romance"—so pronounced that they are best understood as dialectical. The crucial turning points in his intellectual life and in his cultural and political interpretations are, therefore, marked by the ideas or figures in which the conflicting terms of the dialectic reach a synthesis.

Yet this is to anticipate the future, to clarify what was only dimly evident, if at all, to the busy Harvard senior. The weeks were punctuated with shopping trips, though Parrington's sartorial desires were restrained by his finances; with Saturday evening dancing classes in Somerville, which were predictably followed by bouts of feeling "overcast"; with concerts and plays, including hearing Eleanora Duse in "Cavalleria Rusticana" and Ignace Paderewski in a solo performance and seeing Julia Marlowe in *As You Like It* and Helena Modjeska in *Henry VIII*. He sat for his senior photograph, wearing a cutaway, a turn-down collar, and a dark, fluffy four-in-hand. But he was disappointed in the proofs and scheduled a second sitting, which elicited the comment in his diary: "It's a serious matter, you see, that of being handed down to posterity; for what if we should become celebrated. See?" In the fall there were Harvard football games, and in late January Parrington turned in his name as a candidate for the varsity baseball team, looking forward to the practice sessions in the cage whether or not he made the team (which he found out in May he had not) and sealing his hopes by investing $3.75 in a Harvard sweater.

From Emporia came reports of the oratory team's topics and scores and of several trips by the Judge to Washington to oversee the Whidby Island property settlement. In February came the troubling news that Vern Cook's eye had been removed, followed in March by the surprising announcement of Parrington's brother's marriage proposal to a local girl, Mary Wright. He was moved by the deaths of Tennyson in October and Phillips Brooks in January. During the fall campaign season, he attended several Republican torchlight rallies. When election returns showed William Henry Harrison's defeat and widespread Democratic successes in state races, he exclaimed, "The worst has happened!" and was "too sick of it to be very amiable." But he duly recorded Grover Cleveland's inauguration in his diary in March.

In addition to these activities and his regular courses, during the spring term Parrington audited Arthur E. Marsh's comparative literature class, which traced fabliaux, or verse stories, in Italian, French, Spanish, and German literature. He also completed much of the reading in A. S. Hill's nineteenth-century poets course (this included selections from Poe, John Godfrey Saxe, and Nathaniel Parker Willis and from E. Clarence Stedman's anthology) and copied a friend's notes from the nineteenth-century prose writers course, a complete set which he deemed would be "an immense assistance in any serious work which I may undertake."

As this diary entry reveals, that "serious work" seemed to be teaching. In early February Parrington wrote to Professor Reuben S. Lawrence at the College of Emporia about the possibility of obtaining a position there the following year, after his parents had broached the idea in a letter. In May he also wrote inquiring about a vacant position at Milton Academy in Maine and was hopeful of his prospects, asking for a recommendation from his uncle Mark Dunnell, now living in Minnesota, who had taught at several Maine academies. In early June he cast his net wider, following Dunnell's advice to contact the superintendent of higher education in Minnesota. But this step was taken only after hearing from John Dunbar Hewitt, the president of the College of Emporia, who feared that Parrington was not "actively religious" enough to be considered for a position there.[23] "Damn!" was the reaction registered in his diary, which perhaps justified Dr. Hewitt's Presbyterian fears.

Those fears would have been confirmed by Parrington's occasional lack of church attendance (his diaries still regularly recorded the Sunday services he observed and the featured sermon), as he chose to stay in his room and study or work on his second thesis for Lewis Gates. This behavior coincided with a campus visit in April by Henry Drummond, whom Parrington heard speak three times in the space of a week. The first time rated no comment; the second elicited "Interesting"; the third, "I do like the man."

Twenty-five years later, in his 1918 autobiographical sketch, Parrington claimed that Spencer's *Data of Ethics,* read in Palmer's philosophy course, was "the first book of Victorian speculation to make a deep impression on me, and served as my introduction to a stimulating field of thought." He explained further that while at Harvard, "pure literature was still my chief interest, although, I began to feel the fascination of the writers on evolution." Of these, Drummond "came somewhat later to be my chief guide, his *Ascent of Man* seeming to me to be a wonderfully inspiring account of man's origins." This book may be taken as representative of the Glasgow scientist-turned-preacher's attempt to reconcile evolution with Christianity by arguing that although man had progressed biologically in the past, spiritual progress under Christian doctrine—the "ascent" of the soul rather than just the development of the body—could be seen as a more recent manifestation and continuation of evolutionary principles.

To the author of "God in History," influenced by the "conventional orthodoxy" of Emporia's William R. Kirkwood and required to question the sufficiency of that orthodoxy when he encountered Spencer's utilitarianism his first semester at Harvard, Drummond's appeal should be obvious. He was another synthetic figure who allowed Parrington to unite the vacillating forces of social relevance and spiritual expression in his two theses completed for Eighteenth-Century British Literature. As Parrington points out, however, that synthesis did not result during Drummond's Harvard engagement.

If anything, at that point it deepened the fissures created in his conventional orthodoxy when upon numerous Sundays he was exposed to milder versions of evolutionary thinking in the preaching of Phillips Brooks and Lyman Abbott. This pulpit exposure was further reinforced by his initial reading of Taine, the earliest evidence of which is the diary entry for February 25, 1893, during his final semester while he was studying with Lewis Gates. Both Parrington's current religious and secular sources were conveying a similar message. The weight of the message was strengthened by the evident harmony it demonstrated between church and school, the realm of spiritual and philosophical idealism and the realm of practical, literary scholarship. Those two realms had also coexisted in Emporia, but how differently they were defined in Cambridge!

His awareness of those differences assumed the proportions of a religious crisis by the middle of Parrington's second year at Harvard. He did not return to Gorham to stay with the McLellans over Christmas vacation but spent the holidays on campus. The denial of contact with family and friends accentuated Parrington's introspective mood. The weather was bitter, he had not funds to buy presents for he had received no mail from home, his room was too cold to study in, he accomplished little even when he went to the library, he lost the address of a potential date. On Christmas Eve he confided in his diary: "Hang it, I felt kind of pessimistic for a spell. What the deuce does this life of ours amount to after all? I doubt if anyone really enjoys it. If he does, he must be of a different temperament from me."

On Christmas Day, after one hour's respite at an elegant dinner on campus with his roommate, Parrington sat in his room and penned another burst of outrage before going to bed: "Hang a Christmas like this. I hate it. . . . Instead of lifting one up, every such day makes one more indifferent and cynical." In this frame of mind, partially alleviated by several hours working in the library, he approached his annual New Year's Eve ritual of self-evaluation. Parrington went to bed early, only to be awakened by the bells and chimes greeting 1893. Then he inscribed the longest single entry in his entire sequence of diaries.

He began by recounting a visit to the gym before dinner, where he weighed himself and found the scales six pounds heavier than before and noticed how tight his Prince Albert had become around the chest. (Parrington achieved his 5'10" height by his late teens and now weighed 159 pounds "stripped," 170 pounds "dressed.") "Well," the nascent evolutionist commented on this exterior, biological means of measurement,

> I can get onto a pair of scales, or put on an old coat, and find out how much I have grown physically during the year. It is somewhat more difficult to ascertain mental growth. It is a thing so subtle, and takes place so gradually as to be imperceptable in the very midst of the transformation.

First, Parrington singled out the positive aspects of his mental development:

> I appreciate the fact that I possess truer and richer views of life. It is growing less and less a petty, isolated affair to me, and is assuming a place in the great ideal, the universal world-life. I do grow discontented at times, but it is this realization—very imperfect tho' it be—of something nobler and grander in our destiny, which renders this petty routine life of a student, not only tolerable but pleasant. It is the larger and fuller realization of this thought that I wish to seek in the years to come.

There is the duty-bound conscience squaring itself with the daily reality of discouragement, the viewpoint of one who saw good resulting from conflict in his prizewinning oration. Next Parrington pondered his academic development:

> I can see that from a literary standpoint the year has brought noticeable development. I am beginning to get an idea of the spirit and meaning of our literature. Never before this past year have I known how to read and study English. My efforts have been desultory and dissipated. Henceforth, I propose to devote my reading to better purpose—now that I have got a start in the right direction.

Finally, he turned—in the habit of the debater—to what he no doubt considered the negative aspects of his year's experience:

> From a religious standpoint there is no longer any possibility of concealing or overlooking the fact that *the past year has been unsettling.* I look on many things now far otherwise than I did a year ago. What I really believe I almost fear to decide. Many of my old beliefs I don't really, vitally believe in any longer, and yet I cannot, for some reason, calmly disbelieve in them. It is taking away too great a part of my life and habits of thought. The question, however, confronts me and must be answered: "What do you believe? What is your faith?" It is a question, awful in meaning and portent. God help me to answer it aright, to read the meaning of nature and our relation to it and to the supreme being truly. Amen. (Emphasis added)

It was a question to which he continued to seek an answer—sometimes in the professional form of teaching, sometimes in political activity, sometimes in poetry and prayer—over the next decades. It was also a question that the College of Emporia's Hewitt wanted answered according to the conventionally orthodox before bestowing faculty status on the increasingly heterodox, cosmopolitan twenty-one-year-old. Parrington must have assuaged the president's—if not his own—doubts, for just two weeks before commencement came the offer of a position teaching English and French. He was disappointed in the $500 annual salary but glad for the chance to be at home and for the opportunity to continue studying.

Louise—but not the Judge, for the family budget could not stretch that far—traveled east for the graduation observances, including baccalaureate, Class Day exercises, and commencement itself on June 28. The speeches delivered by the class of 1893 participants mirrored the concerns of the century's last decade: "Fin de Siècle," "The Greeks Again," "Political Optimism," "Bankruptcy Legislation." Receiving their master's degrees on the same occasion were Irving Babbitt and Paul Elmer More, whom Parrington would meet again on the battlefields of literary criticism.

Afterward, with his mother he spent a few days sightseeing in the Boston environs, visiting the Old Manse and the Wayside Inn in Concord and picnicking at Plymouth, where they viewed graves of some "of the old Puritans." Following a brief visit to John Parrington's Gorham relatives, they left Boston for the long train trip back to Emporia. "Was awfully sorry to leave Harvard and Cambridge," Parrington wrote in his diary. "Have had some disagreeable experiences here, but I love the place nevertheless. The school means more to me now than it has before." Certainly the past year had been unsettling, but Parrington felt that he had now reached "a definite point" and was "no longer a boy." He had a job, and he had two bachelor's degrees, having maintained a respectable B average at Harvard, though he was not among the half of his class that received awards and commendations at commencement. His two-year experiment in self-making was not to be judged by such standards.

3

~

Poetry and Populism
The Return to Emporia, 1893–1897

On the way back to Emporia, Parrington and his mother stopped in Montreal, then went via the Grand Trunk to Chicago, where the Columbian Exposition was being held. The pair spent twelve days in the area, staying with Louise's aunt and sister (Martha Van Osdel, wife of architect John Van Osdel, and Edith Titsworth, whose daughter Gertrude attended the College of Emporia) and visiting various McClellan cousins in Batavia and Aurora, Vernon's birthplace. He also contacted his boyhood chum Vern Cook, who was attending Northwestern University's Garrett School of Theology.

By coincidence, Parrington was in Chicago on July 12, the day Frederick Jackson Turner delivered his paper "The Significance of the Frontier in American History" to the special meeting of the American Historical Association being held at the fair.[1] The paths of these two figures—the twenty-one-year-old graduate just on the threshold of his career and the thirty-one-year-old Wisconsin professor who was just launching a revolution in historiography—were not yet to cross. Parrington first visited the fair on July 10 and "was almost oppressed, . . . it is so big and imposing," but he went again the next afternoon and stayed to view the illumination of the electric fountains ("Worthy a place in 'Arabian Nights' ") in the evening. Lured back on the 13th and 15th, he returned a final time on the 17th, "doing the pictures with Mother. The British and French, especially." But on July 12, Parrington visited the Union Stockyards and toured the Swift and Company establishment. There he watched the "sickening sight" of sheep being slaughtered.

The slaughtering and Turner's paper, however, pointed to the same processes. When Parrington came to analyze the twin forces of westward expansion and economic opportunism and their relation to democratic theory, he found in Turner not a voice of revelation but a congenial spirit that affirmed his own experiences on the edge of Kansas (and later, Oklahoma) settlement. By the end of his four years of teaching at the College of Emporia, he also would be personally touched by the effects of economic depression and become as involved in politics as he ever would—as a participant—in his lifetime.

After their interval in Chicago, Parrington and his mother stopped briefly in Decatur, visiting another maternal aunt, Medora McClellan Mitchell, and playing tennis with her son Clair. Three years younger than Vernon and called by his first name as an adult, this cousin was Wesley Clair Mitchell, who became the Columbia economist best known for his work with the National Bureau of Economic Research (1920–45) and also served as director of the New School for Social Research (1919–31) and as chairman of the Social Science Research Council (1927–30). Although the two had little contact in their mature lives, this coincidental meeting—like the near brush in Chicago with Turner—with someone whose views Parrington later shared, particularly those developed by Mitchell in *A History of the Greenbacks* (1903), could not have occurred at a more symbolic time.[2]

But Parrington's primary confrontation upon his return to Emporia was not with Populism or with economic or democratic theory but with the classroom. Moreover, his initial responses to his native environment were framed in poetry, not political essays. If self-making was the hallmark of his Harvard years, professional self-definition—which eventually included the outlines of a political stance—could be called the hallmark of his Emporia career.

Poetry and the Mission of Poetry

After arriving in Emporia at the end of July, Parrington wrote in his diary: "Well, I am back again. It seems both odd and natural. The place and people are the same, yet they seem different. It is not at all like the east, and while I like Cambridge am glad to be back." He missed seeing his brother, who was working for a St. Louis newspaper, but was satisfied that his sixty-three-year-old father looked "just as he did two years ago." He easily resumed his former Emporia habits which had been interrupted at Harvard: puttering around his parents' home and repapering his bedroom; playing baseball and tennis; going downtown in the evenings; spending time with old friends and taking drives in the country with young women; and going to church—usually twice each Sunday and, as before, attending a variety of denominational services, including Methodist, Episcopalian, Congregational, and Presbyterian. (This practice elicited the comment in his October 8 diary, "How good I am getting.")

The day before his twenty-second birthday (August 3), Parrington had his first "talk on school matters" with John Dunbar Hewitt, the college's new president, a Princeton Theological Seminary graduate long identified with Kansas educational and church interests. Two weeks later he started reading and taking notes on Shakespearian critics, in preparation for teaching the prescribed senior English course. When classes began on September 7, he found he was "just a little embarrassed, but after the first hour— French—got along swimmingly." By the fifth day, he observed, after giving a "successful" lecture on *Richard III*, "Am getting into the work and enjoy it." The only return of feelings of inadequacy noted in his diary—which stops abruptly on October 9 and is not resumed until February 26, 1896, more than two years later—occur on the occasions of conducting chapel, a duty rotated among the faculty.

"I would give much if I had more confidence in myself," he mused before his first chapel experience. One wonders, in light of his crisis of faith, acknowledged just nine months previously at Harvard, whether Parrington's lack of confidence resulted from masking his lack of conviction or simple stage fright, a feeling the former orator knew well. A habit of diffidence and uncertainty in the face of public scrutiny manifested itself in various forms throughout his life and drove his creative and emotional life further inward so that he felt most comfortable exploring ideas mainly in the circumscribed boundaries of the classroom.

In an illuminating 1896 diary passage, Parrington confessed that during the spring and summer of 1895 he had "longed to preach" but decided he was unsuited for it. Thus his religious doubts, once he returned to the bosom of Emporia Protestantism, were not only assuaged but were replaced for a time by a sense of calling to the ministry, perhaps partly attributable to the college's missionary atmosphere.

At Harvard Parrington's religious doubts had occurred in an atmosphere of changing ideas and challenging professors. But the Emporia faculty and the college had changed little in his two-year absence. President John F. Hendy had resigned and been replaced by another Presbyterian clergyman, John Dunbar Hewitt. Students were still required to take a term of biblical history each year. Vernon's favorite teacher, Hugh Kingery, was replaced in Latin by a William D. Ward, yet at least five former teachers were now colleagues. The two temporary English instructors, each serving a year with duties doubling in Latin and natural science, respectively, had departed, along with the professor of French and Greek. More electives were available in the curriculum, but this only further taxed the resources of the faculty.

Enrollment in the Collegiate Department had swelled from forty-six to fifty-six; that of preparatory and special students from thirty-two to forty. Thirty students were preparing for the ministry, a number that gives credence to the 1893–94 catalog's section "Religious Culture":

> This phase of college life is regarded of paramount importance. The faculty emphasize this conviction in every legitimate way. It will be manifest in all our intercourse with our students. Special prominence is given to the Holy Bible as the only infallible rule of faith and practice. Every fitting opportunity is embraced to set forth the life of the Great Teacher as the perfect model after which all lives should be patterned.[3]

No wonder Parrington was nervous about conducting chapel. In his 1918 autobiographical sketch, however, he downplays the college's religious emphasis, claiming that during his student days Bible study was "very badly taught and served no real purpose beyond providing a talking point in appealing to the churches for aid." But that claim was a modification of reality made to fit Parrington's later image of himself.

This same sketch devotes only one breathless paragraph to his four years on the Emporia faculty and gives equal space to teaching and coaching:

> It was a period of swift growth and expansion, of hard work and voluntary discipline. . . . Those were the busiest years of my life. Everything was new: the department was to be organized; each class to be prepared for in detail. I discovered huge gaps in my knowledge of English literature, which I must fill in. I wrote out my lectures almost in full. I was the coach for debates and orations. I was deep in athletics—very deep it seems to me now. Especially football. My second year I began coaching the team, at the same time playing quarterback. Three years . . . I was the sole coach, and sometimes manager and player as well. In addition I wrote verse pretty steadily, and found it the best training for prose style that I have undergone. How I got so much done is a wonder to me now.[4]

The college catalogs published during Parrington's Emporia faculty days reveal not only how much he accomplished in defining and expanding the English Department to reflect more contemporary standards but also how—as the primary member of the standing faculty committee on printing—he brought order and specificity to all Emporia's course listings, obviously using the Harvard catalog as a model. By 1894, following Barrett Wendell's example, he was insisting for his freshman and sophomore rhetoric and composition courses that "the department believes that the only way to learn to write is to write" and had instituted Wendell's pattern of daily and fortnightly themes. He modified the three upper-level courses first introduced by William E. Henderson during his interval at Harvard. The vague junior course in "development of English literature, with studies from representative authors" became a firm figures-oriented sequence with the first term covering Spenser to Fielding and the second Johnson to Ruskin. The one-term Shakespeare course now included sixteen plays and the sonnets as well as traced "the development of Shakespere's mind as revealed by his works" and studied "the English Renaissance, the development of drama, and Shakespere's philosophical teachings." The nineteenth-century poetry course became a study of the origins, development, and philosophy underlying the romantic movement. To this Parrington added, despite his mediocre Harvard showing, two courses "devoted to the study of Anglo-Saxon with a view to reading Chaucer." More propitiously, he offered a new course which studied the theme of realism versus idealism in the context of contemporary prose and poetry and "their relation to present sociological and artistic tendencies."[5]

By 1895, in addition to continuing to carry all the offerings in French and a minimal load in the Preparatory Department, he added a course in pre-Shakespearian drama; focused the second term of the Anglo-Saxon course on Langland and Chaucer; and added a senior thesis course in addition to one in later nineteenth-century poetry, which treated "post romantic, transcendental and scientific movements" and the works of Browning, Tennyson, Clough, Arnold, Dante Gabriel Rossetti, and Swinburne. For 1896–97, the catalog lists the same courses, with the significant addition of the American Sidney Lanier to his roster of later nineteenth-century poets.[6]

The development of the English curriculum's ten primary courses, several of which were cycled on alternate years, reveals much about Parrington's interests and style of analysis. The major portion of his lecture notes that survive from the period, two notebooks covering his 1893–94 junior English course, are of further help here. Following the pattern of his Harvard class with Lewis Gates, the year-long sequence focused on the 1700–1850 period. It included standard pre–eighteenth-century figures—Spenser, Marlowe, Jonson, Dryden, and Milton—as well as Addison, Swift, Pope, Defoe, Richardson, Johnson, Goldsmith, and Cowper; and from the nineteenth century Scott, Dickens, Thackeray, George Eliot, Macaulay, Carlyle, and Ruskin. Bibliographies inserted in the notebooks list not only Taine but also James Russell Lowell's *Essay on English Poets,* Edward Dowden's *Transcripts and Studies,* Leslie Stephen's two-volume *History of English Thought in the 18th Century,* Edmund Gosse's *History of 18th Century Literature,* and Thomas Sargeant Perry's *English Literature of the 18th Century.* Although Parrington's approach in this class—and no doubt in his other English literature offerings—may now seem conventional, it was strikingly up-to-date: all the above sources had been published in the previous two decades. They treated literature as what we are more comfortable terming *intellectual history* than what post–New Critical literary study has conditioned a late–twentieth century audience to expect. This approach Parrington would modify and adapt in his treatment of American writers, historians, and social critics. The constant recognition of the need to bridge the gap between cultural experience and historical eras would mark Parrington's teaching, making him effective and popular in the classroom.

In contrast to throwing a span across the history of ideas, when Parrington turned to George Eliot he focused on a theme more accessible to his students: realism versus idealism. Here also is a reflection of his Harvard thesis on the historical novel, the substance of the course he offered in 1894–95, and the elaboration of two key words that would form the basis of many assessments in *Main Currents* of the relevancy of ideas and of the minds that advanced them. The following extracts from his notebook show how his description of realism and idealism could be adapted to the context of *The Beginnings of Critical Realism in America:*

> The two schools [of Realism and Idealism] differ on the point, should the novel be dominated by the artistic or scientific spirit. Should it endeavor to in-

struct—consciously or unconsciously—as well as amuse. And how can one best instruct? By absolute fidelity to fact; photographic faithfulness; or by idealising, by changing realities to accord with a standard existing in the mind of the artist alone? Is a knowledge of what is, or what might be, most elevating.

The Macaulay, Carlyle, and Ruskin notes are especially significant, for in them Parrington treated a historian, a social critic, and an art critic in a literature course. Even at this early stage he chose to follow broader paths than "the narrower belletristic," the choice he made in describing the "genesis and development" of ideas in American letters which is delineated clearly in the Introduction to Volume 1 of *Main Currents* and reiterated in the Forewords to Volumes 2 and 3.[7]

Parrington's lecture notes show that he did not present Macaulay and Carlyle to his students as exemplars of prose styles. Rather, he focused on their styles of mind, their conceptions of history's purpose and value, and their methods in writing history. Macaulay is judged as "an orator and rhetorician rather than a litterateur, a politician rather than a philosopher; a dramatic scene painter" lacking "a broad philosophic mind, a pure imagination, subtlety and penetration." He is ultimately unsatisfactory as a historian because of his nonscientific approach to his materials based on an interest in simply reviving the past instead of on drawing deduction from an impartial survey of the past. In contrast, Carlyle is judged as "one of the most original minds England has produced," endeavoring "to get at the heart of the past: not content with facts but striving to arrive at the thought-life of an age." Although we should not be surprised to see Parrington criticize Macaulay (similarly evaluated as standing alone, without predecessors) for his Whig biases, he also criticizes Carlyle for making "the saving force to lie in the great man, rather than in society itself" and observes that his opposition to the worship of material progress includes democracy ("the rule of the many the rule of mediocrity").

Underlying Parrington's spirited defense of democracy would always be discernible the Carlyle-like suspicion that "ballot boxes cure no human ills," that there was an aristocracy of thought and culture. These biases—of which he was perhaps not fully cognizant nor sought to reconcile with the general tenor of his political sympathies—are reflected in Parrington's attraction to such American figures as Thomas Jefferson; they help explain his responses to his environment at the University of Oklahoma; and they illustrate the depth of influence of such English Victorians as John Ruskin. The Ruskin section of Parrington's lecture notes provides a crucial measure of the temper of his aesthetic and sociological convictions. For the two are merged, as they are in Ruskin: the appeal to first principles in art, the ethical argument that truth is beauty, entails the correlative ethical function both of the artist and of art in society. As Parrington summarizes: "Art hence educates. It develops the imaginative part of our nature and beautifies life. Falsification of facts—for art depends upon faithful representation of the object—[is] a falsification of life and art. The sphere of art thus widened. The whole domain of aesthetics included, embracing literature."

This Ruskinian solution that Parrington invoked to reconcile the apparent opposition between idealism and realism emerges clearly in his notes on Eliot. This solution also led him to embrace William Morris and to become, as near as Parrington ever came to being, a disciple of any single intellectual and personal model. He had not yet discovered Morris, who eventually was added to the Victorian cultural triumvirate of Carlyle, Ruskin, and Arnold, a linkage brought into clear relief in these early Emporia lecture notes. Ruskin, he wrote,

> belongs to the spiritualistic as opposed to the materialistic school. A disciple of Carlyle, and friend of Arnold. The three are intellectually bound together. Carlyle is the Puritan poet, impressed with the mystery and grandeur of life. Arnold is the Puritan scholar, impressed by the power of the mind; while Ruskin is the Puritan artist filled with the beauty of the universe. All three set themselves against the materialistic tendency of the age.

In addition to the distinctly emerging outlines of Parrington's analytic and critical framework, several other sources help to fill out our picture of the ambitious young English professor. The catalog of his extant personal library shows him investing heavily in books after his first few months of teaching. The titles concentrate on the authors and themes treated in his various courses: Arnold's poetry and essays; Browning's poetic and dramatic works; Carlyle's edition of Cromwell's *Letters and Speeches, Past and Present, Sartor Resartus;* Coleridge, Keats, D. G. Rossetti, Shelley; Tennyson's works and Stopferd Brooke's 1894 biography; J. C. Shairp's *On Poetic Interpretation of Nature* (1892) and *Studies in Poetry and Philosophy* (1893); various editions of Shakespeare's plays. For background, there was the 1894 edition of Volumes 1 through 4 of H. D. M. Traill's *Social England* and the 1895 edition of John Richard Green's *Short History of the English People,* as well as Henry Drummond's *Ascent of Man* and *Natural Law in the Spiritual World.*[8]

During his faculty days the college held about four thousand volumes. (A separate library facility was not acquired until 1901, four years after Parrington left.) Several catalogs note that "the library is especially strong in the departments of History and Biography, but the department of poetry is incomplete, and inadequate for the purposes of the English students." Certainly it was inadequate for the purposes of the English professor, although the periodical collection seems less inauspicious. In addition to the expected dominance of midwestern and religious publications, a fair sampling was available of national college publications including the *Harvard Daily Crimson;* national newspapers, including the *New York Tribune;* and national magazines, ranging from the literary—such as *Scribner's* and the *North American Review*—to the muckraking: by 1897 the library subscribed to *Cosmopolitan, McClure's,* and *Munsey's.*[9]

Such insights into Parrington's sources of study and opportunities for exposure to events beyond Emporia are supplemented by William Allen White's brief comments on his local townsman in his autobiography. There he places Parrington in the "amen corner" of the local bookstore:

> For years that corner in the bookstore there on Commercial Street was a hangout for the young fellows about town, young fellows too proud for pool, too wicked for prayer meetings, too lazy for baseball (though Vernon Parrington pitched a mean outcurve on the Emporia Browns), too sophisticated for the local poker game, and too young and full of visions to let the world go by without trying to understand it.[10]

During his Emporia faculty years Parrington dared to publish his efforts to understand the world and its culture only in the college's newspaper, to which he contributed three articles concerning the study of English language and literature: "The Position of English in College Curricula" in late October 1893, "On Novel Reading" in November 1895, and "Plain English vs. Pedantry" in January 1896.[11]

The first essay discusses the increasing prominence of college study of English and modern languages in relation to declining emphasis on Greek and Latin, whose mastery formerly denoted the "cultured class." Parrington contrasts his father's 1854–55 Waterville College catalog, which offered only a year of rhetoric and no literature or modern language courses, with a copy of his own 1893–94 Harvard catalog, which lists a total of thirty-three English, twenty-nine German, twenty-three French courses, and twenty-three each in Greek and Latin. The ancient languages, he asserts, embodied the highest thought of their civilizations, yet those civilizations seem simple, incomplete, dead in contrast to "the spirit of modern life." This new spirit is "living, intense, complex. . . . Good or bad, it is everything to us. We are in the midst of it and what we are or may be depends on our understanding it. Why not, therefore, live with the living? Why not concern ourselves chiefly with what expresses modern life and modern civilization?" This plea for modernity is qualified in the third essay. There he criticizes the force of "science-pedantry" in current literary study that would substitute "euphuisms, Italianisms, Latinisms and what not for plain, living English" (as in a Yale course title Methodology and Bibliography of English Literature that Parrington would simplify to Books and Methods for the Study of English Literature). He concludes more happily, observing that alongside this pseudo-scientific trend runs the counterforce of "the reawakening of a love for the English element of our tongue," acknowledged as partly owing to the age's scientific impulse, as in the wider study of Anglo-Saxon.

These brief informal essays are best understood not in the relative isolation of Emporia but in the context of the nationwide reforms in language
study that were reshaping curricula during the 1890s. Three months after
the publication of "The Position of English in the College Curricula," in
February 1894 a series of eighteen articles which surveyed the current
course offerings and pedagogues at various American colleges and universities began appearing in the *Dial*. Each focused on a different institution,
ranging from seven older eastern and southern schools to new midwestern
state universities to a group of new private schools such as the University of
Chicago, and was written by a department member from the particular
school. The series promoted lively exchanges in the *Dial*'s letters column
and aroused enough interest in educational circles to be published in book
form (with the addition of two new articles, on Johns Hopkins and the
University of Minnesota) in 1895 as *English in American Universities* under
the editorship of William Morton Payne, who had organized the *Dial* series.

Although Parrington later regularly read the *Dial*, he may not have been
acquainted with the articles in the periodical or book forms. His essays,
however, voice, if not echo, Payne's argument in the book's introduction,
which insists that the study of literature must be adapted to each individual
because "the spirit of literature is not to be acquired by making chronological tables, or tracing the genealogies of words, or working out the law of
decreasing prediction." Clearly, Parrington's opinions on the value and
mode of literary study were shared by a good portion of the departments
surveyed, and the curriculum he developed at Emporia was in keeping
with that of most institutions that had larger faculties. For this he was primarily in Harvard's debt. Barrett Wendell wrote the Cambridge contribution, but he set a predictably higher store on mastering linguistic detail than
Parrington did either in his theme-oriented literature courses or *College
Life* articles.[12]

The foregoing provides a fairly complete picture of the public, professional Parrington—albeit omitting such extraacademic activities as coaching debates and orations as well as coaching, training, and playing star
quarterback with the college football team. But there was a private
Parrington, revealed in his diary entry, quoted below, confessing his desire
to preach. This entry, at the midpoint in his four Emporia years, also revealed that he had found an alternative to this desire. One might say that he
had rechanneled his religious concerns "through the avenue of art." In late
February 1896, he resumed his diary—dropped since October 1893—with
one of his rare lengthy reflections:

> Mon Dieu! how time has got away since I quit this journal business! More
> than 2 years of mighty hard work. Looking back over a time so significant as
> these last several years, it is easy enough to see one's growth. What a young ac-
> ademician I was then! Perhaps still, but certainly less so. I flatter myself I've got

beyond the schoolboy age: at any rate I have found out how little I know and how much I want to know. I wonder if that doesn't mean the beginning of knowledge. These past few months have been singularly important to me: *the determination has been slowly getting itself made to devote myself to creative literature—to poetry.* There it is in black and white! Deep in my heart, stronger than I dare acknowledge even to myself, is a belief in my powers and my work. The causes for this determination are: 1) A deepseated desire to say my say to men. Last spring and summer I longed to preach, but I see now I was not fitted for it. 2) A profound belief in the divinity of poetry and love for it. 3) A supreme joy obtainable for me in that work and nowhere else. . . . I believe with my whole heart that I may do worthy, if not notable things. Esperance! (Emphasis added.)

The tone of this passage and many others during Parrington's ensuing poetry-writing period, which extended from his twenty-fourth year into his early thirties, often seems peculiarly forced, almost posed, similar in accent to his declaration of intent ("God helping me, I must—nay I will—work out a faithful if not brilliant work") upon leaving for Harvard. This is the fourth vocational desire—the first was to paint, the second to teach, the third to preach, the most recent to write poetry—pursued since he was sixteen. Though his efforts as a poet were as inauspicious as his showing as a student in Cambridge, they document developmental facets in his scholarly and political as well as his private and personal life.

Of Parrington's seventy or so extant poems, the earliest date from 1895.[13] At least three ("Knowing—Is What?," "Naughty Falling Star," "The Fight of the New and the Old") appeared in the college newspaper during 1895–97. One characteristic subject of his early poems was the Kansas landscape, the natural environment. It is helpful to read these in reference to the impressions recorded in his diary entries and daily themes written at Harvard, for Parrington began seeing his native place in a new way—indeed, this may have been one of the forces that led him to poetry—after his return to Emporia. In contrast to his crowded streetcar rides between Cambridge and Boston, jostled by strange faces and strange accents, and to his morning walks in Mt. Auburn Cemetery, visiting the ghosts of New England past, the Kansas fields were open, familiar, alive:

> All day I have passed up and down these long rows,
> Drunk in the full life that quivers and glows;
>
> Caught glimpses of tassels that peep into sight,
> Unsheathe their leaf wrappings, reach up to the light:
>
> Looked on to the time of the full-kernelled ear
> And richness of harvest at full of the year.
>
> The long rows are nodding and waving: all pains
> And toils are forgot, with this June in my veins.

> At dusk of the day, in this midtime of year,
> Our corn is a poet, a prophet, a seer.

These stanzas from "Corn," composed in June 1896, illustrate that Parrington's verse was not sophisticated technically, though he experimented with line arrangements, here achieving an impression of corn rows by using long rows of couplets. He generally relied on meter, rhyme, and didactic moralizing instead of imagery, in contrast to what one might expect from the accomplished prose stylist of *Main Currents*. He seemed to owe more to popular magazine fare and James Whitcomb Riley than to Sidney Lanier, who was included in his nineteenth-century poetry course and who had published a poem entitled "Corn" in *Lippincott's Magazine* two decades earlier.[14]

Parrington also memorialized the sunflower ("Mid stress of this heat-time / The golden-rayed disks climb / To beckon and nod at the sun"), which became the state flower in 1903. "The Sunflower," published on August 30, 1896, in the *Topeka Capital,* was among the handful that appeared in print outside Emporia. Though he had been sending submissions to *Harper's,* the *Century,* the *Independent,* and the *New York Tribune,* after a string of rejections he had resolved "to go in for Western papers more." Yet his next poem, "June," the first in a proposed trilogy called "Kansas Summer," was refused by the *Chicago Tribune.* Perhaps too discouraged to write "July" and "August," he next completed a poem titled "Alfalfa":

> Purple of color, deep-rooted in earth,
> . . . .
>   Thou art a lover of heat,
>   A child of the plain;
>   Bright in thy blossom and sweet
>   Though scant be the rain;
> . . . .
> Though summer be blistered and parched by hot winds
> Like furnace breath searing the grain.

Parrington's identification with his subject is evidenced by his personification of nature, as in calling corn "a poet" and alfalfa "a child of the plain." This technique is employed again in "The Sign of the Short Grass" (completed in March 1897), which treats a theme Henry Nash Smith developed half a century later in his chapter "The Garden and the Desert" in *Virgin Land: The American West as Symbol and Myth.*[15] The poem opens with an image of wagons trailing back eastward to the more fertile prairies from the dry upland plains covered with buffalo grass. First described as "Smiling and calling to plowmen, luring them to their doom," the grass then speaks in the treacherous tones of a land speculator:

"Bring but your labor and skill: see how the upland will bloom!

Bountiful harvests are here—look you how mellow the soil!—
Virgin from millions of years, given to you for the spoil!

Corn and alfalfa and wheat—rich the reward if you sow:
Fear not the winds and the sands, moisture will follow the plow!"

In addition to such natural or organic subjects, in his early phase Parrington wrote several topical poems (like "Pike's Peak at Midnight" and "To Beowulf"); a group of poems dealing with facets of humanitarian and mystic love (indicative of his continuing preoccupation with religion); and one—"Past and Present: One Mood"—that expresses a deep sense of disjunction between his daily life and the life he found expressed in the creative literature of the past. The poem first describes two sunrises, one "that splashed with blood and flame the eastern sky" and another where "a blotch of light; / A yellow sickly thing, . . . / Like a spectre hung." The first sunrise is then compared to the "elder days" when "Men dared to feel, . . . / dared to unbar / The prisoned soul," while the second sunrise provokes the response:

> But oh! the drear waste of the latter age!
> Outward I look, upon the toil-grimed street
> And war of things. No soul is there, replete
> With love and faith, no poet-light, but wage
> Of Godlessness. And in my heart fierce rage
> That I am robbed of visions sweet.

This recoil against the present, recorded in late February 1896, elucidates Parrington's commitment both to his private poetry and to his professional subject matter. What rapprochement could be made between the eloquent heart of the past and the materialistic present? His first formal response to this dilemma, the recognition of which illumines his interest in such troubled Victorians as Carlyle, Arnold, Ruskin, Tennyson, and Browning, was the address "Poetry as the Mission of Poetry," which he delivered at Emporia's 1895 commencement.

On this occasion, Parrington was awarded a Master of Arts degree "in course," that is, without completing a prescribed curriculum but honoring personal study. It was the highest academic degree he would ever receive. Thus, though the hopes he placed in his own poetic endeavors outweighed the critical results, he was recognized for the dedication to imaginative life that must have been positively received across the campus community. Yet we must remember that he was only twenty-three, that he was as popular for his prowess in sports as for his careful classroom preparations, that he was a product of a struggling farm as much as of the struggles of the mind that spurred him on at Harvard.

The *Emporia Gazette* reported that Parrington's address was "full of beautiful and poetical thoughts and was an appeal to the students to see the beautiful in life and the concealed poetry in it." That may have been what was heard; that was hardly what was said; but a similarly composed audience had not caught the contradictions inherent in his prizewinning "God in History" oration either. A more apt summation would be that the address was full of criticisms of everyday existence in Emporia and pleaded for the students to raise their aspirations above the merely practical. Parrington's thesis was "to place poetry by the side of science as one of the twin guides of man," which he developed by contrasting the poet and the scientist, present as the world's "two great teachers" since at least the Elizabethan era, although his references include Greek sources. The contrast delineates the choices in styles of mind, approaches to living, available in the past as well as in turn-of-the-century American culture:

> The true poet then is he who is a revealor of inner truth—conceived immediately by the imagination. The scientist on the other hand, deals with facts, relations, laws—the outer shell of things—and apprehends these laws mediately by means of reason. The scientist looking down, gropes upward; the poet lifts up his eyes and sees. The scientist emerges from his search weary and toil-worn and says: "This is law, for so I have demonstrated it." The poet with the light not passed from his face cries: "So I have seen it; this is the truth."

Although Parrington does not explicitly disparage the role of the scientist, the bulk of his address focuses on the role of the poet. Significantly— and here we see another manifestation of his concern with idealism and realism—he argues that though Keats is right when he exclaims, "Beauty is truth; truth beauty,"

> Nevertheless it is not the whole truth. There is more to the infinite than beauty alone. The esthete has conceived only part of the mission of poetry: his worship removes him from men and this everyday world; and the glamour of the ideal is apt to disenchant him of the real. The development of modern poetry since Keats proves that unless it dwell in the midst of men who toil and suffer and hope, it will come far short of its true greatness.

Parrington concludes first by asking his audience to join for the purpose of social renewal in emphasizing "soul-making" rather than mere love, in "the sentiment of Ruskin—the end of culture is to learn to see and to feel." He then insists that in an "age of science when the poet-prophet is discredited," there is special need to stress his mission "to leaven the materialism of science with the spirituality of poetry." Finally, he suggests that the next generation may be entering upon a new age of poetry and faith and that to reach that age, his audience should take heart from the quest of the aged Merlin, who calls out to young England in the last lines of Tennyson's poem, "Merlin and the Gleam":

> O young mariner,
> Down to the haven,
> Call your companions,
> Launch your vessel
> And crowd your canvas,
> And ere it vanishes
> Over the margin,
> *After it, follow it,*
> *Follow The Gleam.*[16]

Politics and History

The excesses in Parrington's commencement address that caused the *Gazette* reporter to overlook its cultural criticism were the same excesses that marred Parrington's own verse. He had chosen the wrong form to convey his content; he could not win the battle "to leaven the materialism of science" with his poetry; he would have to channel his idealism through a more realistic means. This process issued in his involvement with local Populistic politics. But he would reach politics through art, for his poems were the first form he used to respond to contemporary political events and ideas.

A year after delivering his commencement address, Parrington completed a poem titled "As Things Look to Us of the West." His diary notes that he sent it off to the *New York Tribune* but doubted its acceptance "because of silver sentiment." The work blends his emerging political consciousness with his reawakening to his natural environment; indeed, it was written the same summer as "Corn," "The Sunflower," and "Alfalfa." Opening with the jaunty lines, "The corn's looking fine; never saw it so green: / So bursting with sap: such shimmer and sheen," the poem then reflects on why a plentiful harvest will, ironically, result in low prices per bushel:

> A curious world where abundance means dearth
> And hard times stalk forth from this great smiling earth.
>
> The problem is deep. We feel dimly a cause
> For all. Fail to see, so talk vaguely of laws:
>
> Supply and demand, ebb and flow, the rash West
> A debtor to creditor East and the rest.

The poem then argues for the necessity of economic change but closes by recognizing the difficulties in achieving it:

Be sure, at the last, we'll crack Wall Street's gold shell:
Give silver a show; make life somewhat less hell.

We may all be wrong. They've measured our schemes
With New England yardsticks, and call them wild dreams.

. . . .
The world's such a big one; we toilers alas,
Must butt away blindly to bring things to pass.

A month before composing "As Things Look to Us of the West," Parrington completed a long poem titled "Democracy," which he planned to publish in the 1896 commencement issue of *College Life*. In the year since "Poetry and the Mission of Poetry," however, he had learned to take the measure of his audience and changed his mind, substituting the shorter and far more enigmatic "Knowing—Is What?" While this piece ends with the ambiguous lines, "Yet this our lot / That tho' we know, we cannot tell the why," in "Democracy" Parrington is quite explicit about the why that will cure our lot:

Democracy I rather hold to be
The right to cry out where the sickness is,
And freedom to the healer to apply
His herbs. And so this toilworn race of men
Claps a hand to stomach and declares: The pain is here: . . .
Or lifts a foot with nail all hanging loose.

Then sounding very much like a social settlement worker (Jane Addams was only eleven years his senior and had just founded Hull House in 1889), he continues:

And so I hold it for the supreme good
And final hope of this world's betterment
That there are those still dwelling in our midst
. . . .
True prophets who have seen the light of fact
More doctors and more nurses who can heal.

'Tis not that men have not been sick before:
The millions died with never a plaint nor word
To tell whereof they died. But slowly now
This long dumb pain becomes articulate:
The body cries aloud for easement, cure.
So I take heart for there must come a day
For every ill, its tongue—for every pain
Its healing: so at last the promised land.
That were Democracy indeed: but we—
Alas we shall not see the day!

Observe that both these poems end in despair or near-resignation. In mid-August of 1896 Parrington had found a "true prophet," for he recorded in his diary: "All my thoughts of late have run on the money question. I am an out and out Bryan 16-to-1 silver man." By mid-September he had "read on the money question." And on November 3 he broke with his once ardent Republicanism and cast his first presidential ballot for William Jennings Bryan.

Though this act must have produced some dissension in Judge Parrington's household—"Father will stick by the old party and McKinley. I cannot. There is too much at stake," his son commented—it is not easy to assess the depth or the quality of Vernon's political engagement at this time. His diaries give far more space to studying Shakespeare and writing poetry than to reading on the money question. Yet these private records do indicate awareness of national events and influences. For example, the incidents surrounding Chicago's Haymarket Massacre on May 4, 1886, may well have inspired another poem, completed in January 1897, with the incendiary title "The Dream of a Latter Day Anarchist, 1790–1896." Opening with an evocation of the "inspired madness" of the revolutionary "dreamers" of 1776 and the Constitutional Convention, the poem laments that now we only "prate of liberty" while " 'Era of progress!' cries the blatant fool." Parrington feels that " 'The age of iron' were a truer name" for this "harsh metallic cruel age" and hopes for the establishment of

> a new-born commonweal
> Where man will clasp his brothers by the hand
> . . . .
> Where this strange curse of poverty
> That grows more awful as the world grows rich
> Is eased.

The poem grimly concludes:

> But these are only idle dreams our wise ones say
> And we who dream them are called anarchists
> And the world's finger points at us.

Even the parochial College of Emporia was responding to the economic crises its students' families—small merchants and farmers subject to the falling market—were undergoing. Here Parrington no doubt found support for his political break with his father and his sympathy with anarchists. The catalog printed in the spring of 1895 announced the formation of an Academy of Political and Social Science as an outgrowth of interest "created during the past year in social and economic questions." Faculty members were invited to the academy's monthly meetings, which consisted of discussions of readings conducted by students. The same catalog also announced that new stress would be laid on U.S. colonial and constitutional history and provisions were being made for a new course in political economy, "not only as an abstract science, but in some of its more important applications" with a view to a student "becoming an independent thinker reaching his own conclusions and ruling his own conduct on rational and moral grounds."[17]

The academy apparently continued into the 1896–97 academic year, though it is not listed in subsequent catalogs. The promised development in history and political science did occur, as shown by the offerings available in the new History and Political Science division of the Department of Philosophy for the 1896–97 year. The three instructors in the division were Judge Charles B. Graves, who had taught courses in various phases of law since the college's early days; Reverend William R. Kirkwood, who was adding to his courses in mental philosophy (which Vernon had taken) one each in American history, American politics, and political economy; and Professor Parrington, who was slated to teach an upper-division year-long elective in "Outline of English History, with some account of Parliament." The course gave a comparative context for the American courses, was recommended as an adjunct to the English literature offerings, and used John Richard Green's *Short History of the English People* for a text.

It is not certain that Parrington actually taught this course. A fall 1896 diary entry states that all his work was in English and French with "no side issues," and though the course is listed again in the next catalog, Parrington by then had left Emporia.[18] Nevertheless, that he prepared to teach English history, despite his poor showing in history at Harvard, and was acquainted with Green's notably democratic interpretation of the English past, further substantiates his deepening interest in historical movements and change. His 1895 Harper's edition of Green, first published in 1874, survives. Dated September 14, 1895, it is filled with notes and markings; no doubt he referred to it in preparing his literature courses.

Most important, the offering of this course as well as his vote for Bryan show Parrington—a young twenty-five—striding independently away from the warm cocoon of home, from teaching languages and literature, and from the historical interpretation of "God in History." His next public step was taken in early April 1897 when he ran for the local school board.

Running for office was well within family tradition, and his primary qualification was his reputation as a teacher. Although the group that nominated him, the Citizens' Mass Convention, was not clearly Populist, it was surely not nonpartisan, for it was united by its opposition to the Republican candidate for mayor, "a grocer notorious for insisting on prompt cash payment from all customers." Parrington lost the election 203 to 357, but it served to whet his political appetite, for in August he chaired Emporia's first ward delegation to the State Populist Convention, held in his hometown.[19]

In contrast to the excitement a "latter day anarchist" might have expected, his diary described that experience as "a long, tedious time: on the whole amusing. What I have in common with most of those ungrammatical farmers is more than I know." Although his father's farm was suffering the same reversals as their neighbors', the rather dandyish English professor's sympathies with their plight—so idealistically expressed in his 1896–97 poems—withered in this confrontation with the reality of the democratic process. His chairmanship was his last direct political participation in his lifetime. Yet shortly after losing the school board election, he had taken another public step when in April and May *College Life* published a series of his essays, entitled "Some Political Sketches."

Though their composition (initiated four months previously) required shifting the exploration of ideas from poetry to prose, which he felt uncomfortable doing, the essays also guaranteed him a wider audience and forced him to clarify his thinking. The "Sketches" address the problem of how America can discover "the intellectual resources necessary to guide it through unprecedented social and political adjustments forced by industrialization." Divided into four parts, the "Introduction" pleads for students to become interested in affairs of state; "The Business Ideal" criticizes the control of government by the interests of property; "The University Ideal" concludes that scholars have no influence in politics because they are not trained to be leaders; and finally, "The Humanitarian Ideal" proposes that America needs to produce a new kind of statesman with a realistic grasp of current problems who is yet guided by an idealistic sympathy for the rights of men.[20]

Although the "Sketches" are most immediately influenced by the ideas of Ruskin, Arnold, and Carlyle, they also anticipate the concern expressed in *Main Currents* for educating public opinion and facilitating access to information sources. His experience as a teacher, in contrast to that as a political participant, was enabling him to see the instrumental role ideas might play in history and human affairs. The "Sketches" also contain the root of the historical and philosophical perspectives that would flourish in *Main Currents*. "Only after we have studied the past," Parrington wrote in the introductory essay,

> do we begin to look on the present critically and wonder how things came so and whether or not they must remain as they are. When we look at the present conditions from this point of view the truth that so many social writers of late have been dinning into our ears begins to be significant to us. We . . . have been altogether absorbed in the transition from a society based on the aristocratic idea to a democratic society based on the commercial idea. . . . We have been busy establishing a new condition and now we find ourselves today face to face with the results of that condition.[21]

Parrington would always be more interested in discovering the causes in the past that produced present conditions than in analyzing those conditions.

In short, he was by temperament, training, and inclination a historian and not a sociologist or political scientist. These characteristics are also reflected in several 1897 poems, three whose images of man emerging from the slime show how his sense of current social struggles had been marked by evolutionary theory and one that proclaims, "I will go to the past" to reach "for the meaning of things." But his concerns extended beyond both poetry and English history. In the spring of 1896, he had read Justin McCarthy's text *History of Our Own Time;* in late June of 1897, after the close of the school year, he began the six-volume edition of George Bancroft's *History of the United States.* By early August, he had completed his "great work of the year in reading," an undertaking that included five volumes of James Schouler's *History of the United States of America Under the Constitution.* Reading, rather than direct involvement, was a more familiar approach for Parrington to pursue his interests.

Despite his political essays and poems, political activities, and probable participation in the Academy of Political and Social Science, the young professor was not remembered by his fellow Emporians as a firebrand or an overt supporter of the People's party. In his important 1962 essay "The Populist Image of Vernon Louis Parrington," James L. Colwell assessed Parrington's political viewpoint during this early period. Colwell corresponded with several former Parrington students and acquaintances in the late 1950s and summarized their replies:

> "I never knew of any of his 'Populist activity,' " wrote the former proprietor of a bookstore where he spent some of his spare time. "I think he must have been anti-Populist," (responded an Emporia classmate). A former student of his at the College of Emporia wrote that she did not remember hearing anything about his interest in politics, while the sole surviving member of his own class (1892) stated that "if Vernon was active in politics in or out of the Populist party during college years, I never heard of it." A friend and medical colleague of Vernon's brother, John, described both Parringtons as "rank Republicans" and "no extremists."[22]

Yet I would argue that these perceptions, or lack of perceptions, fit perfectly with the clear separation Parrington made between his private and public life—a separation operative at Harvard (in the contrast between his plaintive diaries and dutiful academic performance, between his religious doubts and constant churchgoing, between his image of himself as a scholar and his enjoyment of social activities) and at Emporia (in the contrast between his poems' political implications and his almost decorous run for the school board, between the young professor troubled by Shakespeare and the outgoing football coach, between the Judge's son and the voter for Bryan). This demarcation not only kept him from trespassing the boundaries of behavior that each sphere required, it also caused him to undergo the experience crucial to the developing intellectual: being detached and involved simultaneously, maintaining an interior dialectic between the necessity of thought and the possibility for action.

Though Richard Hofstadter's analysis of Populism in *The Age of Reform* has been criticized for its ungenerous portrait of midwestern farmers, Parrington would have recognized there both his own attitudes toward "ungrammatical farmers" and his lineaments as a dispossessed elite, whom Hofstadter sees forming the vanguard of Progressive reformers.[23] One so concerned about appearances—Parrington reluctantly began wearing glasses during this period—and maintaining a smooth social life had best keep controversial opinions, as well as aesthetic and scholarly aspirations, to himself. This was especially true if he was a fairly prominent figure in a fairly small town, where one's actions were subject to the scrutiny of a vitriolic local press.

The replies in the mid-1950s to Colwell's inquiries may not only have been softened by time but also suggest how thoroughly mid-1890s Emporia was imbued with what was understood as "populistic" after the general post-World War II discrediting of the American left. Parrington's own memories of the origins of his political views consist of impressionistic personal experiences, not of specific discussions of ideological development. A poignant sample occurs in the section of his autobiographical sketch treating his undergraduate years in Emporia. The Parrington sons were spending some of their last days on the farm north of town, "baching" during the hot summers while working in the orchard and cornfield before John left to work in the Indianapolis Associated Press Office (preparatory to medical school) and Vernon left for Harvard. "It was a cheerless and depressing life," he concludes, "and one that we quitted gladly." In retrospect, their mood seemed reflected in that of other local farmers:

> A change, indeed, was coming over the countryside; evil days were already upon it and worse were in store. The buoyant spirit of pioneering times were gone, expectations had not yet been realized, discouragement was spreading widely among the farmers. . . . Ten cent corn and ten per cent interest epitomizes the situation in which the farmer found himself; he could not extricate himself from the toils of falling prices. The dollar was becoming "as big as a cartwheel." Eggs at five cents a dozen and butter at eight cents a pound were to be exchanged for sugar at ten pounds for a dollar. Much of the produce rotted and wasted for lack of a market. Apples lay under the trees, hay fields went uncut to be burnt over the next spring, milk was fed to the hogs, corn was used instead of coal for fuel. Many a time have I warmed myself by the kitchen stove in which great ears were burning briskly, popping and crackling in the jolliest fashion. And if while we sat around such a fire watching the year's crop go up the chimney, the talk sometimes became bitter about railroads and middlemen, who will wonder? We were in fitting mood to respond to Mary Ellen Lease and her doctrine of raising less corn and more hell.[24]

Parrington's diction vividly evokes memories reaped twenty years earlier. These memories would later reverberate in the prose of *The Beginnings of Critical Realism*, which included a resonant section titled "The Middle Border Rises." In the autobiographical sketch Parrington continues his sharply honed reminiscences:

> It was out of such an economic condition that Populism was born, and although it was not to make me a convert until later, the seeds of rebellion were being sown. My antipathy to the whole race of profit-mongers, goes back I think to those far off days. How well I recall the scene when my anger was first awakened against the middleman! We had taken a firkin of butter to Tanner Brothers and Heed in Emporia. The buyer seized a dirty testing iron, stuck it to the bottom of the firkin, and drew out a core of butter, smelt of it, and pronounced it rancid, and then cut the price. My mother protested indignantly that it was the filthy tester which smelt rancid, and while she argued the matter I stood by in silent rage. Had I not churned that butter, and did I now know it to be as sweet butter as ever came from honest cream? Protest was in vain, however, for it was the buyer's business to cut the price and the dirty tester was only his method.
>
> My dislike of bankers runs back likewise to those early days; the great end for which we raised corn and fattened hogs seemed to me to pay tribute to them. The farmers I knew never entered a bank except to borrow money or pay interest; I never heard of one having a checking account. Every three months father drew his pension amounting to sixty dollars, and regularly it went to pay interest. Often I contrast the lot of Pa Cook who died poor after seventy odd years of a life filled with toil, with that of Major Hood, President of the Emporia National Bank, carefully groomed, smug, respectable, given to heading subscription lists, toadied to both by preachers and politicians, the financial boss of the town, the first citizen of Emporia. Pa Cook worked sixteen hours a day, but was too generous, too uncalculating, too honest to get on; Major Hood sat behind his mahogany desk and owed his success to his skill in estimating what percent of interest the necessities of the borrower made it possible to charge—a mean, small, grasping soul, who never missed a Sunday morning sermon or failed to skin a neighbor on Monday. He had got his start with a bull and a branding iron. As a boy I hated Major Hood, blindly, unreasoningly; as a young man I hated him because he tried to use pressure on me when I turned Populist; in later years I have hated his memory as the representative of a race that a rational social system will one day put out of business.[25]

This passage should be placed in the contexts of what it indicates about Parrington's exposure to Populism and of the historical circumstances impinging upon Emporia's environment. Parrington actually calls himself a Populist, noting that he became a "convert" as a young man when he was pressured by Major Hood, who was also chairman of the executive committee of the college's board of trustees during all but Parrington's first year of teaching. While this may correct the memories of his Emporia acquaintances, it must be stressed that the sketch reflects his self-conception at age forty-six rather than at twenty-four or twenty-five. It provides another insight into why the young professor outwardly suppressed opinions that would have further marked him as a misfit on a faculty, half of whose members were Presbyterian pastors, trained at Princeton, then one of the most conservative of American theological schools. Despite the college's response to current events, evidenced by the academy and the enlarged history offerings, great intellectual gaps must have existed between Judge Graves and Reverend Kirkwood on the one hand and Parrington's reading "on the money question" and American history on the other. And great gaps in political effectiveness are illustrated between the town's domination by Calvin Hood and the lot of Pa Cook, an Americus neighbor and father of Parrington's best friend.

Parrington's father had retired from political office when his second term as probate judge expired in 1888 so the family had been dependent since then on his $20 monthly army pension, on the profits from the farm, and, increasingly, on Vernon's salary. In 1896, his parents had tried to augment their income by venturing into the chicken business, and the sixty-six-year-old retired judge spent the winter of 1896–97 on the farm alone, coming into town once a week to sell eggs. The venture was unsuccessful, and most of Vernon's 1897 salary went to pay expenses. He was left with $5 to serve as pocket money, which he supplemented with a $20 monthly wage as coach of the town's summer baseball team. His own family was being reduced in status and class, resembling the Cooks more closely than any of Emporia's sold citizens.[26]

These events help to evaluate the concern with poverty and struggle in his poems of the period. His emphasis there, in his diary, and in the later autobiographical sketch is upon economic factors and economic cures for what a more thoroughgoing Populist would see as major flaws in political theory and structure. His immediate concern was with the plight of the farmer gripped by the hand of the banker. Though he knew agrarian distress was born of the combination of inflation and falling prices for farm products, of the country's increasing industrialization and capitalistic centralization, he had no direct contact with urban environments where these trends were being played out even more graphically, as many novels being written about Chicago and New York showed. As another example of his limited perception, Parrington never indicates awareness of the 1894 Pullman Strike though the railroad was a major factor in a town that shipped livestock and corn.

He had heard the Farmers' Alliance advocate Mary Elizabeth Lease—he confused her nickname "Yellin" with a middle name (Ellen)—as early as 1890, when duties as president of the State Oratorical Association took the nineteen-year-old to Topeka. An active Grange—the Patrons of Husbandry—was organized in Lyon County in 1873; the Lyon County Farmers' Alliance was founded in 1889 (the year Parrington was a college freshman) and is described by a local historian as "the strongest and most important of the farm organizations in the county."[27] Targeting its main problem as solving the situation whereby merchants were controlling agricultural credit by furnishing supplies until harvest, the Alliance was among the more activist cooperative movements of the 1870s and 1880s and had, for example, clashed in Texas with the Grange's policy of self-improvement and self-help that emphasized the increasingly ephemeral myth of the self-sufficient yeoman farmer.

According to Lawrence Goodwyn's massive study, *Democratic Promise: The Populist Moment in America,* the magnitude of the speculative fever in Kansas was unmatched in any other state during the 1880s. Immigration totalled 220,000 between 1881 and 1887 when rainfall neared thirty inches annually; railroad track mileage trebled from 3,104 miles in 1880 to 8,797 miles in 1890, when fully one-fifth of Kansas was in possession by various rail companies; and land values increased as a result of railroad promotion and inflation of capital. But in 1887 the rains stopped. The drought conditions affected the entire Great Plains area, yet they were felt most strongly in Kansas where the boom had been strongest. Corn and wheat production both were cut nearly in half. This crisis, moreover, followed a hard winter that put many cattle ranchers out of business. In Lyon County, one of the state's oldest and most prosperous counties, affordable 9 percent interest had been available since the 1870s on most farm mortgages, attracting eastern speculators as well as homesteaders like John Parrington. Yet by 1887 the mortgage debt equalled 87 percent of the assessed valuation of the county. During the next decade, half of the population of Kansas fled; at the same time the number of foreclosures increased, and the railroads' tax status seemed more and more outrageous as the farmers' tax burden was not adjusted proportionate to the precipitous price decline, which was accompanied by ever-rising freight rates.

Changes had indeed come over the countryside. By 1890, the ringing idealism and anti-corporate stance of Farmers' Alliance lecturers brought the Kansas membership to between seventy-five thousand and one hundred thousand. That same year, the Kansas branch of the People's party was founded in Topeka, the state capital just sixty miles from Emporia, and a Lyon County man was elected secretary. In the fall elections, Alliance, People's party, and Democratic candidates broke the traditional Republican domination of the lower house. In 1892, the year the national People's party was formed in February in St. Louis, presidential candidate James B. Weaver polled over a million votes; Lewelling (for Kansas governor) and the entire Populist slate won, controlling the state senate but losing the house; and Lyon County Populists won every county office except that of school superintendent.[28]

Eighteen ninety-two also saw the narrow re-election by Nebraskans of William Jennings Bryan to Congress, where he began calling for free coinage of silver. An act that brought the support of western mineowners to the midwestern Democrats' monetary campaign, it also signalled the end of the more broadly based cooperative movement that had distinguished the Farmers' Alliance. While silver was politically expedient, fusion around the silver issue was politically disastrous to the farmers' interests. In 1894, the Republicans elected their entire state ticket, and all Populist congressional candidates were defeated. Locally, such events received close coverage. In 1895 when the opponent of Kansas Populism, William Allen White, bought the *Emporia Gazette,* a Populist leader in Lyon County bought the rival *Emporia Times,* although the *Times* became identified with Democratic politics as Populist strength declined.

Whatever Parrington's exposure to Alliance lecturers or People's party organizing, he could not be called an adherent to the grass-roots "movement culture" that Goodwyn sees as central to the initial success of the agrarian revolt. His support of Bryan seems clearly a localized expression of single-issue support for the silver standard. If he had been more firmly grounded in the broader implications of Populist activity and argument, he might have at least supported Weaver instead of focusing his hopes on Bryan, nominated on the fifth ballot as the compromise candidate of the western and southern Democrats and warring Populist groups. However, Bryan's blend of oratory, evangelical Protestantism, and belief in the common mid-American so closely reflected Parrington's current interests and influences that one might safely say that the weakness in Parrington's rather unformed social and political views was Bryan's, writ small.[29]

Further transformation of the midwestern farmers' consciousness would not come through Bryan, defeated by McKinley in a fairly close 1896 election, or through mainstream Democratic politics. Nor would Parrington's. Just as the impact of his Harvard years would come to fruition only through years of teaching and personal study, so also would his years in Americus and Emporia be refined through subsequent experience. In early July 1897, following his year of growing political awareness and activity and of his parents' financial difficulties, Parrington was feeling inexplicably discontented and unhappy. A determination to make a change in his life led to a consultation with President David Ross Boyd of the new University of Oklahoma in Norman, where a position was open. The same August day he chaired the Populist delegation, he received notification of his appointment, which he accepted primarily for its prospective salary. Because Oklahoma was still a territory during all but Parrington's final year there, he was unable to cast an effective vote in the 1900 or 1904 presidential elections.[30] That was one of the disappointments, among many positive though unexpected changes, that his eleven-year tenure in Norman entailed.

4

 ∼

Advance and Retreat
First Years at the University of Oklahoma,
1897–1903

Parrington broke his ties reluctantly and in later years retained a sense that "Emporia was home." Yet one cannot but ask why, if he were willing to undergo such a severing, he did not journey farther away to a more propitious setting for his incipient professional goals. He had enjoyed being a rather big fish in the small, safe pond of the College of Emporia, as exemplified by a photograph of the college's football team in which Coach Parrington is proudly wearing a sweater emblazoned with an apparently crimson Harvard "H." He had not ventured to apply for a position at the Kansas State Normal School, which began holding classes in 1865, well before the denominational college. Perhaps he had not yet established a clear sense of personal and career direction. Several diary entries indicate the belief that he would not enter "a man's estate" until the age of thirty. This self-designed period of maturation—what Erik Erikson calls a "moratorium," often taking the form of a "pastoral retreat" away from routine pressures—thus extended into his early Oklahoma years.[1]

In this choice Parrington was in tune with other members of his generation—like Randolph Bourne, Lincoln Steffens, and Hutchins Hapgood (whose years at Harvard overlapped Parrington's)—who expressed some of their rebellion against their late Victorian upbringings by glorifying the innocence and freedom associated with childhood. Parrington's youth did fit the classic Victorian outlines. His father was "the Judge," the stern disciplinarian whose life revolved around distant, public concerns. His mother was at home, nurturant of her second son's interest in beauty (they both loved flowers) and possibly in poetry and religion: he kept her childhood copy of *The Book of Common Prayer* to the end of his life. And Vernon had lived at home under the sway of parental atmosphere, participating in yearly housecleanings and refurbishings as well as in family financial reversals except for his two years in Cambridge, when he was also dependent on John and Louise's support and approbation.

Parrington did not lack the scholarly drive that might have pushed another talented young professor to attend graduate school. He took the trouble to meet the college's requirements for a Master of Arts degree in

1895. Moreover, in June of the same year, he took preliminary steps toward returning to Harvard to complete a Ph.D. Such a step would doubtless have changed the subsequent course of his life, but it was not carried out. His parents' financial difficulties were deemed paramount then, and in his decision two years later to secure a position with a substantially increased salary—he had hoped to double his annual $700, raised from an initial $500, but was lured at $1,000—that kept him near enough to home to keep an eye on his aging father's health and his mother's welfare. His older brother was finishing medical school and beginning his own practice; John was not relied upon to assume such filial duties.[2]

So on September 8, after a hot and oppressive summer in Emporia and a hot and dusty train ride, the twenty-six-year-old Parrington arrived in Norman. An editorial in the first fall issue of *College Life* paid him a brave though sentimental farewell, another indication of how successfully Parrington had kept incongruent opinions from the accepted angle of the college's vision:

> In every department of College work he was a master. In social life his genial humor and sterling manhood won him a large circle of sincere friends. In the classroom his quiet dignity and brilliant mind held the undivided attention of his students and stimulated them to realize the possibilities of the powers that lay in them. On the athletic field he was conscientious and painstaking, and in match games the life and mainstay of the team. . . . while new duties and responsibilities demand his time and ability, we would wish to have him remember us.[3]

The assumption of those new duties and responsibilities determined the visible outlines of the ensuing six years.

Institutional Responsibilities

After the publication of *Main Currents in American Thought* some three decades later, Parrington was recognized as a pioneer in charting the wilderness of the American mind. When he arrived in Norman he was a pioneer in the truest sense of the term. Kansas may have had its cultural and geographic drawbacks—as William Allen White pointed out (from one end of the spectrum) in his famous 1898 editorial "What's the Matter with Kansas?" and Carl Becker wryly observed (from the other end) in his 1917 essay "Kansas." But at that time, Oklahoma was still ten years away from statehood.[4]

Between 1830 and 1889, all but the Panhandle and the area now mainly comprising Greer County in the southwest corner of the state was Indian Territory. There the federal government under Andrew Jackson's Indian Removal Act first relocated the "Five Civilized Tribes," primarily from traditional lands in southern states, and then various groups of Plains Indians. In the spring of 1889, unassigned reservation lands in the central section of Indian Territory were opened to white settlement. In 1890, the western half of Indian Territory was designated Oklahoma Territory. That same year, citizens who desired the stability and economic benefits that institutions both symbolize and encourage convinced the territorial government to charter several schools, including a state university to be located at Norman. A boom town created by and for commercial interests, its population nearly doubled (from 764 to 1,218) by the following year. After securing a president, David Ross Boyd, a former school superintendent in Ohio and Kansas with an honorary doctorate from Wooster College, and a faculty of four members, the new university opened its doors to fifty-seven students on September 15, 1892. They were all at the preparatory level and were temporarily to attend classes in a downtown office building.

When Parrington joined the five-year-old institution, 359 students were enrolled with the majority (309) still in the Preparatory Department. The new professor of English and modern languages was to teach French and German, in which (as his Harvard grades show) he was not well-grounded, in addition to literature and composition courses. He swelled the faculty roster to thirteen, although these included four part-time music instructors, a librarian, and the president (who taught mental and moral science). Four other recent additions played important roles in Parrington's life: the instructor of oratory and head of the Music Department, Grace King, a fellow Emporian who had recommended the Harvard-trained Parrington to Boyd; the professors of Greek and Latin, Joseph F. Paxton, who also held a B.A. from Harvard, and of mathematics, Frederick S. Elder, who became fellow sportsmen if not friends; and the professor of biology and physics, Alfred Van Vleet, whose training (A.B. Wisconsin, A.M. Johns Hopkins, Ph.D. Leipzig) reflected the most contemporary academic trends. As new and raw as the university was, it provided both a strikingly different intellectual atmosphere and student body from the College of Emporia. Parrington numbered as colleagues none of his former professors, another measure of increasing independence, nor any whose primary commitment was to Presbyterian doctrine. The secular training of the faculty and the practical aims of the students (a pharmaceutical department developed steadily after its 1893 inception) were in harmony with the spirit of the growing midwestern state universities established under the Morrill Act. As the charter, modeled on that of Indiana University, stated,

> The object of the University of Oklahoma shall be to provide the means of requiring a thorough knowledge of the various branches of learning connected with scientific, industrial and professional pursuits, in the instruction and training of persons in the theory and art of teaching, and also instruction in the fundamental laws of the United States and of this Territory, in what regards the rights and duties of citizens.[5]

The practical and ultimately political nature of the school would later cause Parrington deep bitterness and occasion for professional soul-searching. Nor could his introduction to the university be described as auspicious, although a new building was completed by 1894 on forty acres of donated land located half a mile beyond the Norman city center. An essay he wrote in 1905 for the first yearbook, the *Mistletoe,* dryly reminisced:

> I had never been in Oklahoma, and as I got off the train, that September day, what lay before one was disheartening. The afternoon was insufferably hot and dry. A fierce wind was blowing from the southwest, and great dust clouds—that I have got better acquainted with since—greeted me inhospitably. I asked the way to the University, and set out along the plank walk that the heat had drawn the nails half out of. My mind was busy with the weather, the ugliness of the raw little town, the barrenness of the streets and yards.
>
> As I came on to the campus I stopped—this was the University! The word had always meant—well, something very different to me. A single small red brick building—ugly in its lines and with a wart atop—a sort of misshapen cross between a cupola and a dome—stood in a grove of tiny elms. Across the front and especially about the door, some ivy had made a fine growth and was the one restful thing that met my eyes. The weather had got on my nerves, and it was in no pleasant mood that I went inside. The first person whom I met was a boyish looking fellow who told me . . . he was part freshman and part secretary to the president. He showed me around. It didn't take long.

The Kansas immigrant was impressed by the well-equipped chemical laboratory in the basement but dismayed by the library on the second floor:

> The room was fair-sized and pleasant, only where were the books? . . . There were perhaps three or four hundred books, all told, but of those that could be used for the work in English, there were not fifty. They were so few, it was with downright pleasure that I found a set of the "English Men of Letters," Taine's "History of English Literature," and Gosse's "History of Eighteenth Century Literature." For a year they were the stock and trade of the English department.[6]

Developing yet another English Department, of which he was again chairman and sole member, was Parrington's primary task. At first he could not put in place the series of courses developed at Emporia because of the lack of upper-division students. Parrington also taught composition in the Preparatory Department because the university functioned initially as a secondary school. The first prospectus lists no literature or language instructor, yet evidently the position was filled from 1893 to 1895 by James S. Griffin, who had a master's degree from Eureka College. During 1895–96 English was jointly covered by Mary Overstreet and James S. Buchanan, the history professor, French was taught by the mathematics professor, and German was not offered.

During Parrington's first year, only one collegiate-level English class, in composition, was possible. Its dozen students included the librarian and M. Jay Ferguson, who became a close friend and completed graduate work under Parrington. The following year, Parrington was promoted to full professor and these students advanced to sophomore courses in argumentation, modeled on his Harvard forensics class, and composition, featuring the history of the English language with an emphasis on etymology and dialect. Although the 1898–99 catalog listed four upper-level courses (a survey of English literature, Shakespeare, a nineteenth-century literature course focusing on poetry and "with special consideration of the subject of imagination," and an independent study), these could not be fully instituted until 1900–1901. By then, Parrington had also added courses in Chaucer and advanced composition as well as restructured and retitled most of his prior offerings. The first two B.A.'s had been awarded, and the enrollment had grown enough (393 total, with 64 in arts and one graduate student) to warrant introduction of the elective system, increased library holdings (to nearly two thousand volumes), and a second laboratory.

Beginning in the fall of 1899, tutors from among the advanced students started assuming the preparatory load until full-time preparatory instructors were employed two years later. Parrington was freed from teaching French and German when a full-time modern language instructor was hired in 1900, although he continued to teach two courses in French yearly. Released to concentrate on upper-division offerings, Parrington designed a master's degree program. Finally, in 1903 he was joined in the English Department by Wilbur Raymond Humphreys, a slightly newer product of Harvard's English curriculum. After receiving his B.A. in 1900, Humphreys took graduate work in Anglo-Saxon and Germanic philology—two areas in which his chairman was weak—and earned his Harvard M.A. the year he came to Norman. A colleague's presence made it possible for Parrington to take a year's leave during 1903–4. When he returned, Humphreys took over some of the composition and English prose style classes and taught a group of courses (historical grammar, Anglo-Saxon, Anglo-Saxon poetry) in Old English. During 1903 to 1908, the two were usually given a hand in the burgeoning lower-level courses by a series of part-time instructors. But Parrington continued to teach writing and retained primary responsibility for directing required bachelor's theses as well as for a group of courses dealing with "the development of English literature from the time of Chaucer to the present." By 1902–3 these included Chaucer, the eighteenth- and nineteenth-century novel, English literature from Spenser to Defoe, English literature from Pope to Carlyle, Shakespeare, Browning and Tennyson, the French Revolution and English poetry, and a series of seminary lectures on selected topics.

Within six years Parrington had not only substantially duplicated his Emporia offerings but had inaugurated two new courses (the seminary lectures and the novel course, covering Jane Austen to Thomas Hardy); modified his survey course (the delineating figures were no longer Fielding, Johnson, and Ruskin); remolded his romantic movement course under the influence of Dowden's volume *The French Revolution and English Literature;* and narrowed his later nineteenth-century poetry course to the two authors (Browning and Tennyson) who had so strongly influenced his 1895 "Poetry and the Mission of Poetry" address. Nor was this all. In the falls of 1900 and 1904 he again ventured outside his department, this time into philosophy, a move for which Palmer's Harvard class had partly prepared him. There he taught Introduction to the Study of Ethics, described in the catalog as "an examination of certain first principles, such as conscience, goodness, duty, with special attention to the teachings of modern hedonists."[7]

With a few significant exceptions, only a smattering of lecture notes survive from these early Norman years. A disastrous fire on the night of January 6, 1903, destroyed the original campus building, the old University Hall, which had been remodeled and renamed Science Hall. Student records, the chemistry equipment, historian Buchanan's books and maps, and some of President Boyd's papers were saved. Nothing was saved from the third floor, which housed the chapel and library, except the books that were checked out. There is no record of the fate of the first floor English offices, but the lack of materials, including any course syllabi or departmental proceedings, for these years in either Parrington's effects or the university archives suggests that the fire may have erased all but the personal books and papers he kept at home. His diary was neglected during 1902 and until July 1903 so no note of the event is there.[8]

Parrington's collegiate-level courses at Oklahoma and at Emporia up through 1903 were by title and content still focused on English and not American literature. The university's *Bulletins* provide a guide to the early stages of the teaching of American subjects. Courses in American literature were regularly offered in the Preparatory Department, and familiarity with three representative American authors was required for admittance to the College of Arts and Sciences, as distinct from the Schools of Pharmacy and of Music, after the former was established in 1899. Parrington's predecessor, James S. Griffin, first bore the title of professor of history, English and American literature and offered a sophomore course that was to study American classics, which included works by Irving, Poe, Longfellow, Emerson, Cooper, Hawthorne, and Lowell. At that point, however, only one student—a freshman—had risen above the preparatory ranks. This course disappeared the following year but reappeared slightly revised as a freshman course in the catalog printed the year Parrington arrived, along with a grammar course that incorporated readings from Hawthorne, Irving, and Longfellow. During Parrington's first year, he taught an American classics course in the Preparatory Department. Until the first full-time preparatory English instructor was hired three years after that, Parrington may well have had responsibility for this as well as a second preparatory course in representative American authors that used Brander Matthews's *Introduction to American Literature* as a text.

Thus in its initial decade, instead of developing American literature at the collegiate level as its first catalogs had intended, the university relegated it to the Preparatory Department. American literature and civics were deemed, as they are now, necessary components of an adequate secondary education. For the next few years, the Norman curriculum continued to reflect the general national trend of focusing postsecondary literature study on English subjects. One verification of this bias against the advanced study of native literature is the 1894 *Dial* survey, in which of the twenty institutions surveyed only a handful include any reference to American literature as a subject taught in its own right. Parrington thus participated in the perpetuation of widely accepted national curriculum standards, as seen in his department's offerings and in the university's substitution of English for American literature in its college candidacy requirements.[9]

His exposure to American writers at Harvard and his early delight in Poe and Hawthorne had certainly prepared him for these duties, but his attention and tastes still ran heavily to the English mid-Victorian period. His personal reading, though, contains one harbinger of the future. In early November 1898, Parrington noted in his diary that he "got hold of *Leaves of Grass* for the first time." Reading Walt Whitman again in February 1900, he found "some fascinating poems with the glimpses reaching out into the infinite—cosmic, elemental."

But Parrington's schedule left few moments for such leisurely pursuits. In coming to Norman, he also brought along football, becoming the university's first legendary football coach, and chairing the faculty Athletic Committee. He had to train the team from the ground up, spending his afternoons in daily practices, but he succeeded in leading the first Oklahoma team to a cumulative 9-2-1 record during its four initial seasons.[10]

In addition to his grueling duties editing the successive catalogs, his responsibilities on the Publication Committee expanded to include the campus's first student magazine, athletically titled the *University Umpire,* started the year before he arrived. Parrington served as editor for a year and a half, from the fall of 1898 to mid-February of 1900, then as advisory editor until the spring of 1905. The editorial columns Parrington wrote for the bimonthly *Umpire* constitute his primary publications during his Norman tenure and help supplement speculations about his intellectual development.

Less formal than his last *College Life* essays, the twenty *Umpire* columns form a running counterpoint to facets of Parrington's courses and current thinking.[11] Several reveal a preoccupation with assumed Anglo-Saxon traits that border on the jingoistic nativism so prevalent in the 1890s when immigration—especially of darker-skinned, non-English-speaking eastern

Europeans—increased. Although Parrington had had Germans and Bohemians for neighbors and schoolmates, one of the penalties of living in the Southwest was a reinforcement of cultural prejudices that helps explain his attraction to Beowulf and Chaucer but jars unsettlingly with the social idealism expressed in the political sympathies manifested in Emporia. For example, the celebration of Thanksgiving provoked the following reflections:

> In spite of the ill-smelling hordes of Poles and Italian[s], Russians and what not, who had landed at Castle Garden and scattered through the length and breadth of the land, in spite of the strange ways and strange doctrines which the millions have brought with them, the fibre and sinew of this nation is puritan. As individuals we may be French or German, Irish or Scandinavian, but as Americans we are Anglo-Saxon. . . .
>
> Our great middleclass have inherited the Mayflower ideals. The farmers scattered over these prairie states, the villagers of New England, the plain people north and south, for the most part are kin to the psalm-singing puritans of King Charles' day.

The positive identification here of Puritan, Anglo-Saxon, and middle class suggests what a vast shift in political and cultural education lay ahead before the interpretative framework of *Main Currents in American Thought,* which relies heavily on delineating the warping features of Puritanism and of the middle class, could be built.

In another piece, Rudyard Kipling (currently visiting in New York) is praised as "the great English writer of our generation," who appeals to the Anglo-Saxon world because of his "vigourous, manly, forthright nature" that is the "product of a society given over to democratic ideas—to commercialism, to the conquest of the world by the Anglo-Saxon middle class." The essay ends by criticizing Kipling for having "a stern sense of duty . . . but no love; fellow feeling and grim pathos but little tenderness; vigourous thinking but no brooding." The more mature Parrington would see that it was Kipling's Anglo-Saxon traits that marred his writing. Similarly, Parrington's Anglo-Saxon jingoism mars his understanding here. When that component was eliminated by exposure to more cosmopolitan influences, it helped clarify what "democratic ideals" could mean outside the boundaries of his own narrow environment.

An editorial provoked by the shallowness of speeches at a Lafayette Day celebration reflects ill-consorting prejudices and idealistic strivings in Parrington's thinking. For here he questions the meanings given to the word "liberty," first pointing out that to John Knox liberty meant intellectual freedom and to Cromwell it meant political freedom. Then he insists that the term must be redefined to keep pace with changing conditions. To men thrown out of jobs by machines or experiencing poverty,

> some other definition of the term freedom must be found, and it is because such men as Edward Bellamy and Henry George have defined it otherwise that they

appeal to so many men today. To these later fighters, liberty means something very much more than the right to cast a ballot; it means the right to live. . . . The great mass of men have been forced to struggle for mere bread, their birthright has been stolen from them, and their poor stunted souls cry out for vengeance on a world that has enslaved them. It is this cry that is ringing in our ears.

Such impassioned rhetoric would mark, for example, Parrington's portrait of Roger Williams in *Main Currents* and his introduction to Ole Rölvaag's *Giants in the Earth*. Significant also is the evidence of Parrington's acquaintance with Bellamy and George, both of whose reform programs would be scrutinized in the third volume of *Main Currents*.

Two other editorials are of special interest because they show how much firmer ground Parrington occupied when he wrote from the basis of his professional expertise in literature. In one Parrington outlines and then illustrates, through an explication of Longfellow's "Psalm of Life" that cheerfully deflates the revered status of this "household god," two rules of criticism that he advocates for students to follow. The first is to "approach the work from the point of view of the writer; be in sympathy with that which he had done," for "without sympathy one can never hope to understand anything or know it through and through." The second rule follows from the recognition that "something more than sympathy is necessary; we must challenge what we read. We must criticize it asking what it means and if it be worth our while. We need constantly to put the question that Audrey put to Touchstone: 'I do not know what "poetical" is; is it honest in deed and word? Is it a true thing?' "

Here we also gain the flavor of what it might have been like to sit in one of Parrington's classes, where close reading and independent judgment were valued by the professor and expected of the student. These same characteristics, as well as the rhetorical verve of the Lafayette Day passage, mark a later column in which Parrington takes on the task of distinguishing, in a pithy paragraph, the recent "fashions" in literature by comparing them with changing fashions in dress:

> Sixty years ago the style was Byronic—the poet wore flaring collars and held conventions and decencies in supreme contempt—a spoilt-child prose. Thirty years ago the mode was set by Matthew Arnold—a melancholy longing for other days and other ways—a poetic sorrow at finding himself so much better than the age in which he was forced to live. Today the style is to affect neither the flaring collar nor the robe of melancholy but to put on a blue flannel shirt and mix with the world's work. Not to sigh for other ages but to live very eagerly in this present one—to write about Armenian massacres with William Watson, or about socialism with William Morris.

Not only does the sartorial imagery illustrate one of Parrington's teaching strategies—visualizing ideas in sharp, concrete forms—it also reverses the nativism of his Thanksgiving editorial. Most important, it contains one of his earliest references to William Morris, the English poet-craftsman-socialist who had died just three years earlier and was soon to become Parrington's primary intellectual model. Morris's carefully constructed arguments on the relation between art and politics would inspire Parrington to weave the divergent threads illustrated in his *Umpire* editorials into a coherent philosophical fabric.

The editorials may be understood as the transforming remains of Parrington's political participation during his later Emporia years. Like those activities and his Norman teaching responsibilities, they were public acts. But just as his Emporia life had its private counterpoint, so also did this period in his Norman existence. Coming to Oklahoma had given him opportunities to advance professionally, gaining an increased salary and freedom to develop new courses. But it also made it possible for Parrington, despite his heavy institutional burdens, to retreat, to enter a meditative period in which he could grapple with the religious and personal issues that had been running like silent streams under the currents of poetry and Populism.

The Claims of Life and Faith

Living alone away from home in the heady Cambridge atmosphere had produced physical discomfort, a crisis in confidence, a crisis in faith, a dedication to "the genius of work," and a gradually augmenting social life. When Parrington was thrown back again on his own resources in Norman, this pattern might have repeated itself. He gained twelve pounds eating hotel fare until he located a better place to take his meals, at the home of Louise Williams, where several other faculty members boarded. After his apprentice years of teaching in Emporia, he never lacked confidence in his powers of accomplishment, but he was troubled by the pace and effectiveness with which he reached his goals. He took the time necessary to satisfy his own harsh conscience, though adherence to personal standards might cost him more immediate rewards.

At first he was certain he would like the faculty and his courses, despite the heavy preparatory load. He anxiously led an initial September chapel service, much less an ordeal than at the Presbyterian College of Emporia. But after the first long hours alone in his room in Norman, Parrington found the routine of life disheartening, the auxiliary demands—playing first base in a ball game against Oklahoma City ("Univ. 26, Ok. 1"), attending a dance, teaching a Sunday school class, writing an article for the *Umpire* ("A Little Homily"), and plugging through Ben Jonson's "Everyman in His Humour" ("stupid"). He was troubled by the lack of time for "my work," which often meant writing poetry.

Spells of dreaminess and moodiness were frequently recorded in his diary, which became confessional in tone and nature.

After a few October outings gathering persimmons along the banks of the Canadian River, Parrington felt rejuvenated, inspired to write a poem responsive to his new landscape. One of his most successful efforts, the lyrical "To the Canadian River" (published in a mid-March 1900 issue of the *Umpire*) contains these appropriately flowing, imagistic stanzas:

> Wilderness river that comes from the Alkali lands,
> Stretching from West to East with long fleshless hands,
> Telling the lowlands strange tales of the far upland sands,
> . . . .
> Passed the wild wind with a desolate shrill,
> Restlessly seeking in river-bed, upland and hill—
> Ceaselessly wailing and loving the loneliness still.
> . . . .
> Silent the river: it may not reveal what it knows:
> Gone are the older days: only the wind as it blows
> Swishes its way through the rushes and shrieks as it goes.[12]

Then during Thanksgiving recess, shortly after receiving a letter from his friend Vern Cook, who was succumbing to the ravages of tuberculosis, he was moved to write in his diary:

> God has been very good to me in the years just past, and I am not heedless of it. *I am becoming more and more religious, more and more grave,* yet ever more clear of what our duties in this life are. While I am granted the strength I will do faithfully what comes to hand, leaving the needless worry and the fret. (Emphasis added)

In this reflective, dutiful mood—spelled by one "jolly time" in Oklahoma City at a dance with a "jolly girl"—he returned home for the Christmas holidays. Home was once again Americus, John and Louise Parrington having moved from Emporia back to the farm when Vernon departed for Norman. It was a grim visit. In town, he met his College of Emporia successor, John Van Schaik, whom he found likable but no scholar. In Americus, the once idealistic Populist confessed to his diary: "I can live anywhere, but certainly there is little here to fire a man to large thoughts. I seem to become half comatose under the influence of farm air."

On the last day of the year, he ended his visit, regretting his mother's tears and loneliness. His annual New Year's Eve stocktaking illuminates how far he had retreated from optimistic political solutions to economic problems:

The struggle with the money has taken the sweetness out of things and left the bitter. Under it I fear I have grown sterner and gloomier in my beliefs and outlook. Everything is unsettled: and I think it cannot be otherwise to the end of the chapter. We have glimmerings that are only half vision, and by them we must guide our vision. Yet I have no fear. God has made us so and the world so, and we have only to keep knocking at the doors: it is no fault of ours if they are not open to us. *And I have knocked and been denied, but I have grown the more religious thereby.* (Emphasis added)

His New Year's resolution was to publish a volume of poetry by the summer of 1899. The first new poem, labored over in periods of feeling blue during a dreary January made worse by eyestrain, was titled "Behold I Stand at the Door and Knock." In it Parrington contrasted the "vibrant" chant of "the morning of my day" when he was certain God would answer his knock with this despairing chant "in the evening of my day":

> Phantoms the spirits that cry me:
> Mad are the hopes that belie me:
> Keyless the gates that deny me
> Passageway on to my goal.
> . . . .
> I had knocked and still the doors
> were bolted fast;
> I had squandered health and found
> scant truth at last.

The claims of poetry and religion, instead of poetry and Populism, began to grip his private concerns. The fulfillment of university duties was interpreted not as a component of his professional persona but as part of his troubled faith: "Never may I dare do my work lightly or carelessly; or I blaspheme the Holy One," he vowed one evening after church. A week later came the news of the death of Bertha White, a former Emporia student with whom he had become seriously involved the summer he moved to Norman.[13] Over the next thirteen months he nearly ceased writing in his diary, pouring much of his reflective time into writing a series of "memorial verses" dedicated to Miss White. Titled "A Plain-Song," this sixteen-page effort was the longest poem he would ever write. In the midst of this therapeutic process, he completed other short poems and began a poem titled "Amos." His attempt—which went through many revisions and emendations and was never finished—was to build into verse the experience of the Old Testament shepherd who stood on the starlit Syrian hills and responded to God's call: "And God took me as I was following my sheep, and the Lord said unto me: Go, prophesy unto my people Israel" (Amos 7. 15–16).

In "Amos" the linkage of poetry and religion seems to indicate a return to Parrington's earlier desire to preach, buried since his second year at Emporia, and the decision to dedicate himself to poetry. Now the dedication is to the role of the prophet, his identification not with late Victorian poets lamenting the eroding of English culture by industrialization but with the Old Testament voices in the wilderness decrying the spiritual emptiness of the children of Israel.

Progress on his memorial verses was interrupted by a summer trip to Chicago, where he studied Restoration drama in the public library and at the new University of Chicago library. The fall term began, followed by a period of fruitless socializing that deflected him from preparing for his courses. Such behavior violated a stern mid-September diary command: "For the present one source only of happiness—work. . . . Do this and thou shalt be happy—or what is better—blessed. Do it not and thou shalt be—unhappy." He spent another Christmas in Americus, where his parents' financial struggles had eased only slightly. For the first time in his years of diary keeping, he made no New Year's resolutions. His eye trouble flared up again, and he missed the first day of classes in five and one-half years of teaching.

Then in early April 1899 came the news of Vern Cook's death. A series of couplets dedicated to his longtime friend was incorporated in "A Plain-Song." A little over a year later, his brother's young wife died in childbirth. Mary Wright Parrington's was the fourth death that marred his first three years in Norman, for John Hewitt, the College of Emporia's president, had died in late April 1898. These deaths not only further severed his ties to Emporia and Americus, they help explain his sense of growing both gloomier and tenderer and his identification with the lonely convictions of Old Testament figures.

It is no surprise that "A Plain-Song," finally completed in May 1899, concludes with an attempt to reconcile the sense of estrangement from the certainties of faith in "Behold I Stand at the Door and Knock" with an Amos-like vision of a sunset from a prairie hill and an expression of being set adrift by the loss of his Emporia moorings:

> Yesternight I watched the setting of the broad sun in the West
> As it dropped in orange splendour down the prairie hills to rest:
>
> And the sky grew purer, deeper, with all hear-stains washed away—
> Till a star of evening standeth in the tender orange-gray—
>
> Standeth like a tongueless prophet of high things of mystic worth—
> Pure-eyed watcher o'er the night-dreams of this restless, troubled earth.
>
> . . . .
>
> Till from all the troubled broodings of the long months comes release—
> God hath stretched His hand in blessing: whispers, "Peace, my brave
> earth, peace!

Thou art mine and I do love thee; through the years that come and go
I will wipe away thy tears and ease thy heart of the long woe."

And no more I vex the quiet with the riddle things that are,
For I know above the storm-clouds thou are shining O my star!

Though the way be long and rugged to the far-off golden West,
Lo, thou guidest Ishmael, wanderer, till he sleeps upon God's breast.

There can be no doubt about the inward struggle Parrington's verses convey, whatever reservations we might have about their quality as poetry. The day the final copy of "A Plain-Song" was completed, he observed gloomily in his diary: "It is humiliating to look squarely at a thing and say: This then is the best that you can do, the highest that you are capable of. Good or bad however, it is behind me. I am the stronger for the work, so I go on to new and better work, I hope. . . . Gott sei dank! 269 couplets."

Release from "A Plain-Song" betokened another crucial stage in Parrington's achievement of personal independence. Shortly after he began teaching a Shakespeare course in the university's 1899 summer term, he moved from his hotel lodgings into a room at Louise Williams's, where he had taken his meals for the past two years. The change provided more than shelter; it afforded daily companionship. Although Abram Williams was a successful local businessman, he seems to have been unable to satisfy his wife's ambitions. The former Mary Louise Stewart was a sprightly and sympathetic conversationalist. Twelve years Parrington's senior, she was still a regally beautiful woman, and she had two charming daughters: Julia, who was then sixteen, and her younger sister, Eloise. This household quickly became a second home to Parrington. When he traveled back to Americus for his brother's wedding at the end of June, he cut short his stay by four days. "I am never happy here at the farm," he wrote, and "was not sorry to be in Norman once more."[4]

At Mrs. Williams's he spent the morning hours on his "new and better work," the Amos cycle, as well as polishing his composition notes into a pamphlet and reading Longfellow's "Christus" (which he found adhered too closely to the gospels), Joseph Ernest Renan's *Vie de Jésus,* and a volume of Edwin Markham's poems. At the end of August he departed, with his new Kodak camera, on a three-week trip to Colorado to visit his brother and sister-in-law. At the foot of Pike's Peak, he found himself wishing he was not alone; after a day riding in the Telluride hills, he felt closed off from the prairie, "a stranger in a strange land"; the next day he was happy to "face homeward" and assume his fall teaching duties. Although Mrs. Williams visited his parents in early January, that Christmas he did not return to the Americus farm but went on a hunting trip with some colleagues in the Keechi Hills. His year-end diary again omitted any resolutions or reflections. When his mother became ill at the end of March, he sped back to the farm, only to depart for Norman when Mrs. Williams became ill in his absence.

This last brief trip produced the idea for "a short Hebrew prayer" to serve as an introduction to the volume of poems he still planned to publish. In "Jehovah, Father, Unto Thee," Parrington identifies with another Old Testament figure, the shepherd-poet David. The poem asks for steadfast faith "lest should I fall through my much pride" and quietly argues: "The tears and grief are good for us—/ Yea and the breaking heart." This sense of pride and grief, produced by the long process of separating from his own family, was intensified by a visit to Norman by his aging father and a subsequent trip back to Emporia for the funeral of his sister-in-law, Mary Wright Parrington.

While his brother, John, returned with his infant daughter to live at the elder Parringtons' home and establish a medical practice in Emporia, Vernon returned to Norman and wrote a poem—"Yea Master I Do Speak to Thee"—in which he asks for mercy and calls himself an Ishmael, as in the last lines of "A Plain-Song":

> Fear with me though I wander far
> And wound thee grievously;
> For Ishmael hath a heart of love
> And sorely needeth thee.

Parrington was not taking his bearings here from *Moby-Dick*'s narrator but from his and Melville's mutual Old Testament source, the outcast son of the union of Abraham and his dark concubine, Hagar, regarded as the founder of the tribe of Mohammed. These poems show Parrington clinging to his faith, but they also show the cost to his conscience of breaking away from the farm and his own tribe. Whatever it cost, such a break is a necessary step in the consolidation of a young person's identity, and Parrington was nearing twenty-nine.

On July Fourth he heard Theodore Roosevelt speak in Oklahoma City and recorded the event on his Kodak. "Duly impressed" by the Republican vice-presidential candidate's rhetoric, he noted in his diary—in virtually the only political entry during his early years in Norman—that he did not agree with his ideas. Parrington went home and began hand-coloring significant passages of Leviticus and Deuteronomy in his Bible, purchased nearly a decade earlier in his first weeks at Harvard. Then he embarked on the highly symbolic project of redecorating his room. Earlier he had arranged a corner with a beaded Indian blanket and other Indian artifacts. Now he repapered the walls in a subdued tan and bought a Morris chair and a Wilton rug. He concluded these rites, which outwardly projected the identity of an aesthetic-minded Oklahoma professor rather than an emergent Emporia

Populist, with a photo session. Seated casually in the Morris chair, Parrington is flanked by a wall of books and holds what may well be his own volume of poems. The photograph also reveals the growth of a stylish beard and mustache.[15]

Having created a new image and a new setting for himself, Parrington required only one more anchor. He did return to his parents' home for Christmas, perhaps partly because he felt more certain of his autonomy and partly because—since they had moved back to town after John and baby Louise joined them—he did not have to endure the farm. But on December 30 he received news that Julia, Mrs. Williams's older daughter, was ill with smallpox, and he departed posthaste for Norman. The only prior mention of Julia in his diary occurred a year earlier, when she gave him a desk felt for Christmas. Now he was relieved to find her better than he feared. Later that spring of 1901, after going on a duck hunting trip with Professor Van Vleet and his wife, he decided to give the completed version of "Amos" to her. Then on the night of May 10, the sweet-faced eighteen-year-old and the nearly thirty-year-old professor became engaged. Parrington inscribed in wonderment in his diary: "A great change in my life has taken place—suddenly."

The couple set a wedding date for mid-December, then Julia left to spend the summer with a close family friend (Julia Rochester, for whom she was named) in Seattle. A few weeks after her departure, Vernon decided to join her there for a brief vacation. After traveling by train through Los Angeles and up the Pacific Coast, which he had never seen despite his father's former Whidby Island holdings, Parrington arrived in Seattle on July 19. Many tender, cherishing letters had passed between the pair, which helped advance the courtship. ("We cannot be happy away from each other . . . and it makes me the happiest man in the world to know that you have given yourself to me so completely. I hope and pray that I shall make my little girl happy, and I know I shall," he had written in early July.)

They were married at once, on July 31, 1901, by chance in the city where they would spend most of the rest of their lives. A few days later, on this thirtieth birthday, Parrington asserted in his diary: "Here I am at last arrived at a man's estate." They began their honeymoon in Snoqualmie Falls, just north of Seattle. Then they sojourned in the "charming English town" of Victoria, British Columbia, before returning by train to Norman, a route that included a refreshing day's stopover in the Rockies and a difficult week in Emporia. Parrington had delayed telling his mother of his engagement, then had married with no family present. Now both his mother and wife were unwell, and he found it "hard work to keep cheerful." The newlyweds gladly returned home, where they indulged in the pleasures of rearranging a room together in the Williams's house.[16]

Parrington began inquiring about purchasing land in Norman on which to build a home. But his salary—which had been raised to $1,500—

would not conveniently stretch that far so the living arrangement at his mother-in-law's seemed practical. Their first year of marriage contained the usual joys and problems. Julia was pregnant and endured morning sickness while Vernon immersed himself in a new fall term. There was conflict between the mothers and perhaps some unexpected adjustments between the couple, for Parrington spent Christmas away from his young bride on a hunting trip in the Arbuckle Mountains. Their daughter, Elizabeth, was born on April 27, 1902.[17] (Parrington stopped keeping his diary several months after his marriage so these events are not recorded there.) Two months later, Parrington was in Emporia, helping remodel the Rural Street home, a project that kept him away from Norman on his first wedding anniversary. There would be other trials and separations in the future, but Parrington called 1901 "the golden year" in his autobiographical sketch, and his children remembered their parents' relationship as filled with warm affection and thoughtful consideration.

Parrington's marriage put a stop to his football coaching but not to his religious explorations. Significantly, these now moved beyond private modes of reflection to more public forms. In early October 1900 he had ventured to print "Jehovah, Father, Unto Thee," the Hebrew prayer intended as the introduction to his proposed poetry volume, in the *University Umpire*. In the fall of 1901, in addition to his regular courses, Parrington began offering the series of seminary lectures on special topics. The lectures provided a format for him to discuss some of the spiritual and theological issues that he had been confiding in his poetry. They also reveal painstaking study of the Old Testament, which illuminates his poetic identification with scriptural prophets and outcasts and his practice of color-coding his Bible.

The university *Bulletin* announced the subject of the first series of seminary lectures as "the lyric and prophetic poetry of the Old Testament, with a special study of Isaiah." Preliminary lectures were to consider "The Canon of the Old Testament; the technique of Hebrew lyric and epic poetry; Prophecy in Israel and Judah; The development of Hebrew thought before the dispersion; and, The influence of the exile upon Hebrew literature," followed by an "examination of the first thirty-nine chapters of Isaiah and a comparison with chapters XL to LXVI." During the next year, 1902–3, the subject was announced as "The Book of Job, with some account of the Book of Ecclesiastes," and the preliminary lectures were to consider "The canon of the Old Testament; The development of Hebrew thought before the dispersion; the II Isaiah; The Church nation of the time of Ezra; and the sources of Job."[18]

Among the few documents preserved from Parrington's Oklahoma years is a small notebook labeled "Notes on the Old Testament." Dated September 1901, it contains nearly fifty pages of both polished and scratch notes keyed to the various seminary lecture topics. In addition, there exists a typed nine-thousand-word essay titled "A Layman's View of Isaiah," which

Parrington began in the summer of 1900, concurrent with "Amos" and his room redecoration project. Completed in 1902, the essay—as well as the notebook—reflects not only imaginative reading of Scripture but, in the heyday of form criticism, an acquaintance with standard historical and exigetical literature. His notes list as sources Samuel R. Driver's *Introduction to the Literature of the Old Testament* (1891) and Herbert Edward Ryle's *Canon of the Old Testament* (1892). Parrington's essay contains only one footnote, to a passage in the distinguished Bampton lectures, still given biannually at Oxford, delivered by Thomas K. Cheyne in 1889 and published in an 1895 American edition as *The Origin and Religious Contents of the Psalter.*

Parrington's notebook contains only a few pages on Job, so it is unclear whether the second series of lectures continued as planned or how he approached those subjects. However, the approach in "A Layman's View of Isaiah" is striking. His primary concerns were to describe the characteristics of Isaiah's multiple authors and textual problems. These are more the concerns of an intellectual historian than a seeker of solace and revelation. The latter focus might be expected from perusing his poems, tempered by our knowledge of the historical and philosophical emphasis in his literature courses and by the critical reading standards he advised in his *Umpire* columns. For example, at the outset of his essay, Parrington insisted that the Bible is

> the work of many hands and of different ages jumbled together in its present form. . . . To attempt a study of the bible in any other than an historical way is folly. Order must be brought out of chaos; . . . The words of the writer should be studied in their time order, with a view to following the development of the mind of the prophet or poet. Moreover[,] the words must be taken in their evident sense, as they appealed to those to whom they were addressed. Later meanings and symbolism must not be read into them. . . . Finally[,] it must be kept in mind that sporadic verses are of little significance; it is the total philosophy of a given writer that we are interested in.[19]

The development and application of such methods illustrates the intellectual and scholarly strides he had made since the ungrounded claims in his "God in History" oration a decade earlier. But most important, it illustrates how well Parrington would be equipped when he turned to the fields in which he would make his reputation. Several other features of "A Layman's View of Isaiah" help trace the emergence of the author of *Main Currents in American Thought*. For instance, Parrington's discussions of Puritan theology in *The Colonial Mind* were certainly informed by his understanding of such fundamental issues as the role of the idea of the covenant in Jewish history. It was an idea that played a similarly crucial role in early American religious and political history, from William Bradford to Jonathan Edwards.

The essay also reveals a love for Hebrew poetry, which influenced the cadences and imagery of Parrington's mature prose style. Finally, the merging of Parrington's long private religious struggles with his public Old Testament studies helps explain how he became able to express sympathy for such figures as the conservative Charleston lawyer and intellectual Hugh Legaré, who "like old John Winthrop two hundred years before . . . found the words of the Hebrew scriptures rising to his lips in moments of deep emotion."[20]

Despite its generally objective tone, the essay offers insight into Parrington's personal attraction to Isaiah, for he located the core of the book's persuasiveness in the selections known as "The Servant Songs." In these, the writer accepts the task of placing his faith in the service of God's word. Two other poems Parrington wrote in this period—one on his honeymoon titled "Prayer" and one in the fall of 1901 titled "Great Master Builder That Hath Shaped"—also stress the necessity of assuming the humble role of the servant. The seminary lectures and essay mark another transformation—from the desire to preach to the layman—in Parrington's search for an avenue to channel his beliefs. Their emphasis on the servant role accords with the duty-bound conscience that drove him on at Oklahoma in his institutional responsibilities and in his personal scholarly and creative endeavors. Yet he had yet to solve the problem of combining these two major facets of his life with the social conscience manifested in his Emporia political activities. Identity as either poet, preacher, prophet, or scholar alone was too narrow. Neither alone offered a means to develop his longtime interest in art, or to reconcile his aesthetic concerns with his background as a farmer's son, toiling to survive and yet deeply responsive to the beauty of nature, or even to place in perspective the passionate nature that prompted his decision to marry.

The roots of a role that would combine all of Parrington's commitments, interests, and yearning can also be found in this period. They lay not in religion or poetry but in the professional sphere, in preparations for the new course on the eighteenth- and nineteenth-century novel to be taught in the fall and spring of 1902–3. Another of the remaining documents among Parrington's Oklahoma papers is a small notebook titled "The Novel" and dated 1901–2. Although this notebook is interleaved with scraps of obviously later notes, the first sequence is of particular interest here. It consists of dated entries responding to his reading of four Thomas Hardy novels during the summer of his engagement and marriage. Hardy—who after 1896 devoted himself to poetry until his death in 1928 (only a year before Parrington's own)—was a new and fortuitous discovery. Parrington had purchased his *Wessex Poems* the year after they appeared (1898), when he was deep in his own poetry phase.

Now he first read *Far from the Madding Crowd* (1874) and judged that its realism fell short because it emphasized the romantic, personality, and plot at the expense of the "social idea." Yet we can imagine the appeal of the title and story—the relationship of farmer Gabriel Oak to the socially superior Bathsheba Everdene—to the former farm boy now identifying with Old Testament shepherds and rural prophets. He then read the more recent *Tess of the D'Urbervilles* (1891) and recommended it in a late June letter to Julia. His notes emphasize the Puritanism of Angel Clare, son of a clergyman, who idealizes farm life and abandons his young bride when he discovers her sullied past, and its "bitter, intensely modern" philosophy, expressed in Tess's and Angel's reconciled love pursued against the current of social forces. Next Parrington backtracked to *The Return of the Native* (1878), in which a Sophoclean tragedy is played out on the evocative Egdon Heath. He observed in his notebook: "It shows the clash and failure resulting from the philosophies of two worlds: . . . The old pagan with its zest for the joys of physical life and . . . the modern with its dominant social feeling and its chastened spiritual life." Did Parrington recognize something of himself in the returning native, Clym Yeobright, who damages his eyesight by late night reading and whose mother interferes in his relationship with the young, unschooled Eustacia? The old pastoral world is always both idealized and fading in Hardy, but the new world, though it seems to promise freedom from crippling social customs, can scarcely be deemed an improvement, as he continually symbolizes by the pulling down of medieval churches and houses and their replacement by contemporary architectural monstrosities.

It is the elaboration of this clash of old and new, again played out in romantic relationships, that also distinguishes Hardy's last novel and masterpiece, *Jude the Obscure* (1895). Jude's dilemma was in many ways Parrington's. Raised in a farming village, Jude became fired by the nearly unattainable goal of attending Oxford, called Christminster. To supplement his scanty education, he taught himself Greek and Latin; to support himself he learned the trade of stonemason. When he arrived in Oxford, he nursed his scholarly dreams by lamplight and by day repaired the outer walls of the buildings he could never enter because of his birthright. Jude aspires to the Anglican clergy and studies the church fathers as well as contemporary Tractarian writings. But his passion for his cousin Sue Bridehead causes him to abandon first his priestly then his scholarly dreams. Jude ultimately returns to his original stonemason's trade and class position only to lose the woman whose love changed the direction of his life.

Parrington's notes on this novel were dated the day after his marriage. No grimmer reflections on marriage and divorce can be found than in *Jude;* Hardy seems inappropriate fare for a honeymoon. That this series of novels markedly influenced Parrington will be seen in the next chapter. But what Hardy offered him now was a counterpart to his own divergent image. The thirty-year-old Parrington described Jude, who dies at age thirty, as "a medieval mystic, an enthusiast and dreamer, but with the restless intellectual ambition of the present," and noted how in the central reversal in the story "Jude becomes the free thinker." Jude's aspirations all fail, but for a time he embodies the multiple identities of preacher, scholar, and workman. The idealization of and reverence for this last facet finally provided the means for Parrington to transform his Kansas background and redefine himself as a craftsman, a role that unified—in its modeling upon William Morris—the poetic, the aesthetic, the literary, the spiritual, and the political.

The Morris model was but a short step away. Meanwhile, Jude's craft of restoring Gothic architectural features, based on Hardy's long-practiced profession as an architect, surely struck a chord in Parrington. Architecture became a passionate avocation, again spurred on by Morris. Always responsive to design and detail in his personal appearance and lately in arranging his Norman rooms, Parrington now turned his attention to domestic architecture and published his first article in other than a college organ. In January 1903, "On the Lack of Privacy in American Village Homes" appeared in *House Beautiful* just as he was beginning to teach the nineteenth-century novel course that included Hardy. Neither the article nor the magazine fit the outline a scholarly literature professor might be expected to fill. Rather, both bear witness to the emerging craftsman image. Further, the article illustrates the merging of the aesthetic with the social in its characteristically Progressive concern with city planning.

Parrington's complaint was against Americans' "curious love of publicity," which caused them to sacrifice comfort and privacy in order "that our place may be spoken of approvingly by those who go driving in the evening, that strangers may admire as they look over the town from street-cars." He argued that homes should face inward, away from the street, instead of outward, with "the company rooms in front, where they get the best exposure, and the work and living rooms on the side and rear." Advocating well-designed, private garden areas, he condemned parklike front lawns that beautify the neighborhood but do not serve the dweller. Parrington's plan combined the advantages of urban living with the virtues of rural life, while it criticized the attempt of home builders to create an artificial sense of community. In the "older days of scanty populations," he wrote, "the thing sought was not solitude, but companionship. . . . Today, however, we are in a different mood. A city life has tired us of the crowd, of publicity. When we go home we feel like shutting the world out and lounging as we may desire." Much like Whitman, Parrington preferred to "loafe and invite [the] soul."[21] But the essay seems less nostalgic about the nineteenth century—the setting of Hardy's novels and his own village boyhood—than it is critical of contemporary Norman.

Writing about the rearrangement of physical life was another manifestation of the process of rearranging his intellectual life. But that process was not further stimulated in Norman. The hiring of Wilbur Humphreys made it possible for Parrington to take a year's leave of absence from the university at the close of the spring term. Celebrating Elizabeth's first birthday and then bidding his family farewell, he embarked on a fourteen-month "grand tour" of England and France. At last, he could add this finishing touch to his education, a touch that many another bright, financially secure Harvard graduate would have acquired a decade earlier. As callous as it may seem to leave a wife of less than two years, surely it would have been difficult for Elizabeth to make the trek. His many letters to Julia over those months state frequently his regret at the financial necessity of going alone. Like Jude, circumstance and character prohibited him from pursuing conventional patterns. But in Parrington's case the delay in Emporia and retreat in Norman produced fruitful results.

5

~

Dwelling Between Worlds
Europe and Norman, 1903–1906

England and France, 1903–1904

When Parrington set sail from New York on July 7, he was, we might say, heading toward his own version of Hardy's Christminster. The lure of England and France for a professor who had lived and breathed their literatures and languages is more than understandable. His expectably rigid plans for study, however, were often revised as he encountered environments vastly different from Norman's dry climate and barren culture.

The contrasts began as soon as Parrington boarded the *Carpathia*, a Cunard Line vessel bound for Liverpool, carrying second- and third-class passengers only. After the long train journey from home, with stops to visit Emporia and relatives in Aurora and Chicago, it seemed "strangely unreal" to watch the ship leave the New York wharf. The nine-day crossing was blessed by fine weather and a relatively cosmopolitan array of fellow passengers. Among the representatives of the professional class, all no doubt attracted by the modest fare, were a Cornell University professor and student, going to Germany to study theology; several lawyers; a Boston artist bound for Paris; a botany professor from the University of Nebraska; an Irish priest from St. Louis; and "a delightful old Yankee" on the staff of the *New York Outlook*. Parrington was armed with a letter to the London representative of G. P. Putnam's Sons, given to him in New York by the firm's senior partner, George H. Putnam, whom he described to Julia as "an exceedingly courteous and intelligent man."

Upon arrival in Liverpool, he quickly toured several art galleries, finding works by the American Edwin A. Abbey the "best" and those by Dante Gabriel Rossetti, Holman Hunt, and John Everett Millais "magnificent also." He thought the John Ryands Library a splendid example of modern Gothic and was amused by discovering the ale firm of Harding and Parrington. After a brief stop in Manchester, he settled in London at 41 Upper Bedford Place, off Russell Square. In a letter home to Julia, he exclaimed: "Here I am at last in London, and I never was more surprised at a place nor so pleased in my life. It is delightful—so big and roomy with breathing spots everywhere. Not crowded together like Chicago but at every turn a small square or garden brilliantly green." In his first three days he attended Sunday services at Westminster Abbey and was deeply moved by the spirit of the place. He visited the Tate Gallery and the British Museum, found paintings by Raphael, Titian, Rembrandt, Reynolds, and Hogarth in the National Gallery "past imagining"; toured St. Paul's, whose Renaissance style appealed to him less than the Gothic, and the Tower, where he felt overpowered by the "history that is clinging to the walls." Returning to Westminster on a weekday, he noted, "I am a bookman after all, and when I stood by the graves of those whom I have studied so lovingly it came closer to my heart than all the splendid pictures of the galleries."[1]

A few days later, Parrington's thoughts had turned from literature and art to economics and home. He confessed in his diary:

> O this London! A beautiful place with the wealth even of the far countries in its hands and yet with misery unspeakable. It oppresses me so, and yet it lifts me up. As I go in and out among the streets and curious lanes I am delighted, and yet my heart cries out for the hills and the quiet places. *I am a child of the country after all,* and already I am beginning to long for the smell of the dew on the wild grass. There is something here that brings home too closely the thought of mortality and its hopes and fears that are vain alike. My heart goes out across that stretch of miles to those at home. God bless them and keep them. Yet sometimes that cry of poor Juliet's is mine: "O God, I have an ill divining mind." Only I try to put it by resolutely. (Emphasis added)

A key to what was troubling him, and perhaps to another reason he had escaped to Europe, comes in an anniversary letter to Julia, where he expresses the fear that she had not been "as happy as you should have been and as you had a right to be." "I blame myself more than you think for it," he added, then swiftly changed from the personal, citing his growing reverence for old builders and his intention to write an article for *Country Life in America* or *House Beautiful* based on the notes he had taken at Kew Gardens. There were intervening tours of the Temple with its Romanesque architecture and the grave of Goldsmith, St. Bartholomew's, St. Giles's Cripplegate where Milton is buried, and Grub Street. The dark emotional theme was resumed shortly afterward on August 3, his thirty-second birthday:

> I am always a bit depressed of late years on my birthday: It is a time of stock-taking, and that is not growing a pleasanter task as the years pass. A certain distrust of myself, of my ever getting out what I feel to be in me, seems to grow stronger from year to year and acts like a blight. The past two years have been bitter, bitter ones in many ways: I have fallen so short of my ideals—drifting sadly. But I am stoutly bent now on doing my utmost to make good what I can of the lost time. And the dear ones that have been so good to me, I must make for them a larger and better future. The path has not been pleasant to their feet of late. God help us all.[2]

That he described the past two years—the years of marriage and father-hood—as bitter is not necessarily a reflection on Julia, living patiently with her mother and Elizabeth in Norman. Rather, the accusing finger is pointed toward Parrington's demanding conscience, which insisted that productive work rather than enjoyment of normal human pleasures was the measure of a fulfilled life. How far away were the days when "pleasant" was his diaries' dominant adjective! Yet he was thirty-two, and what did he have to show for it except the transitory achievements of organizing two English departments, some victories on the collegiate football field, a few minor essays, and a sheaf of poems tucked away in a drawer?

Three days later Parrington arrived in Cambridge for a three-week stay. There the graduate of the American Cambridge began "getting out what I feel to be in me." The mode this time was not poetry or religious essays but prose fiction. On August 7, he took satisfaction when noting in his diary: "After a long time and many delays I got to work this morning on my projected novel. It has been lying in my mind for months, and I propose giving my best hours this year to it. Today writing a preliminary chapter and outlining. It will be drawn largely from my own life and hopes—a sort of apologia pro vita mea. I feel a good deal uncertain but hopeful nevertheless."

Throughout his Cambridge stay, most days were spent quietly working in his room, making up for lost time, and the hours passed quickly. Midway, he wrote his first poem in nearly two years. "Come, love, and let us wander down / And bathe us in the golden light / That shineth upon field and town" one stanza runs, in Jude-like tones. But it was not an idle production; he planned to incorporate it in a critical romantic chapter that occurred well into his novel, eventually titled "Stuart Forbes: Stoic." Parrington devoted his grand tour's best hours to this project and continued working on it when he returned to Norman. Yet it was never completed, and he never sought to correct the impression that the manuscript was destroyed in a fire. He tucked the thick packet of completed chapters, partially developed scenes, and working notes—all in a minute, thin-nibbed variant of his usual backhand script—into a green leather folding notebook and filed it away in his desk with the poems he also would never publish.

Encompassing well over three hundred 6-x-8-inch pages, the extant manuscript is covered with revisions and emendations, often written crosswise over the original. Some of the sections are dated; these can be correlated with diary entries so that the compositional stages can be generally determined. But a reconstruction of the novel, or even accurate transcriptions of the most polished sections, is a prohibitive task. And because of the highly personal nature of the plot, perhaps much of it should remain as silent as Parrington preferred to leave it. Nevertheless, "Stuart Forbes: Stoic" is a highly significant index to his current intellectual stance as well as to his evaluation of fin-de-siècle culture.[3]

The plot turns on an unconsummated love affair between Stuart Forbes and a woman named Elizabeth Ashleigh. In Cambridge Parrington first worked on this emotional core of the novel, referred to as the "love book," then over the course of his European stay backtracked to write the opening scenes and key portions of later sections. The fictional couple "sacrifice their happiness to the great ideal of justice"; Elizabeth dies; and Stuart goes on to pursue a university career in which his "chief desire was to rise superior to the law of nature." Failing in this, or choosing an alternative to university life, he sets out to adapt a stoic philosophy to the conditions of late Victorian culture, a philosophy that centers on overcoming selfishness and leading the life of an honest workman, "not too much of an artist—not too many ideals, too much thinking, but wholesome, natural." In Stuart's dilemma the reader is to see a "sense of irony of our position in striving to establish an ethical system based on altruism in a world of self where the survival of the fittest is the law."

Stuart is, of course, Parrington himself. His first name appears to be a combination of two streams of maternal influence: a Scottish clan, in recognition of his mother's McLellan ancestry, but Stewart was also his mother-in-law's maiden name. Forbes may be an aural cognate for "fortitude" or a Carlylian echo ("refurbished") from *Sartor Resartus* ("the tailor retailored"). Elizabeth Ashleigh is modeled on Bertha White, the young Emporia woman memorialized in "A Plain-Song." His wife, Julia, makes her appearance as Mary, the betrothed to whom Stuart ultimately keeps his commitment, while his mother-in-law, Mrs. Williams, is disguised as a Mrs. Arnold. The parallels to *Jude the Obscure*'s main characters are obvious: Stuart is Jude, frustrated in his choice of vocation by both vocational and emotional aspirations; Elizabeth is Sue Bridehead, the woman Jude cannot marry because each of them believes that love can only be fettered by the marriage contract. In Parrington's variant, Elizabeth/Sue dies instead of Jude, and Stuart/Jude rather than Elizabeth/Sue returns to initial personal commitments. Mary is certainly a softer version of Jude's coarse wife, Arabella, and Mrs. Arnold may play part of the role of the elderly teacher Richard Phillotson, to whom Sue returns after their divorce in a fanatical attempt to justify her affair with Jude by adhering strictly to the letter of the law—the biblical injunction against divorce and adultery—rather than the spirit, which had characterized her relationship with Jude.

When Parrington traveled back to London at the end of August for an additional two months before departing for a half-year's sojourn in France, his schedule included a good deal more than daily writing. But his experiences fed the novel's undeveloped major theme and second plot line as well as furnished nonliterary influences on his thinking. After isolation in the scholarly environs of Cambridge, Parrington hurried to the American Express office and skimmed a back pile of American daily newspapers. The side that cried out, "I am a child of the country after all," upon first arriving in London took special note of the good crop reports in the *Kansas City Star.* Then the bookman asserted himself and located the site of the Globe Theatre and the graves of John Gower, Francis Beaumont, and John Fletcher. He attended two performances of *Richard II* and was mesmerized by the spectacular staging. "How gorgeous the old pageants must have been! I often wish I had lived then," he exclaimed in his diary in an outburst of medieval romanticism. He also saw one Harvard discovery, Eleonora Duse, in Gabriele D'Annunzio's *Francesca da Rimini,* a badly staged play saved by Duse's "wonderfully interesting" smoldering style.

Several cold, rainy afternoons were passed in the British Museum, completing the "love book," then studying stoicism and reading Marcus Aurelius. At this point Parrington sketched out his "own system of stoical philosophy" and decided firmly upon his novel's title and purpose: "Showing how stoicism is innate in the Puritan and how, as the dogmatic Christian life dies out, the stoic remains to contend with." These last exertions were followed not by renewed energy but by a week of severe eyestrain. This recurring problem, manifested first at Harvard, may well have had more than a physiological cause. For it was not solved by the glasses prescribed while he was teaching at Emporia and seemed to flare up at critical junctures either of intense study or of despondency resulting from dissatisfaction with his personal life or failure to achieve work goals. Not surprisingly, he again framed his reflections in poetry.[4]

One of these, "In Smock and Frock," illustrates Parrington's early employment of architectural imagery in a Jude-like conjunction of identification with "workmen." The final stanzas, which follow an invocation humbly welcoming God's judgment on the products of labor, also show Parrington laboring under his sense of lost time, the religious spirit that dominated his early Oklahoma years, and a resurgent social conscience:

> If we have built no lordly pile,
>   Nor fashioned marbles of great worth,
> Yet have we toiled with all our will
>   To make a nobler place of earth.
>
> Our huts are but for homely use
>   And builded out of common brick,
> But thou wilt judge us how we loved
>   Our weakling brothers, maimed and sick.
>
> And so in workman smock and frock
>   We stand with all our ways confessed;
> Judge thou, if we have laboured well,
>   Or if we scanted of our best.

With that confession off his chest—perhaps he felt he had only been idling over another indulgent aesthetic tangent in Cambridge—Parrington set off to spend a week studying in the British Museum. He did not study economics or politics, subjects that might shed light on how to love "our weakling brothers," but landscape gardening. In his devotion to architecture and gardening, Parrington, like so many figures caught up in the late nineteenth-century arts and crafts movement, felt that improvement in the exteriors of existence would react positively on the inner and the social life. Moreover, simplification meant the yoking of art, of beauty, with the rude sphere of work, with a consequent emphasis on reviving handcraft skills and cottage industry to protest the spiritual devaluation resulting from the separation of art and industry, the worker and his product, labor and capital.[5]

By 1903, all the prophets of nineteenth-century culture and politics Parrington had studied had died: Carlyle in 1881, Arnold in 1888, Morris in 1896, Ruskin in 1900. But some of their disciples were bravely carrying on. Among these were the architect C. R. Ashbee, son of a prosperous Bloomsbury family. Ashbee, born in 1863 and to live until 1942, attended King's College, Cambridge, in the 1880s, where his closest friends included the humanist and historian Goldsworthy Lowes Dickinson and the art critic Roger Fry. The atmosphere at King's closely paralleled that at Oxford's Merton and Balliol three decades earlier, when William Morris, Dante Gabriel Rossetti, and Edward Burne-Jones were students. There, under the influence of Ruskin and the early phases of Pre-Raphaelitism, they displayed their view of the function of beauty and art by decorating the walls of the newly built Oxford Union with scenes from *Morte d'Arthur* and floral designs. Yet not only the university and the times had shifted but also the chief influence—from Ruskin to Morris—and the central blazing concern—from art that sought to revive art to art that sought to revive society and politics.

The subtitle of E. P. Thompson's biography of Morris precisely indicates the change: "Romantic to Revolutionary." For nearly a quarter-century Morris had exercised his prodigious energy and talents as a poet and translator of Icelandic legends and as chief mover in the interior decorating firm that revolutionized late Victorian taste by its insistence on medieval simplicity of style and handcrafted (rather than machine crafted) textiles, furniture, wallpapers, and stained glass. Now, during Ashbee's youth, the middle-aged Morris began his association with the Social Democratic Federation, from which he withdrew and founded the Hammersmith Branch of the Socialist League. Named after the site of his workshops in the London suburbs, the league was an attempt to model political action on the medieval English and Italian Renaissance craft guilds, the model for Morris's workshops.[6]

In 1886, Ashbee had gone to Hammersmith to attend a lecture on private property by Edward Carpenter. Influenced as much by Walt Whitman's linkage of personal freedom and democracy as by Morris's advocacy of the value of manual labor, Carpenter was a leader in many of the reform movements of the 1880s, which might all be gathered under the rubric of "the Simple Life." Carpenter's persona and Morris's ideas inspired Ashbee to found the Guild of Handicraft in Whitechapel in 1888. The guild, with its attendant School of Handicraft, helped realize Ashbee's "yen for simple useful things produced by honest toil; his hope that the British working man could build a new society; most of all, his burning faith in the reforming zeal of comradeship." Ashbee's guild was one of the most successful that proliferated in the late nineteenth century. As his biographer Fiona McCarthy writes, such guilds were "very much a symptom of their time, the thinking person's protest in an age of increasing mass production and a worsening environment." She adds that they "looked back, with varying degrees of sense and eccentricity, to better days before industrialization when craftsmen took pride in their work and found joy from it."[7] Ranging from the professional to the inept, these contemporary guilds began with Ruskin's own Guild of St. George, set up in the 1870s, and included London's Toynbee House, which provided Jane Addams with a model for the American settlement house.

In 1891 the Guild of Handicraft moved its workshops to Essex House in Mile End Road. Shortly after Morris's death, Ashbee took over his pioneering Kelmscott Press (and most of his printers), establishing the Essex House Press. By the end of the century, "guild craftsmen were working in copper, brass, and iron; making silver and jewelry, some of it enamelled; cabinet making, modelling and carving, and carrying out whole restoration and decoration schemes." Then in the spring of 1902, the guild sought to incarnate the simple life by moving its seventy workmen, their families, and their equipment bodily to the site of an old silk mill in the small Gloucestershire town of Chipping Campden, in the Cotswolds.[8]

Ashbee had by then become a well-known figure, and many visitors sought out him and his workshops. Among them were Jack London, who lived in Ashbee's London house while dressing as a tramp to gather data for his 1903 exposé of the appalling poverty in the East End, *The People of the Abyss*. Another was V. L. Parrington. Parrington may have discovered Ashbee and his guild through persuing *House Beautiful* and John Lane's *Studio*. Contemporary copies of the *Studio*, which carried articles on Essex House and the Arts and Crafts Exhibition Society, survive in Parrington's library. In mid-September, while working on "Stuart Forbes" in the British Museum, he had taken at least one afternoon out to read some of Ashbee's "intensely interesting" writings. Although Parrington did not specify titles, these could have included an account of the guild's London origins, *From Whitechapel to Camelot* (1892) as well as *A Few Chapters in Workshop Reconstruction and Citizenship* (1894) and *An Endeavour Towards the Teaching of John Ruskin and William Morris* (1901). In early October he wrote to Ashbee, then the two met in Chelsea, where Ashbee extended an invitation to Chipping Campden. Delaying his planned departure for Paris so he could accept, late that month Parrington ran up to spend a week-end at the guild's new establishment, now called the Essex House of Arts and Crafts.

Staying in the Ashbees' "quaint old stone house" built in 1398, he met Ashbee's wife, Janet, "a frank whole-souled woman of perhaps 28"; William Strang, a Scottish artist friend visiting from London; and George Loosely, an English painter who had recently settled in a lodging house in Chipping Campden. The Ashbees' "wholly unconventional and simple" life, with its "quaint simplicity and directness about everything" (including sexual attitudes as well as other modes of behavior, dress, food, and speech) impressed Parrington. But he was not so charmed as to lose his critical perspective. He found a lecture by Strang that first evening "rather stupid," although he enjoyed sitting around the fire afterward while Strang told Scottish yarns. The next day, when he toured the guild works, he "came away with the feeling that more artists were needed: One man cannot project himself into so many different lines, and the work suffers in its higher aspects."[9]

Only five years later, the guild went into liquidation, but not because Ashbee diffused his control. Rather, the cause was the guildsmen's independence, which had increased by the move out from London. The breaking up of Essex House—many of the workshops continued to be run as private businesses—may have seemed like failure from the viewpoint of the artists who had sought a moral and philosophical utopia. For the majority of guild workers and families who became entrenched in the local community, the experiment seemed a success.

That in Chipping Campden Parrington was seeking more a model for his own character and aspirations than of the "Simple Life" for export home is illustrated by his October 24 diary account of a long evening's conservation with Ashbee on the guild workings and the relations between England and America:

> I find in such men as Mr. A. an appreciation and understanding of America that is surprising. It is only by knowing such men that one understands the strength of the English aristocratic institution. The English gentleman is a splendid fellow, and more sons of the noblemen are of the better type than I thought. Ashbee himself—and his wife—is absolutely democratic in dress, speech, and bearing. The young men of the guild he treats as social equals and opens his house to them.

On his final evening, after a day's ramble through the country, Parrington democratically "took dinner with a dozen guild boys at their club." It was St. Crispin's Day, and the meal was followed by Ashbee reading the king's speech before the battle of Agincourt from *Henry V.*

How much did Parrington see, or want to see, of himself in Ashbee, an aristocratically refined democrat, talented, artistic, visionary, who read

Shakespeare and lived in a country town? Did he identify the guild with the university, the guildmaster with the professor and the candidate for the Emporia school board, the guild workers with students and ungrammatical farmers? Parrington's weekend produced a notation in Ashbee's journal to the effect that a "charming young American professor from Kansas (or was it Oklahoma?) had come to investigate the Guild's workings."[10] It also resulted a few weeks later in a short essay in which Parrington sketched Essex House's history and evaluated its various handcrafts and its future.

The essay indicates that he was drawn to Chipping Campden as the best representative of the Ruskin-Morris spirit and tradition. He was well aware that Morris's Kelmscott Press had been subsumed by Ashbee's and that Liberty's had taken over Morris's Merton Abbey dye works. But Parrington's major concern was to elaborate two questions posed in his diary. The first was whether the guild had "developed in its workmen artistic power sufficient to enable them to compete successfully with the great shops." Parrington's answer was a gently couched no, for he feared that the master designer's (Ashbee) energies were too diffused to keep all the crafts functioning at the highest, most efficient standard and that his role was too strong. "Such a course defeats the purpose of the guild," he commented, "which is based on the principle that hand and brain should work together and the finished product should be the product of a single workman." The second question, which Parrington posed to a guild woodcarver, was whether Essex House was "being welded into a whole that will enable it to survive the withdrawal of the master." Again, the answer was negative: the majority of workmen "have failed to understand the guild idea and still regard it as an ordinary workshop and have no other idea in their work than that of making a living." Moreover, the inner circle of sympathizers with the guild's idea were not sufficiently "homogeneous in spirit and aims as to be able to carry on the work themselves."[11]

Ashbee's fate bore out Parrington's perceptions, and the issues his visit raised may well have tempered an enthusiastic optimism about the Simple Life experiments. What must be stressed is his thorough knowledge of the arts and crafts movement, its ideological underpinnings, and its current influences, which by the turn of the century had reached America. There they would assume such diverse forms as Frank Lloyd Wright's domestic architecture (Wright was one of Ashbee's first American enthusiasts), the glass studios of Tiffany and Company, Gustav Stickley's craftsman furniture workshops, and Elbert Hubbard's Roycroft Colony in Aurora, New York, a patent though pale and maudlin imitation of Kelmscott Press.

Despite his well-grounded perturbations, the idea of the guild and the ideal of the artist-workman continued to engage Parrington's reflections and his grand tour activities. He left Chipping Campden armed with a half dozen letters of recommendation to Cambridge and Paris connections.

The next weekend he returned to Cambridge, where he observed a rugby game and dined twice in the preserved hall of Henry VIII at King's College, first with a King's fellow and classics tutor named Nathaniel Wedd and then with Ashbee's close friend G. Lowes Dickinson, who taught modern political thought at King's and the new London School of Economics. Parrington also attended an Anglo-Saxon class of Walter A. Skeat's, upon whose edition of Chaucer Kelmscott's most lavish printing venture was based, the last supervised completely by Morris. The lecture he found "a prosy affair," a judgment he asked Julia to convey to Wilbur Humphreys. He also found his mind fashioning contrasts to Harvard, and Harvard came out much the better, both as an institution and for its "certain crispness of frosty mornings" that in retrospect made some of his own Cambridge days appear "marvellously beautiful."[12]

On November 2, Parrington sailed for France, arriving two days later in Paris and settling by mid-November in a cheap room in the Hôtel Fénélon on Rue Férou. This location, near the Luxembourg Gardens, would be his home for the next five months. His ostensible reason for coming to Paris was to improve his French, but he soon discovered that most people spoke English, and he put his card for the Bibliothèque Nationale to other uses: French architecture and, when he had had his fill of that, early Italian painting.

In plan Paris struck him as magnificent, but with the exception of his delight in churches and Gothic cathedrals, French architecture made no appeal. The heavily ornamented Louvre and Opéra, the "glittering prison" of Versailles, the domestic architectural drawings on display at the Salon Champ du Mars convinced him that "the French genius is essentially unpoetic and unidealistic. The finer soul of beauty that makes one glad of art and glad of life they do not understand." Although the arts and crafts devotee judged the jewelry and bookbinding also on display at the salon "excellent," a visit to Fontainebleu elicited the comment, "How much better the flat beamed ceiling is than the Louis XIV domed and arched ceiling!" And though the formal French garden style employed at Versailles impressed him as having some advantages (if only a little less geometric and with more flowers), he declared firmly that "English gardeners know better how to do things than the French—there is nothing in Paris to compare with Kew."[13]

Driven indoors by a surprisingly unsatisfactory environment and by Parisian winter weather, Parrington's days took on much of the flavor of those he spent during his second year at Harvard. He did manage short sightseeing tours—to Montparnasse, Le Petit Palais, Notre Dame (several times), St. Denis, Chartres, the village of Bellevue, among others—often in the company of young women met through the American Girls' Club. Instead of having his photograph taken "for posterity," he engaged a sculptor,

Mme Tollenaar, to make a life-sized bust. After several months of sittings, the bust fell and smashed beyond repair shortly before he was to leave Paris. The resourceful Mme Tollenaar proposed a bas-relief silhouette as a substitute. This Parrington had cast in bronze, and the original hangs today in a granddaughter's home. In early December, he began attending lectures at the Sorbonne, which, as he explained in a letter to Julia, he could understand if the lecturers spoke distinctly. A good many evenings were spent at the theater, where he filled in his knowledge of contemporary and classical dramatic trends. But he also included a few lighter excursions to cabarets and the Moulin Rouge. He viewed his Harvard passion, Sarah Bernhardt, in Sardou's *Tosca* and *La Sorcière* and witnessed Stéphane Mallarmé's verse drama *Hérodiade,* Henrik Ibsen's *Ghosts* (judged "fearful"), a French version of *Oedipus Rex,* and a splendid production of Wagner's *Tannhäuser.*[14]

Parrington passed many daytime hours in his room working steadily on his novel. By Thanksgiving, when he wrote a touchingly private note to Julia and admitted that he missed his daughter, the second book—titled "The University"—was well under way. The traceable literary influences of the equally autobiographical second book are more diffuse, apparently including the expository sections of *Sartor Resartus* and the utopian vision offered by William Morris's 1889 novel *News from Nowhere.* These portions of "Stuart Forbes: Stoic" gave Parrington the most difficulty. He acknowledged that he lacked the resources to make sufficiently dramatic Stuart's articulation of his stoic viewpoint and advocacy of the life of the "honest worker." Here Stuart/Parrington is shown in conversation with two friends: Jack Cade, a pseudonym for his boyhood chum Vern Cook, and Watson Randolph, the real name of another College of Emporia student used here to disguise his friend Vern Byers. Forbes is also shown delivering a series of speeches to groups of university men, perhaps idealized versions of Cambridge or Norman classrooms or colleagues.

Many of these speeches and other ostensibly descriptive passages drift away from a novelistic purpose and become vehicles for commentary on such subjects as contrasts between the English and American college and university, the heritage of Puritanism in American life, and the meaning of democracy in contemporary American culture. The most revealing sections were composed after Parrington's return to Oklahoma though the conversations between Forbes, Cade, and Randolph took shape when Parrington was midway through his tour.

As nearly as can be determined by correlating diary entries and the extant manuscript, these conversations were completed in late November, by which time much of the novel's outline was also thought out. "Quelle joie de travaille!" the watchful conscience inscribed in its diary. This concentrated period was followed by a week in bed nursing neuralgia in the right eye. Before this setback, Parrington had composed these remarkably explicit passages extracted from "The University" section:

The first great crisis in the mental life of a young man is the theological crisis: most thoughtful young men pass through the priest period. Some men and most women remain in this stage; their minds take on finally the theological cast, and they become the official keepers of the church.

Stuart Forbes entered this period rather later than most young men. Whether it was the influence of the art ideal—the early paganism that was in him or simply the fact that he developed more slowly than common—it was not until his 22nd year that the theological instinct was thoroughly awakened.[15]

After this introduction, Randolph speaks first, in a dialogue whose transposition from the College of Emporia to a setting in Stuart's university rooms was suggested by its author's exposure to graduate work at Cambridge:

"I envy you, Jack. Ever since you were 19 you have known what you were going to do. You make no false starts; you have your aim clearly in view. . . . And here I am fretting and stewing and trying a dozen things and giving them up, and at 23 with no idea what my work is to be. This being called to the ministry saves a lot of worry." . . .

Jack laughed and then was grave. . . . "I fought against it for years, but I had to give in."

"You really believe you were called, do you?" asked Stuart half-laughing.

"I know the place and the moment when the summons came. It was a revival service. . . . A hand seemed laid upon me." . . .

Watson unlocked his long legs, leaned forward and said, carefully weighing his words, "But don't you think it might be explained on other grounds: . . . The records of the church are full of visions and marvels that are really curious psychological phenomena."

Jack smiled and replied, "My dear fellow, perhaps you think I have not considered that, but I have threshed it all out."

Randolph then interrupts Cade's explanation of this conviction of his calling:

"You and Stuart and I have been working side by side here in the university. We have grown up together. We are agreed that modern science is fast undermining the old dogmatic position, that the very foundations are giving way—the doctrine of original sin, the fall of man, for example. Now what I want to know is, what reply have you for those doubts and uncertainties?"

The face of the young preacher lighted up with the challenge and in an earnest voice he said, "I have only one message: I shall preach Christ and him crucified. . . . Life is more than philosophy, and Christ is greater than the schools."

. . . Stuart looked at him fondly and said, "I like to hear you talk, Jack, whether I follow your reasoning or not. You'll do more good in the world than Watson and I with our doubts and analyses." . . .

They all laughed, and Jack walked to Watson, put his hand affectionately on his shoulder and said, "You see, old fellow, it is a difference of temperament. I am a mystic; I feel first and think afterwards. You are a pagan rationalist; you think first and feel afterwards."

"And what is Stuart here?" said Watson laughing. "Oh, he is a composite, a bundle of contradictions. He has some of your rationalism, but not enough to damn him; and some of my mysticism, but not enough, I fear, to save him. He is a little pagan, a good deal puritan and the rest not yet known."

Parrington's manuscript continues with a prose commentary that further delineates the intellectual stance of the three young men. Here it is possible to view Cade as occupying the stage Parrington had until his marriage and to view Randolph as occupying the stage he would reach in his maturity. The characterization of Stuart is noteworthy for its emphasis on art, the facet lacking in both Cade and Randolph.

Jack, who had been his closest friend since early boyhood . . . was at bottom a primitive Methodist, with the religious emotionalism of the old sect tempered but not eradicated by university training.

The other friend . . . represented an opposite type. . . . The problems of society appealed to him and instead of studying pure biology he was applying his mind to the study of social conditions. His enthusiasms were social rather than religious, and in this respect he was the most modern of the three. Jack represented a type that was disappearing; Watson Randolph, a type that was becoming everyday more numerous.

Stuart Forbes at this time was neither a religious nor a social enthusiast. Since his early youth he had dreamed of art, by which he meant at that time painting easel pictures; but of late years he had passed into the theological period of his development. And in this he represented the mean between his two friends.

The brief plot sketch of the "love book" provided earlier shows that although early in the novel Stuart describes himself as a mean between his friends, he is actually closer to Jack's position. In the course of the story he will move toward Randolph's, but it will be a movement that combines "the study of social conditions" with art, not biology. This final position owes its influence to Morris and Ruskin and not to Herbert Spencer and redefines theology into the secular ethical code that characterized such American contemporaries as Walter Rauschenbusch. In addition, Parrington's description of Stuart as a mean between the theological and the social within the context of the intellectual change demarcating the nineteenth and twentieth centuries, and his emergence at a further stage that synthesized two prior influences, is fundamentally dialectical.

Certainly Parrington's intellectual development as detailed heretofore, with its polar shifts between art and literature, poetry and politics, literature and religion—and now art and social thought—also accurately fits a dialectical model. And as in Stuart's case, Parrington's successive syntheses appear as "a bundle of contradictions"; they do not mark firm upward points on a linear mental graph but more closely resemble crablike progress. Parrington's delineation of Forbes's evolution, with its sympa-

thetic awareness of the often convoluted dynamics of change, illustrates another use (others being manifested in "God in History," "Some Political
Sketches," "Poetry and the Mission of Poetry," and "A Layman's View of
Isaiah") of the form—dialectical—and the content—intellectual and cultural change—employed in *Main Currents in American Thought*.

One measure of the effect of expatriation was Parrington's clarification
of his (alias Stuart's) reflections on his past in prose, a form that demanded
sequential explanation of motives and influences. Such reflections had formerly been couched in diary entries and poems, periodic forms that usually
omitted the connective tissue allowing the observer to place abstractions
within the daily processes of thought and feeling. Another measure of expatriation was the contrasts between his former and present holiday seasons. After his week in bed with neuralgia, Parrington spent Christmas on
the Champs Élysées. Back home, Julia made a yuletide trek to the Americus
farm for her husband, taking Elizabeth to see her Parrington grandparents
for the first time and enduring some difficult periods with her mother-in-
law. On the final day of 1903, instead of reflecting on the year's significance,
Parrington polished some architectural notes and bought a secondhand box
of drawing instruments. On New Year's Day, instead of making resolutions,
he strolled happily on the Boulevard St. Michel and revisited Notre Dame.

The pull of the theological was still strong enough to produce a poem on
Isaiah in late January. About the same time he toiled over a sermon ("If all
sermons are so difficult, I pity the ministers") preached by Jack Cade "sum-
ming up the old faith" for his novel. By early February he put his drawing
instruments to use and began designing plans for building his own home in
Norman. A month later he decided to insert in his novel "a chapter on how
Stuart at last built his house: that Great American ideal that for years he
had longed for, had planned and seen his plans overthrown. . . . Built by
hands of friends and comrades—honest, simple, beautiful—untainted by
lust of money and greed of gain." In March he thought seriously about going to Germany rather than returning to England as planned. But this shift
in itinerary fell by the wayside as he worked at least four to five hours daily
on his novel.[16]

As the date of his departure from Europe drew nearer, Parrington's
expatriation provided grist for "Stuart Forbes." From what can be determined from dated manuscript sections, composed according to Parrington's
mood and not according to the order of his overall outline, Stuart returns
to America (Omaha instead of Emporia or Norman) after his university
stint. There he resumes his work, apparently architecture instead of teaching, and retreats alone to a glacial wilderness (in a section titled "Wild
Columbines") before visiting the grave of Jack Cade some two years later
in Colorado Springs. The American settings of the novel, written in the
socially free atmosphere of Paris after his confrontation with England,
apparently turned Parrington's thought to delineating the features of

the American character. In an unrevised passage intended for the third book of "Stuart Forbes," Parrington wrote:

> In spite of their modernity the Americans are still a primitive people—separated from the time of Charles II to the time of Victoria—cut off in a way that we today forget from intercourse with Europe, the American people escaped the silent but tremendous social changes of the 18th century. Left to themselves confronted by a virgin land which they must conquer, they gave themselves to this material work. . . . During these generations they were developing a common national character—that at bottom is a mingling of Scotch and English characteristics—that in spite of later floods of Irish, German, Scandinavian, and southern Europe immigration has not only maintained itself, but has stamped itself upon American life and institutions. . . . We owe our temperament to our Scotch-Irish blood and our taste to our English. After all how intensely English we are in our homes, in our laws, in our ways of looking at life—in our national prejudices and enthusiasms.[17]

Parrington's argument here reflects both the subject of his 1898 *Umpire* editorial and the biographical projection that would remain traceable in *Main Currents:* his mother was Scotch-Irish and his father was English. Dwelling in Paris between the worlds of England and America, Parrington came to see "in a hundred different ways" that he was English and not French.[18] This realization was first stimulated by his negative response to French architecture and suggests that the younger aesthete—studying art and teaching French—had identified France as his spiritual home, as did so many expatriates of his own and the World War I generation.

The continuation of the "Stuart Forbes" passage illustrates a version of the novel's synthesis of art and social awareness that points toward one of the major themes of *Main Currents,* that of the necessity for Americans to interpret their past in light of European experience, particularly European political experience:

> Just before the Civil War we discovered Europe and since that time we have gone over in increasing multitudes year after year. The effect of the first invasions was first to awaken the slumbering artistic feeling of the people. Under the long rule of Puritanism art was dead. But of later years the lesson which America is learning of Europe is not so much the artistic or civil. For a hundred years after the formation of the constitution, the American people rested content on their work—in the exuberant belief that the final word had been said, the final battle for freedom had been fought. But during the last generation there has been a distinct change—While we were resting on our oars, England, Germany, and France had been fighting steadily and it gradually became plain that we had been surpassed in the work for good government. The carelessness born of overconfidence had produced great evils at home—[19]

Parrington does name those great evils; that indictment appears in later portions of the novel when Forbes develops the contrast between art and industrialism, culture and democracy. But Parrington was sufficiently immersed in European political events of 1903–4—and capable of reading French and German papers—to focus his observations in a short essay sent home and published in the *University Umpire* on April 1. "Most Americans are brought up to regard France as our natural friend and England as our natural enemy," he began lecturing his absent students in tones Mark Twain would relish.

> As a matter of fact that is a bit of antiquated prejudice. Our liking for France is purely sentimental and is not I believe shared by the French themselves. The French people generally do not like Americans; and they still look on us with the same contempt they are quick to accord all foreigners. England, on the other hand, is our best friend in Europe. The great body of the English people have and always have had a real affection for the American people; and they have never sympathized with the Anti-American policy of the government from the days of George III to those of Lord Palmerston.

The essay continues with comments on the disruptive effects of the Boer War:

> On the surface everything is diplomatically correct; there is much talk of arbitration, "rapproachments," and the like, but they hate each other! They all want to fight—especially Germany—but they are afraid. . . . Germany and France of course are frankly enemies, and England is hated by the entire continent with the exception of Scandinavia and Italy . . . . We Americans need to look to our Monroe doctrine for some fine day we shall have to back down from our position or fight and naturally we don't want to do either.

Parrington then shifts gears and dryly concludes that American libraries are better catalogued and equipped than European ones:

> It takes from ten to fifteen minutes to get any [books] in "Boston Library," from twenty to thirty at the "British Museum," and from forty to sixty minutes at the "Bibliothèque Nationale." Fancy what pleasant things you think of the management while waiting an hour for a single book.[20]

Parrington's days of waiting for books in Paris were almost at an end. On May 11 he returned to London and his room at 41 Upper Bedford Place, feeling—as a newly identified Anglo-American—"right glad to be back." He was delighted to see the tulips and rhododendrons abloom at Kew, and he pursued his political interests by visiting Parliament in early June. At the House of Commons, he heard Joseph Chamberlain ("an excellent speaker," whose tariff protection movement he had followed closely in October), Arthur Balfour ("rather diffident"), Sir Henry Campbell-Bannerman, Sir William Harcourt, Henry Labouchère, and Winston Churchill (who rated no comment). The following day at the

House of Lords provoked the quotation from Gilbert and Sullivan, "They do nothing in particular / And they do it very well."[21]

Until late July, when he left London for the last leg of his tour (in northern and western England and Scotland), Parrington concentrated on his novel, returning to the British Museum not for books but for a place to write. During those two months he added over a hundred pages to his manuscript, most of them developing Stuart's relationship with Elizabeth Ashleigh (for example, a chapter titled "Hill Idylls" chronicles part of a vacation in America) and his marriage to Mary. Yet his last day at the museum produced this despairing diary entry:

> Have worked hard these past weeks and begin to see that if I had only another year I should get something done. I feel sometimes that the past year has been a failure, but I know it hasn't, for I have settled many things, and I have also grown very much older. It is the irony of life that impresses me more and more—yet with a much more fixed and certain philosophy than ever before.[22]

Perhaps it was the return to London, which felt like home territory after Paris, that caused the realization that his novel was not a welcome to the future (the Watson Randolph position) but a benediction, in Arnoldian accents, over "the sadness of the passing of the old faith." Neither Stuart Forbes nor Parrington was ready to relinquish the familiar theology of Jack Cade, no matter how much they were being called to enter the modern world.

After brief side trips to Windsor and Canterbury and a last call at Kew, Parrington left London for good. His first stop was Oxford, where a convention cut short his planned stay to four days. It was the "loveliest town" he had ever visited, despite a steady rain. Magdalen, New, and Christ Church colleges appealed to him the most. Why he delayed a pilgrimage to Hardy's Christminster until this point in his tour is not known. But his best friend in Paris was a Cambridge man who believed that although Cambridge emphasized mathematics and science and was rigorous and Germanic, it produced as graduates merely "an older public schoolboy." Oxford emphasized the humanities, was more catholic and less exact, more French, yet produced graduates who were men, more interesting socially and stronger physically. Parrington must have felt as if he were back at Harvard, a greenhorn making all the wrong choices, having spent (from his friend's viewpoint) most of his university time in the wrong place.[23]

Whatever regrets he may have harbored were set quickly in the background as he left Oxford via Stratford and Lincoln for York. On August 3, he celebrated his thirty-third birthday "very quietly in the county seat of my forefathers." He lovingly photographed the cathedral "that some of my far off ancestors may well have helped to build," as he had at Lincoln, then set off for a two-week stay in Edinburgh. At this point his diary for 1904 stops.

A few notes collected in an additional European notebook titled "Odds and Ends" show that as he faced the end of his tour Parrington was preoccupied with the conflict between what he called the "puritan" and "pagan" in his own and Stuart Forbes's personality. Another consequence of expatriation was Parrington's finding a label out of the American past that described the workings of his conscience even though it had lost its force as a creed. Yet the pagan—what he termed the art influence but might have defined as Bohemianism born of the confluence of a franker psychology and the Simple Life—had its pull. Parrington's paganism would never express itself in the "lifestyle radicalism" that Christopher Lasch has identified as one of the hallmarks of his generation, the first generation to form a true intellectual class in America. But Parrington's yearnings toward that term in the dialectic of his own nature would be the controlling force in the next few years of his personal and professional life.[24]

Indeed, the final days of his tour, as he rambled mostly by foot from Edinburgh (where he bought a McClellan tartan) back to the *Carpathia* and the Liverpool dock on August 24, seemed the most Bohemian, conscience-free part of his travels, a "Wanderjahr" compressed into a week. He ventured into the highlands and heard the melancholy plaint of bagpipes. He spent two days in the Lake District, buying Elizabeth a tiny silver spoon at the Keswick Arts and Crafts shop and, after losing his way in the hills above Grasmere, visiting William Wordsworth's home, Dove Cottage. At Coniston he glimpsed Brantwood, Ruskin's home during his final years. Ruskin was the last of the "great dead" he sought out in Europe. By September 10, after stops in Aurora and Emporia, Parrington was back in Norman.[25]

The contrasts between his narrow, provincial world and the broad, cosmopolitan world he had left had altered his entire spectrum of thinking and behavior. One of the last passages in his "Odds and Ends" notebook, spoken by the fictional alter ego of Stuart Forbes, summarizes the past fourteen months and forecasts the coming years:

> In my younger days I used to sum up life as a Puritan in terms of deity. I have come to see that happiness—abiding satisfying happiness that leaves a good taste in the mouth—is the truer end. Let me be understood. I do not mean selfishness—of that no good can come to you or to others and certainly not happiness—but [the] content and peace of mind (of which I spoke). Not alone to see that beauty of things, of humble everyday life; that is much, but it is not all or the chief thing. Not so much to see beauty as to make it, to build, shape, fashion with your own brain and hand until something lovely has taken the place of ugliness: that is what I mean by the worship of beauty. Creation—work—not mere appreciation of other men's handiwork or even of nature.
>
> But you will reply that the answer to these theories of Ruskin is his own life; the sad tragic ending of a brave, good and unselfish life. Well, I do not say that happiness can be found, that men have a cure-all for the sorrows of life, a

mustard plaster, but I do say that happiness can best be found in the way I have spoken of. *And if Ruskin failed, was it not partly because he was rather a preacher than a doer, a critic than a workman?* (Emphasis added)

William Morris in America

During both stays in England, Parrington had felt and written about a sense of dwelling in the world of American culture. In Paris, he felt alienated and longed to dwell in the world of English culture. Now back in America, he experienced the returning sojourner's clarification of perspective that caused him to dwell intellectually in the European world he had left. The reconciliation of the ideas and ideals stimulated by his European exposure with the reality of his American existence took three separate, though closely related, forms. First, he began making himself over; second, he began making Norman over; and third, he began making his professional life over.

In each of these three tasks, Parrington followed the model of the doer and the workman epitomized for him by William Morris rather than that of the Ruskinian preacher and critic. The date of Parrington's engagement with Morris is critical and difficult to establish. There is no mention of him in the context of reading Ruskin in his art class at Harvard or in his Emporia or Norman course descriptions from 1897 to 1903. Morris's death on October 3, 1896, was reported the next day in leading American dailies. The *New York Herald-Tribune* and the *Chicago Times,* both available in the Emporia library if not at the *Gazette* office, ran obituaries side by side with news of the Bryan campaign, which Parrington was no doubt following. The earliest evidence of any acquaintance with Morris dates from the summer of 1898. In Chicago studying Restoration drama, on his birthday Parrington purchased a copy of Morris's best-known Icelandic saga translations, *Sigurd the Volsung and the Fall of the Nibelungs.* In May 1899 the comment on Morris as a workman appeared in one of the *Umpire* editorials. Then around Thanksgiving of the same year, still deep in his poetry-writing phase and working on "A Plain-Song," he purchased a four-volume edition of *The Earthly Paradise,* Morris's best-known contribution to English poetry.

By the spring of 1903, just before Parrington left on his grand tour, two of the university's first graduates wrote their required English bachelor's theses on Morris. One, a thirty-one-page effort titled "William Morris' Conception of the Relation of Art to Society," was by George A. Bucklin, the part-freshman and part-assistant to the president who met Parrington after his hot, dusty walk to the barren campus. The other, "The Social Views of William Morris," reached fifty-seven pages and was by A. M. Edwards, who completed a master's degree under Humphreys's guidance the next year. In 1906, Adelaide Loomis, Parrington's favorite Oklahoma student, who became a department assistant before marrying another Norman English major (George B. Parker, later chief of the Scripps-Howard newspaper bureau), took the medievalism of William Morris as her thesis topic. In addition, at some point during the 1903–5 composition of "Stuart Forbes: Stoic," Parrington incorporated in titles for chapters treating Elizabeth Ashleigh and Mary the names of two Morris heroines: Gudrun from *The Earthly Paradise* and Brynhild from *Sigurd the Volsung*.

His interest in Morris's writings and ideas, on both art and society, before his grand tour helps substantiate Parrington's comment in his 1918 "Autobiographical Sketch" that while in Paris, "as a disciple of William Morris I loved everything medieval and hated everything classic." Yet aside from his mention of the closing of Kelmscott Press in the short essay on visiting C. R. Ashbee in Chipping Campden, this is the only explicit mention of Morris made in reference to or while on his grand tour. While he viewed Ruskin's grave at Coniston, he did not apparently make a pilgrimage to Morris's grave at Kelmscott Manor. Perhaps his contact with the living, in the figure of Ashbee, was deemed sufficient.

Twenty-five years later, Parrington commented in the Introduction to *The Beginnings of Critical Realism in America* on how "many feel, as Matthew Arnold felt fourscore years ago, that they are dwelling between worlds, the one dead, the other powerless to be born." Here Parrington is paraphrasing the famous lines from Arnold's poem "Stanzas from the Grande Chartreuse." In Europe as he worked on "Stuart Forbes: Stoic" and the novel's theme defined itself as "the sadness of the passing of the old faith" (another Arnoldian line, on the passing of Greek paganism and the Carthusian monks' creed, runs, "For both were faiths, and both are gone"); as he studied Gothic architecture in light of Ruskin's well-known essay "On the Nature of Gothic" from *The Stones of Venice;* as the medievalism of the arts and crafts movement shaped his personal taste and his view of the debate over which form fin-de-siècle utopian thinking should assume, Parrington was drawn to the emphasis on spiritual renewal in the Victorian critics.[26]

This emphasis can also be understood as a more mature expression of the religious issues treated earlier in his poems and seminary lectures. Architecture and art provided a means literally to externalize theology, just as the form of the novel demanded that he explicate the relationship between theology, art, and social criticism. All these pursuits were undertaken and followed independently, without the guidance of, for example, formal graduate study. The self-making that had been a personality key since his Harvard days was thus reconfirmed, although in a variety of forms, by his experience of dwelling between worlds and his attraction to the aesthetic, not political, strain in the theories of William Morris.

The process of making himself over upon his return to Norman is most dramatically illustrated in Parrington's diaries. Instead of recording his professional activities, social intercourse, interior life, or creative and scholarly pursuits, the diaries from then until his death are almost exclusively devoted to gardening plans. Indeed, Parrington began to call them "garden books." Instead of depicting the "child of the country" who missed the dew on the wild grass in London and had responded to the Kansas prairie and farms in verse, the garden books suggest the outlines of a tamed, conscientious horticulturist. Following the last 1904 diary entries made in Edinburgh, there is a break of six months. Then in early 1905 Parrington begins recording:

> *21 January. Saturday.* Today began spring planting by putting some tomatoes, pansies, columbine, and campanulas in boxes.
>
> *27 January. Friday.* A lovely day—after a cold, disagreeable spell. Put in the day thinning trees and pottering around.
>
> *28 January. Saturday.* Misting all day. Finished trimming outside trees. Was to have plowed, but the ground still frozen.
>
> *30 January. Monday.* Today sent off for flower seeds to P. Henderson.
>
> *1 February. Wednesday.* Very cold. Today the first appearance of the plants sown ten days ago. No sunshine since Friday. I never knew such a cold, dark Jan. in Oklahoma.

While the botanist is the scientist who goes on field research to find new plant species, the horticulturist is the intellectual who controls the further development of species by manipulating evolution. The former could be said to perform primary research, the latter to work from secondary sources. Kew Gardens, where Parrington had lavished time and notes, is an international horticultural center, and the height of English horticulture is the perennial bed, designed to provide changing masses of color year-round. The garden is unnatural, whereas Parrington's own prairie landscapes were natural. He had kept a herbarium of wild, native Kansas flowers and grasses; now he artificially contrived a garden that emphasized non-native species created for perennial borders. He had worked in the fields and orchards and among the animals on his father's quarter-section farm; now he tilled a quarter-block-size family garden. Like the roses—one of the most highly manipulated of all flowers—that he carefully selected and grew, Parrington can be seen as a root stock onto which a genetically different fruiting stock is grafted. The rose cannot exist without aid of the rooting stock; nor could Parrington have become the gardener he did without the aid of his prairie roots. He knew what it was to be wild, to be a pioneer. Now he became a cultivator, a husbandman.[27]

The contrast between the intellectual workman who now contentedly crafted his handmade garden and the scholarly professor who before his grand tour had escaped the pressures of Norman life by retreating into the wilderness is mirrored in the contrast between Parrington's garden books and an essay written in February 1901 after a duck hunting expedition. "Happy is the man who has his specific for the ills for the spirit as well as for the ills of the flesh," Parrington commences. The essay then lyrically elaborates:

> When I begin to long for the outer world where the multitudes hurry about their own business forgetting their fathers, when I begin to watch wistfully the smoke of the north bound train lying on the horizon, then I have mine own specific that cures infallibly the devil of restlessness. . . . It is not to plunge with the train into the great city, for I know only too well that happiness is not there, but instead, the worry and the fever of life. Rather my cure is to plunge still farther into the back woods, where the whistle of the rushing trains does not come and where the life of men is still primitive. With three or four tried companions I load tent and bedding and camp gear on a prairie schooner and set out for the lakes in the Chickasaw Nation. I am no disciple of John Burroughs. As a true Englishman I want to kill something, and yet my hunting trips are very much more than hunting trips. . . . It is not the shooting alone—whether I bag much game or little, it is still the same. I have had my outing. I have smelt the wildness, have watched the ducks sail by overhead far out of gunshot, have seen the twilight come and the dusk and then the lonesome night.[28]

After his grand tour, it was no longer the wild but the cultivated that Parrington was happy to claim as his specific for the ills of the flesh and spirit. Not the primitive westerner but the cultured English workman became his personal model, a model that at last unified his personal and intellectual life. The result of dwelling between worlds was not fragmentation but consolidation of identity. Concomitantly, the figure emerging from Parrington's garden books closely resembles the Morris-like main character in "Stuart Forbes: Stoic." During the summer of 1905, most of which he passed in Emporia and at his parents' farm, Parrington spent his last concentrated period working on his novel. At this point, Forbes had reached the realization that unjust economic and social conditions and the challenges to traditional culture posed by science and industrialization required a more engaged response than an isolated university life offered. As Stuart explained to a group of colleagues, in one of many similar speeches that appear inspired by Ruskin's epistolary *Fors Clavigera* and Morris's lectures on the relation between art and industry: "Life and work—here, my friends, we are at the heart of the matter . . . how shall we combine them and in reality make our work our life . . . ? Knowledge and culture give us a larger outlook, but they do not bring happiness. . . . Much study is a weariness to the flesh. . . . The more we know and think, the lonelier becomes our position and the sadder our cast of mind." And thus Stuart—and Parrington—commits himself to the life "of the honest worker," a less alienated existence in which work shall be free, creative, the apprentice to the ideal of beauty, and "absorb the whole man—muscle, brain and heart."

Parrington's self-making, modeled on the craftsman ideal and symbolized by the change of his diaries into garden books, entailed an even broader commitment to art. Yet it also marks the virtual end of his poetry writing. As he revised and reshaped the passages in his novel in which Forbes expounds on the relation of life and work in the context of the changing values assigned to culture and education in a society reeling under the impact of industrial capitalism, Parrington was no longer writing fiction. He was still writing autobiography, but it was intellectual autobiography. This concentration, in prose, on the evolution of ideas marks a crucial transition in forms of expression that drew Parrington increasingly away from the literary and religious and poetic toward the historical and analytical and political.

Both Parrington and Stuart Forbes can be understood as vacillating between the terms of a dialectic: the heritage of American Puritanism, the determining, Weberian feature of their personalities; and the modernism of the English arts and crafts movement, the catalytic, Morrisian feature of their thinking. The synthesis of the dialectic's terms was not to transform society by participating in communal or organized political renewal but to transform the self by individual thoughts and actions. It was a very American solution, with its antecedents in Emerson's ideal of the active scholar (combined with the theological personalism of the "Divinity School Address") and Thoreau's patient reconciliation of the naturalist, the Greek pagan, the dutiful farmer, and the social moralist.

Parrington's models in his own intellectual and personal odyssey were not yet Emerson and Thoreau and the other heroes of *Main Currents in American Thought*. The next phase in the dialectic would bring the transforming self in conjunction with a transforming society that insisted on organized, not individual, solutions. From that conflict would shortly emerge the synthesis that distinguished Parrington's mature thinking and writing.

Parrington's adherence to individual self-making was certainly reinforced by his isolation in Norman. Whereas the political ferment in Emporia had resulted in his grappling with Populism, here Parrington found himself a cosmopolitan among provincials, an idealist among realists, an outsider among insiders. This dilemma was resolved through architecture, another artistic avenue as highly visible and symbolic as his gardening. In 1903 Parrington had begun serving on the University of Oklahoma's Committee on Buildings and Grounds. That year's catalog carries a sketch, in Parrington's hand, of a proposed campus plan designed upon two modified quadrangles. The plan—vestiges are discernible in the contemporary Norman campus, where the oldest buildings are grouped around a grassy, tree-studded oval now named for Parrington—was buttressed by a report submitted to the Board of Regents four years later. *On Recent Develop-*

ments in American College Architecture summarized Parrington's survey of twenty-five campuses, two-thirds of them state schools and the rest private institutions.[29]

The report demonstrates his acquaintance with the work of such Gothic revivalists as Ralph Adams Cram as well as his Morrisian allegiance to the architectural theories outlined in Ruskin's "Nature of Gothic." It also could be considered a tangible outcome of the architectural studies pursued on his grand tour. His activities can be seen as efforts to transform the Norman environment—the larger, public sphere—by means of an American adaptation of the Cambridge and Oxford model. Interestingly, they do not express the views of education and culture that Stuart Forbes espoused. But neither the report's nor the plan's recommendations were executed during Parrington's tenure at Oklahoma.

Parrington did succeed in transforming his own immediate environment into a setting consistent with the self-made craftsman ideal. His garden books were begun when he and his small family still lived with Julia's mother. By the summer of 1906 he laid aside the manuscript of "Stuart Forbes" and gathered his polished poems ("Amos," for example, was omitted) in a booklet titled "A Plain-Song and Other Poems," which he tucked away in his desk. This farewell to creative writing marked a break with his youthful and romantic past. Although he spent most of the summer of 1906 in Emporia, from early July to early September, the concept of home, the desire to establish his own dwelling, gained intensity. Near their fifth wedding anniversary on July 31, Julia became pregnant a second time. Parrington began refining the house plans he had sketched in Paris, virtually living out a plot sequence in "Stuart Forbes," that had been suggested by his architectural studies and his impressions of the Ashbees' late medieval home. In early March 1904, he had noted in his novel manuscript: "Insert a chapter on how Stuart at last built his house: that great American ideal that for years he had longed for, had planned and seen his plans overthrown but had come at last to be ready. Built by hands of friends and comrades—honest, simple, beautiful—untainted by lust of money and greed of gain."

The explicit mention of building a house as "that great American ideal" shows Parrington in nearer relation to the native pole of the Puritanism/art, American/British dialectic than does his gardening. Although his gardening seems clearly inspired by his visits to Kew and study of English landscaping, building a home in itself did not jar with Norman's climate or values. And there was the precedent of his 1903 *House Beautiful* article that criticized the lack of privacy in American village homes. The self-making Parrington would have his privacy, turning the front of his house away from the street and nestling it in an English garden.

In his study *The American Home: Architecture and Society, 1815–1915,* David P. Handlin observed how much at odds Parrington's domestic architectural proposals were with most American suburbs laid out after the Civil

War and with the post-1865 discussions of home gardening carried out in periodicals such as *Country Life in America* and in books such as Frank J. Scott's *Art of Beautifying the Home Grounds,* published in 1870.[30] Parrington would not plant an American garden; nor would he build a typically American home. Although the theoretical antecedents for building a home to express and contain the individual personality could be directly traced to Emerson's metaphor of building a house as a form of soul-building and to Thoreau's carefully crafted cabin that sheltered only three chairs, Parrington's design for his home was the English cottage. Of course, it was the traditional cottage remodeled according to arts and crafts movement taste: "honest, simple, beautiful."

The exterior of the two-story house was to be brick with half-timbering and leaded windows. The interior featured rough-beamed ceilings, built-in cupboards and wooden seats (as a variation on the high-backed medieval settle, so favored by Morris and Company decorating projects), an open-work wooden stairway that resembles the one at Kelmscott Manor, as well as the Arthurian-inspired furniture that Morris preferred. By the turn of the century such furniture was being manufactured in America and labeled the Mission Oak style.[31]

Construction did not begin until the following spring, when Parrington helped with the foundations and other tasks, although the project did not quite proceed according to Stuart Forbes's visions. Meanwhile, the process of symbolically arranging his personal life was accompanied by striking modifications in his professional life. The catalog printed in the spring of 1905 shows that Parrington changed the names of the figures demarcating his late eighteenth- through nineteenth-century English survey course. Pope to Carlyle gave way to Dr. Johnson to William Morris. In the fall of 1906, he began offering a new figures course on Ruskin and Morris, which studied their chief works and gave "special attention to the medieval movement in Victorian art." He also separated his Tennyson and Browning course into discrete semesters focusing on a single figure. Developing these new courses was facilitated by the addition of a departmental lecturer who assumed some of the work in composition, as the student body had grown to over five hundred.

Yet the most profound change was registered by the seminary lectures announced for 1905–6. Instead of Old Testament prophets—the Isaiahs and the Jobs with whom Parrington and Stuart Forbes had wrestled and upon whom Jack Cade (Vern Cook) had drawn for parallel gospel lections—the lectures' post-grand-tour topic was medievalism in art. According to the university *Bulletin,* the new lectures were to

> deal with such questions as: The structural beauty of Gothic architecture; The arts and crafts in medieval village life; The incoming of a foreign architecture, and the decay of Gothic; Creative and formal Renaissance architecture, and the

parallelism between the architecture and the literature of the seventeenth century; The revival of Gothic in the nineteenth century; Ruskin, Morris, and the Pre-Raphaelites; and Present day arts and crafts in England and America.[32]

This description manifests the breadth of interests and the interdisciplinary approach to culture, treated within a historical, developmental context, requisite for an intellectual historian. The old faith was indeed passing.

Parrington's professional duties were still primarily focused on English culture, but the boundaries between the ideal world of William Morris and the real world of Norman were beginning to shift. In the process of making over himself, his environment, and his courses, Parrington was also entering new intellectual terrain. Again it would be reached through the avenue of art, again Morris and his grand tour would provide guidance, and again his professional life would take new directions.

6

~

Transitions and Closures
1906–1909

Parrington had included American authors in several courses conducted in his first Oklahoma year, encouraged his composition students to be aware of American speech, and recommended grounding in American literature as a requisite for undergraduate standing. But only after his grand tour did he become vitally engaged with the native branch of the Anglo-American literary and linguistic tradition. Expatriation allowed him to gain perspective and to place form on American culture. Later, when the first shoots planted in Norman were cultivated into *Main Currents in American Thought*, Parrington never forgave an American who failed to broaden his or her mind through confrontation with European thought and culture. England taught him that he was not French; France and England taught him that he was an American. Parrington, however, did not return to Norman in a mood of nostalgic reembracement. Rather, he returned with his critical faculties honed, seeing and hearing with the double-edged senses of the dweller between worlds. He learned in greater proportion than his Harvard journey produced what it meant to be an immigrant. His homecoming made him an intellectual, and it made irony one of the most telling terms in his vocabulary.

The earliest evidence of Parrington's serious inclusion of American subjects in his courses just predates his grand tour. In the spring of 1903 he first taught The Novel in the XIX Century, the course prepared for by reading Thomas Hardy that included "a special study of realism." His well-thumbed notebook "The Novel," dated 1901, indicates that this study was pursued comparatively, with major British novelists—including George Meredith, Hardy, and Kipling—set over against the major American realists—Howells, Twain, and James. Parrington's pedagogical concern with realism dates to his Emporia course on George Eliot, but the Norman novel course illustrates a more detailed treatment of the issue.

Parrington's grappling with these three still living American authors caused him to break the reigning assumption that criticism should be undertaken from the supposed vantage point of death. It also caused him to reflect on the definition and purpose of the novel, a genre being reshaped in content as well as form by post–Civil War American authors. His own reading taste had been influenced by the English mid-Victorians. But English reality was not American reality, and realism as a theory depended on the accurate portrayal of the environment and dynamics of the tangible daily world. Parrington had advanced much of the basis of the theory of realism in his Harvard forensics on the historical novel. The crucial additions in his new course were, first, that he treated American as well as British works and, second, that those works heralded the entrance of the common person into the domain of literary acceptability.

Parrington's notebook opens with a defense of the novel as a legitimate form that, unlike poetry, drama, and the essay, embraces the three major types of pure literature—"the symbolical expression of the beautiful, the emotional expression of the real, the meditative expression of the true." Then he demarcates three sorts of realism: that with an insistence on the facts, human documents; the commonplace; and the base. The only surviving note on Henry James states that he is an example of the first sort, and Howells is identified with the second. Additional brief entries on Howells are instructive when contrasted with Parrington's opinion of Howells expressed in the Harvard daily themes written a decade earlier. Then Howells had been a crude realist; now he was "the dean of American letters," "a kindly genial soul, generous to younger writers, a tireless writer and reader of novels."[1]

Those early comments were made under the influence of Barrett Wendell, who in his just published *Literary History of America* (1900) had criticized Twain and other western writers as too unskilled and uncouth to be considered a viable movement in American literature. This was precisely the point on which Parrington now disagreed. "The west has come into its own," he proclaimed; "Howells is from Ohio, Twain from Missouri." The bout was on. One of the first fruits of Parrington's post-grand-tour identification as an American was a parallel identification with his own geographic region that dissented from his former professor's.[2] Parrington had struggled with the possibilities of fiction and achieving realism in writing his own novel. Now what he had so typically learned by doing alone sharpened what he said in the literature classroom. But it was in Parrington's composition courses that the most resounding impact of his grand tour was heard. Heard—not felt or observed—because it was the contrast between English and American speech, in its Norman variants, that succeeded in shocking Parrington into analyzing the relations between language, literature, and culture.

From the English Language to American Literature

Parrington's experience at Harvard, away from Kansas farms and small towns, had enlarged his perspective on midwestern politics. His European experience had even more far-reaching effects, altering his conception of culture. An instructive analogy can be drawn between what Parrington saw and heard in Oklahoma upon his return in 1904 and the themes developed in *Main Currents*, and between historian Carl Becker's experience teaching at the University of Kansas (after leaving Iowa farms and small towns to study at Wisconsin and Columbia) and the point of view expressed in "Everyman His Own Historian" (1931). For Becker, the issue might be summarized as how to make history relevant to the layman concerned with his daily round of activities. For Parrington, it was how to make language and literature relevant to the student seeking a practical education.[3]

Toward the resolution of this issue Parrington may well again have drawn on the example of William Morris. The sociological conditions of the early 1880s in England had penetrated to King's College, Cambridge, where C. R. Ashbee, G. Lowes Dickinson, and Roger Fry were students, giving impetus to the Simple Life movement. In London, full of political refugees from Germany, Russia, France, and Austria, where the starving armies of the unemployed were demonstrating angrily in the West End, socialism was deemed the comprehensive solution to bridging the gap between rich and poor, cultured and unlettered, elite and dispossessed. Morris, still engaged with his various artistic ventures pursued through the guild-craftsman system, began manifesting the acute attack of conscience that would lead him shortly on the road of revolutionary politics. In mid-October of 1881, he confessed in an address to the School of Science and Art connected with Wedgewood Institute at Burslem:

> As I sit at my work at home, which is at Hammersmith, close to the river, I often hear some of that ruffianism go past the window of which a good deal has been said in the papers of late, and has been said before at recurring periods. As I hear the yells and shrieks and all the degradation cast on the glorious tongue of Shakespeare and Milton, as I see the brutal reckless faces and figures go past me, it rouses the recklessness and brutality in me also, and fierce wrath takes possession of me, till I remember, as I hope I mostly do, that it was my good luck only of being born respectable and rich, that has put me on this side of the window among delightful books and lovely works of art, and not on the other side, in the empty street, the drink-steeped liquor-shops, the foul and degraded lodgings. I know by my own feelings and desires what these men want, what would have saved them from this lowest depth of savagery: employment which would foster their self-respect and win the praise and sympathy of their fellows, and dwellings which they could come to with pleasure, surroundings which would soothe and elevate them; reasonable labour, reasonable rest. There is only one thing that can give them this—art.[4]

As Philip Henderson, another biographer of Morris, has stressed, by art Morris meant much more than his youthful Pre-Raphaelite painting that now appeared "out of touch with 'the general sympathy of simple peoples.' " Rather, like Stuart Forbes and Parrington, whose first career desire was to paint, he meant art, reflective and productive of an essentially moral quality, "in its widest application to our whole material environment." Just a little over a year later, in January 1883, Morris enrolled as a member of the newly founded Democratic Federation. He began studying *Das Kapital* in its French translation, confessing that he found Marx's pure economics "stiffer going than some of Browning's poetry."[5] But his life manifested the contradictions that marked Parrington's upon his return to Norman.

Morris was a craftsman; Parrington consciously became a craftsman. Morris grafted socialist political activity onto his art when nearing fifty; Parrington grafted art onto Populist political activity in his mid-twenties. Parrington was a professor in a state university that soon would be the victim of a corrupt political power system; Morris was elected an Honorary Fellow of his college, Exeter, at Oxford almost the same day he joined the Democratic Federation. Their mutual dilemma was to reconcile their personal elitism (Morris's by birth, Parrington's by intellectual bent) with "the general sympathy of simple peoples" (in the London streets and workshops, in the Norman streets and classrooms), or, to put the issue in the terms both Morris and Parrington would, to reconcile art with democracy.

"Art and Democracy" was the title of an address Morris was invited to give by the Russell Club, "a society of Liberal undergraduates with Radical tendencies," in Oxford's University Hall in November 1883. By then he spoke with the authority not only of a well-known poet and head of the influential Morris and Company but also of a Fellow of Exeter and a Federation member. One of the members of the audience, who must have felt "his mantle had fallen upon broader and more vigorous shoulders," was John Ruskin, Oxford's Slade Professor of Fine Art. Morris began his lecture by stating that his real subject was art under plutocracy, that he was not going to criticize or plead for any particular school or style of art or artists, that art was bound up with the general condition of society, and that he therefore thought there was a feeling of despair over the future of art, broadly defined. He contrasted, as he had in his study at Hammersmith, his ideal of art and culture with the reality of current social conditions and external surroundings:

> Go through Oxford streets and ponder on what is left us there unscathed by the fury of the thriving shop and the progressive college. . . . Not only are London and our other great commercial cities mere masses of sordidness, filth, and squalor, embroidered with patches of pompous and vulgar hideousness, no less revolting to the eye and the mind when one knows what it means: not only have whole counties of England, and the heavens that hang over them, disappeared beneath a crust of unutterable grime, but . . . our civilization is passing like a blight, daily growing heavier and more poisonous, over the whole face of the country. . . . So it comes to this, that not only are the minds of great artists narrowed and their

sympathies frozen by their isolation, not only has co-operative art come to a standstill, but the very food on which both the greater and the lesser art subsists is being destroyed: the well of art is poisoned at its spring.[6]

Morris then set forth a defense of handiwork as opposed to machine civilization that was echoed in "Stuart Forbes: Stoic" two decades later. The ideas Parrington elucidated in his novel were helping frame the next stage in his intellectual dialectic, when art—including language and literature—was brought into confrontation with the conditions of his professional life—a life that began to include the formal study and teaching of American literature and history in an effort to develop an explanation for the state of contemporary American (at least midwestern American) culture.

Several of Parrington's pre-grand-tour *Umpire* editorials indicated that he encouraged his students, as an aid to their writing, to collect examples of informal conversational vocabulary patterns and local idioms. As early as 1900, Parrington's interest in language sparked one of his first graduate students, Carleton Ross Hume, to compile a master's thesis titled "A dialectical history of the eastern and southern portions of the United States: being an attempt to trace certain peculiarities of those regions in their origin and development." The fifty-six-page project, accompanied by color-coded maps and a book list, was the subject of much campus interest. It was followed in 1904 by another, less scholarly master's thesis by A. M. Edwards (who had written his bachelor's thesis on William Morris), titled "The Speech of Joshua, or a few dialectical peculiarities of Northcentral Texas." Edwards's effort, however, had the virtue of focusing on his home environment: it was embryonic local linguistic history. It was not abstract philological discussion but was written at a time when philology was the vogue for bringing the study of language into conformance with the reigning model of scientific objectivity.[7]

Several brief essays that date from Parrington's later—probably post-grand-tour—Norman years clarify that it was not the interests of the philologist, concerned with abstract structural changes, but those of the social linguist, concerned with the dynamics between environment and speech, that increasingly animated his composition courses and hours of reflection. For example, in one informal essay titled "Western Speech" Parrington describes characteristics of speech patterns among American blacks and midwestern farmers' wives. Here he was searching for a "broadly human" rather than a scientific explanation of the relationship between frontier experience and the "flat and monotonous" western dialect.

In these personal and student-oriented projects, Parrington was again pioneering. The classifying and analysis of regional American speech was a new area of academic study. The American Philological Association had been founded in 1869, but the more narrowly focused American Dialect Society was not established until 1889. Founded at Harvard with Francis J.

Child, the specialist in English and Scottish ballads, as president, the society's original members included most of Harvard's literature and language faculty, several of whom Parrington had studied with: Robert L. Sanderson in French, Edward S. Sheldon in Italian, and George Bendelari, who taught Spanish and Italian in addition to European history. A journal, *Dialect Notes,* was promptly begun, although it appeared irregularly over the next five decades. The journal did make its way to Oklahoma, for C. Ross Hume's thesis lists the first volume among its sources.[8]

The Society can be seen as formalizing the literary explorations of dialect by pre-Civil War Southern and New England writers. But it remained for such post-Civil War realistic writers as Edward Eggleston, in his 1871 novel *The Hoosier Schoolmaster,* and Hamlin Garland, most influentially in his 1891 collection *Main-Travelled Roads,* to portray varieties of midwestern speech and to portray them for their sociological importance instead of for their primarily comic value. As Garland had predicted in his essay on "The Local Novel" published in *Crumbling Idols: Twelve Essays on Art Dealing Chiefly with Literature Painting and the Drama* (1889),

> Both drama and novel will be colloquial. This does not mean that they will be exclusively in the dialects, but the actual speech of the people of each locality will unquestionably be studied more closely than ever before. Dialect is the life of a language, precisely as the common people of the nation form the sustaining power of its social life and art.

Now, in addition to Parrington's consideration of realism in the formal context of his novel course, he was led to evaluate the western realists' crusade, with its clear cultural (anti-Eastern), economic (anti–middle class and anti-industrial), and political (pro-democratic, if not explicitly socialistic) components. Like Garland, born and reared on impoverished Wisconsin and Iowa farms, then gleaning his education in the Boston Public Library before returning to the Midwest to write about the people and locale he knew best, Parrington began treating his own autobiography objectively (as he had in "Stuart Forbes") as the viable basis for class discussions and lecture notes. This rapprochement with the past that he had yearned to escape at Harvard and again on his grand tour determined the tone and perspective of much of his subsequent teaching and writing. Like Eggleston, Parrington's interest in native speech would lead to a deeper interest in native literature and then to history. During all his vacillations between poetry and politics, religion and novel writing, the one constant had been his role as a professor of English. And it was, as historiographical critic Gene Wise might describe it, along the two fault lines of language and literature that Parrington's explanation of reality finally cracked.[9]

This process is dramatically revealed in an essay, "Thoughts on the Teaching of Literature," written in 1906 after his European trip. The essay echoes Morris's despair over hearing English abused outside his Hammersmith windows and his criticism of the machine civilization that was darkening the future of art made in his 1883 Oxford address. In addition, it is stamped boldly with Matthew Arnold's critical vocabulary and view of culture as "the best and the brightest" of civilization, most influentially contained in *Culture and Anarchy*, whose first edition appeared in 1869. The essay precisely defines, in clear expository prose rather than in the unwieldy fiction of "Stuart Forbes" (on which work had apparently stopped a year earlier), the process of what is best called Parrington's conversion from Arnold to Morris. Arnold had reinforced the prejudices that caused townspeople and students to see Parrington as an aristocrat, an aesthete, in both Emporia and Norman—despite his baseball playing and football coaching. And Arnold's early life and career, like Parrington's, was pursued in education—first as son of Thomas Arnold, the headmaster of Rugby School and principal creator of the modern English public school system, then as inspector of schools, a post held from 1851 until two years before his death in 1888. Also like Parrington, Arnold pursued a second career as a poet and essayist, although he had the advantages of background and talent that allowed him to succeed in balancing two vocations when most of his contemporaries and followers would fail, by comparison, in succeeding in one.

Parrington's conversion was freighted with his experience of dwelling between two worlds as well as by the paradoxes manifested in his personality. If he was going to reconcile art and democracy, it would be only by vigilantly maintaining a critical observer's suspended judgment about both art's and democracy's possibilities and liabilities. He was a teacher who was both suspicious of dogma and ideological rigidity and committed to the role of education in shaping the values of students and citizens. He made himself upon the craftsman model, but the result more closely resembled an eighteenth-century English gentleman farmer than an early twentieth-century communist. He was a disciple of William Morris and not of Karl Marx. He would become a Jeffersonian democrat and not a member of the American political left. He was an intellectual, and his personal experience as an outsider and own self-effacing nature were inextricably bound up with his scholarly and avocational interests and detached perspective on the course of American culture.

"It is now thirteen years since I left the yard in Cambridge," Parrington's 1906 essay begins, identifying positively with his Harvard years,

> to become a teacher of the English language of the English literature to the philistines of the undergraduate world. If love for English letters be enough to give one the right to call oneself a bookman, then I was a bookman. . . . Arguing from my own life, I believed firmly that most young college men and women love books and need only a little wise encouragement to find each for himself the wealth that lay ready for them. And I would try to give that wise encouragement.

The shortcomings of my own teachers, their insistence upon learning rather than upon letters, I would supply. They had "eat paper and drunk ink," whereas I would feed to the untrained mind the "dainties that are bred in a book." . . . Especially I would steep them in the Elizabethans until they loved the vernacular of the "English of the golden time." Once they had tasted the savour of this right English speech they would be saved. Journalism and journalistic novels could have them no longer. They would become bookmen and true lovers of letters.

That was thirteen years ago. I was an idealist of course and very ignorant. I am an idealist still but my teaching creed has been overhauled until most of the articles are so patched and twisted that I hardly know them myself. . . . [N]ow that I found myself in a small school where I soon came to know most of the undergraduates, I looked with some perhaps unfounded misgivings on the number claimed by the laboratories and shops. . . . Two-thirds of the undergraduates learn nothing outside of the laboratory during four years of college work. The day I came to this conclusion was a dark one for me. I became sensitive on the point. I was very young and I worried over it; and for several years I could not understand it. I knew of course the conventional statements—that science was the real rich working field of the 19th century—that Germany had taught the American university the value of experimental research in mind-training—and the like. But I was a bookman with the traditions of five hundred years back of me. I felt a vague distrust and dislike of it all. It did not seem to me to make for culture—in those days I placed culture very high.[10]

Parrington then distinguishes between the "college" like Oxford, designed to train the elite, and the "university," designed to train "engineers, shop foremen, businessmen, farmers, foresters." He sympathized with the need for such a "democratic" institution but complained, "They have neither time nor money to cultivate a love of the dainties that are bred in a book. Elizabethans—talk to them of the Elizabethans. They are young Americans. . . . The very English on their tongues is often of a single generation." Again, one overhears the Arnold/Morris debate and sees the irony of the University of Oklahoma professor ensconced in Cambridge on his grand tour, sees the reluctant immigrant returning under the spur of a dutiful conscience to till rocky fields. What role could he play in this new system, as the nineteenth century gave way to the twentieth? "The bookman," the essay continues,

is slow to grant that science as taught to the undergraduates can take the place of the older fashioned "culture studies." We look with suspicion upon overmuch "shopping around in the laboratories" and we dream of a return in part to the older ways. But we hardly expect it.

Having got my mind cleared on this first point, I saw that as a lover of letters it was my business to make the most of the remaining . . . "remnant," . . . the leaven to leaven the vast lump of nationalism based on "progress." They were to be the handful of cultured men and women to overcome the noisy preachers of the "doctrine of getting on."

> But . . . in studying my remnant . . . I found that very few cared for letters. Now and then one of them would stray into a Shakespeare class but he did not feel altogether at home and his curiosity about English literature usually was satisfied with this dip into Shakespeare.

Another way to interpret Parrington's dilemma here is to compare him with Henry Adams. Adams was also fond of quoting Arnold's "Stanzas from the Grande Chartreuse" whose lines—"wandering between two worlds / one dead, the other powerless to be born"—seemed so aptly to describe fin-de-siècle experience. Parrington was similarly a troubled product of nineteenth-century Victorian culture who was both attracted to and repelled by the twentieth century. And thus, like Adams, he often found himself looking fondly backwards to the presumed certainties of the eighteenth century.[11] Intellectually and emotionally, Parrington remained caught between those two worlds the rest of his life; professionally, he experimented with ways to bridge the gulf.

Whether the intended audience for "Thoughts on the Teaching of Literature"—which, like almost all the other writings undertaken during Parrington's Norman years, remained unpolished and unpublished—extended beyond the author himself is not known. But the essay marks a definite point of pedagogical departure. The university *Bulletin* had announced that the first course in undergraduate American literature since Parrington became department chair was to be offered in the fall of 1905, just before he composed "Thoughts on the Teaching of Literature." The catalog description for English XVIII reads:

A study of the literary production of America, from the settlement of the colonies to the present time. The colonial and revolutionary periods are treated only in a general review. Special attention is given to Irving and Cooper, to the New England and Southern schools, and to recent men of letters. Throughout the course, the development of literature in America is studied in relation to its contemporary development in England.[12]

This course is distinguished by its early inception in comparison with the curricula of many other universities and colleges. In 1827 Amherst had pioneered with perhaps the first collegiate level course, Lectures in English and American Literature, that included some proportion of native topics. Vermont's Middlebury College appears to have the longest continuous tradition of American literary study, beginning to list a course in Critiques of British and American Classics in 1848–49. But not until after the 1870s (as Parrington observed in his Emporia essay "The Position of English in College Curricula") did either English language or literature begin gaining prominence in American higher education. By the 1870s most highly ranked colleges had expanded their traditional oratory and rhetoric offerings with English-related courses. Courses taught in at least twenty-four institutions included American writers, and the first college-level course devoted solely to American literature was initiated by John S. Hart at Princeton in 1872.[13]

During the post–Civil War period, as the newly reunited nation sought to redefine itself, interest in American culture was reflected in a broad spectrum of formats, of which periodical literature was both a barometer and a thermostat, providing a wide range of reading matter (including serialized fiction and short stories and poetry) to a heterogeneous public with heterogeneous tastes and critical acumen. The Centennial Exposition held in Philadelphia in 1876 gave impetus to the organization of scores of state and local historical societies; a shared interest in newly respected Americana was manifested in higher as well as secondary education. Yet when Johns Hopkins University was founded in 1876, the Centennial year, its stress on the scientific model made it a center for philological study. Thus in the 1870s were apparent two cross-currents, one leading toward the study of American literature within its biographical and historical contexts and one leading toward the study of languages and emphasizing its abstract and structural properties.

Shortly following the Centennial, the first scholarly study of American literature appeared, Moses Coit Tyler's *History of American Literature, 1607–1765* (1878). George H. Putnam had contracted with Tyler, educated at Yale and Andover Theological Seminary and since 1867 a professor of English at the University of Michigan, to write "a manual of American Literature" in 1875. Tyler's painstaking research, completed at a time and a place in which primary sources were difficult to locate and secondary sources nearly nonexistent, was sufficient to persuade Cornell University to appoint him to the first professorship in the country wholly devoted to American history in 1881. Renouncing his earlier Calvinism, he was ordained an Episcopal priest in 1883. In 1887 he published a work in his Cornell field, a biography of Patrick Henry, then in 1897 blended his historical and literary interests to produce in two volumes *The Literary History of the American Revolution,* which brought the American canon to the eve of the eighteenth century. Tyler's mix of history, literature, and theology marks him as a member of the fluid preprofessional generation, but it also foreshadows the major interests of Edward Eggleston and Parrington, who likewise made their reputations primarily as historians of ideas.[14]

After Tyler's initial work, the major studies of American literature in the last decades of the century were written by those trained or practicing well within the literary fold. Most of those works, such as Charles F. Richardson's two-volume *American Literature, 1607–1885* (1886–88), Fred Lewis Pattee's *History of American Literature* (1896), Brander Matthews's *Introduction to American Literature* (1896), Henry S. Pancoast's *Introduction to American Literature* (1898), and Walter C. Bronson's *Short History of*

American Literature (1900), were aimed at or scarcely above a secondary or preparatory audience. (Parrington's copy of Matthews belonged to Julia, who attended Norman's Preparatory Department, and he purchased Pattee the year of its publication when he was focusing entirely on English literature at Emporia. In 1895 he evidently purchased his first American literary study, an 1894 primer by Mildred Cabell Watkins, *American Literature*.) One virtue of Wendell's *Literary History of America* (Parrington owned the first and not the 1907 revision), despite its attempt to cover the period from Jamestown to the present in a single volume, is that it was directed at a more sophisticated audience and prefaced each chronological period of literary development with comparative chapters on English and American history.

At Harvard, Wendell taught only one American literature course, the American authors course, which Parrington attended, that evidently used an anthology by E. Clarence Stedman for a text, but it was peripheral to his interests as it was to most professors' in the 1890s. Overall, the condition of the texts reflected the prevailing status of American literature: an adjunct to high school civics, a lowly provincial appendage to the glittering body of English belles lettres, not wholly worthy of formal collegiate study. For example, of the twenty institutions canvassed by the 1894 *Dial* surveys, thirteen mention American literature, but in all cases it was regarded as an aspect of English literature, and both were now treated from the aesthetic point of view instead of from the broader perspective of the mid-nineteenth century, before the impact of specialization progressively fractured the monolithic identification of "literature" with "letters." On the one hand, this fracturing hindered the serious study of American literature, for native productions suffered on a belletristic standard in comparison with the British corpus. On the other, it made the discrete study of American literature possible, for the application of belletristic standards showed at least that American literature was different from its British forerunners and contemporaries.

By 1897 at Brown, Lorenzo Sears became the first to hold a titled professorship in American literature. (Sears published his own text, *American Literature*, in 1902.) During the same decade, Brander Matthews and William Peterfield Trent at Columbia, A. G. Newcomer at Stanford, Fred Lewis Pattee at the Pennsylvania State University, Katharine Lee Bates at Wellesley, William B. Cairns at Wisconsin, Killis Campbell at Texas, C. W. Kent at Virginia, and Isaac Demmon at Michigan were beginning their careers. Charles F. Richardson at Dartmouth continued the work begun in the 1880s and in 1895 sponsored one of the first students to pursue graduate work in American literature. At the beginning of the century, both graduate and undergraduate possibilities in the field increased as additional institutions began offering courses. But at no time until the 1950s—and then only on campuses with strong interdisciplinary programs in American Civilization or American Studies—did offerings in American literature approach in number those in British.[15]

Parrington's emerging interest in American literature may be placed in the context of his early twentieth-century colleagues by noting that three years before Oklahoma offered its first undergraduate American literature courses, Arthur Hobson Quinn began teaching the subject at the University of Pennsylvania. The same year, Leonard Lemmon sent a complimentary copy of his and Julian Hawthorne's new *American Literature: A Textbook* (1902) to Parrington. In 1905, the year English XVIII was announced, Quinn offered the first course in American literature solely for graduate students and Percy Holmes Boynton began his career at the University of Chicago. Thus Norman's course does not rank among the pioneering 1890s curricula; its cross-cultural emphasis on British and American relations looks backward to the 1850s perspective, but its contemporary emphasis sets it far apart from Wendell's critical standards.

Unfortunately, it is not clear whether English XVIII was actually taught or whether Parrington taught it. Forty pages of notes for English XVIII, with an initial book list, survive among Parrington's Norman papers and are in his handwriting. The catalog lists his colleague Wilbur Humphreys as instructor, although nothing in Humphreys's background suggests that his interests were turning to nonphilological and non-British subjects. The two men's concerns and Harvard training had dovetailed in the area of composition, and in 1907 the university published their jointly authored rhetoric, *Handbook to English I.* The approximately fifty-page pamphlet owes its model to Wendell's example and 1891 text, *English Composition,* and its distillation to their experience teaching ill-prepared, practical-minded midwesterners as opposed to more elite eastern students. Interestingly, after Parrington changed his seminary lecture topics from the Old Testament to medievalism in art, Humphreys began offering a class on the English Bible as literature. And when Parrington began his new Morris and Ruskin course, Humphreys took over the second semester of his chairman's course on the novel. Their working relationship thus seems compatible, perhaps to the extent that Parrington sat in on Humphreys's lectures.[16]

Curiously, the American course was withdrawn from the regular listings for the academic year after the fall of 1905. But when English XVIII reappeared in the summer session of 1908, with precisely the same catalog description, Parrington was beyond doubt the instructor.[17] The surviving course notes, which emphasize movements and trends influencing American literary production and character and only cursorily treat colonial authors, break off with a few comments on the eighteenth century and could well date from the summer of 1908. Certainly they bear the marks of Parrington's post-grand-tour thinking and the tone of the author of *Main Currents in American Thought.* In the main, English XVIII runs counter to Parrington's interest in contemporary American speech and literature.

Nevertheless, turning to the past as a means to provide a context for understanding present experience is entirely characteristic of Parrington's teaching and avocations up to this point. The voice that can be over-heard in the notes is compounded of a Stuart Forbes who has matured beyond his theological phase, the returning immigrant's Anglophilia, and the interpretation-seeking Emporia professor who knew J. R. Green and read doggedly through Bancroft and Schouler after voting for William Jennings Bryan.

In developing an American literature survey before specialized figures or theme courses, Parrington was within the pattern of other English depart-ments and could provide his students with texts and primary sources. The notes list, as the initial reading assignment, a thirty-five-page selection from Volume 1 of Bancroft's *History of the United States;* the first fifty-five pages of Wendell's *Literary History of America;* the first seventy-eight pages of William Peterfield Trent's *History of American Literature, 1607–1865* (1903); and about ninety pages of selected readings from E. Clarence Sted-man and E. M. Hutchinson's *Library of American Literature* (eleven vol-umes, 1889–90). Next follows an "Introduction" that begins by insisting that the following points must be kept in mind while studying American literature:

1. That it is a part of the great body of English literature.
2. That starting from the common source of Elizabethan England, it has de-veloped independently of English literature and is therefore doubly interesting, because of its likeness as well as its unlikeness to the literature of the mother country.
3. That in its earlier development it was the creation of a compact and ho-mogeneous body of Englishmen. The first migration to New England, i.e. 1620–1700, exclusively English. Of these the vast majority came in the years from 1620–1640 when the outbreak of the war stopped the movement. In the year 1640 in New England 21,000 settlers scattered in 50 towns and villages.
4. That we shall do well to leave the flag out of the discussion.
5. That for the early period we shall confine ourselves to the literature of New England.

Having chosen to void the issue of nationalism (point 4), as a dweller between worlds interested in raising American literature from a civics ad-junct would wisely do, and to ignore the colonial literature of the South (al-though the notes stipulate 1607–1765 as demarcations for the colonial period), Parrington then firmly states two basic theses. Both deal with the relationship between Puritanism and colonial (he interchangeably calls it "immigrant") literature. In the first thesis, he contrasted Puritanism in En-gland and America, developing a comparative perspective focused on a his-toric, ideological movement and not on belles lettres as promised in the English XVIII catalog description. In the second, he counterposed the "dwarfing . . . theological conception of life" with "broadly human interests"; stressed the necessity of recovering a "broader humanism" from Europe, by two American authors with extensive European experience, Longfellow and Irving (one reflection of the impact of Parrington's grand tour); and then negatively evaluated the entire corpus of American literature to the present day (a reflection of Parrington's lingering post-grand-tour Arnoldian view of culture also expressed in the 1906 "Thoughts on the Teaching of Literature"). In all these instances Puritanism is the damning culprit. Indeed, a long section of the notes details the tenets of Calvinism.

Though perhaps reinforced by subsequent reading of the first volume of *Main Currents*, a memoir written sometime after 1941 by a former Parrington student at Norman, Sardis Roy Hadsell, indicates that the professor's attitude was crystal clear: "Parrington's classes in American literature were popular, and fresh, for he was studying incessantly. His special abhorrence in those days was puritanism." Hadsell, who went on to write a doctoral dissertation on the Arthurian romance at the University of Chicago in the 1920s, also helps verify Parrington's conscious self-making in the image of Morris: "Parrington said that if there was one Englishman he would rather be than any other that was William Morris. He was more like William Morris than any other. He was socialistic in tendency. He was versatile. He liked to make things. He was especially interested in architecture; therefore Thomas Hardy interested him also."[18]

This juxtaposition of anti-Puritanism with the Morris model defines more exactly what Parrington meant by "humanism" or "the broadly human," a phrase he had counterpoised to philological concerns in the essay "Western Speech." Although the term in one common sense is identical with the Renaissance revival of classical learning associated with the beliefs of the humanists, both humanism and humanist share another common meaning: the emphasis on human (including literary) interests as distinguished from divine. This denotation of humanism became current, according to the *Oxford English Dictionary*, in the second half of the nineteenth century, when traditional literary culture was set on the defensive against the power and values of industrial capitalism's machine civilization.

Parrington's opposition of Puritanism and humanism marks another stage in the dialectical thought processes traced in Chapter 5. Autobiographically, it reveals that he had found a label for the attitudes, specifically in their American form, that hindered the development of culture as well as a label for the attitudes, specifically derived from Morris and Ruskin, that promoted the development of culture. In developing the ramifications of the Puritanism label, the course notes assess the impact of colonial immigration:

> 1. They left behind them a beautiful and settled land, the home of their friends and the resting place of their fathers. *Such a break with the past is a serious business.*

2. They left behind a noble literature and the vital forces which produce literature.

3. They brought with them: (1) Their English speech; (2) a sturdy morality and a solid culture; (3) the common law; (4) a Calvinistic theology which should not only prevail but which should suffice—*to exact this theology, they were content to lose the rest.* (Emphasis added)

Couched in such terms, the magnitude of the loss to a lover of humanism is starkly clear, if not historically accurate. But Parrington was not as concerned with accuracy as with interpreting the sources of the thin shallowness of American culture. In developing the ramifications of the humanism label, the course notes predictably apply theories of Ruskin and Morris:

> Such a theology may develop strong and upright men and women, but it will hardly bring forth a literature. It is concerned with truth and art, with beauty. The great prayers, long vigils and passionate imaginings brought forth intensity, but they closed the eyes to the facts and wonders of the outer world of reality. Too much contemplation of the glorious city of God encircled by its jasper walls shut the eyes to the beauty of this world.

Finally, Parrington draws a knife-edged parallel between colonial New England and contemporary Norman: "Pioneer life is not productive of books. In her 19 years of existence Oklahoma has written nothing of worth, and yet we have a million and a half people and the public schools and newspapers."

Having determined as nearly impossible the task of teaching "the dainties that are bred in a book" or talking of the Elizabethans to students whose mastery of English was but a generation, what could Parrington himself do at this cultural impasse, in this cultural wasteland? The solution was professorial, scholarly, and typical: he began pinning his thoughts to paper, shifting genres from the prose fiction of "Stuart Forbes: Stoic" to prose in the service of historical and cultural interpretation. The genesis of *Main Currents in American Thought* can be traced directly to Parrington's post-grand-tour experiences and can be found among his later Norman papers. Among many pages of sketchy comments and tentative outlines handwritten on the backs of examination report forms and soiled university stationery is a typed "Introduction" that discusses the relations between culture and literature, rich social life and individualism, aristocracy and democracy. Two typed though unpolished chapters from the work for which this introduction was prepared also survive. The first is titled "Puritanism" and develops the theses in Parrington's course notes. The second is titled "The Revolution" and describes the point of political severing between English and American culture.

The existence of these chapters, obviously designed as part of a longer work, in addition to Parrington's teaching of American literature first as a component of preparatory courses, then on the undergraduate level during the 1905–8 period, sets back the widely held dates of both his engagement with American literature and his initial work on what became *Main Currents*. The former is generally attributed to the catalyst of political scientist J. Allen Smith at the University of Washington, where Parrington was shortly destined to assume a position, the latter generally pinpointed as 1910 or 1913. Although it will probably remain difficult to date either event with much more accuracy, all available evidence points to the earlier manuscript date and to the true catalyst as the conflict between "high" English Victorian culture and "low" American Progressive culture. That conflict—or dialectic—characterized the full range of Parrington's behavior and thinking during and especially after his 1903–4 European journey.[19]

The second half of Parrington's eleven years in Norman was a time of crucial intellectual transition. The dynamics and components of that transition were, it is true, refined and focused once his Oklahoma chapter reached closure and he began his nearly twenty-one-year tenure in Seattle. The events that occurred during that closure process further colored his view of American culture, leaving a dark stain on his entire midwestern experience and adding to the range of his critical palate.

Professionalization and Its Discontents

By 1908, then, Parrington was well under way with a manuscript, a product by that time regarded as requisite by leading institutions for professional advancement. It was presumed, of course, that a doctoral degree would either contribute toward or precede one's first book. But Parrington had only his Emporia M.A. Yet armed with his self-making propensities and driven by his self-tailored scholarly and creative outlets, he had begun offering graduate degrees in Norman's English Department. Only three years after his arrival, one of the first master's degrees was awarded, to Carleton Ross Hume for his "Dialectical history of the eastern and southern portions of the United States." With no or sparse assistance, Parrington had developed a curriculum that reflected current academic trends, maintained rigorous scholastic standards, and attracted an enthusiastic following among his students (though perhaps not those who were satisfied with a "dip into Shakespeare").

S. R. Hadsell's memoir provides two vignettes of the teaching style Parrington began honing in Emporia in 1893. One concerns Parrington's methods in his composition courses, which Hadsell took before receiving his B.A. in English in 1904 and then assumed teaching in 1908.

> I am sure that many early graduates who came under Parrington's influence feel that his method, learn to do by doing, was right for the early days. We wrote a theme every day, an outline for a long paper on Monday, the finished long theme on the following Monday. . . . We wrote many short themes on the

blackboard, and Professor Parrington would proceed to tear them to pieces, ridicule our mistakes, glow with enthusiasm at our successes, pick out the misplaced commas, question our handwriting, and magnify our misspelled words. How we loved it, even when he reduced us to tears, or made us angry, for we felt that Parrington was interested in us, and we knew that he hated shoddy English.

"If style is the man, it should be easy to write about Parrington's style," Hadsell continues in a second illustration that highlights Parrington's personality as well as his classroom methods.

People everywhere were charmed with him, with his appearance and with his manner. Among students, he made disciples. . . . I do not know how he did it, but he made a student feel that he was personally interested in him, in his life, his ideals.
. . . He lectured in class a great deal. His English was sweet upon the tongue. He charmed us, even when he was wrong. For the first fifteen minutes of a class hour he would ask questions, provoke discussions concerning what he had said the day before. He would polish his eye glasses, with a clean handkerchief, hold them up to the light, and say "Is that clear, Miss Barnett?" Miss Barnett . . . with a roguish smile would answer, "I think it should be clear, you have polished it enough." There was always good fun, good spirit in his classes. That searching analysis at the beginning of the hour made us squirm, if we had not reviewed the notes, if we had not understood their import. Then for forty-five minutes he would advance the subject. We felt that not a word was to be lost. He never made more than three or four points. . . . He would start toward a point, go round and about, then suddenly he would arrive . . . using the inductive method. . . . By the time we arrived we were almost out of our seats. Or, he would state a point and illustrate it from all angles . . . until it stood forth clear. . . . He never preached; he was orderly and clear.[20]

With the exception of his year's leave of absence, his poetry, and his novel, most of Parrington's attention had been taken by institutional duties, largely by the teaching that Hadsell so memorably described. Still, his plans to publish a volume of poetry and to complete "Stuart Forbes: Stoic" never reached fruition. He had published only one article (the 1903 *House Beautiful* essay) and that not in one of the emerging professional journals in his field. He might have contributed a piece on western speech to *Dialect Notes*, published since 1890. His and Humphreys's rhetoric, *Handbook to English I*, a competent though brief text, was published by the university for a university audience. The classroom provided immediate rewards based on the effectiveness of the student-teacher relationship; his garden provided immediate rewards based on the effectiveness of the husbandman's relationship with nature; the rewards of publishing remained largely intangible. The pattern did not auger well for his latest project.

One trial title for what became *Main Currents* was "The American Mind: A Study in National Ideals," which aptly applies to the surviving Norman "germs" of *Main Currents*.[21] Surveying scholarly terrain that generally would not be developed or debated for two decades, its scope went far beyond the usual simplistic or adulatory literary judgments and easy nationalism of the American literature textbooks available up to that time, Tyler's two histories still being the only major scholarly works in the field. Among Parrington's usually handwritten drafts that probably postdate his English XVIII course notes and certainly precede the typed and more polished "Introduction" and chapters on Puritanism and the Revolution is a brief preface which begins:

> The following study is founded upon the belief that no understanding of American letters can be had without first coming to know the American Mind & the deeper ideals to which in the midst of an unlovely material development we cling to, even though our clinging to these ideals does not seem to be of effect upon our life. For some reason as yet no foreign critic of American letters has been able to grasp this American mind—the very simplicity of it, deceives him— he is looking for complexity, subtlety, and the very openness of the secret keeps it obscure.
>
> The second belief that runs through this work is that the student of letters must not lay aside his literary judgment in the presence of ideals however excellent to other purposes, but which do not produce literature.

In the remainder of the preface, Parrington continues arguing that the application of aesthetic standards will reveal the paucity in American letters. Additional notes from the same period show that Parrington's analysis of American culture and its ideals was stimulated by the contrast between English speech and literature and American speech and literature.

For example, in a handwritten outline titled "The American Literary Spirit," Parrington argues that "literature is the glorified expression of life in the common speech. All art is but the expression of life and the art of letters is only one form of the larger art expression. Heretofore American literature has been sporadic, individual, never the art speaking of the American people." He then characterizes American speech as "shallow, nervous, emotional—gifted with ready wit, but not mellow idiomatic beauty." Significantly conjoined with Parrington's emphasis on the humanism of English literature are comments on "the note of friendliness if not of fellowship, in Chaucer" and Shakespeare's ability "To see life as a whole— open-hearted, honest, sympathetic . . . whereas in all puritan literature there is a certain aloofness from the coarse & groin, a certain virginity that is pale and unreal." Parrington finally advances into the political sphere and insists that "we need but a fuller realization of a new social ideal—humanism that is the outgrowth of true democracy."

He also merges speech, literature, humanism, democracy, and the impact of immigration (discussed in his English XVIII notes) in several pages of notes treating "the literary spirit of the west." Here Parrington vaults from

the revolutionary to the contemporary period, observing that western settlers, including Oklahomans, aided by the post–Civil War railway expansion, brought with them the Puritan and revolutionary ideals but added a
third social characteristic: "a free and easy informality." In addition, the
West—in part because of climate, geography, and social conditions—"developed a new vocabulary & a new accent," though "the several dialects
are now merging into the common western speech." Coincident with the
development of a freer, friendly spirit (the traits admired in Chaucer and
Shakespeare) and new speech is "a firm belief in democracy . . . based on
the idea of nature's nobleman but influenced by Whig ideals . . . and commercial ideals." Every man must be given the "chance to make of himself
what he will. But implied in this is the feeling of free competition both in
the field of business & the field of politics."

Parrington was still mining the vein developed in his 1897 "Some Political Sketches" with their stern criticism of the "business ideal." But those
sketches, whose criticism of the "university ideal" can be seen as a foreshadowing of Stuart Forbes's mature opinions, proposed as a solution for
contemporary social problems the "humanitarian ideal." This ideal was
embodied in a new statesman with a realistic grasp of current problems yet
guided by idealistic sympathy for the rights of men. Such an Arnoldian solution surfaces again in his Norman notes in the context of describing the
declining force of "our old national faith": "Not of least importance in the
decline of the political ideal is the fact that whereas in the earlier days the
better men—men of social position and learning—were the leaders. Leadership passed from them to the less educated."

The problems of adequate leadership and the declining force of political
ideals considered in the nexus of influences determining the western literary
spirit also led Parrington to comment on Populism. In one case Parrington
identifies Populism as one of the new social forces molding the new western generation, first praising Populism's attempt to critique Whig principles of government, then soberly concluding about the movement that "the
chief thing to notice however is the vigorous self-confidence with which ill-
trained thinkers solved all our social problems and the confidence in theories & idealisms which proved their Americanism." In another case, instead
of criticizing Populism in light of its leadership problems, he focuses on
Populism as an aspect of the philosophy of western life. And here we can
again hear—as in his brief notes for the novel course treating Twain and
Howells—the voice objecting to the eastern domination of literary criticism:

> To understand the spirit of the west one must have lived among western people.
> When the panic of 1893 brought to a head the widespread political movement
> known as populism, the East laughed and derided what to this day it has not
> understood. That populism was an honest attempt on the part of level-headed
> men to criticize & supplement the principles of Whig government has never been

widely understood. It was the attempt of men who lived in a world that still believed in a social democracy to apply to the Whig principles of government popular in the East certain principles of political democracy. It was the revolt of a less highly organized industrial world against a more highly organized that had taken advantage of its machinery to exploit the younger and the weapon it found ready to its hand was the weapon that for a hundred years had been used more or less successfully—namely political machinery.

These late Norman-era comments on Populism—nearly more extensive than those in *Main Currents*—show Parrington coming intellectually full circle, reviving his latent Emporia political interests after his long bout with religion and art. But his most recent bout with art had pitted him on the side of William Morris, and Morris offered, through the ideal of the guild, a system that united aesthetic standards and a form of political organization designed to encourage the friendliness and human fellowship that Parrington found in English literature. It is no surprise that at one point in his notes Parrington calls Morris a humanist. Here again is the conjunction of politics and art with humanism in English culture, allied against the conjunction of Whig politics and hostility to letters with Puritanism in American culture.

At last, Parrington located an American counterpart of the Morris ideal: Walt Whitman. Interestingly, his brief comments on Whitman emerge in an evaluation of the impact of French revolutionary political ideas on the American colonists. At this point—perhaps because of the force of his Parisian discovery that he himself was English and not French—Parrington insists, taking a position he would reverse in *Main Currents,* that French revolutionary ideas have dominated unhealthily American national life and proved also a "literary calamity":

> When we find a man who has wholly sloughed off these alien ideas, we exclaim him as unamerican and when as happens rarely we find a man who has cast off as well the still older and equally outworn ideals of 17th century puritanism we thrust him out as an apostate. This is the explanation of our American dislike for Whitman—he is neither republican nor Puritan but democrat, frank, material, chaotic. A half-man because regardless of the past—a composite of Morris and Whitman must be an ideal.

Whitman thus is not judged a full humanist because of his present-mindedness. But he is one of the first American writers to rate Parrington's approbation, in addition to the praise accorded Irving and Longfellow in the English XVIII notes for their exposure to European ideas and effort to develop the "foreign critic's" perspective. One other writer is treated in these early notes: Nathaniel Hawthorne. Not unexpectedly, Parrington's evaluation (almost exactly paralleled in *Main Currents*) places him in the opposite corner from Whitman. Hawthorne is identified with the past, with

Puritanism, with the "distrust of the flesh of humanness," although, applying his critical standards, Parrington judges him "luminous" as an artist.[22]

The inclusion of Hawthorne adds another dimension to the full-circle effect of Parrington's current thinking, for Hawthorne had been his delight and literary model at Harvard—ironically, a discovery made under Wendell's guidance. Whitman adds a third, for deep in Parrington's poetry phase in his early Norman years he had bought his own copy of *Leaves of Grass*.

Thus all of the components that animated Parrington's thinking and analysis since leaving Harvard were coming into dynamic interplay as he planned his new book, refining its theses and writing its initial introductions and chapters. In 1907, several events in his personal life happily fitted into the sequence of intellectual progress. On April 29, Julia gave birth to a second daughter, Louise Wrathal, named after both of her grandmothers (Mary Louise Parrington and Mary Louise Williams) and Vernon's grandmother Ann Wrathal, the wife of the Yorkshire weaver who settled in Gorham, Maine.[23] During the summer Parrington spent much of his spare time helping to build his new house, and the newly enlarged family was able to move there in November.

Then the ax fell. The very forces Parrington had been seeking to explain in turning his attention to American culture cost him his job. One University of Oklahoma historian, Roy Gittinger, who was on campus at the time, describes the 1907–8 year as opening "with a feeling of unrest. . . . Rumors were already current that considerable reorganization not only of the university faculty but of the university itself, might be expected under the new state government." Total enrollment had grown to 790, including 191 in the College of Arts and Sciences. To the mood of political uneasiness and to strained campus facilities was added discouragement when a disastrous fire destroyed University Hall on December 20.

A year following a constitutional convention in Guthrie, Oklahoma and Indian territories were unified and admitted to statehood in mid-November of 1907 by proclamation of President Theodore Roosevelt. What happened in Norman after that Richard Hofstadter has called "one of the most scandalous episodes in American history." Ironically, the new governor, Charles N. Haskell, had run for office as a Bryan Democrat. In the power jockeying that followed statehood, Haskell acceded to the demands of a group of self-interested Southern Methodist reformers. In March 1908, control of the university was taken from the Board of Regents and placed with the State Board of Education. David Ross Boyd, a Republican who had served sixteen years as president, was removed and replaced by Arthur Grant Evans, a Democrat and an ordained Southern Methodist minister. Evans had served in Governor Haskell's campaign and been president of a Presbyterian Indian school, Henry Kendall College in Muskogee, in the former Indian Territory. He was deemed a helpful political asset because of his influence among the tribal population, a result of his opposition to the linkage of Oklahoma and Indian territories. Members of the faculty who could be targeted as supposedly immoral noncoreligionists or outside nonsympathizers with Oklahoma interests were investigated. Beginning in April, the case was taken up as a small cause célèbre in the *New York Outlook* with an editorial titled "Serious Educational Blunder" that criticized the partisanship involved in Boyd's firing.[24]

Parrington, a highly visible and popular campus fixture, nevertheless was guilty of smoking cigarettes and apparently of cutting too aristocratic a figure. Perhaps the building and occupancy of Stuart Forbes's dream house, symbolic of so much that was antithetical or foreign to midwestern and southwestern culture, engendered the final blow. On these points S. R. Hadsell provides substantiation, observing that, like Jefferson, Parrington seemed to have sympathy with the common man but was "an aristocrat. . . . In his dress, deportment, talk, tastes, interests." "He could never have been elected to an office in Norman," Hadsell continues, in a passage that reads like a replay of the 1897 Emporia school board election:

> He could never campaign in a hickory hat and with one suspender fastened to a nail as "Uncle Buck" [James Shannon Buchanan, the history professor] . . . did when he ran for membership in the constitutional convention. He was not well known, not well understood on "main street," yet he enjoyed people. He never felt above them. He liked to work with his hands, like a common laborer, yet how he kept himself so immaculate, when working in the garden, coaching athletics, or using a saw and hammer I don't know; he must have had an innate taste for cleanliness. In the faculty picture, 1903, he is almost the only one in a high collar, white tie, and dress suit.

Later in his memoir, Hadsell comments that he "never heard of Parrington dancing or playing cards." Although these were two diversions he had enjoyed since his youth, they were evidently pursued away from the eyes of Main Street. Hadsell then adds that, although Parrington smoked neither a pipe nor cigars,

> he did smoke cigarettes, in the early days when dancing, playing cards, and smoking cigarettes was something no church member would do. He was therefore considered a bad example for youth, because he smoked. Professor Buchanan could smoke a cob pipe, but Parrington with his cigarettes! Who thought that in a few years women everywhere would be at it. . . . They tell a story in this neighborhood about the investigation which the Board of Regents conducted in 1908. When Parrington was called in the board asked him if he smoked. He replied, according to the story, "Yes, but not on the street, or about my class room." A little later Professor Paxton [Joseph Francis Paxton, the professor of Greek and classical archaeology] was called in. "Do you smoke?" they asked him. "Yes, but I don't go behind the barn to do it, I smoke in the open

when I feel like it." The room was blue with cigar smoke at the time, for the Regents were smoking. I don't know which answer pleased them.[25]

Clearly Paxton's did, even though he had received a Harvard M.A. in 1895, the year before assuming his Norman position. At this point Parrington was preceded in seniority only by two original (1892) faculty members, President Boyd and Edwin DeBarr, the chemistry professor, as well as by Buchanan (hired in 1895) and Paxton. It was not his Harvard degree that convicted Parrington but the way he wore it. Of the most senior teaching faculty, only Parrington would lose his job.

The power grab following statehood was not the first campus political eruption, although its effects were the most far-reaching. For example, when Parrington was in England in the late spring of 1904, one faculty member was not retained (Lewis E. Coles, the instructor in economics and sociology), another left (Lawrence N. Upjohn), and Parrington suspected the board was taking action against a third (Frederick S. Elder). He wrote frankly to Julia:

> The only men in the faculty who are "safe" are Paxton, who is too lazy to care what the President does, Cole [Lawrence Wooster Cole, the professor of psychology, who received a Harvard M.A. in 1904], who is his protégé, and Gould [Charles Newton Gould, professor of geology and head of the School of Mines], who is so busy writing about himself for the papers as to pay no attention to what is going on. The rest of us know too much of the inside workings and are too anxious to change things—to be altogether safe. Someday Van Vleet will get knifed and then DeBarr, etc. All of which doesn't worry me in the least. Altho I am not quite ready to be kicked out and shouldn't like the idea of being kicked out even if I were ready and should probably fight. I am not dependent on the one position, and before many years I shall give it up anyway.

This prescient letter described Parrington's attitude once the investigations were under way. He fought. By the end of May, William Allen White and a cashier at Norman's First National Bank had sent letters on Parrington's behalf to the board. More testimonials followed in the ensuing weeks, including one from a surprising ally, Lee Cruce, the president of both nearby Ardmore's National Bank and of the Board of Regents. A letter arrived from Morrell Sayre of the Carnegie Foundation for the Advancement of Teaching expressing concern over the university situation.[26]

All these efforts were to no avail. On June 14, Parrington replied in acid understatement to the charges of immorality to W. E. Rowsey, the board secretary: "My life may not be as Cotton Mather said of an old Puritan divine 'A trembling walk with God'—that high faith seems not to be given to men of our generation—but it is I believe, a serious attempt to find out what is sane and just and honorable and to make them prevail." But it was not the charge of immorality but a second charge questioning his teaching qualifications that cut Parrington to the quick. To Rowsey, he stated flatly: "I know how to teach my subject better than any other man in the southwest. That may not seem modest, but it is a fact." He also eloquently addressed the charge regarding his qualifications two days later in a letter to the Reverend L. N. Linebaugh (later elected to the Board of Regents), pastor of a McAlester church and evidently a member of the Southern Methodist coterie responsible for most of the upheaval:

> No one holds the profession of the teacher in higher respect than I. If I did not have a high opinion of the profession I should not be a teacher. You may be sure it is not the pay: I could make more money laying brick and I should not be a victim of the meddling tongues and busy-bodies in that case.
> ... If I believe that my influence were bad or if indeed I were not certain that my influence is strongly and positively for good I should not have [been] teaching all these years. I look upon my work very much I suspect as you look upon yours—as missionary work. Officially I am a teacher of English literature, but in reality my business in life is to wage war on the crude and selfish materialism that is biting so deeply into our national life and character, and I do it by teaching whomever I can lay hands on that the worship of materialism can never make a people either noble or great, but that if we hope to become men we had better study to learn what things produce manhood. Whatever gifts are mine are devoted to teaching the need of a high civic and personal morality: and I mean by morality that integrity of purpose that keeps one upright and just and honorable, and that endeavours to enlarge the realm of sanity and justice and honor in this world.

This remarkably explicit apologia, couched in the context of the criticism of materialism that was spurring on his study of American literature, pleased the Reverend Linebaugh as little as Parrington's reply to the Board of Regents about smoking. Apparently controlled partly by external pressures, the board met a week later, on June 23. Evans was officially elected president, and seven faculty members were terminated, including Lawrence Cole (hired in 1900, the protégé of President Boyd); Henry Daniel Guelich (1903), the head of the School of Fine Arts and professor of music theory; and Roy Philson Stoops (1903), acting dean of the School of Medicine and professor of anatomy. On June 30, Parrington's notice—addressed carelessly to "V. L. Carrington"—was sent by Rowsey, who enclosed a private note expressing regret over Parrington's termination after learning about his work.[27]

Parrington's protégé M. Jay Ferguson had resigned as university librarian in January to assume a position as assistant in the California State Library in Sacramento. By the time the board's decisions were announced, five more faculty members had resigned in protest, including Parrington's English colleague W. R. Humphreys (1903), who had already secured a new position at the University of Michigan; James D. Barnett (1905), the professor of political science and fellow graduate of the College of Emporia; and Parrington's close friend Dr. David C. Hall (1902), the director of physical training and instructor in pharmacology, who would also secure a position at the University of Washington.

President Evans began his administration with twenty-eight new faculty, for while the old teaching staff had been reduced and replaced, additional staff was hired. Parrington's replacement, selected at the same meeting at which he was fired, was Theodore Hampton Brewer, appointed chair of the English Department at the rank of full professor. On paper his academic credentials were no more extensive than his predecessor's: Brewer received both his B.A. (in 1906) and M.A. (in 1907) from Vanderbilt University. (He chaired the department until 1938–39 and taught until his death in September 1940.) Brewer's credentials illustrate that the Board of Regents was not calling into question Parrington's teaching qualifications on the basis of his lacking a Ph.D. It was concerned with his influence over his students in those spellbinding courses, not with his cigarette smoking.[28]

Parrington's shoes were impossible to fill—and neither the board nor Governor Haskell's political creditors wanted them filled. To a degree his influence was carried on in the department by Adelaide Loomis, Parrington's favorite student. Loomis began as a preparatory instructor in 1904 and wrote her B.A. thesis in 1906 on the medievalism of William Morris.

Seeing the writing on the wall, Parrington had not waited for his termination notice to pursue alternative plans. In early June, he had written to his cousin Wesley C. Mitchell, then on a year's leave of absence from the University of Chicago working for the U.S. Immigration Commission in California, to investigate the possibility of openings at Berkeley. The results were negative. Whether he sought other positions that month is not clear, but the expenses of his newly enlarged family and new house demanded decisive action. These responsibilities, in addition to the desire to clear his name, help explain why he fought the patently spurious dismissal charges at all. He later described his eleven years in Norman as filled with "few highlights and much monotone." One wonders, watching his sense of despair and puzzlement over the state of American culture, especially in the Midwest and Southwest, with its emphasis on materialism and business, why he did not leave Norman after returning from Europe.[29]

The university's political upheaval did have the positive effect of forcing him from an environment in which his actions were privately carried on in opposition to the Main Street status quo. But it took a crisis to make him consider other options, as it had taken the deaths of his youthful acquaintances to cut many of his ties to Emporia. Among his last Norman writings are several short sketches of this environment, which appeared as hostile as it had the day eleven years earlier when he walked the wooden planks in searing heat out to the barren campus. One illustrates his sensitivity to speech as a barometer of culture and predicts that fifty years hence the Oklahoma accent will not have been absorbed into a general western accent. (He also abjured his two Oklahoma-born daughters never to imitate the local pronunciation.) In another, he discusses the drive toward statehood in the context of immigration and the effects of breaking with the past, as he had discussed Puritanism in his English XVIII notes.

In a third, he vents the frustrations of his recent struggle, locating their cause in Norman—but in the town and the forces that controlled it, not in the people:

It is fallen into the hands of speculators who are exploiting the land for their own gain.

It is a machine made civilization.

In years to come it will be a good land to live in—today it is not. The life is raw and crude. Why shouldn't a man give himself over to business and politics? There is little to interest. In the winter you have a few plays, for the most part poor. In the summer you have Delmar garden with its melodrama, moving picture shows, and professional baseball. For sports there is driving and for a few, motoring—but unfortunately there is nowhere to drive. There is no country club with golf and tennis, no water, no pleasant roads or charming bits of scenery. There is little music, few intellectual interests, no stirring of the art impulse. Everywhere business, business, business. And to counteract this, there is the church—or rather let us say churches. This southwestern country is religious—surely this will prove to be the leaven that shall leaven this crude mass. What a work stands ready to their hands!

To this bitter conclusion had led Parrington's efforts at transforming himself into the image of William Morris. That image had helped shape not only his external life and his imaginative life but also his classroom life, as glimpsed in this profound and lovely extract from one of those fifteen-minute lectures he delivered to sessions of composition courses:

We are members of a huge guild—a great body of craftsmen seeking to shape the noble thing called English prose. We must serve our apprenticeship to learn what has been found out in long practice of the craft. We might refuse to join the guild and work independently: but that is foolish. We put by the accumulated experience of many workers & fall into elementary mistakes. But there are orders within the guild: the apprentice, the journeyman, the master craftsman. . . . Today everyone must be at least an apprentice.

Parrington had served far beyond his apprentice years at teaching. But at this juncture, when he had every right to vociferate against his profession, his guild, he sketched the following thoughtful stanzas on the back of the

caustic comments on Norman quoted above. The full poem is alternately
titled "The Teacher" and "Apologia Pro Vita Mea."[30]

> What life has taught me with the years
>   That I have counted gain;
> What, open-hearted, I have learned
>   Gladly I teach again.
>
> . . . .
>
> And so the market holds me cheap,
>   And grudges daily bread;
> A teacher poor in other friends
>   Except the noble dead.
>
> I am content. I go my way
>   And teach with open eyes;
> Yet they who hold me in contempt
>   Would fear me were they wise.

Financially and institutionally bereft, Parrington decided to take the advice against working independently delivered to his freshman composition
class. For the second time he considered returning to Harvard for a Ph.D in
English. The day before his official termination notice was addressed, he
wrote to the secretary of the Harvard Graduate School. Parrington briefly
outlined his current dilemma at Norman and the losses caused by the fires
of 1903 and 1907, claiming that most of his European notes had been destroyed. Then he explained that he felt "some of the results" of his composition teaching were "ripe for publication"; that he wanted to develop a
comparative study of how "changes in economics and other conditions" affected American, Canadian, and Australian literature; and that he planned
a thesis on "the influence of the Renaissance upon English prose" that compared developments in architecture and literary style from 1500 to 1800.[31]

When this ambitious project, which he hoped to complete in one year,
and his plea for financial support were rejected, Parrington considered appealing to Irving Babbitt, professor of French at Harvard and dean of the
New Humanist critics. This seems a remarkable step in view of Parrington's
later identification with the socially responsive scholarship of the New
Historians, a group that included James Harvey Robinson, Charles Beard,
and Carl Becker. Parrington would come to hold precisely the opposite
evaluation of Rousseau as Babbitt, who deemed Rousseau and Bacon the
sources of most of the pernicious liberalisms of the tradition-scoffing,
future-oriented present. Yet the socially conservative aestheticism of the
New Humanists did resonate the long-held Arnoldian chord in Parrington's
view of culture, as his 1906 essay "Thoughts on the Teaching of Literature" makes clear. And he had just read Babbitt's volume *Literature
and the American College,* published in 1908, whose first chapter, "What

Is Humanism?" sought to define the very term the Oklahoma professor had seized as the counterbalance to Puritanism.

The part of Parrington reflected in his Populist involvement and enthusiasm for William Morris would prevent him from agreeing, even then, with much of Babbitt's discussion. But at least Babbitt was concerned, as those on Norman's Main Street were not, about an attitude toward life that machine civilization was not fostering. Parrington drafted a letter, first indicating interest in the views expressed in *Literature and the American College,* then venting his frustrations at the professional standards that were evidently closing off his one claim—his Harvard degree—to academic respectability. The years of self-making as well as those of institutional organizing had derailed Parrington from the academic track that was being built at the same time, ironically, as American literature was being included in higher education curricula. "I have a far riper and broader knowledge of my subject," the veteran of fifteen years of full-time college and university teaching wrote,

> than any young doctor whom I have happened to know. Now should all this count for no more than the work of . . . a boy who has just taken his bachelor's degree. The answer of course is that my work was not done under "expert guidance"— it has been merely "undirected study." I shall probably need "training in special research" etc. etc. To all of which I feel very much inclined to reply bosh. . . . I do not take very seriously the big talk about "methodology" and the like.

Having rejected professional standards, which deemed his Emporia master's degree completed "in course" unacceptable as graduate credit, Parrington then took the crucial step of rejecting the acceptable content of English doctorates. Instead of a thesis on the Renaissance and English prose, he proposed "a study of the literary spirit of the middle west." "I know the west," he argued; "I don't want to be forced into work in philology or Anglo-Saxon or Middle English." But the letter, which remained unmailed, ends with the audible tremor, "What shall I do."[32]

What he did do was go farther west, accepting in early August a position as assistant professor of rhetoric at the University of Washington. Washington's president, Thomas Franklin Kane, had visited Norman in July and had dinner with the Parringtons in their new house. Parrington followed that meeting with a letter including a statement of his teaching philosophy: "As my knowledge of English letters ripens into understanding I find myself more & more puzzled how to set before the student the vital ideas of English literature so that they will become a part of his life instead of an incident in his 'education.' And when it comes to capturing for his use the spirit of English prose, I grow even more puzzled."[33] Fortunately, the University of Washington was ready to risk the intellectual and professional independence that Norman and Harvard were not.

Among Parrington's last tasks in Norman was selling the Stuart Forbes dream house, lived in less than a year. One effect of the university upheaval, rationalized as it was by hypocritical piety, was to confirm even more darkly Parrington's attitudes toward dogmatic creeds. The firing further rechanneled his personal struggle with religious doubt and belief into the more broadly based cultural criticism on which rested his new studies in American literature. This process—converting what would have been nineteenth-century religious enthusiasm into what would be twentieth-century social or intellectual activism—was undergone by many other members of Parrington's late Victorian generation. Most, like Parrington, turned to art in their critique of mass society. Art, and for Parrington especially architecture, had framed most of his European and post-grand-tour experience. But he would never again wear so much of his heart on his sleeve.

7

~

Retreat and Advance
First Years at the University of Washington, 1908–1914

The Parrington family arrived in Seattle on Labor Day of 1908. It was Vernon and Julia's first return to the city where they were married almost exactly seven years before. They put Oklahoma behind them forever, along with the dreams invested in the Stuart Forbes house. That summer, serving under a new president and with both his contract termination notice and Harvard graduate school rejection letter in hand, Parrington had endured teaching American literature in Norman's summer session. One can imagine in what a mood he prepared for his English XVIII classes, pondering Roger Williams's *Bloudy Tenent of Persecution,* Jonathan Edwards's *Freedom of the Will,* Irving's struggle to make a living wage, Cooper's distrust of democracy, Hawthorne's tale of a cursed house in *Seven Gables,* Garland's stories of hope and despair on the middle border in *Main-Travelled Roads.* When ten years later Parrington described his eleven Oklahoma years, so crucial in his intellectual and personal development, as containing "few highlights and much monotone," it is evident that the institutional upheaval had pulled a grim, gray curtain across those chapters in his life.[1]

Fortunately, the door to a new position opened in a place holding positive memories, located in a climate the antithesis of Norman's—and remarkably similar to England's. And it opened just at the point when his interests in American literature and culture were revealing new scholarly fields. Seattle thus provided a much needed retreat as well as the setting in which Parrington's American studies would rapidly advance and produce pedagogical and professional growth.

In accepting the position at the University of Washington, Parrington took a cut in pay (from $1,800 to $1,500 annually), a cut in rank (from full professor of English to assistant professor of rhetoric and oratory), and a cut in status.[2] After spending his entire previous career as department chairman, he became simply a member of a department, headed by an austere, Yale-trained Spenser specialist, Frederick Morgan Padelford. These major changes in the structural features of Parrington's job initially produced a more immediate effect on the further focus of his interest in American subjects than new contacts with colleagues in the social sciences such as J. Allen

Smith or the relatively cosmopolitan atmosphere of Seattle. For instead of putting his energies into extracurricular institutional demands, Parrington put them into study and writing. Within five years he would develop two year-long sequences in American literature and begin directing graduate seminars in American topics. Within six years he would be ready to send to New York publishers the major portion of his first full-length book, the nearly 450-page manuscript of "The Democratic Spirit in American Letters, 1620–1870," the one-volume predecessor of *Main Currents*.

A pervasive image of *Main Currents in American Thought* is that it was an isolated product of an isolated mind working at an isolated western academic outpost. Richard Hofstadter has claimed that "Parrington, with his singular vision of his task, his undismayed persistence, and his isolated and unpracticed energy, appears to be less a typical product of the academy than a phenomenon of natural talent, another of those lonely American originals." Ralph Henry Gabriel has argued that "the mid-twentieth century, too owes a debt to the lone explorer who appeared suddenly over the western horizon in 1927 . . . a scholar from the American hinterland." David W. Noble has provocatively described Parrington as "the unknown outsider whose life was almost over . . . a voice crying in the wilderness."[3]

There is a good deal of truth in the image of Parrington as isolated, based on his self-directed studies and avocations and his self-making personal behavior. Washington nurtured both those traits, and Parrington recognized the prices he paid to remain there. But the image is essentially untrue in its implications that Parrington worked outside the currents of contemporary thought, that he lacked professional contacts, and that the university functioned in a static environment. After Norman, Seattle provided a dynamic intellectual, social, economic, and political milieu. It was not Cambridge or New York, but it had its own lively history. It was not the Middle West, but there the westerner in Parrington found a congenial home.

The Seattle Setting

During his first winter in Washington, Parrington wrote his last known poem, an ode to the Alaska-Yukon-Pacific Exposition. At the invitation of the university trustees, who were influenced by a group of prominent Seattle citizens, the exposition was held on the campus, a lovely wooded site on a hill giving a clear view—weather permitting—of the Olympic Mountains and Puget Sound. Founded in 1861, when Washington was still a territory and Seattle had a population of only 302, the university was originally located in a stately two-story frame building in the center of town. The campus was moved to its present location in 1895, when land was purchased north of downtown Seattle near Lake Washington. By the time Parrington came, the student body had outgrown its quarters in Denny Hall and Science Hall. The trustees planned that the structures built for the exposition would be converted, after its close, to classrooms and other facilities.

The construction of the permanent and temporary exposition buildings necessitated the clearing of one hundred acres of the wooded campus. Formal gardens and footpaths were designed to cover the raw spaces between the new buildings, and the present campus layout began to be discernible. By 1915, under the leadership of the newly appointed president, Henry Suzzallo, a new building program was authorized by the state legislature. A committee that included Parrington determined that the general design of the upper quadrangle would follow a Tudor Gothic architectural conception. The new library, to occupy a dominating position between the upper and lower quadrangles, was conceived as "a monumental cathedral-like structure . . . emphasizing in its design the inspiration and the spiritual qualities which should infuse the quest for knowledge."[4] Thus the Alaska-Yukon-Pacific Exposition, which celebrated the growth and achievements of the Pacific Northwest region, gave impetus to the physical and academic development of the university, a development that would precipitate its involvement in several important political and economic events in the early twentieth-century history of the state of Washington.

The story of Washington's economy has largely been the story of the exploitation of its natural resources, especially of its vast timberlands. Spurred on by the post–Civil War dream of westward expansion—the dream that had caused Parrington's father to move to Kansas—nearly one hundred thousand people came into the Washington Territory during the first two years after the Northern Pacific Railroad linked its rails from Lake Superior to the Columbia River and then to Puget Sound in the 1880s. By the time Washington achieved statehood in 1889, these early adventurers and settlers who had been drawn by the lure of fortunes to be made from wheat, lumber, and easily mined mineral deposits were joined by "thousands of capitalists" from banks and offices in New York, Boston, St. Louis, and St. Paul. This latter group of men bought land, planned towns, and called "for the machines that would industrialize their exploitation of an almost untouched wilderness." By 1892 it was rumored that James J. Hill, "the Empire Builder," would bring the main line of his Great Northern Railroad over the Cascades, that Frederick Weyerhaeuser would come from Minnesota to oversee the development of the timber industry, and that John D. Rockefeller wanted to build a second Pittsburgh at Everett (a town just north of Seattle) because of recently discovered iron, coal, oil, and gas deposits.

The Panic of 1893 for a time severely crippled many of these exploitative visions and schemes. But by 1906, when the first plans were made to locate the Alaska-Yukon-Pacific Exposition on the university campus, the expansive spirit had caught hold again in the wake of economic recovery, partially stimulated by the Yukon gold rush of the early 1900s.[5] By then, the spirit of Progressive Era reform had also caught hold in Seattle and at the university.

As one university historian has pointed out, "for some years Washington had been a battleground where questions of land monopoly, railroad regulation, and political manipulation had been fought out," and the university was "regarded as a focal point" for the debate between the forces of exploitation and the conservationists and reformers.[6] Indeed, the university itself was accused of being involved in land speculation, for it derived revenue from the lease of the Metropolitan tract (its original downtown Seattle site) and from the sale of rich timberlands and agricultural lands it owned in three adjoining counties.

The university's governing Board of Regents, the state government, and the Seattle community were generally Republican, pro-business, and conservative. Their inability to tolerate criticism of their political philosophy and economic practices by university students and faculty was illustrated by Governor Albert E. Mead in his 1905 inaugural address in which he expressed fear that "students were being taught to believe 'that our system of government is based upon fallacious principles and should, therefore, ultimately be overthrown.'" Mead also promised, in a veiled reference to J. Allen Smith, that "any instructor 'engaged in the exploitation of such un-American ideas' would be dismissed immediately." Smith had become widely known in the state as a Progressive leader because of his criticism of streetcar franchises, yet he did not aspire to elected office, preferring to make his influence felt through the classroom and research. Governor Mead received letters from Progressive community members testifying to Smith's loyalty and ability; students defended Smith at public meetings; President Kane expressed his respect by allowing Smith to continue teaching and by appointing him dean of the Graduate School four years later in 1909.[7]

Kane had received his Ph.D. from Johns Hopkins in classics and held a chair in Latin at the university before assuming the presidency in 1902. Tolerant of independence of judgment on the part of the faculty and trusting of young people, he treated disciplinary problems arising from student dissent tactfully yet sympathetically. Such leniency, coupled with his handling of problems created by the university's rapid expansion (problems beyond his control because the legislature played a large role in determining policies and directions), weakened the Board of Regents' confidence in him and resulted in his firing in 1914.[8] Kane's difficulties with his own regents are especially ironic in light of the role he played in Parrington's career.

Thus when Parrington came to Washington he was entering a milieu in which such issues as academic freedom, the role of the university in influencing and educating public opinion, the role of the state and corporate interests in controlling the university administration, and municipal reform and other topics central to the Progressive critique of American society were hotly debated. Certainly the author of "Some Political Sketches," written in Emporia just after his first involvement with Populist politics, had found fertile soil to nurture and sharpen his own political sympathies, which had been reawakened by the unjust circumstances of his Oklahoma firing.

The interplay between the Seattle setting and the American literature curriculum Parrington would shortly develop at the university is forecast in his ode to the A-Y-P Exposition. The poem also offers a measure of the impact of characteristic Progressive Era concerns on the political critique that had been maturing, primarily under the model of William Morris, since Parrington wrote the silver sentiment–inspired "As Things Look to Us of the West" back in Kansas in the summer of 1896.

Two versions of the ode survive among Parrington's papers. The shorter, seven stanzas and nearly four pages in length, emphasizes in its conclusion the role of art and imagination in redeeming the human spirit from the greed manifest in the exposition's worship of the god of trade. Here Parrington seems to have taken a geographical step—employing Seattle's physical environment and recent past—but not an ideological one: the solution for twentieth-century exploitation is the Morrisian solution for nineteenth-century exploitation offered in *News from Nowhere*. The longer version, however, which includes ten stanzas and runs to a full six pages, exhibits characteristics of the Progressive political critique, which focused more precisely on urban challenges to democratic theory than did the agrarian-rooted Populism. One of the added stanzas develops this critique in diction compounded of Herbert Spencer, Rebecca Harding Davis, and the former farm boy, and reads like an antithesis to Carl Sandburg's *Chicago Poems* (to be published in 1916):

> Was it for this that we possess the land,
> to rough-hew with a careless hand,
> Despoiling what the centuries held dear?
> Have we no better guidance to our feet
> Than the blind wisdom of the street,
> That bids us in this pleasant place uprear
> A megalosaurian giantry of trade—
> Huge, steam-begotten, toiling all asweat
> To snatch its profits from the smelter's jaws:
> Stoking the giant monster it hath made,
> Unthinking, strong, intolerant of let,
> And bowing only to the dragon's law?
> Surely the god of trade hath made this people mad.
> . . . .
> We have forgot the worth
> Of the fair life of men upon this earth;
> Like spendthrifts we have scorned our heritage,
> Master vulgarians of a vulgar age.

The seventh stanza, almost identical to the other version's fourth stanza, then provides an alternative view, compounded of so much of Parrington's thinking and life-style in his post-grand-tour Norman years:

It was not always so,
For in a wholesome, elder day,
There wandered to and fro
Among the poppy blooms of English lanes,
And in the market-place of walled towns,
The gentle god of artistry.
He came and went like summer rains
Across the pleasant downs,
. . . .
And oftentimes he laughed
To see the workman busy at his craft.

Both versions conclude, after developing the opposition between the god of trade and the god of artistry, with a Ruskinian apostrophe to Seattle to "let not the smoke of traffic blind thy eyes / To the unhasting judgment of the wise" and with pleas for peace and to enwreath life "with unbought loveliness of art." But interposed before this in the longer version is a stanza that suggests a transition in Parrington's intellectual mentors. For Parrington does not hew to the view that art is sufficient to save the masses but widens his scope beyond the national to a vision of international cooperation:

Brave freemen of the world's democracies,
On whose undaunted lip
Abides the ancient cry of fellowship.
To them the coming years belong:
. . . .
For day by day
The stern, unhasting discipline of thought,
Lays bare the law,
And day by day
Long buried loyalties rise in new birth
And walk this troubled earth
To do men good:
Slowly the dragon lusts are beaten down,
Slowly is being wrought
With stern relentless skill
The fabric of a true, imperial state,
Just, wise and strong, to set the beast at naught.

These passages suggest a dim view of essential human nature, and Parrington might rue his use of the term "imperial." But the stress here on the formation of a just, wise, and strong state to control the excesses wrought by the god of trade can be seen as linking Parrington forward to J. Allen Smith's arguments regarding American government rather than backward to Morris's arguments epitomized in "Art and Democracy." Another possible reference to Smith's controlling idea—the contrast between the democratic spirit of the Declaration of Independence and the fundamentally undemocratic law embodied in the Constitution—is contained in the lines "The stern, unhasting discipline of thought / Lays bare the law."

Smith has been seen as the essential catalyst to Parrington's thinking. The unfolding logic of *The Spirit of American Government* clarified and directed Parrington's political sympathies and analysis, providing a structure that similarly explained, for example, the behavior of Emporia's Major Calvin Hood and of the University of Oklahoma Board of Regents. Yet Smith could be a catalyst because Parrington had worked to a parallel solution in his studies of literature and art.[9] He would always, as he confessed in his 1906 essay "Thoughts on the Teaching of Literature," place culture "very high." The central feature of Parrington's years at Washington, especially the initial decade, was the rapprochement between culture—under which concept were now subsumed art and literature—and history, defined in its emerging contemporary sense as incorporating political and economic thought as well as the view that the study of the past was an aid to understanding the present.

Parrington's literature courses had always contained a historical dimension. But history was the stage upon which the drama of culture unfolded. At Harvard he had missed the offerings that might have earlier turned his attention to the political, economic, and social dynamics of American life. Emporia's faculty included no full-time or professionally trained historians or social scientists. Norman's included James "Uncle Buck" Buchanan in history, James D. Barnett in political science, and a few in psychology and education. But the trends in social science training and research being pioneered at Johns Hopkins and debated when the American Social Science Association broke apart in 1906, under the stimulus of the professionalization of individual disciplines, were by contrast far more evident at Washington. As the events of 1907–8 illustrate, Oklahoma could then scarcely be said to value dissenting faculty behavior and opinion, especially if this last veered in the direction of criticizing the impact of commercialization on both the student body and the town.

Although J. Allen Smith provided the primary intellectual and personal model for Parrington during the early years of his Washington tenure, he was only one influence among many on the faculty and, indeed, in the larger community. William Savery, who received his Ph.D. from Harvard in 1899 and came to the university's Philosophy Department in 1902; Edward McMahon, who was hired in the History Department in 1907 after receiving his M.A. from Wisconsin, where he studied under Frederick Jackson Turner; and his wife, Theresa Schmid McMahon, who began teaching political science courses in 1911 after receiving her degree at Washington under Smith, were also recognized as liberal faculty members and became some of Parrington's closest faculty associates. The McMahons, for example, held open house on Friday evenings, "where spirited discussions took place on issues of public interest."[10]

In *Seattle, Past to Present*, Roger Sale has described how the city grew from its founding in 1851 to become the "premier city of the Northwest" during the decades from 1890 to 1910. But the end of World War I also brought the end of the economic boom that had stimulated Seattle's growth. After 1918 "Seattle settled in as a provincial commercial city, content to live off its past achievements and its continuing role as processor and shipper of northwest raw materials—lumber, wheat, fish." During the 1920s "each minor recession was felt hard in Seattle, and the Depression of the thirties laid the city as low as any in the country." Writing of the city's effect on Parrington in a chapter titled "Seattle Between the Wars," Sale observes:

> Seattle in the years of Parrington's maturity still had its own populist tradition, a thwarted one to be sure, but more vital than it could still be farther east. Seattle was not mean and drab, but lush, green, quiet, filled with beautiful houses and invitations to formality and seclusion. That it was static may have been part of its appeal. Here he could settle, and feel both the thwarted romanticism of his frontier populist belief and the quiet formality of his temperament gain strength, direction, flexible life. He lived on 19th Avenue Northeast, in a comfortable house a few blocks from the university, where he worked on his garden and in his greenhouse and on his great book all in the same spirit, quietly and slowly. He did not need what Seattle could not have given him: the abrasiveness or constant challenge of one's peers, the visible signs of an older culture. But from here he could look backward into American history and find more than a buttress for his own thwarted populism, though he could find that too.[11]

This description may fit the Parrington and the city of the 1920s, but it is not an accurate portrayal of the Parrington of 1908. It does not indicate the sense of contrast Parrington must have perceived between the midwestern agrarian provincialism of Emporia and Norman and the bustling commercialism of a seaport city, between a university that apparently fired professors for smoking and dancing and one that generally tolerated, if it did not always foster, the free exchange of ideas. Sale is concerned here with describing Seattle between the wars, and he does not deal with the effect of the prewar city on Parrington or with Parrington's anything but quiet and slow innovations in the English Department curriculum and the classroom.

Radicalism in the Curriculum and the Classroom

When Parrington came to Washington, rhetoric and oratory courses were taught in a separate department from English language and literature. Since he was hired to teach rhetoric, during his initial year (1908–9) he may not have taught courses in the English Department, although one professor is cross-listed in both departments in the catalog printed before Parrington was hired. In the next catalog he is listed as an assistant professor in the English Department, yet he probably continued teaching rhetoric until the departments merged in 1911–12.

The English Department had only four other members and was dominated by the academic interests of its chairman, Frederick Morgan Padelford, the Yale-trained Spenserian who had come to Washington in 1901. The course offerings, like the year before, were heavily weighted toward British subjects such as Medieval Chronicles and Tales, Chaucer and His Contemporaries, Old and Middle English, Shakespeare, the Development of English Drama, and the Victorian Poets. Until then no American literature courses had apparently ever been offered, but that same year Parrington started a new tradition and taught another survey course, simply titled American Literature. The university catalog describes the first semester as "a study of the literary production of America from the settlement of the colonies to the rise of the New England School, emphasis being laid upon the revolutionary writers, upon the beginnings of nineteenth century letters, and upon the Knickerbocker school."[12] The second semester was to be "a study of the New England and Southern Schools, and of later movements in American letters, special consideration being given to the relation between contemporary English and American literary development."[13]

From these beginnings, similar to English XVIII at Norman, Parrington developed more and more diversified American literature offerings at Washington. But he also continued to teach British literature, always maintaining a wide and respectable interest in the entire Anglo-American literary tradition and its various genres. In the 1911–12 academic year, Parrington taught Technique of English Verse, XIX Century Prose Styles, the Georgian Poets, and the Victorian Poets (curiously, these poetry courses were listed in the catalog as "Open to women only") as well as the American sequence. This was the third time Parrington had taught the sequence, and the changed catalog description indicates his increasing familiarity with its materials and consequent refinement of focus. The fall semester was now "a study of the literary production of America before the year 1820, with special attention to social forces and ideals. The greater part of the time will be given to the investigation of puritanism and the beginnings of democracy." The emphasis had shifted from the more purely literary content of 1909–10 and 1910–11 to stress "social forces and ideals," "democracy," and "puritanism," although like H. L. Mencken and other later critics who equated Puritanism with moral rigidity, he did not capitalize the term. The spring semester, likewise reflecting increasing specialization, now focused on "XIX century American culture as revealed in the literature. Special attention will be given to the New England school, to Cooper and Whitman, and to the rise of a literature of democracy." That same year, Loren Milliman, an assistant professor who had begun his Washington career in the Rhetoric and Oratory Department shortly before Parrington and began teaching part-time in the English Language and Literature Department in 1910–11, started offering a major figures sequence that focused on American writers. In the first semester Emerson and Hawthorne were studied, in the second, Longfellow and Lowell.[14]

By 1912–13, the English Department ("Language and Literature" had been dropped from its official appellation) had expanded to thirteen faculty, and Parrington was promoted from assistant to full professor. Milliman continued to teach his sequence on Emerson, Hawthorne, Longfellow, and Lowell. Parrington again taught Technique of English Verse, which included practice in verse writing, "recent English Prose Styles," and the American sequence. In addition, he added a new course: a two-semester sequence called American Literature Since 1870, described as "a study of current literary ideals."[15]

The curricular changes in part reflected the growth of graduate-level studies. Washington's Graduate School was established in 1899 but was not permanently organized until 1911. The first Ph.D., in chemistry, was granted in 1914. The first woman to receive the doctorate, Kate Leila Gregg, an English major, was graduated in 1916. Her thesis title, "Thomas Dekker: A Study of Economic Influences in Literature," indicates that the point of view associated with Parrington, her adviser, was making itself felt in the department. Always one of the largest contributors to graduate enrollment, the English Department had begun offering graduate seminars in British and American topics several years earlier. In 1912 Parrington began offering a graduate seminar which he taught thereafter almost every year. Reflective of his teaching approach, the subject matter was usually determined by the wishes of the students and changed from a focus on American literature since 1890 (in 1914–15 and for several following years) to early American literature (beginning in 1924–25).

During 1913–14, Parrington again offered the two undergraduate sequences. Now listed as American Literature from the Beginnings to 1870 and American Literature Since 1870, they would be taught for the next two years. Their catalog description remained essentially unchanged yet still indicated the basic shift in Parrington's interest away from a purely literary approach and toward treating literature as a repository of ideas and of cultural experience. The early course was fixed as "a study in the development of national ideals. Emphasis will be laid upon the reflection of theological, political, and social movements in literature" and on "the social forces that produced" the body of American literature. The contemporary course, "an introduction to current literary movements and ideals in America," was designed to deal with recent work and "such men as Mark Twain, Howells, Henry James, Riley, Norris, Herrick, and Moody."[16]

Parrington's reading lists included not only assigned texts but related supplementary novels and works of criticism, literary history, historical and political analysis, and articles in current journals such as the *Dial, Yale Review,* and the *New Republic* (founded in 1914). For example, the reading lists for English 19a, American Literature from 1870 to 1890, taught in the fall of 1914, includes selections from George William Curtis's column "From the Easy Chair," written when he was editor of the reform-minded *Harper's Weekly,* and from the poems of Bayard Taylor and suggests the students "sketch" (he means skim) Taylor's translation of Goethe's *Faust.* It lists four novels by Mark Twain and asks that Albert Bigelow Paine's biography of Twain and John Macy's *Spirit of American Literature* be consulted. Students are to read three novels by William Dean Howells as well as his essays in *Criticism and Fiction* and, among other supplementary sources, to consult Émile Zola's *Les romanciers naturalistes,* William Morris's *News from Nowhere,* Bellamy's *Looking Backward,* and H. G. Wells's *Modern Utopia.* Finally, the syllabus includes poets Sidney Lanier and James Whitcomb Riley, a biography of Lanier, stories by Bret Harte, fiction by Thomas Bailey Aldrich, and Paul Elmer More's *Shelburne Essays, Seventh Series.*[17]

The mere teaching of an American literature survey course, at Oklahoma or Washington, placed Parrington in the vanguard of curriculum reformers. But the teaching of contemporary American literature at this early date places him on the cutting edge of innovation. The reigning critical attitude had been clearly expressed by Barrett Wendell in his Introduction to *A Literary History of America,* published just twelve years before Parrington began teaching Washington's contemporary undergraduate sequence and graduate seminar: "Contemporary life is never quite ripe for history; facts cannot at once range themselves in true perspective; and when these facts are living men and women, there is a touch of inhumanity in writing of them as if we had already had the misfortune to lose them . . . so far as our study concerns individuals, we must confine it to those no longer living."[18]

Three years after Parrington began his contemporary sequence appeared Fred Lewis Pattee's *History of American Literature Since 1870* (1915). Pattee's study used the same initial date as Parrington's course, but he paled at discussing authors whose major work was not completed before 1892, under the stimulus of the Civil War years. But the major difference between Parrington and Pattee—who had pioneered in the teaching of and publishing about American literature since 1896—was that Pattee, like Wendell, was concerned with establishing literary value and not with analyzing the culture that literature revealed.

While Wendell and Pattee indeed contributed to raising American literature to the level of college study acceptability, another work—John Macy's *Spirit of American Literature*—was closer in approach and aims to Parrington's in his courses. Published in 1913, Macy's volume shared four-fifths of the title as well as the anticonservative viewpoint toward national sacred cows with Smith's *Spirit of American Government,* which appeared six years earlier. As Parrington's reading lists show, he employed Macy's volume of seventeen critical essays (all but one on general characteristics dealt with figures ranging from Irving to Henry James) as a supplementary source in his contemporary courses.

Macy's position regarding the inclusion of living authors in critical works is irreverently stated in his Preface: "To be sure, the historian avowedly and properly puts emphasis on writers who are dead in the flesh, and finishes off his contemporaries briefly because they are not yet established and are too numerous to mention. But it seems well, in books about literature, not to discuss writers admittedly dead in the spirit, whose names persist by the inertia of reputation." And his attitude toward the acceptable content of American literature is succinctly argued in his chapter titled "General Characteristics":

> Our dreamers have dreamed about many wonderful things, but their faces have been averted from the mightier issues of life. They have been high-minded, fine-grained, eloquent in manner, in odd contrast to the real or reputed vigour and crudeness of the nation. In the hundred years from Irving's first romance to Mr. Howells's latest unromantic novel, most of our books are eminent for just those virtues which America is supposed to lack. Their physique is feminine; they are fanciful, dainty, reserved; they are literose, sophisticated in craftsmanship, but innocently unaware of the profound agitation of American life, of life everywhere. Those who strike the deeper notes of reality, Whitman, Thoreau, Mark Twain, Mrs. Stowe in her one great book, Whittier, Lowell and Emerson at their best, are a powerful minority. The rest, beautiful and fine in spirit, too seldom show that they are conscious of contemporaneous realities, too seldom vibrate with a tremendous sense of life.[19]

Voices like Macy's, in which one can overhear the pre–World War Bohemian accent that characterized such publications as the *Masses,* founded in 1911, were, however, the independent exception rather than the scholarly rule.

During the years from 1909 to 1914, Parrington's thinking is best documented by the changes in emphasis in his American literature courses and by the syllabi and reading lists developed for them. No publications, not even in University of Washington campus organs, exist for this period. There are only a few letters, and his diaries—even in their transmuted form as garden books—remain silent (possibly lost or destroyed) between late April 1908 and late January 1917. Parrington was channeling his energies into finishing a book, on which he drew as he prepared his syllabi and which in turn was fed by his experiences teaching his new American courses. It was not yet titled *Main Currents in American Thought,* although there were many similarities to the later work. Both the new book and courses incorporated materials not usually coupled together in literature classrooms. Parrington might be said to be searching for a way, as John Macy suggested, of striking "the deeper notes of reality."

Syllabi that date from the first two years Parrington taught American literature (1909–11) show that he already had separated the first two hundred years of American history into distinct units and chosen figures who typified prevailing points of view.[20] The first semester was divided into five sections. "The Emigrants (1620–1686)" discussed the English backgrounds of Puritanism, the differences between Congregational and Presbyterian church government, the clash between the Puritan magistrates and the emerging democratic yeomen, the rise of an indigenous culture and the decline of Puritanism, and such figures as John Winthrop, John Cotton, Roger Williams, Anne Hutchinson, Anne Bradstreet, Michael Wigglesworth, and Cotton Mather. "The Fall of the Charter and the End of the Puritan Dream (1686–1725)" dealt with the village world of Samuel Sewall, Mather's defense of the old order, the arrival of Joseph Dudley as a sign of the minister's lack of power, and the rise of a merchant class. The 1725–60 period included sections on doctrinal discussion (Arminianism, Deism), on Jonathan Edwards, the Great Awakening, and Benjamin Franklin. "The Break with England and the Rise of Parties, 1760–1800" included Crèvecoeur, "the shift from theological to political discussion," Sam Adams, John Dickinson, Tom Paine, Philip Freneau, Alexander Hamilton ("philosopher of Federalism"), Jefferson ("philosopher of democracy"), and the Hartford Wits. The last section, "The Beginnings of a National Literature, 1800–1830," studied Charles Brockden Brown and Washington Irving.

The second semester, "Beginnings of the Nineteenth Century, 1820–1840," was not as ambitious. The first section, "The Second Transplanting," discussed the establishment of village democracy in the inland empire. The second section's topic was the rise of the city and the transportation revolution. "The New Sectionalism" described the commercial East, the aristocratic South, and the democratic West. "Changing Social Ideals" dealt with "the ideal of material progress" and manifest destiny and "The Jacksonian Revolution" described how village democracy triumphed over "the 18th century ideal of gentlemen serving as trustees." "The New Literature" was treated as "the product of a maturing civilization; not the record of current change" and as examples cited James Fenimore Cooper ("A Whig Squire at War with Village Democracy") and William Cullen Bryant ("The poet of a decaying puritanism").

By the spring semester of 1912, the third time Parrington had taught this sequence, in addition to Cooper and Bryant he included Edgar Allan Poe ("The Artist"), Henry Wadsworth Longfellow ("The poet of emerging New England culture"), Nathaniel Hawthorne ("Literary flower of Puritanism"), and Ralph Waldo Emerson ("The emancipated soul of Puritanism") and expanded the time period from 1840 to 1860. He also added a section that covered the period 1850 to 1890, which was to include James Russell Lowell (significantly, in light of his later Oklahoma thinking, called "The Humanist"), Walt Whitman ("The Leveler"), Mark Twain (" 'The Lincoln of our Literature' "), William Dean Howells ("The Flowering of American Culture"), and James Whitcomb Riley ("The Poet of Jacksonian Democracy"). Parrington here considered figures—Whitman, Twain, Howells, Riley—who would be treated in the third volume of *Main Currents*. But with this exception and his failure to deal with southern writers, the first and second semesters of this sequence, respectively, correspond fairly closely to the first two volumes of *Main Currents*.

By 1914–15, Parrington supplied an introduction for his first semester syllabus that highlights its ideological thrust:

I. The Study of literature: (1) As a record of individual aspiration; (2) As an art product; (3) As a phase of Kulturgeschichte—the record of social forces and ideals.

II. Back of the cultural is the economic; civilization an expression of the master group. Social equality follows economic equality, and social inequality follows economic inequality.

III. The creative ideal in American life the ideal of democracy. The problem therefore to determine: (1) How the economics of America have conditioned the growth of the democratic ideal; (2) To what extent American literature reflects this democratic drift. Two phases: The literature of democratic propaganda and the literature of aristocratic protest.

IV. Four great periods of democratic advance: (1) Puritan democracy—Rhode Island; 1630–1650; (2) Agrarian democracy, culminating in the appeal to arms—1720–1783—and followed by the reaction—1785–1800; (3) The rise of Jacksonian democracy—1820–1840—and the reaction following upon slavery agitation; (4) The struggle for industrial democracy—1870–1915.

The syllabus for the second semester also contains some significant changes. Parrington now included Daniel Webster ("Defender of the Constitution") in the section "The Beginnings of a National Literature," and he added a seventh section, "The Mind of New England, 1830–1870," discussing Transcendentalism and Emerson (now called a "Spiritual Democrat"). Although the South was still omitted, the outlines of Books Two and Three of *The Romantic Revolution* were beginning to emerge. Even more clear was the direction that Parrington's book, titled similarly to Macy's and Smith's works—"The Democratic Spirit in American Literature: 1620–1870"—was taking in its interpretation of the relations between art and democracy.

Parrington's continued active and respectable interest in the entire Anglo-American literary tradition, as evidenced by his teaching of various British and prose style courses, did not forestall the division of the English Department into two camps. The "nontraditionalists"—generally younger professors who were interested in American literature and as yet unsanctioned methodological approaches—became identified with Parrington. The "traditionalists"—generally older professors who taught British literature and adhered to an aesthetic approach—became identified with Frederick Morgan Padelford, the department chairman. From 1912 until 1916, Parrington and Padelford were the only full professors in the department. Until Parrington's death in 1929, when four more professors had achieved full professorial status out of a department that had grown to twenty-eight members, excluding graduate assistants, he was the only Americanist who ever attained full rank, although the only two associate professors (Milliman and Joseph B. Harrison, who admired Parrington and assumed some of his courses) were also American specialists.

The divisional lines seem to have been drawn on the basis of personality and possibly attitudes toward students, as well as on areas of specialization and approaches to subject matter. Students were prone to say "they just love Mr. Parrington" and to remark about "his wonderful hair and his charming manners." In this respect, there had been no change since the professor's days at the College of Emporia or the University of Oklahoma, even though he now had almost entirely withdrawn from nonclassroom campus activities. In contrast, Padelford has been characterized as "tall and thin and New Englandish. . . . A very good teacher but not a warm person." Parrington, however, could hardly be described as outgoing; rather, as in his former positions, he was "a person who kept sort of alone, but had more of a relationship with students than with other faculty members." One former Washington professor has stressed that although Parrington might have appeared "wild and woolly" in his political opinions and classroom technique, "he was really a very courtly guy who conducted himself with finesse"; and another has described him as an "Aristocrat and Artist."[21]

But perhaps the major difference between the two men was that Parrington, like his father, was "stubbornly independent, refusing to toady, not taking orders well," while Padelford manifested the characteristics that made him a longtime department chairman (1901–20), a longtime dean of the Graduate School (1920–42), and a president of the Modern Language Association (in 1942, the year of his death). Parrington did not relish administrative tasks, even though he had been a department chairman for fifteen years before coming to Washington. Padelford was the kind of scholar, loyal to the interests of the guild, who would edit the *Variorum Edition of the Works of Edmund Spenser;* Parrington was the kind of scholar, restive with conventional disciplinary boundaries, who would win a Pulitzer Prize in History.

Parrington's growing radicalism in political and social thinking did not go entirely unnoticed either in the English Department or on the campus at large. Yet there is very little substantiated evidence of his political opinions, outside of his new book manuscript, until he began publishing book reviews on such topics in the early 1920s. Nor is there verifiable evidence of participation in political affairs during his Washington years. Like J. Allen Smith, he preferred to make his influence felt through the classroom.

During these years many events did occur, both on the university campus and in the state of Washington, that undoubtedly further shaped Parrington's convictions. For example, in the spring of 1912 the university students wanted to bring political speakers to campus. The Board of Regents denied the request. President Kane, who opposed the cutting off of political discussion, was forced to explain to them that only a few students could vote and that politicians might "take advantage of the rights of free speech." The students protested the decision on the grounds that a university should encourage interest in civic affairs. The regents subsequently allowed nonpartisan meetings to be held, but the students were still unsatisfied and "staged some kind of 'strike,' " then decided to hold meetings off campus where the content could not be controlled.[22]

The issues surrounding the election of 1912 worked themselves into a section of one of Parrington's course syllabi called "Democracy and Literature in America." The document first explains how democracy developed in America "not as a result of conflict, in the midst of a complex society, but as the natural expression of a decentralized society" that was shaped by the "leveling environment" of the frontier and thus possessed "the social philosophy of the frontier." With the passing of the fluid frontier environment, "this hereditary democracy has outlived the conditions which brought it forth" and "is now facing the problem of carrying over into a complex world the independence, the equality, the equity, the friendliness, created by the frontier and the village." In addition to citing these positive traits (perhaps reflective of his experience in Americus and Emporia), Parrington criticizes the frontier philosophy for manifesting "a crude anti-social individualism, an inadequate social ideal, the provincialism of inexperience" (these traits perhaps reflective of his experience in Norman). Then he comes to the core of the matter:

> In the presence of the new industrialism, our ancestral democracy, grown profoundly conservative during three hundred years of unchallenged development ... must equip itself with a new philosophy suited to the new centralization ... against the new plutocracy, it is pitting the ideal of equity, the "square deal." But socialized equity means socialism. Unconsciously this anti-social democracy of a primitive decentralised society, in order to preserve its deepest instinct, is moving toward a bourgeois socialism, under the leadership of Mr. Roosevelt.[23]

Here Parrington refers to Theodore Roosevelt's leadership of the Bull Moose party, whose 1912 platform incorporated the Progressive principles that the university students wanted to hear debated. The "Democracy and Literature in America" syllabus contains one of the most explicit statements of the mission of Progressive reform—how to carry over into a complex world the positive traits of a democratic theory derived from the experience of a simpler world—that Parrington had yet made. In Kansas, he had witnessed the effects of the encroachment of business practices on the agrarian economy of the once primitive Middle Border. Now in Washington he could perceive how another simple society was being made over by industrialization and how both former frontiers needed to develop a new political theory that could preserve the "solid gains" of democracy while adapting to the complexities of the early twentieth century.

Meanwhile, Parrington's personal life had its own complexities and joys. Less than a year after the move to Seattle, in early April 1909, seventy-nine-year-old John William Parrington became gravely ill. His youngest son rushed back to Emporia but arrived the morning after the Judge died. "I wished I might help you in your sorrow," Julia wrote. The household became increasingly though happily cramped in late April 1913, when a long-awaited son, Vernon Louis Parrington, Jr., was added to the family. Then in 1914, Julia's father committed suicide. Her parents had earlier moved to Seattle, and now Mrs. Williams came to live with her eldest daughter and son-in-law, thus reestablishing the living arrangements that had prevailed through most of Parrington's Norman years. Daughters Elizabeth and Louise were old enough to remember summers spent at "Camp," the colony of faculty cabins across Puget Sound near Kingston, after their father was asked to join the University Outing Club during his second year. Seven families eventually owned parcels of Camp, including the Padelfords, and each moved its entire household via moving van and ferry out of the city in June. Departmental dissensions and tensions were set aside in these months of nearly communal living.[24]

Parrington usually taught during the summer sessions and commuted to the Outing Club property on weekends. There he could swim, potter around the cabin, plant yet another garden, and roam in the woods. Camp became his new frontier. He was also finishing his new book, and he would soon begin thinking about a new scholarly identity, as a historian rather than a literature professor alone.

8

∼

Democracy, Economics, and Literature

1914–1918

The Democratic Spirit in American Letters, 1620–1870

In late June 1914, Parrington received word from R. R. Smith, manager of the Macmillan Company's College Department, that Macmillan was "very favorably impressed by the scholarly character" of the completed portion of "The Democratic Spirit in American Letters, 1620–1870." But the company was unwilling to undertake the risk and expense of publishing the work according to the author's present design.[1] Over the next ten years, this manuscript—in several substantially altered versions—would rate similar comments from half a dozen other editors. But Parrington persisted, as he had not with earlier projects of lesser scope, the poems he privately labored over during a period of crisis in his late twenties and the unfinished novel that occupied so many hours of his 1903–4 European sojourn. By the decade's close he held a publishing contract in his hand.

That contract applied to a study trebled in length over its 1914 progenitor, the work of a man who saw American culture through the dark lenses of post–World War I disillusion rather than the bright promise of Progressive Era optimism. *Main Currents in American Thought* was more complexly argued and organized, because its author was wiser and more troubled, than "The Democratic Spirit in American Letters." The change was paralleled by the difference between Parrington's mid-1890s Populism and his post-grand-tour view of the relations between art and democracy. The former was shot through with the sharp, single-minded purpose of youth; the latter manifested the virtues of study, exposure, and synthetic analysis. Much was gained in the transition, but something irreplaceable was lost. To use Parrington's own later formulation, romantic idealism gave way to critical realism.

Parrington had sent R. R. Smith (the two had met when Smith stopped at the University of Washington on his way through Seattle that spring) the completed manuscript of the first volume of a projected two-volume work and the table of contents for the proposed second volume. It was the two-volume plan that gave Macmillan pause. Smith provided two options: Parrington might resubmit the manuscript after the second volume was

1. Vernon Louis Parrington (right), age five, and his brother John M. Parrington, age eight. Photograph taken in Chicago in June 1877.

2. Stuart Hall at the College of Emporia, Emporia, Kansas, where Parrington was first a student and later a faculty member.

31. Parrington en route to Europe in spring 1929. He died while in England that June.

32. After Parrington's death, the University of Washington honored his memory by renaming the old Science Hall, built in 1901, as Parrington Hall. It was dedicated August 3, 1931, the

3. Parrington in 1893 at Cambridge, Massachusetts, while attending Harvard.

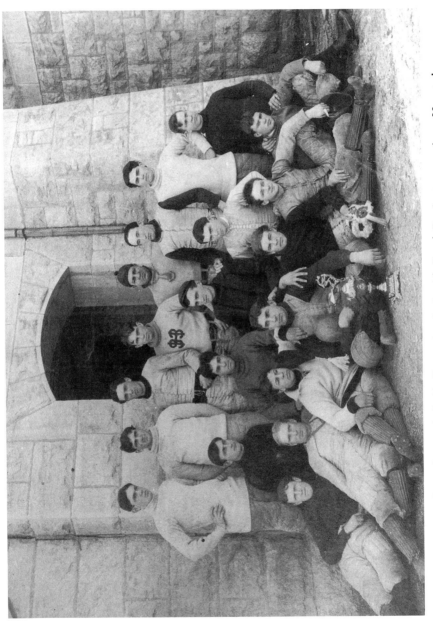

4. The College of Emporia football team in 1896, with Coach Parrington wearing a Harvard "93" shirt (middle of back row).

5. Vernon's brother John M. Parrington at Emporia, Kansas, circa 1899.

6. Louise McClellan Parrington, Vernon's mother, in February 1899.

7. John W. Parrington, Vernon's father, at his farm outside Americus, Kansas, in March 1900.

8. The family farmhouse, with John W. Parrington seated on steps, April 1900.

9. The new University of Oklahoma at Norman, Oklahoma Territory, as it looked when Parrington began his teaching years there in 1897.

10. A scholar's retreat. Parrington's study in Norman.

11. Vernon Parrington at work in his study, circa 1900.

12. Parrington as hunter, in camp in the Keechi Hills near Gray Mountain, Oklahoma, December 1899.

13. Julia Williams (center), who married Vernon Parrington in July 1901, with her mother, Louise Stewart Williams, and younger sister Eloise. Photograph taken circa 1901.

14. The young wife and mother Julia Williams Parrington with her daughter Elizabeth, September 1902.

15. Julia Parrington, circa 1903.

16. The Williams family house in Norman, Oklahoma, around 1904. Vernon and Julia began married life here.

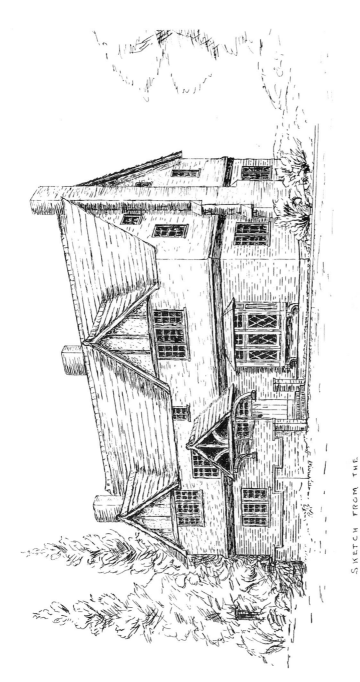

SKETCH FROM THE
SOUTHEAST

17. In 1906 Parrington drew sketches and plans for the house he and Julia built in Norman the following year.

CORNER OF LIVING ROOM

AUGUST 3 '06

18. Parrington dated his sketch of a corner of the living room August 3, 1906, his thirty-fifth birthday.

19. Vernon Louis Parrington, around the age of thirty-five, at Norman.

20. Commencement 1909 at the University of Washington, Seattle. Parrington, at right, is with his friend Dr. David C. Hall.

21. Parrington holds his newborn son, Vernon Louis Parrington, Jr., in 1913.

22. The Parrington children at "Camp," near Kingston, Washington, around 1916. Left to right are Vernon, Louise, and Elizabeth holding Philip Padelford on her lap.

23. The summer colony "Camp" near Kingston was a gathering place for members of the University of Washington Outing Club and their families. Parrington is at front left, his daughter Louise is second from left in the middle row with Julia right behind her. Vernon, Jr., is at center (face turned away from the camera), and behind him is his grandmother, Louise Parrington, Vernon's mother. Photograph taken circa 1916.

24. The Parrington children pose for the camera around 1920. Left to right are Louise, Elizabeth, and Vernon, Jr.

25. Summers at Camp gave Parrington a chance to garden (shown here in the early 1920s).

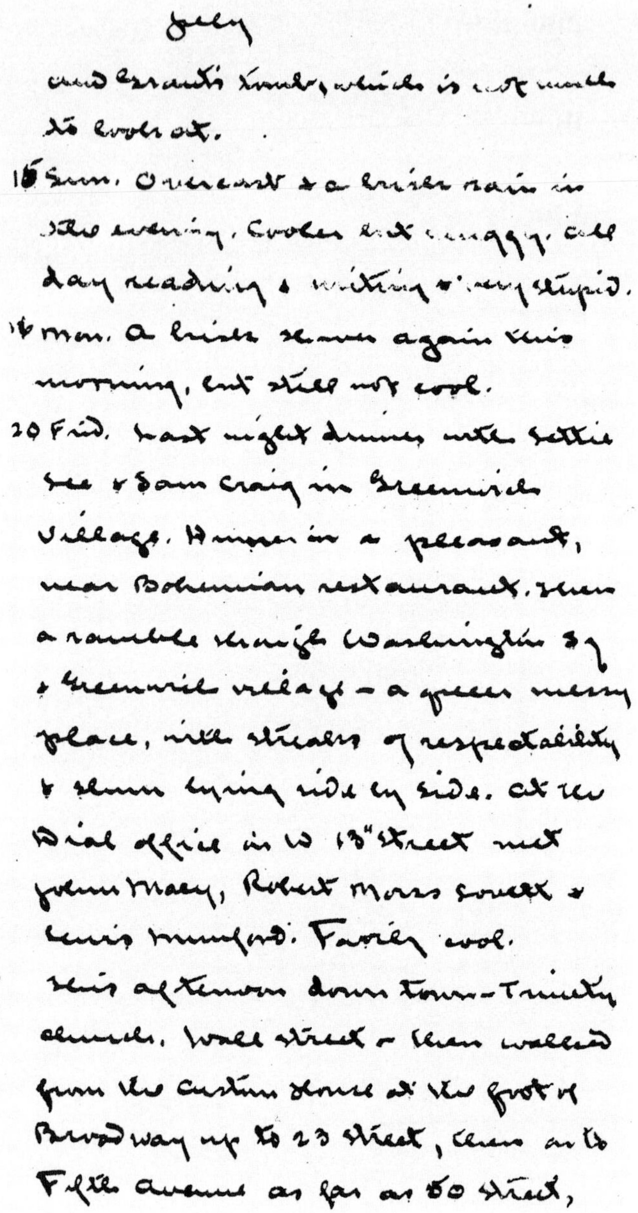

July

[handwritten journal entry in cursive]

26. Sample of Parrington's handwriting, taken from his 1923 journal.

27. Enjoying Seattle's snow are Parrington and his daughter Louise, around 1927.

28. The dapper scholar V. L. Parrington on Mt. Ranier, Washington, circa 1928.

29. Julia and Vernon Parrington on Mt. Ranier.

30. Vernon Louis Parrington at the peak of his career, shortly after earning the Pulitzer Prize in History in 1928.

completed, or he might follow the literary adviser's suggestion "that the material in the present volume be very considerably condensed so that the entire work might appear in a single volume." At Parrington's request, Smith forwarded the details of the adviser's comments:

> It is an able book, well planned and well written, and deserves publication. I cannot, however, see any chance for a considerable sale. This colonial history has been raked fore and aft many times, and of late there have been some efforts to change the balance of judgment in favor of the forerunners of democracy and against the aristocrats and theocrats. The author's development of this point of view seems too elaborate and too detailed to win any attention. If he had written a brief book on his subject, he could have dealt with all the colonial persons in 50 pages, and then gone on to trace the continued growth of democratic spirit in later periods. As it is, a good deal of his book seems rather beside his subject, and other portions too much in the nature of a doctor's dissertation: there is also necessarily a good deal of repetition. For example, in talking about democracy among the Puritans, he has only one Puritan among the early emigrants who had any notion of democracy, that was Roger Williams; but many pages are given up to the discussion of Winthrop, Cotton, Hooker, Elliot [sic], and the others, simply because they were opposed to democracy.[2]

The adviser's opinion helped forestall the appearance of what might have been one of the more richly textured, multidisciplinary efforts of the immediate prewar years. As the final sentence illustrates, what the adviser found weak was the strength of "The Democratic Spirit in American Letters" and later of *Main Currents:* the debatelike quality of its structure. This quality stemmed from Parrington's perception of the way ideas were played out in the political (e.g., the Constitutional Convention) and cultural (e.g., the work of the Hartford Wits and H. H. Brackenridge) spheres. The "efforts to change the balance of judgment in favor of the forerunners of democracy and against the aristocrats and theocrats" included J. Allen Smith's *Spirit of American Government* (1907) and more recently Charles A. Beard's *Economic Interpretation of the Constitution of the United States* (1913), the latter published by Macmillan. Under Macmillan's aegis had also appeared the adventure tales and socialist-influenced novels of Jack London as well as James Harvey Robinson's pathbreaking essays collected in *The New History* (1912) and Herbert Croly's *Promise of American Life* (1909) and *Progressive Democracy* (1915). No wonder Parrington hoped for a sympathetic reading. But none of these "raked" colonial history "fore and aft." That job was presumed unnecessary, even as late as the mid-1930s, when at Harvard Perry Miller began his reexamination of Puritan theology that culminated in *The Seventeenth Century* (1939), the first volume of *The New England Mind*.[3]

Macmillan was no doubt correct in its estimation of the public's and the college's dull appetite in 1914 for the thorny dogmatics of the colonial past and keener taste for the triumphs of democracy in the still rosy glow of the nineteenth century. Thus Parrington's title and the positive side of his manuscript appeared compatible with the view of the company and much of the nation, concurrently witnessing the presidential campaign of Woodrow Wilson, optimistically believing the world could be made safe for democracy. Parrington would vote for Wilson in November, but he hardly believed democracy was safe. To him, it was and always had been the radical cutting edge of politics, economics, and culture, always on the defensive against the encroachments of power and the vested interests threatening that fragile construct, the will of the people. That was why he had begun his book. His regular teaching of American literature survey courses ensured continual contact with the past as he traced the history of American literary production. But Parrington was as thoroughly immersed in the present as any of his contemporaries as a result of his innovative teaching of recent American literature.

Parrington knew and valued the double vision of the critic. He should have been innured to the adviser's suggestions. Perhaps he was not because of a lingering lack of confidence in his professional training: in some ways "The Democratic Spirit in American Letters" was his doctoral dissertation. Parrington followed the spirit of the suggestions but not the letter. He reduced his manuscript to a single volume, but he did so by cutting the final half of the proposed second volume, effectively bringing his story down only to the close of the Civil War instead of to 1885 as originally planned.

Completing the retained half of the second volume and slightly revising and expanding the original first volume occupied Parrington until the spring of 1916. Resubmitted to Macmillan, the manuscript met the same fate as its predecessor, although this time primarily on the grounds that "present manufacturing costs are abnormally high, the increases above normal ranging from 20% to as high as 80%" and the near impossibility of obtaining paper at any price. Smith did tender a publication offer under the condition that Parrington assume part of the expenses. This was not feasible on a professor's slim salary, now stretched to support three children, a wife, and a mother-in-law. A few weeks later, cautious but not undaunted, Parrington wrote to Houghton Mifflin asking whether there was enough possibility of publication to warrant sending "The Democratic Spirit" to Boston. The firm was "not entirely sanguine of our ability to make a publishing success" of Parrington's book, and nothing resulted from that brief negotiation.[4]

It is difficult to guess what else might have been involved in Houghton Mifflin's and Macmillan's decisions. We are on much firmer ground in identifying Parrington's intentions in writing his book. The introduction, boldly titled "Democracy, Economics, and Literature," concludes with the declaration: "To aid in democratizing our history by giving to the open facts of our literature a democratic instead of a tory or Whiggish interpretation, is the underlying purpose of the following pages. Whether such an interpretation is true or false to the spirit of American life, is not for the writer to determine." The final sentence is a misleading disclaimer to a crusading volume built upon the following plan:

> It is to concern ourselves mainly with the dramatic periods, fastening attention upon the great proponents of democracy, inquiring into their hopes and considering their programmes, judging them by the standards of the world through which they moved. We shall summon their chief opponents to challenge their arguments, and endeavour to understand wherein they succeeded and wherein they fell short of their hopes. Such an investigation, surely, is worthwhile if, as we are coming more and more to see, the democratic ideal is the great end and aim towards which American society has been tending from the first and which it must eventually realise if it is to be true to itself.[5]

Parrington chose five "dramatic periods" during 1620 to 1870 around which to organize his materials and arguments: "the period of incipient Puritan democracy" ("the story of the old-world democratic hope brought to America, and what came of it"); "the period of Revolutionary aspirations" ("the story of a raw colonial democracy coming to blows with old-world toryism"); "the period of the constitutional struggle" ("the story of the conscious alignment of agrarianism and capitalism in the great struggle over the control of the government"); "the period of Jacksonian aggression" ("the story of the new agrarianism of the West and how it was submerged by the struggle over slavery and the rise of modern industrialism"); and "the period of transcendental propaganda" ("the story of radical idealisms, rising from the ashes of Puritan dogma, to re-order the world").

He explains that these dramatic high points of struggle and conflict at most significant "to the historian of democratic radicalism," whereas "the historian of *belles lettres*" would find the less dramatic times in between—calmer periods more productive of culture—most important. After giving a capsule summary of English literature, Parrington states that American literature has repeated its predecessor's history with spans of peacetime producing belles lettres and times of rebellion producing hardier, more serviceable writing. Then he hammers his point home, asserting that, as a result, American literature is

> prevailing undemocratic, an expression of the forces which have persistently opposed the democratic advance. . . . The impulse to radicalism has come from the back-country; the impulse to literary creation has come from the coast centres of wealth. Our democratic ideals are native to the new-world environment; our literary culture is largely alien, an importation of foreign ideals. The hero of our literature has rarely been the frontiersman with his gospel of levelling, or the free-hold farmer with his agrarian economics. . . . It has been curiously unresponsive to the actualities of our American life. . . . In the total body of our

literature the democratic record is small in quantity and too rarely distinguished by excellence. Such as it is, however, it has preserved the democratic hope through evil days as well as good; and he who wishes to hear the authentic voice of America, speaking in native accents, must seek out the record where it lies covered with the dust of neglect, and read it in the light of our economic history. Whoever thus reads it will discover to his surprise that in such neglected records beats the living heart of radical America.[6]

This paragraph epitomizes the Parrington of 1914–18, the world war years during which he fought his own battles on the classroom front on behalf of "the authentic voice of America." Parrington at this point clearly identified "radical" with "democratic." Certainly his autobiography—his experience at elite, coastal Harvard, with Kansas Populism, with laboratory-loving Oklahoma undergraduates—can be deduced from this section of the introduction to "The Democratic Spirit in American Letters." All of this is much more transparent than when he composed the measured phrases of the prefaces to *The Colonial Mind* and The *Romantic Revolution in America* and eliminated the term "radical" in favor of "liberal" in their texts.

Despite major changes in political and cultural attitudes that produced both structural and thematic differences between "The Democratic Spirit" and *Main Currents,* Parrington's theoretical view of the relationship of literature to culture remained constant. "It is a truism that the masters of society in every generation make the law, and shape the institutions, and determine the culture," he announced. "Before a different social ideal can prevail, not only must it wrest supremacy from the present masters, but it must remake the law, and reshape the institutions, and recreate the culture; and it is not until these secondary triumphs have been achieved, not until the creative spirit of the new has permeated society as a whole, that it rises into spontaneous expression in literature."[7] This view was obscured in "The Democratic Spirit" by its urgent political equation of radical with democratic and in *Main Currents* by its focus on the evolution of ideas. For Parrington, literature was a touchstone that measured prior changes in the cultural, social, and political environments. As a critic he believed that art, at the moment of production, was not a weapon but a mirror. As a historian he believed that mirrors made in the past could serve as weapons in the battle to understand the present. As a critic he was thus less encumbered by environmental determinism and cultural relativism than he often was in his role as a historian. But it was being a historian that excited him and made the crucial difference in the scale and quality of his scholarly achievements after the mid-1910s.

After reading the Macmillan adviser's report, Parrington had eliminated the fourth book of "The Democratic Spirit," which covered 1865–85 and was titled "Democracy and Capitalism." This section was nearly identical to what Parrington covered in his University of Washington contemporary literature course, which he began teaching in 1914 and which treated the 1870–90 period. Parrington therefore cut the most "radical"—in the sense of challenging prevailing literary standards—part of his manuscript. It was a fatal choice, for Parrington then delayed Book Four's subject matter to what became the third volume of *Main Currents,* which was incomplete at his death. Five portraits—of Walt Whitman, Henry George, Mark Twain, William Dean Howells, and William James—were to be included, along with chapters titled "The New Spirit and the Old Culture" and "The New Nationalism" as well as a conclusion to the entire work. From these proposed chapters Parrington saved only the one on Whitman ("Prophet of Democracy"). He grafted this onto Book Three ("Democracy and Individualism, 1800–1865," primarily treating New England and the South) as a final section called "The Flowering of Individualism."

This rearrangement served to disguise an obvious similarity to Barrett Wendell's *Literary History of America,* published fourteen years earlier. Wendell's study also concluded with a section containing a portrait of Whitman and four other chapters: "New York Since 1857," "Literature in the South," "The West," and "The Present Time." Parrington's book can, in fact, be read as a point-by-point refutation of his former professor's opus. Certainly this is true of the Whitman chapter. Parrington's opinion is largely signified in his titles, "The Flowering of Individualism" and "Walt Whitman—Prophet of Democracy"; Wendell's in the patrician observation that Whitman's "literary anarchy" is a reflection of political confusion that goes against the tide of American common sense. The older critic claims that the poet's "conception of equality, utterly ignoring values, is not that of American democracy, but rather that of European. His democracy, in short, is the least native which has ever found a voice in this country. The saving grace of American democracy has been a tacit recognition that excellence is admirable."[8]

One way Parrington gained his intellectual independence was to hone his ideas on a Harvard whetstone. As a B student in Wendell's English 12 course, he had endured his professor's withering comments on several creative efforts and had swallowed wholeheartedly his critical judgments. Parrington was in a position now to fight page with page, chapter with chapter. That he had *A Literary History of America* in mind as a model, if not as a foil, is evidenced by a penciled note across the top of one of his preliminary tables of contents for "The Democratic Spirit": "Manuscript runs about 415 words to a page. At 330 words to the printed page, the size of Wendell's *Literary History of America,* a book of 600 pages would require 480 pages of manuscript." Parrington evidently planned to best Wendell in both theme and length, for Wendell's book contains not 600 but 530 pages of text.

In the form that it reached R. R. Smith in 1916, "The Democratic Spirit" ran to approximately 442 pages, with the intended average of about 415 words to a page. The text was distributed over its three large divisions with Books One and Two roughly corresponding to the first volume of *Main Currents* and Book Three to the second. Book One, "Puritanism and Democracy, 1620–1720," was eighty-eight pages in length and contained one thematic chapter and seven portraits (of Roger Williams, Thomas Hooker, John Cotton, John Winthrop, John Wise, Cotton Mather, and Samuel Sewall). After 1916, sections of the early manuscript were taken apart, reorganized, and expanded as Parrington's purposes and political viewpoint changed.

An example of Parrington's changing political emphasis is the chapter on Roger Williams, the one Puritan among his selection in Book One "who had any notion of democracy," according to the Macmillan literary adviser. Of course, Williams occupies a place of primacy in *Main Currents*. Parrington specifies in the Introduction to Volume 1 that "the line of liberalism in colonial America runs through Roger Williams, Benjamin Franklin, and Thomas Jefferson."[9] Labeled a "Seeker" and treated in a section detailing "The Puritan Heritage, 1620–1660," and a subsection discussing "The Contributions of Independency," Williams is portrayed as one voice in the colonial religio-political conversation, the voice of theological liberalism and independence in political as well as religious matters. Along with Thomas Hooker, he is contrasted to the theologically conservative and more institutionally committed voices of John Winthrop and John Cotton. In "The Democratic Spirit," however, Williams's portrait is not only hung prominently as the first chapter but also assigned the epithet "Puritan Radical," the only one to achieve the distinction of a variant of "radical" in Book One. (John Wise does earn a close second with "Village Democrat.") Williams is grouped with Hooker, Cotton, and Winthrop in a section whose title, "The Old-World Democratic Hope, 1620–1640," indicates a more overt preoccupation with the relations between theological bent and political practice.

Such structural differences are an index to the more complex development and careful argument of *Main Currents*. But with one as concerned professionally and personally with writing style as Parrington, the shift in political emphasis—the change in the urgency of his theme—is immediately recognizable by a shift in tone. The opening sentence of "The Democratic Spirit," and of the Williams chapter, is designed to shatter traditional expectations regarding the New England past: "There is possibly no episode in early colonial history better known than the banishment of Roger Williams from the godly precincts of Massachusetts Bay." Having sounded the rebel yell, Parrington brandishes his bayonet, polished to hyperbolic brightness:

> This stormy petrel came out of England, fluttered and clamoured for a while about Boston and Salem, and after arousing many a vexatious perturbation in

the breasts of good and honest men, was driven away to find what resting place he might, there to bring forth according to his kind . . . . the shrewd leaders of Massachusetts Bay read the purpose of Roger Williams more clearly, and discovered in his motives a more significant intention than later men have commonly seen: they saw in this advocate of religious toleration a social rebel, one who had lifted up his hand against all established authorities, who would have no others rule over him, and who dared to go out as a single David to make war upon the principle of absolutism in state as well as church. An agitator notable in a generation that bred a surprising number of agitators, a dreamer and idealist significant in an age that fed largely upon dreams and ideals, this lonely emigrant whose enthusiams brought so many trials upon his devoted head, . . . must be accounted the most prophetic figure thrown upon the American coast by the social forces then laboring in the bowels of England.[10]

The 1914 Williams bears resemblance to his creator, who identified with "a single David" in several Oklahoma-vintage poems and felt like a "lonely emigrant whose enthusiams brought so many trials upon his devoted head." He would also, it seems, make good copy for *The Masses,* a journal with which Parrington was sufficiently familiar. The diction of the passage—"social rebel," "agitator," "social forces"—links it to the pre–World War I terrain inhabited by Jack Reed, Big Bill Heywood, and frequenters of Mabel Dodge's Greenwich Village salon. The chapter continues in this rhapsodic vein, dealing in generalities rather than specifics, quoting little other of Williams's writings than *A Bloudy Tenent of Persecution.*

The 1927 Williams is still most significant as an embodiment of the principle of rebellion, "a rebel against all the stupidities that interposed a barrier betwixt men and the fellowship of their dreams." But Parrington tempered his prose with the times, and Williams emerges as a nascent supporter of the League of Nations: "A humane and liberal spirit, he was groping for a social order more generous than any theocracy— . . . greater than sect or church, village or nation, embracing all races and creeds, bringing together the sundered societies of men in a common spirit of good will."

Parrington's discussion is rooted more firmly in Williams's texts and thought, with the majority of the *Main Currents* chapter focusing on his ideas, supporting the claim that Williams was "primarily a political philosopher than a theologian." By the time he wrote *Main Currents,* the philosopher rather than the agitator was of more interest to Parrington, and it is as an ironic observer rather than as an enthusiastic partisan that Parrington writes the later 1927 Williams's opening message:

> The gods, it would seem, were pleased to have their jest with Roger Williams by sending him to earth before his time. In manner and speech a seventeenth-century Puritan controversialist, in intellectual interests he was contemporary with successive generations of prophets from his own days to ours. His hospitable mind anticipated a surprising number of the idealisms of the future. As a transcendental mystic he was a forerunner of Emerson and the Concord school. . . .

as a speculative Seeker he was a forerunner of Channing and the Unitarians, . . . as a political philosopher he was a forerunner of Paine and the French romantic school. . . . Democrat and Christian, the generation to which he belongs is not yet born.[11]

Although Parrington enlarged Williams from a "Puritan Radical" to a "Democrat and Christian," he also placed him more securely within the American intellectual tradition. This broadening of scope as reflected in writing style, including emphasis and structure, distinguishes *Main Currents in American Thought* from its predecessor. Although the issue of changing emphasis becomes immediately apparent in examining Book One of "The Democratic Spirit," the issue of changing structure becomes more critical in Book Two.

In the 1916 collation, Book Two was titled "The Emergence of Parties, 1720–1800" but was called "The Colonial Democrat" in most prior tables of contents. Running to 196 pages, it contained five thematic chapters (primarily on the revolutionary and constitutional debates), ten full portraits (of Franklin, Crèvecoeur, Samuel Adams, Paine, John Dickinson, Thomas Hutchinson, Hamilton, Jefferson, John Adams, and Philip Freneau), and nine briefer portraits—all of literary figures—in several consolidated chapters.

With several exceptions, the general order of chapters in Book Two of "The Democratic Spirit" and Books II and III of *The Colonial Mind* is similar. But the glaring omission of Jonathan Edwards precisely illustrates how Parrington's early manuscript lacks the complex sense of the interplay of ideas that distinguishes the elegantly arranged contents of *Main Currents*. In his later work Parrington specifies that "the line of liberalism in colonial America runs through Roger Williams, Benjamin Franklin, and Thomas Jefferson." But there he also specifies that over against these "must be set the complementary figures of John Cotton, Johnathan Edwards, and Alexander Hamilton. . . . The Carolinian Seeker and the Jacobean theocrat, the colonial democrat and the colonial Calvinist, the Physiocratic republican and the capitalistic financier, embody in concrete forms the diverse tendencies of primitive America; and around these major figures lesser ones will group themselves."[12]

Neither the Williams/Cotton nor the Jefferson/Hamilton contrast is as clear in "The Democratic Spirit" as in *Main Currents*. In the former, these figures appear simply in contiguous or nearly contiguous chapters in the same topical subsections; in the latter, they are linked in contrasting subsections containing related figures, Jefferson and Paine (called "The French Group") versus Hamilton and Adams (called "The English Group"). Without the Edwards/Franklin contrast, "The Democratic Spirit" is missing a key element. The omission is all the more curious because Parrington included Edwards regularly in his colonial literature survey courses beginning in 1909–10.[13] "The Democratic Spirit," however, lacks not only a major eighteenth-century intellect but an explanation for the decay of Calvinism that was occurring concomitantly with the rise of rationalism represented by Franklin. Here structure is brought into the service of theme at the price of historical oversimplification. In both works Franklin is described as achieving "a class triumph," for "the figure of the self-made democrat, with some three million of his fellows at his back. . . . was entering upon a worldwide struggle for political mastery."[14] In *Main Currents* Franklin's achievement is clearer and more dramatic because it is counterpoised to Edwards's. The two in effect debate together in the pages of *Main Currents;* what emerges from the debate is "the awakening of the American mind," the title of the section following their portraits. In "The Democratic Spirit," Franklin is called "Colonial Democrat" instead of "Our First Ambassador," is lumped with Crèvecoeur in a section titled "Native Democracy, 1720–1760," and then is followed by another section militantly titled "The Appeal to Arms: 1760–1785." Democratic radicalism may thus appear to triumph, but in *Main Currents* the ideological battle and not the victory would intrigue Parrington.

Parrington's treatment of Williams and Franklin also points out a third characteristic of "The Democratic Spirit," one that ties it to rather than separates it from *Main Currents in American Thought.* The direct result of Parrington's intention to trace the thread of democracy announced in "Democracy, Economics, and Literature," it also ties "The Democratic Spirit" closely to other Progressive Era histories and documents. This is the charge of "contemporaneity," of Parrington's seeing in the past aspects of the present. For example, in *The Progressive Historians,* Richard Hofstadter describes the structure and methods of *Main Currents* as follows:

> We are in the presence of two great historical currents that course through our history, the currents, roughly speaking, of democratic and antidemocratic thought. Through changing intellectual assumptions and through various phases of manner and speech, we deal in substance, always and recurrently, with the same age-old controversy. The major thinkers of the past are summoned up, in effect, as contemporaries of each other and ourselves. The colonial Americans, for example, were "old-fashioned only in manner and dress," and the subjects they dealt with were at heart "much the same themes with which we are engaged and with which our children will be engaged after us." . . . There is, as he sees it, a hidden core, a basic substance, to history; and once we have found this, the essential thing, we have reached reality and have come to the point at which the actual contemporaneity of history can be clearly perceived. The true significance of our ancestors lies just here: in their contemporaneity.[15]

In *Social Thought in America: The Revolt Against Formalism,* philosopher Morton White describe the "certain style of thinking which dominated America for almost half a century—an intellectual pattern compounded

of pragmatism, institutionalism, behaviorism, legal realism, economic de-
termism, the 'new history.' " These constituents of the early twentieth century's "liberal social philosophy" are all, White claims, "suspicious of
approaches which are excessively formal; they all protest their anxiety to
come to grips with reality, their attachment to the moving and the vital in
social life." Although he does not treat Parrington at length, in the Introduction White calls him "the literary historian who parallels" his book's
main subjects (Holmes, Dewey, Veblen, James Harvey Robinson, Beard).
White discusses how Robinson and Beard's famous text, *The Development
of Modern Europe* (1907), " 'consistently subordinated the past to the
present' " to enable the reader "to catch up with his own times; to read intelligently the foreign news in the morning paper," and "construed history
pragmatically, as a study which could and should contribute directly to the
understanding and explanation of current affairs." In a lecture at Columbia
University the following year, Robinson elaborated his views on how to
make history relevant, freeing it from "moralism and estheticism," drawing
upon scientific method yet distinguishing itself from Leopold von Ranke's
stress on recording facts and past events.[16]

Robinson's views reached an audience beyond the classroom in 1912
when a revised version of his 1908 lecture was collected with seven related
essays and published in the volume titled *The New History*. These ideas became so embedded in American historiography, especially through Carl
Becker's elaboration of them in such essays as "Everyman His Own Historian," that they function as a rationale for the wave of "new" social histories since the 1960s which incorporate demographic data and statistical
methods. While Parrington's revolt against the formalism of literary studies
was leading him to develop a methodology similar to Robinson's, he was
already concentrating on the cultural setting to a greater extent than the
New Historians who looked primarily at institutionalization and industrialization. Hofstadter's complaint against a contemporaneous orientation is
not that one is attempted but that it may deny the complexity and integrity
of history by focusing on features extracted from the larger historical picture. In the role of literary critic, it is one thing to observe that a character,
for example, in a contemporary drama is analogous to Hamlet, himself an
imaginative recreation of a historical figure; in the role of historian, it is
quite another to observe that a seventeenth-century Puritan is like a Progressive reformer except for matters of dress and outward appearance. The
former instance is subject only to the rules of reference within the world of
art; the latter is subject to actual fact and may bear directly on the formation of cultural, ethical, and political values that will have actual consequences in the realm of public policy.

Progressive reformers—including such academic ones as Parrington—
hoped, of course, that their writings would have public consequences. But
Parrington was keenly aware, even at the time he composed his early manu-

script, of the methodological issues later raised by Hofstadter as well as by Robinson. For the brief Conclusion to "The Democratic Spirit" exhibits the sound judgment too rarely glimpsed in historians, new or otherwise. "Any study in history is little more than the writer's guess at the meaning of the past from such data as fall under his observation," he begins thoughtfully, arguing,

> and it is vitiated by two weaknesses—an inevitable inadequacy of data, and the philosophical bias of the writer. The demand for scientific history, I take it, is a counsel of perfection. The utmost that the so-called scientific historian can accomplish, is to apply the exact method of science to the gathering and ordering of his data. . . . It is humanly impossible to maintain an attitude of austere intellectual aloofness in contemplating the passionate record of human struggles which passes for history. . . . *We read the present into the past, we guess at lost facts, we seek to restore lifelikeness to the dimmed features; and we end by painting our own portrait masquerading in the clothes of other days.* (Emphasis added)

Turning specifically to his own work, Parrington then writes:

> Very likely the account herein given lies open to such criticism. . . . In assuming that the movement towards democracy has been the master impulse in determining our native thought and institutions; still more, in assuming that the democratic struggle has been sharply conditioned by economic forces, and that our literature bears the indelible mark of class antagonism—one challenges vigorous dissent. Nevertheless the student who is dissatisfied with a mere chronicle of literary and biographical fact . . . must risk such dissent.[17]

As we might expect, Hofstadter's charge of contemporaneity is even more applicable to Parrington's early manuscript and is well illustrated in the third book, "Democracy and Individualism: 1800–1870." Originally 156 pages in length, this section contained three thematic chapters, ten full portraits, and five brief portraits in one consolidated chapter. It provides the basis for Volume 2 of *Main Currents, The Romantic Revolution in America, 1800–1860.* Tripled to 485 pages, the later work contained fifty portraits and devoted the remaining one-ninth of the text to analytical or transitional material. The most striking structural change was from subdivisions that carried out the general title's emphasis on democracy—"Economic Sectionalism and Literature: 1800–1865"; "Democracy and Slavery: 1830–1860; "The Democratic Mind of New England: 1830–1870"; and "The Flowering of Individualism"—to subdivisions characterizing the intellectual styles of the major regional sections of the nation: "The Mind of the South," "The Mind of the Middle East," "The Mind of New England."

In the process of trebling Book Three, the overall emphasis shifted away from searching for and justifying the antecedents of present-day democracy toward a generous illumination of the often ambiguous processes at work in the evolution of American culture. For example, the chapter that appeared in *The Romantic Revolution* as "John Greenleaf Whittier—Puritan Quaker" first bore the subtitle "Primitive Democrat." While the later chapter discusses Whittier's poetry primarily in the context of the abolitionist movement, "The Democratic Spirit" once ranged well beyond the nineteenth century. In reference to the use abolitionists made of poetry, Parrington writes, in a passage that would have caught Hofstadter's attention:

> Unpoetic though we may seem today, our propagandists write better poetry than the Abolitionists write, as a glance at *The Masses* will show. Our syndicalist radicals now and then strike a living spark of the divine fire, for they know by experience the bitter reality of which they write. They bear in their own souls the sear of social injustice, and their words quiver with passion. Arturo Giavanitti is a truer poet of the white slave, than Whittier, or Longfellow, or Lowell of the black slave, for he dwells in a world of reality, carrying in his heart the wrongs of the proletariat with whom he is one. How those old abolition poems smell of the closet when set over against the vibrant passion of *Arrows in the Gale*, or the tender sadness of Morris Rosenfeld's *Songs of Labor?*

The paragraph, elided for *Main Currents*, tells us more about Parrington's current reading than it does about Whittier's writing. Certainly it exhibits a present-mindedness that surfaces only occasionally in his finished work, as in the striking instance when he interjects the term "Fascist" to characterize opponents to William Lloyd Garrison.[18]

Politics lie very close to the surface of "The Democratic Spirit." Indeed, Parrington's desire to illustrate his book's political thesis is the motivating factor in his drawing contemporary analogies. Like Whittier's, Thoreau's early epithet—"Anarchist"—indicates his place on the political spectrum, not his role—he is a "Transcendental Economist" in *Main Currents*—in the larger mid-nineteenth-century New England cultural life. At one point, after quoting several long passages from *Civil Disobedience*, we find Parrington commenting: "Shift such principles to the field of economic endeavour and they become strangely like syndicalism. The Direct Actionists might well go to Thoreau for a motto to inscribe on the red banner: 'Let your life'—not your act alone—'be a counter friction to stop the machine.' "[19]

Similarly, after writing derisively of James Russell Lowell's opinion that civil service reform would cure late nineteenth-century social injustices ("Let only capable gentlemen be secure in their tenure of office, and the political Saturnalia must vanish, like witches on broomsticks at the first cockcrow"), Parrington accuses Lowell of being "no more than a brilliant bookman, a clever amateur in social philosophy. . . . One has only to read his essay on *The Independent in Politics*, in the light of such studies as Simond's [sic] *Social Forces in American History*, or Beard's *Contemporary*

American History, to perceive how helplessly inadequate was his analysis of an American in the clutches of a feudal industrialism, and how hopeless was his proposed cure." In *Main Currents,* Lowell is grouped with Oliver Wendell Holmes, Sr., in a section delineating "the authentic Brahmin," where Lowell wears the perjorative title of "Cambridge Brahmin." Holmes and Lowell are evaluated as "poets of the library" and seen as true products of their environment rather than as victims of later social critics. "The Democratic Spirit" chapter—in which Lowell serves as an example of "the subsidence of the ferment" of the New England Renaissance—opens with a contrast between Thoreau, the outdoor rebel, and Lowell, the indoor bookman; the contrast is then developed without acknowledgement of Thoreau's and Lowell's differences in background and breeding.[20] In "The Democratic Spirit," vital connective and analytic tissue that allows placement of figures within their proper social-cultural milieu is usually missing. Parrington's judgments are hasty; his portraits impressionistic.

These traits, conjoined with an overriding political agenda, are clearly apparent in his early portrait of Emerson. In "The Democratic Spirit" Emerson is labeled "Spiritual Democrat"; in *Main Currents,* "Transcendental Critic." In "The Democratic Spirit" Parrington reaches back in time to observe that "Roger Williams was his own brother to him; and if the tyranny of theology has reacted less heavily upon the mother, persuading her that such offspring could be no other than base-born, Roger Williams might have become an elder Emerson"; in *Main Currents* he stresses Emerson's relation to the thought of William Ellery Channing, his contemporary and immediate predecessor in the liberalizing of Unitarianism.

By failing to treat the development of Unitarianism or Channing's ideas, Parrington has no way to explain how "Nature" could have been written in 1836. He states that it signals Emerson's long-delayed birth, metaphorically set back by Jonathan Edwards (the base-born offspring described in the above paragraph), whose portrait is, of course, missing from "The Democratic Spirit." He calls "The American Scholar" Emerson's "declaration of intellectual independence" but fails to mention "The Divinity School Address," stressing Emerson's contribution to political thought in his later essays.

As in his Thoreau chapter, Parrington notes in his early manuscript that "the whole social philosophy of William Morris is compressed" within a few sentences in the essay "The Method of Nature," but he accuses Emerson of not seeing, as Morris did, that the "function of art in society" was to redeem workmen from the bonds of industrialization. In *Main Currents* he would write that Morris would have endorsed Emerson's critique of industrialism in "Man the Reformer." But in "The Democratic Spirit" he jumps to the conclusion that Emerson was too much the New England idealist to make room in his thinking for "the philosophy of economic interpretation" and flatly states:

This is the inevitable weakness of Emerson in the eyes of the present day democrat. . . . He was reluctant to probe the relation between his master conception of
the worth of the individual and the ideal of commercial efficiency. . . . The fierce
heart of our democratic problem is the economic, as we understand clearly today; the struggles of social classes is the struggle for economic advantage. Inspired by a common purpose Emerson and the modern radical part company to
follow different paths to a common end.[21]

Parrington continues this passage in a vein that indicates more about the
formation of his own political attitudes than it informs us about the development of Emerson's social thought and style of mind, the focus of the
Main Currents chapter:

The economic interpretation of history was one of the illuminating achievements
of that generation, but though Emerson like Carlyle, looked the world over in
search of great men, he failed to see the significant figure of Karl Marx, or learn
the message of the great thinker of modern democracy. What a pity he should not
have known the one man who could have supplied the lack in Emerson's social
philosophy. Doubtless he would have recoiled from the apparent materialism of
the Marxian interpretation, but he could scarcely have failed to question more
deeply the meaning and outcome of the industrialism which was riding mankind.

Then in a few concluding sentences, Parrington observes:

But failing to grasp the significance of the economic in society he stands as the
last of the older school of democrats who base their programme upon aspiration;
whereas the great German with his English mind, is the first of the new school
who base their programmes upon the solid fact of economic impulse. Emerson
and Marx are complementary spirits; they are the twin halves of the democratic
whole; the one the prophet of the spiritual, inadequately equipped with social
understanding, the other the prophet of the new determinism armed with knowledge adequate to its needs.[22]

Perhaps it is harmless to imagine Emerson and Marx as friends. But to
omit Emerson's relation to the development of Unitarianism; to "pity" his
lack of acquaintance with Marx when the first volume of *Capital* was
not translated into English until 1886, four years after Emerson's death;
and to convict him of not being influenced by economic philosophy when
he lived at the height of nineteenth-century communitarian experimentation is to distort the physiognomy of the New England Renaissance, a period Parrington would describe with considerable skill in *The Romantic
Revolution.*
The decade between the completion of "The Democratic Spirit in American Letters" and the final revisions on the first volumes of *Main Currents
in American Thought* saw the metamorphoses of key seventeenth-,

eighteenth-, and nineteenth-century figures from sometimes rough manne-
quins on which Parrington hung his emerging ideas about democracy and
culture to realistic, often imaginative and insightful portraits of artists and
social thinkers in the process of formulating their characteristic ideas within
the framework of their prevailing climate of opinion.

Those years also saw the maturation of Parrington's own political attitudes and of his interpretation of the course of American history. In contrast
to the bright convictions in democracy's future trumpeted in the 1916
manuscript, Parrington drew this dark picture of the past in his Foreword to
The Beginnings of Critical Realism:

> After three hundred years' experience we have returned, intellectually, to the
> point from which we set out, and the old philosophy brought to the new world
> from the compact societies of Europe, with its doctrine of determinism and its
> mood of pessimism, has come back in changed form to color the thinking of our
> generation. *Emersonian optimism, that was the fullest expression of the romantic
> faith, is giving way to Dreiserian pessimism, and the traditional doctrine of
> progress is being subjected to analysis by a growing skepticism. Our intellectual
> history thus conceived falls into three broad phases: Calvinistic pessimism, ro-
> mantic optimism, and mechanistic pessimism.* Between the first and last lies the
> America of yesterday that shaped the American mind and American institutions;
> and with the submergence of that native world we are in the way of repeating
> here the familiar history of Europe, with its coercive regimentations reproduced
> on a large scale and in more mechanical fashion. Once more a gloomy philoso-
> phy stands on the threshold of the American mind. Whether it will enter and take
> possession of the household, no one can predict.[23] (Emphasis added)

The "traditional doctrine of progress" had been justified by a linear view
of history, which, in turn, was based on the social application of evolutionary theory. The so-called Progressive historians—Turner, Beard, and Parrington—are usually judged as adherents of a linear view of history.

This view rests on the assumption that man is basically good, that history is a record of the conflict between corrupting institutions and purifying
environments in which men can develop naturally and of the conflict between absolutistic, formalistic ideas based on abstract dogma and fresh,
practical ideas drawn from the reality of social, political, and economic experience. Conflict is the dynamic of progress, and progress is always good
because its goal is a democratic society in which the common welfare is assured. The welfare is assured because men, through their inherent good nature, will contribute to it individually without coercion, avoiding the
establishment of corrupting institutions and formalistic ideas. To achieve
this end, conflict must always be resolved: liberalism must defeat conserva-
tism, democracy defeat aristocracy, idealism defeat materialism. The central
charge against the limitations of this view of history is that the Progressive

historians saw such a close linkage between democracy and agrarian ideals that the rise of an urbanized, industrialized order challenged their democratic faith as well as their belief in progress, for progress was moving in the direction of a caste society based on the exploitation of wealth and resources made possible by the Machine Age.[24]

When *Main Currents* is read as a Progressive document, in the sense described above, inconsistencies in Parrington's thinking and anomalies in his historical explanation have been identified. For example, in *American Historical Explanations* Gene Wise has described a "Parrington (I)" and a "Parrington (II)." Parrington (I) is totally within the paradigmatic Progressive tradition, as in *The Colonial Mind*. But in *The Romantic Revolution,* some cracks in his Progressive explanation become visible and Parrington (II) comes into being, although he does not fully develop until *The Beginnings of Critical Realism*. The (II) form is characterized by Parrington (I)'s form breaking down as a result of "anomalies between his sensed experience and his characteristic mode of ordering things." As Wise explains,

> Parrington (I) . . . pictured himself battling effete intellectuals, "poetasters" of the "genteel tradition." He, in contrast, would "enter sympathetically into a world of masculine intellects and material struggles." But when he gets to volume 3, Parrington betrays doubt about this vigorous life. For vigor in his post–Civil War America is expressed not only by progressive intellects, but by the captains of industry, by the Babbitts, by all those compelled to "make it" in the American land of promise.[25]

Similarly, in their essay "Vernon Louis Parrington: The Mind and Art of a Historian of Ideas," Robert Skotheim and Kermit Vanderbilt observe that

> by the early chapters of Volume II, Americans had struggled out of the confinements of Puritanism to the wider vistas of Jefferson and Jackson. Here we were standing on Pisgah. Through the political and economic storm clouds of the early republic, we had caught a glimpse of the promised land. But we failed to pass over. . . . Before the middle of Volume II, Parrington was quite clearly writing American history as tragedy and betrayal.[26]

Seeing Parrington as writing history as tragedy and betrayal seems more accurate than portraying his view of history as linear and progressive, but Skotheim and Vanderbilt do not find this pattern emerging until well into his second volume, the same place that Wise sees Parrington (I) beginning to break down.

One of the most significant passages added to *Main Currents* but entirely absent from "The Democratic Spirit" occurs midway in *The Colonial Mind*. Here Parrington forecasts the conflict between the imaginative forces that nurture culture and the economic forces that breed middle-class values. This claim appears long before the final defeat of agrarianism in Volume 2 and the triumph of a plutocratic society rationalized by science in Volume 3.

After positing that the American Revolution resulted from the clash between home rule and imperial centralization, Parrington writes that the Revolution overthrew the monarchial principle and established the principle of republicanism. As a result, "for the first time the middle class was free to create a civilization after its own ideals." What were those ideals?

> Dignity and culture henceforth were to count for less and assertiveness for more. . . . The charm of the older aristocracy disappeared along with its indisputable evils. . . . A franker evaluation of success in terms of money began to obscure the older personal and family distinctions. New men brought new ways and a vulgar clamor of politics went hand in hand with business expansion. The demagogue and the speculator discovered a fruitful field for their activities.

And what form did the new society take?

> The new capitalism lay on the horizon of republican America, and the middle class was eager to hasten its development. But a new economic order required a new political state, and as a necessary preliminary, the spirit of nationalism. . . . *Americanism superseded colonialism, and with the new loyalty there developed a conception of federal sovereignty, overriding all local authorities. . . . This marked the turning point in American development; the checking of the long movement of decentralization and the beginning of a counter movement of centralization*—the most revolutionary change in three hundred years of American experience. The history of the rise of the coercive state in America, with the ultimate arrest of all centrifugal tendencies, was implicit in that momentous counter movement.[27] (Emphasis added)

This passage shows tragedy and betrayal occurring concurrently with the Revolution; it shows the breakdown of the Progressive paradigm almost before it can be established. Conflict is resolved, but even at this early stage it does not resolve into liberal, democratic, idealistic tendencies. Crucial here is the emergence of the middle class and its role in creating the "coercive state." The middle class, like this foreshadowing of Volume 3's theme of the middle class's hostility to imaginative freedom and open-minded analysis, as well as its concern with economic advantage at the expense of social justice, is also absent from "The Democratic Spirit," with its narrower focus on radical versus aristocratic cultural and political attitudes.

Clearly Parrington revised the first two volumes of *Main Currents* in light of his changing understanding of historical processes. This transformation took place between 1916, the date of his early manuscript's completion, and 1926, the date *The Colonial Mind* and *The Romantic Revolution* were sent to Harcourt, Brace—not between 1926 and 1929, the date of his death and his last possible work on *The Beginnings of Critical*

Realism. The apparent inconsistencies between the first two volumes and the last have been attributed to Parrington's abandonment of Progressive categories—supposedly adequate for explaining seventeenth- through nineteenth-century experience—under the pressure of the complexities of twentieth-century experience. In light of such textual revisions just illustrated in *The Colonial Mind,* that abandonment actually occurs in the process of revising "The Democratic Spirit in American Letters" to bring what became the first two volumes of *Main Currents* in accord with the argument being pursued in its third volume. This third volume had its roots in a manuscript begun in 1917. The origins of Parrington's increasingly ironic view of history, coupled with his enlarged perception of the components of class conflict, are visible in *The Colonial Mind.* But *Main Currents* as we know it was made possible because he completed his early manuscript and because he began identifying as a historian.

"A Literary Refugee Among the Drilled Hosts of the Historians"

Despite the Macmillan literary adviser's opinion that colonial America had been "raked fore and aft many times," he remembered Parrington's particular raking sufficiently to mention "The Democratic Spirit" to Carl Van Doren. Van Doren was then teaching at Columbia's Brearly School and serving as one of four editors of *The Cambridge History of American Literature.* Modeled on the fourteen-volume *Cambridge History of English Literature,* the American *Cambridge History* was the first collaborative work in the field, with chapters written by experts in various chronological and thematic areas of American literature. Its best-known recent predecessors in literary history were widely varied in viewpoint and organization: Barrett Wendell's *Literary History of America,* William B. Cairns's *History of American Literature,* John Macy's *Spirit of American Literature,* and college texts by F. L. Pattee.

In mid-January of 1915, Van Doren wrote to Parrington asking him to submit to the editors the manuscript sections treating "the Puritan divines to the death of Cotton Mather." Parrington promptly responded and was awarded a contract for an eight-thousand-word chapter by the end of February. By mid-March, he was complaining that the word limit was cramping. Van Doren attempted to assuage his complaints by observing that many of the problems of colonial writers had been dealt with in the *Cambridge History*'s English volumes, that the two volumes (eventually three) reserved for the American phase "were probably proportionate on the basis of importance," and that "under the circumstances we are doing all we can to represent the American spirit, but it is simply impossible to undertake the culture history which we should like and which should certainly be done, sometime, by someone."[28]

Van Doren's former observations may have been a red flag to a champion of American literature, but his last statement regarding writing "culture history" may well have appeared as a green light. For Parrington had revised and completed "The Democratic Spirit in American Letters" by the spring of 1916. In the meantime, despite the unfavorable space limitations, Parrington submitted his chapter, "The Puritan Divines, 1620–1720." When the first volume of *The Cambridge History of American Literature* was published in 1917, he appeared in the company of such recognized figures as literary critic Paul Elmer Moore and historian John Spencer Bassett as well as the four editors (Van Doren, John Erskine, William Peterfield Trent, and Stuart Pratt Sherman), all of whom contributed chapters and had published in the field. In fact, Parrington was using Trent's *Library of American Literature* and Moore's *Shelburne Essays* in one of his classes at Washington.

The "Puritan Divines" chapter was a long-delayed professional leap since his first (and last) national publication on domestic architecture in *House Beautiful*. He now had a context and a network to ease his further entrance into the scholarly community. And he had at last found a mode in which to channel the religious interests earlier manifested in the desire to preach and to write penitential poetry. Appearing in *The Cambridge History of American Literature* did not take the place of publishing his own book, but it was probably the most crucial academic lifeline in his career.

The self-styled historian of democratic radicalism was concerned, as Van Doren rightly perceived, with "culture history" and not literature narrowly construed and was no doubt in substantial agreement with the Cambridge editors' intentions: the project was to "be a survey of the life of the American people as expressed in their writings rather than a history of belles-lettres alone." The separately written chapters were thus unified by an interpretative viewpoint that reflected a contemporary but alternative outlook on the teaching and study of American literature:

> To write the intellectual history of America from the modern aesthetic standpoint is to miss precisely what makes it significant among modern literatures, namely, that for two centuries the main energy of Americans went into exploration, settlement, labour for subsistence, religion and statecraft. . . . But the . . . belated expansion of their purely aesthetic impulses, unfavourable as it was to the development of poetry and fiction, was no serious handicap to the production of a prose competently recording their practical activities and expressing their moral, religious, and political ideas.[29]

Parrington's turning toward American subjects in his later Oklahoma years had been accompanied by a hard-won lessening of his own adherence to the aesthetic tradition in the study of English language and literature. He would always retain—sometimes even surprisingly insist on—a respect for the formal properties of literary craft. But in the mid-1910s Parrington's major intellectual influences were neither literary nor aesthetic but broadly social scientific. In this direction he was encouraged not only by Washington colleagues such as his friend J. Allen Smith but by current trends in historiography.

Sending the partially completed manuscript of "The Democratic Spirit in American Letters" off to Macmillan, the act that opened up the world of scholarly publication to Parrington, was one outstanding event of 1914. Another took place that summer, when Frederick Jackson Turner came out from Harvard to deliver the 1914 commencement address and then stayed on to teach during the university's summer session. There is no record that the two ever met. A penciled invitation list for a reception given by Edmond S. Meany, the History Department chair and an active member of the Washington Historical Association, fails to list Parrington's name. But it is difficult to imagine that the pair did not at least make each other's acquaintance, if not pass a pleasant Seattle afternoon. After all, Parrington's colleague Edward McMahon, who taught American topics in the History Department and American economic history in J. Allen Smith's omnibus department that included political science, economics, and sociology, studied with Turner at Wisconsin before receiving his M.A. there in 1907. His wife, Theresa Schmid McMahon, also taught in Smith's department and had received her Ph.D. in economics from Wisconsin in 1909, the year before Turner's departure.[30]

Whether or not their paths crossed on campus, Parrington would have attended commencement and heard Turner's speech, "The West and American Ideals," later collected among the essays in *The Frontier in American History* (1920). The opening words of the address certainly echoed sentiments of Parrington's and could even be a source for the final title of the English professor's opus:

> This attitude of self-examination is hardly characteristic of the people as a whole. Particularly it is not characteristic of the historic American. He has been an opportunist rather than a dealer in general ideas. Destiny set him in a current which bore him swiftly along through such a wealth of opportunity that reflection and well-considered planning seemed wasted time. He knew not where he was going, but he was on his way, cheerful, optimistic, busy and buoyant.
>
> To-day we are reaching a changed condition. . . . The swift and inevitable current of the upper reaches of the nation's history has borne it to the broader expanse and slower stretches which mark the nearness of the level sea. The vessel, no longer carried along by the rushing waters, finds it necessary to determine its own directions on this new ocean of its future, to give conscious consideration to its motive power and to its steering gear.

Parrington would have fully assented with Turner's general theme: in a rapidly changing world, "in place of old frontiers of wilderness, there are new frontiers of unwon fields of science . . . there are frontiers of better social domains yet unexplored." He would have nodded in agreement with the description of how "the Populist revised the pioneer conception of government" when "the Western radical became convinced that he must sacrifice his ideal of individualism and free competition in order to maintain his ideal of democracy." And he would find resonant the elegiac spirit of Tennyson's Ulysses ("Tis not too late to seek a newer world") with which Turner closed his address.[31]

The quality of Turner's impact, direct or indirect, on the slightly younger man is clear. On one hand, Parrington's geographical autobiography and much of his experience in Kansas and Oklahoma and now Washington found ready reflection in the transplanted Wisconsin scholar's explanation of the relation between democracy and western development. On the other, Turner's emphasis on environmental and economic influences, however persuasive or truthful, was fundamentally at odds with the side of Parrington that was committed to culture, to letters, to the life of the mind. The conflict between two contrasting modes of explanation, between economic determinism and the history of ideas, would become markedly apparent in *Main Currents*. In the later manuscript, as Parrington modified his stress on radicalism, he was generally freed by his focus on intellectuals and ideas from reliance on economic and environmental explanations.

But such explanations more obviously formed the theoretical core of "The Democratic Spirit in American Letters," which was not finished until two years after Turner's visit. Notably, Turner's name does not appear in the index to *The Colonial Mind*, while a lengthy section on the colonial period in "The Democratic Spirit" treats Turner more explicitly than any other in Parrington's writings. In a chapter titled "The Impulse to Freedom" included with the portraits of John Wise, Cotton Mather, and Samuel Sewall in a subdivision tellingly called "The New-World Environment and the Democratic Hope: 1640–1720," Parrington elaborates:

> If democracy were to take possession of America it would result neither from the proseletyzing of a handful of intellectuals like Roger Williams, nor from the discontent of rebellious underlings; it must grow up out of the new environment, discovering in the free soil congenial sustenance, and spreading over the land as naturally as the wholesome apple transplanted from English cottage gardens. . . .
>
> Professor Turner has demonstrated the importance of the frontier in determining the characteristics of our American democracy. The wilderness is a great leveller, and pioneer life with its rough economic equality, with its stern self-reliance, is a training school in assertive individualism. In this new world the play of economic forces was to take place in a larger and freer fashion than had been known to men since European civilization took form. . . . [32]

In this passage speaks the Populist bent on legitimizing the history and experience—including, we feel, his own—of the pioneer, the farmer, the wilderness survivor, the practical students in their laboratories who did not know the Elizabethans and spoke accented English. But as the Populist was subsumed by the worldview of William Morris, so the champion of radicalism would come to defend the hesitancies of Thomas Jefferson, the economic determinist, to soften under the liberal spirit. In *Main Currents*, completed in the postwar years, these two streams that so long dominated Parrington's outlook are intermingled, often successfully enough so the argument sails on smoothly without backtracking. But in "The Democratic Spirit" the radical stream is the major current. (The early manuscript could almost be retitled *The Main Current in American Thought*.)

Local, national, and world events contributed to Parrington's heightened political temperament. Although his precise views on American response to the European war are not known (Parrington's diaries are missing between 1908 and 1917), he did vote rather unenthusiastically for Woodrow Wilson in the 1916 elections. Growing nativism, partly a product of and partly encouraged by the United States's isolationist policy, combined with suspicion of foreign ideologies. Active among the Pacific Northwest's lumber mills and logging camps, the Industrial Workers of the World (IWW) was facing local political and corporate resistance that climaxed in the Everett massacre in November 1916. Five Wobblies were killed, thirty severely wounded, and over a hundred more jailed in Seattle when the Everett sheriff tried to stop union members and sympathizers from cooperating in a lumber mill strike. In 1917 many Wobblies were beaten and jailed in nearby Yakima and Ellensburg during a strike for the eight-hour day. Later, in 1919 after the Armistice Day parade in Centralia, Wesley Everest was castrated and lynched by a group of American Legion members who had raided the IWW hall on grounds that the Wobblies were Bolsheviks.[33]

Fears of radicalism and sedition were heightened by U.S. entry into World War I, leading to passage of the Espionage Act (1917) and Sedition Act (1918). The University of Washington played a direct role in preventing labor agitation and supporting state and corporate interests (which supported the university financially). President Henry Suzzallo was appointed chairman of the State Defense Council. In this capacity he became involved in settling labor disputes that threatened the spruce lumber industry, vital to wartime airplane construction, and in the fall of 1918 he was called to help stabilize labor discontent among shipyard workers.

The students in Parrington's undergraduate contemporary American literature classes were no doubt kept aware to some degree of national and world events by their professor's expectation that they read the *Dial* and the *New Republic*. Parrington himself also read the *Nation* and the *Masses*—until its suppression in 1917—and could scarcely have remained ignorant of the circumstances surrounding the February and October phases of the Russian Revolution. The contemporary course began using as a text

Charles Beard's *Contemporary American History* just after its 1915 publication. On the literary side, the students were now reading Progressive novelist Winston Churchill's *Inside of the Cup*, Frank Norris's *Octopus*, Booth Tarkington's *Gentleman from Indiana*, Edith Wharton's *House of Mirth*, and short stories by Sarah Orne Jewett. On the cultural side they were studying William Jennings Bryan's "Cross of Gold" speech, Walter Weyl's *New Democracy*, Herbert Croly's *Promise of American Life*, and Walter Rauschenbusch's *Christianity and the Social Crisis*.[34]

The constellation of viewpoints and figures in this array, conjoined with his relationship to Frederick Jackson Turner on one hand and James Harvey Robinson on the other, indicates Parrington's intellectual orientation far more accurately than the almost accidental inclusion of his Puritan Divines chapter in *The Cambridge History of American Literature*. By profession he belonged among literary critics such as Van Wyck Brooks, whose updated version of Emerson's "American Scholar" address, *America's Coming of Age*, appeared in 1915 and whose memorably titled "On Creating a Usable Past" appeared in the *Dial* in 1918. But in practice he partook of "the revolt against formalism," and by desire he claimed membership among the New Historians.

As an outgrowth of his contemporary course; of his awareness of recent trends in history, political science, and cultural criticism; and of Seattle's political and economic climate, in the late fall of 1916 Parrington began working on a new book. The revision of "The Democratic Spirit in American Letters" had just been rejected by Macmillan, and his Puritan chapter would soon appear in *The Cambridge History*. Perhaps he felt personally free, if not socially compelled, to concentrate on the present. Parrington started by retrieving the materials he had omitted from his manuscript's original design when he followed the suggestion to trim its length. This section, "Democracy and Capitalism: 1865–1890," became the basis for the first section of his new work. Tentatively titled "The Spirit of Radicalism in Recent American Literature, 1870–1916," it was the nucleus of *The Beginnings of Critical Realism in America, 1860–1920*, which would not be published for fourteen years. The original title reflects the spirit of radicalism that the now forty-five-year-old Parrington had invested in "The Democratic Spirit"; the final title reflects changes in tone (a political stance replaced by a term drawn from both philosophy and literature) and content (a narrower focus on one aspect of American literature broadened to tracing the development of a cluster of ideas) similar to those to be undergone by *The Colonial Mind* and *The Romantic Revolution*.[35]

At the same time he was designing his new book, Parrington was evidently testing out its apparent theoretical political and economic bases in his graduate seminar in American literature. For the past several years, his graduate students had been considering the period since 1890. He planned to launch the opening months of 1917 with such themes as "the beginnings of an examination into the economic origins of social problems," which included Lincoln Steffens's *Shame of the Cities,* Charles Edward Russell's *Stories of the Great Railroads,* and Mary Wilkins Freeman's *Portion of Labor* among its readings, and "the theory of collectivism," which included John Spargo's *Socialism* and John Graham Brooks's *American Syndicalism.*[36]

And yet the overall tenor of Parrington's thinking, writing, and teaching remained in balance, although that balance must have been bought at the price of intellectual—if not emotional—tension. For during the months of planning his new book's contents and his graduate seminar, Parrington was developing an essay that provides grounds for refuting critics who have accused *Main Currents* of mechanically treating literature according to its extrinsic content and ignoring its irreducible aesthetic aspects. Variously titled "Economics and Criticism," "Economics and Literature," and "The Economic Interpretation of Literature," one version contains some of the clearest statements of Parrington's understanding of how an economic interpretation may be applied to literature and to ideas.

In the essay Parrington first argues that "ideas are not godlings that spring perfect-winged from the head of Jove" but are "themselves conditioned by social forces." Then he states that "to understand those forces is the economist's first business" but goes on to insist—as we might expect in light of his years spent writing and teaching poetry, composing "Stuart Forbes: Stoic," and studying art and architecture—that

> there is much for which the economist has no explanation. If literature be the product of estheticism and not of protest and propaganda; if it has had its birth out of that persistent love of beauty which is the mainspring of creative art, it is a thing spiritual or esthetic rather than economic. . . . It is a glorious imaging of the flux of personality which discovers delight in reordering its gallery of pictures. In this world of emotional experience fetters have no place; the economic is not master there.[37]

Here Parrington makes a crucial distinction between literature that is primarily aesthetic in conception ("the product of estheticism") and literature ("of protest and propaganda") that originates in the author's explicit desire to portray ideas in his or her work. He claims that an economic interpretation is applicable to this second type of writing, that the first type must be judged by artistic standards alone. He maintained this distinction throughout *Main Currents.* But in "The Democratic Spirit in American Letters" and in "The Spirit of Radicalism in Recent American Literature," if he was to trace either democracy or radicalism in literary forms, he would need to choose as examples those works that lent themselves to his purposes. They were not ones that made life comfortable in an English Department.

As was Parrington's wont, he toiled over the phrasing and images of the essay, which seems to have been intended as his new book's introduction.

One version bears the marks of his father's legal background, of his Kansas farm boyhood, and of his dissatisfaction with formal literary study. It opens with a wry, yet brutal, scholarly confession:

> I am not a critic. In moments of intellectual stocktaking I am compelled to acknowledge to myself that the wise finality of the literary judge is beyond me. However ardently I may wish to assume the high prerogatives of criticism, honesty bids me acknowledge that I am too little read in the common law of art to mount the bench. I have turned over many a volume in the legal library of criticism, but I could never lay my hand on any authentic Coke or Blackstone to open to me the great principle of literary art. That such exist my friends assure me and talk of Aristotle and other great men who are dead; but the *Poetics* affords me little confidence, and human perversity whispers to me that there aren't any authentic Cokes and Blackstones at whose feet I may set. Nor, I must acknowledge further, am I a scientist, to content my soul with gleaning in the field of Teutonic origins, bringing home sheaves of philological roots and precious grains of ablaut changes. The philologists, to borrow Dr. Johnson's homely figure, seem to me to have gone to milking the bull. I could never fancy the butter which they hope to churn from the whey of their milkpails. If the bread of scholarship must be spread with such it must prove a lean feast. *And so because I can be neither a critic nor a scientist, I am perforce driven into the camp of the historians, to conduct myself in such seemly fashion as is possible to one who has retreated from outposts that he could not hold. A literary refugee among the drilled hosts of the historians, must needs bear himself modestly.*[38] (Emphasis added)

Parrington certainly had no credentials as a historian and precious few as a critic. He did not seek to establish networks of professional relationships, so necessary to the conditions of modern academic life, either personally or through correspondence. But he knew where he wanted to stand. The epigraph on the title page of "The Democratic Spirit in American Letters" was taken from Carl Becker's review in the July 1912 *Dial* of James Harvey Robinson's *New History:* "The business of history is to arouse an intelligent discontent, to foster a fruitful radicalism."[39]

9

~

"I Become More Radical with Every Year"

1918–1924

Definitions and Declarations

Parrington's attention to the business of history fostered not only "The Democratic Spirit in American Letters" and "The Spirit of Radicalism in Recent American Literature." In February 1918 he turned to personal history and wrote the brief but illuminating "Autobiographical Sketch." By the war's end, two other events occurred that help delineate Parrington's particular brand of radicalism. In May ground was broken for a new house, at 5248 Nineteenth Avenue N.E., in Seattle's University District. Except for the feature of a first-floor study whose windows overlooked the gardens in back, the dwelling was indistinguishable from much other modern housing. Leafing through the blueprints, one feels the romantic days of Stuart Forbes and William Morris were gone, replaced by the practical concerns of family care and, perhaps, a wish to present a smooth surface to an inquisitive campus world. Architecturally, it was a democratic little house, designed to fit in with its neighbors, although what went on in the confines of the study was often at odds with the appearance of settled conventionality. The Nineteenth Avenue house was Parrington's mid-1910s version of his 1903 article "The Lack of Privacy in American Village Homes."[1]

This dichotomy between public and private that so marks Parrington's behavior had first become evident in the diaries kept during his Harvard years. Interestingly, the third defining event of 1918 was Parrington's reply to the request for contributions to the Harvard class of 1893 *Secretary's Sixth Report*. Instead of containing his thoughts behind conventional walls, Parrington burst the bounds of his usual decorum: "The past five years I have spent in study and writing, up to my ears in the economic interpretation of American history and literature, getting the last lingering Harvard prejudices out of my system. *I become more radical with every year,* and more impatient with the smug Tory culture which we were fed on as undergraduates" (emphasis added). Admitting proudly that he had not been in Cambridge since receiving his bachelor's degree twenty-five years earlier, Parrington continues, somewhat cynically: "Very likely I am wrong in my judgment, yet from what little information comes through to me I have set the school down as a liability rather than an asset to the cause of democracy. It seems to me the apologist and advocate of capitalistic exploitation—as witness the sweet-smelling list of nominees sent out yearly for the Board of Overseers."[2]

Why did Parrington choose this official format to assume the role of rebel against his Harvard experience? The 1918 report marks the first time he declared the anti-Cambridge sentiments that have become so linked with his historiographical image. Granting that the class reports were issued sporadically, the last having appeared five years earlier, previously Parrington had sent the "customary bland replies" of a dutiful alumnus. In 1898 only his name and address were included. In 1899 Parrington replied that he was "a plain school teacher" and a member of the Elks Lodge, certainly not a radical organization. The 1903 report mentions only that he is a member of the University of Oklahoma faculty. The 1910 report states that he had been fired from Oklahoma and assumed a position at the University of Washington. Publishing the news of his dismissal may be an indication that his rebellion against Harvard was under way because after that incident he had not been accepted for doctoral study. For the fifth report (1913) he returned a blank questionnaire.[3]

The real clue to the quality of Parrington's 1918 response is found in the *Sixth Report*'s section on publication. There Parrington announces that he had finished the five-hundred-page manuscript of "The Democratic Spirit in American Letters: 1620–1870." Surely such a title helped back his claim of radicalism. The manuscript had not yet met with editorial success so the report informed an influential sector of the professional world—no matter how smugly Tory—that he was a contender in the academic lists. Besides, one of the chief practitioners of the economic interpretation of history—Turner—was ensconced in Harvard's history department.[4]

The completion of "The Democratic Spirit" also provides the clue to why Parrington turned in early 1918 to writing personal history. The approximately fifty-page "Autobiographical Sketch" abruptly closes with a paragraph recounting the 1908 firing and subsequent move to Seattle. But on the penultimate page he began explaining:

> When I quitted Norman the economic interpretation of history had not yet risen for me, but it lay just below the horizon and was soon to become the chief luminary in my intellectual sky. My new interest in American literature opened a fresh field for me and in that field I applied the economic interpretation more and more rigidly. I came to see that from the first two rival economies struggled for supremacy in America: the economy of the farmer and the economy of the merchant. . . . To the expansion of this thesis I devoted my studies between the years 1910 and 1916, and it is worked out in the volume, *The Democratic Spirit in American Literature: 1620–1870*. This is the best and maturest work that I have done, and from the beginning to end it is a study in radicalism.[5]

Again, Parrington coupled a declaration of radicalism with a book announcement. His modified feeling about Harvard is not only paralleled by the architectural differences between his Norman and Seattle homes. Both the modification and the differences are part of a more thorough revision of self-image contained in his "Autobiographical Sketch." Parrington's book manuscript had concluded: "We read the present into the past, we guess at lost facts, we seek to restore lifelikeness to the dimmed features; and we end by painting our own portrait." One can imagine that after sketching the intellectual portraits of so many others in "The Democratic Spirit," he decided to draw his own.

Like most autobiographies, Parrington's sketch has a purpose, to trace the development of his radicalism and to explain how he came to write his book. The latter required a shift in professional fields (from English to American literature), and this shift was accompanied by a change in allegiances from art to politics. These shifts had occurred gradually but not easily, as the foregoing chapters have detailed. In February 1918 Parrington was nearing forty-seven years of age and may have felt, as he had written about James Russell Lowell, that he was "a man of many contradictions. . . . The course that he sailed was marked by much veering and tacking, to the sad confusion of those who would chart his progress."[6] Parrington had begun keeping his diary again in 1917 after the lapse of a decade, but it remained primarily a garden book. Writing an autobiography, even as short as his sketch, can often serve as a way to explain and to consolidate one's identity as one seeks to understand it at a particular moment in time. Parrington, however, does not present himself as a man of contradictions; rather, he presents his life as a consistent unfolding of tendencies that flow naturally out of his heritage and experience. The creation of that consistency may have been his object in writing his autobiography, and the appearance of consistency may be a result of ordering experience chronologically.

In the sketch's opening paragraph, Parrington inscribes its ostensible intention:

> In order that my children may know something of the line from which they come, I am minded to set down such facts as I retain in memory concerning my family, together with bits from my earlier life. They will be fragmentary at best, and of little significance except to those who may care. It is commonly said that when one begins to turn back lovingly to the past, it is a sign that the years begin to lie heavy upon him. It may be true in my case although I am not as yet conscious of the burden of the years.

Like most autobiographers, Parrington was mindful of posterity. Yet his reflective mood hardly seems motivated by familial concerns. His three children were still young; Elizabeth would have been fifteen, Louise ten, and

Vernon, Jr., just four. Parrington was still in good health despite his habitual cigarette smoking. His mother, who figures only briefly in the sketch, was still living in Emporia, yet his father, who died nine years earlier, figures prominently. Giving such prominence to the Judge, who had seemed so distant in Vernon's youth, may be part of the design of Parrington's 1918 identity, for the sketch credits his paternal line with most of his formative political attitudes. Yet one reason why the facts are fragmentary is revealed early in the sketch when Parrington confesses he knows little about his father's boyhood because "the trick of being close-mouthed seems to be a Parrington characteristic."[7]

The comment that the sketch may be of significance only "to those who may care" hints at the private nature of a self-revelatory task. Yet the work is hardly a confession; it omits almost all details concerning Parrington's emotional life and focuses on his intellectual development. And even the facts chosen to illustrate his exterior changes are highly selective. It provides another example of Parrington's persistent public/private dichotomy.

The sketch must be relied on for life data available nowhere else. But it is most important as a record of how Parrington wanted to see himself and to be seen in early 1918. For example, the first six pages of the autobiography discuss his family heritage. Here his grandfather John Parrington, the 1829 immigrant, is portrayed as "a free soul and a rebel against injustice . . . partly because rebellion seems to be in the blood" and partly because the Yorkshire weaver

> was a follower of Tom Paine. What light that . . . throws on his character! To be a follower of Tom Paine in the early years of the last century was to respond to the best and cleanest radicalism then making appeal to intelligence against sordid interest. To do one's own thinking in politics and religion is a job worthy of a man. . . . He was a democrat, I take it; one who has thrown off the aristocratic and monarchical prejudices.[8]

Clearly a follower of Tom Paine was a worthy ancestor for a grandson who looked for the origin of political attitudes and personality traits in people's heredity and environment.

In evocative prose, the sketch's next seventeen pages recollect Parrington's childhood from his birth in Aurora through his years in Americus. Stress is laid on those experiences that qualified Parrington by native environment as a Populist but one receptive to the nostalgic note in Turner. After describing his boyhood on the Americus farm, Parrington first writes that

> Hamlin Garland has pictured truly in his *Son of the Middle Border* the life that I knew and lived; every detail of discomfort and ugliness and rebellion which he sets down vividly, I can match from my own experience. The cow lot was deep in

manure in rainy weather, the stable was reeking and steaming with fresh droppings, the pig-pens were miry and foul-smelling, the chicken houses must be cleaned, which meant getting nits all over us.

Garland's autobiographical work, just published in 1917, may have been the primary stimulus for Parrington's reflections. Yet he immediately qualifies the preceding description: "It is not these discomforts that I think of when I recall those years. Life was not a drab or hopeless existence; it was filled with poignant emotions; it palpitated with unreasoning joys and baseless terrors." Now, because both the wild, primitive poetry and the hard reality of the border had passed, he feels he was "permitted to know what later generations of American boys can never know."[9]

These reminiscences are continued in one of the loveliest sections of the sketch in an idyllic passage containing the mature distillation of a subject his youthful verse could not capture. Although those later generations of midwesterners "will have their poetry of course,"

it cannot be compounded of the tameless booming of the prairie chicken in the golden morning, or of the wild fascination of a prairie fire in the soft darkness of a spring night. To go to bed with the pleasant acrid smell of the freshly burnt-off land in the nostrils, with the mind full of the excitement of backfiring, of watching the low flame running before the wind, of wielding of the broom against all dangerous vagrant tendencies; and then to wake in the morning to the call of the prairie cock from a low ridge half a mile away—a call that was compact of the dawns and freedoms of the untamed places—was not that to sleep and wake in the very land of Desire? . . .

The prairie fires have long since died out, the prairie chickens have left forever fields that have fallen to the base servitude of the plough—so much is gone definitely out my life to its loss. How much I came later to realise, when one evening in the spring of 1896, off southwest of Emporia, I heard the old distant boom of the prairie chicken again. With a rush of emotion the old border days and memories came back to me; the note was sad now rather than exultant as if the old freedoms were gone with my youth. I tried to put the emotion into verse, but failed. The wildest, most vibrant note that my ears have ever heard, refused to be prisoned in words. Since then I have not heard it; nor shall again.

In this passage the historian in Parrington seems to be reawakening the latent literary artist. Like Mark Twain in *Life on the Mississippi,* Parrington paradoxically laments that his experience has vanished forever, "at the very moment he renews it through poetic expression."[10]

Following his impressionistic prairie memories, the sketch veers from the pastoral to Parrington's first political memories: a ditty from the 1876 election ("Hayes on a white horse, Tilden on a mule, / Hayes was elected and Tilden was a fool!") when he was five, Garfield's assassination when he was ten, attending a James G. Blaine rally when he was thirteen. The next ten pages are devoted to Parrington's years in Emporia. His account of baseball, oratory, and school life concludes with a long section detailing the changes "coming over the countryside" that were to help confirm his later Populism.

After apportioning thirty-three pages to his first twenty years, only seventeen pages of the sketch remain to cover the twenty-seven-year period from 1891 to 1918. From journey out to return, Harvard receives five pages; three pages are given over to the period that includes teaching at the College of Emporia; the last nine pages cover the eleven-year span in Norman, although almost half of these describe his European grand tour. Part of this problem of disproportion is resolved by lopping off the chronology in 1908. But the apparent disproportions are themselves keys to Parrington's emphasis. His scholarly and professional life up to 1908 is subordinated to his experience of intellectual rebirth congruent with his move to Seattle, the place where he would accomplish his "best and maturest work."

After describing the effect of William Morris and of the "agrarian proposals," Parrington writes that he

> had entered upon a train of thinking that must lead to a complete readjustment of my social philosophy. It was a process of growth rather than a violent rupture, and carried farther for that reason. With every passing year my radicalism draws fresh nourishment from large knowledge of the evils of private capitalism. Hatred of that selfish system is become the chief passion of my life. The change from Oklahoma to Washington marks the shift with me from the older cultural interpretation of life to the later economic.

The change was far-reaching enough to take on the qualities of a conversion experience, as James L. Colwell has suggested. Indeed, Parrington's conversion to his new social philosophy is dramatically emphasized by the sketch's complete silence regarding his own deeply held religious attitudes and long struggle to shape his faith. Perhaps Parrington found his religious concerns too private to explain in the sketch, even to his children, its supposed readers. As a father, he seems to have approached religion professorially. Julia, perhaps influenced by her husband, did not attend church, and none of the children was baptized. Louise attended Sunday school a few times when invited by girlfriends and was encouraged to take a college course in the Bible as literature. But "religion was not part of the Parrington family's life in *any* way," Louise emphasizes. When she asked her father "if he believed in God, his answer was invariably that he was an agnostic."[11] Certainly Parrington's earlier concerns jarred with his now preferred image as a radical, although the story of Parrington's religious life would have added a complex dimension to the sketch's portrait.

Although Parrington omits the role of religion, he also seems apologetic about his former allegiance to "the older cultural interpretation of life" as well as about his means of changing commitments to the "later economic." During his last four years in Norman, after returning from Europe, Parrington explains in one of the sketch's central passages,

> I was still the bookman, drawing my nourishment from *belle lettres*. Consciously I was neither radical nor conservative, and yet my reading was drawing me inevitably out of the narrower field of polite literature into the new world of social thought that was rising about me. Carlyle, Ruskin, Morris became increasingly my teachers—above all others Morris. I have always been a rebel, I think, but with the bias of my training in art and letters I must enter the field of radicalism through such an avenue if at all. My economics must be sugar-coated for me. Shelley ought to have aroused me, or William Blake; but they did not. And it was not till William Morris came with the charm of his prose style that I was shaken out of the lethargy of the cultural. *To enter the field of modern social thought through the avenue of art*, may seem strange to a younger generation; but it was a common experience in days when Ruskin and Morris were prophets to a world content with its smug Manchesterism.[12] (Emphasis added)

By the 1930s it would again become common for American intellectuals to express their political views through art forms. Although Parrington states that his intellectual development "may seem strange to a younger generation," many members of the generation who came to maturity after World War I would find his approach to politics through culture congenial. They would form part of the audience greeting *Main Currents* with praise, especially for its evaluation of the central part the life of the mind had played in the past and was coming increasingly to play in the postwar years.

In 1918, however, Parrington obviously felt that he needed to justify the literary origins of his radicalism to his social science–oriented Progressive contemporaries. He may have been particularly concerned with differentiating his own ideas and interests from those of J. Allen Smith and other close Washington colleagues outside the English Department. Yet Parrington was not alone among his generation in entering "the field of modern social thought through the avenue of art."

Parrington's declarations manifested in his new house, his Harvard class letter, and his "Autobiographical Sketch" powerfully support his inclusion with the group of intellectuals described by Christopher Lasch in *The New Radicalism in America, 1889–1963: The Intellectual as a Social Type.* These intellectuals came of age around the turn of the century, rebelled against the restraints of their Victorian upbringings, and went on to develop a searching critique of the imaginative and moral poverty of pre–World War I American culture. The evidence in Parrington's sketch, diaries, and such early writings as "Stuart Forbes: Stoic" suggests that his childhood and adolescence contained the salient characteristics that Lasch describes as necessary for developing the new radicals' attitudes toward culture and politics.[13] In addition, Parrington shares with the new radicals another significant trait, the autobiographical impulse.

Earlier, speculations were made regarding what motivated Parrington to write his autobiography in 1918 when he was forty-six and the major phase of his career was still in the offing. The earliest forms of autobiography tended to be written at the end of a long and generally successful life, recollecting a past that might serve as a model for posterity. In the American tradition, Benjamin Franklin's *Autobiography* is the prime example of this form. Throughout the nineteenth century, Franklin's work stood as the arbiter of autobiographical form and molded the conception of the kind of person an autobiographer should be.

In the twentieth century both the kinds of persons who wrote autobiographies and the forms chosen to cast such analyses began to change. These options relate directly to the impact of industrialization, urbanization, and immigration on the traditional agrarian image and experience of American society and to the accompanying dislocations in values, job roles, and sex roles. One result was that potential autobiographers began to reflect on who they had been and who they might become and to record those reflections at various stages in their lives. The determining motivational factor began to be not professional and public achievements but the state of one's personal and private life.

At least one traditional feature of autobiography remained. Such works were still usually written by exceptional persons—exceptional because of access to superior education, wider cultural experience, and leisure to reflect and write than, for example, a factory worker. The artists, writers, and intellectuals who came of age during the Progressive Era were the first group of Americans to experience acutely the need for a new identity, to rebel against their nineteenth-century Victorian backgrounds (often including a cramping Protestantism), and to write about the process in autobiographies. In *The New Radicalism in America,* Lasch has persuasively argued that these persons constituted a new social type because they mark the emergence in America of an identifiable intellectual class. They faced the dilemma of lacking a place in the new commercially oriented social structure yet feeling out of place in the stifling cultural conventions of the Victorian world. Their solution—obviously not a cohesive effort but a pattern traceable in representative individuals—was to carve out a new social role.

Lasch describes how Jane Addams achieved a new social role by founding the settlement house movement in the United States and providing a meaningful way for culturally advantaged young men and women to help economically disadvantaged immigrants and city dwellers. As other examples, Charlotte Perkins Gilman advocated cooperative living situations that would free women to live more productive lives. Randolph Bourne pleaded for a new education that would nurture children's curiosity and freedom instead of regimenting their thought and behavior. Mabel Dodge Luhan wanted to unshackle the taboos of Victorian morality by replacing the ethic of work with the ethic of sex. Lincoln Steffens developed an advocacy journalism that provided a forum for exploring political organization and changing political values.[14]

Lasch argues further that these disparate individuals shared a common faith in radical politics. Urban industrial America clearly was not fulfilling the promises of a democracy based on a relatively static agrarian economy. The intellectuals, who themselves had been dispossessed of a social role, thus began to identify with the economically and politically dispossessed. Radicalism offered both a niche from which they could fulfill the traditional function of an intellectual class, that of critiquing society and developing new ideas, and a solution for their feeling of uselessness in having no structurally approved function. The expanding middle-class business ethic was shouldering aside the ideal of literary culture that had given a role to nineteenth-century intellectuals. Lasch's intellectuals could agree with Parrington in his sketch's conclusion that "it is this merchant economy that has written our laws, shaped our institutions, fastened upon us our constitution, determined our culture, coloured our literature."[15]

Another similarity between Parrington and the new radicals is their mutual concern for aesthetic values and for encouraging a rich cultural life. Lasch maintains that the new radicals saw culture and politics all of a piece, much as did the Simple Life practitioners in England such as C. R. Ashbee, who drew on the ideals of William Morris. Thus developed a "life-style radicalism" through which, as outsiders to a society that did not value their contributions, they could enact their ideals by living them as individuals and expressing them through their own creative channels.

In *The End of American Innocence,* Henry May describes these life-style radicals as participating in an "innocent rebellion." Lasch expands on May's analysis by explaining that in their innocent confusion of culture and politics, they failed to grapple with hard political realities. Thus after World War I crushed their hopes in radical politics as a cure-all for American cultural ills, many became disillusioned with politics in the 1920s.[16]

Parrington was no life-style radical. Except for the streak of Bohemianism evidenced in his attraction to the arts and crafts movement, he led a fairly conventional life, at least in its outward features. In the 1920s he may have despaired over America's failure to subject the idea of progress to rational scrutiny, but he channeled his rebellion into his work. His new identity as a historian helped save him from "the lethargy of the cultural," although he felt apologetic about his professional background. He did retain the sharp sense, expressed by many other intellectuals of his generation, of feeling outside the main current of contemporary life. But his concern with interpreting the present, both his own and his country's, in light of past experience, did not issue in disillusion but in a cogent perception of the role intellectuals play in American culture. "The Democratic Spirit in American Letters"—and ultimately, *Main Currents in American Thought*—can be understood as Parrington's attempt to carve out a new social role for himself, an attempt that resulted in his carving out new territory for the field of American intellectual history.

Writing and Teaching

In 1920 Parrington acted upon the declarations of radicalism in his "Autobiographical Sketch" and Harvard class's *Sixth Report* by casting his presidential vote, along with nearly a million other politically dissatisfied citizens, for Socialist party leader Eugene V. Debs. Then imprisoned in Illinois, Debs was serving a ten-year sentence after being tried under the Espionage Act for questioning, in wartime, the concept of patriotic duty. In the next national election, Parrington voted for Progressive party candidate Robert M. LaFollette. Endorsed by Debs, the Wisconsin senator received five million votes but carried only his home state.[17]

The intensification of Parrington's left-wing political sentiments, measured by the shift between his votes for Wilson and for Debs, resulted from pressures inside and outside his study walls. He continued to organize materials for "The Spirit of Radicalism in Recent American Literature" into the early months of 1917. By the end of January he had fixed the work's time span as 1870 to 1900, dropping his initial ambitious desire to carry it up to the midwar years. Parrington did not build upon the excluded section from "The Democratic Spirit" that treated contemporary nonliterary intellectuals such as William James, restricting the contents to literature and not letters. But the restriction hardly blunted the volume's thrust. The first half, or book, of the new work was titled "The Industrial Revolution" and included four subdivisions ("The State of Literature in 1870," "The Realities of America," "The World of Ideas," "Literature Considers the State of America"). The second half was titled "Old and New Radicalisms" and included three subdivisions ("Radicalisms Out of the West," "Literature Becomes Democratic," "Old World Radicalisms"). One of the most tantalizing portions of Book Two was never, unfortunately, revived for *Main Currents*. An emendation to "Literature Becomes Democratic" in Parrington's hand lists "The 'down and outs' in literature: negro, waif, outcast, poor (Mrs. Wiggs), small boy."[18]

The down and outs were soon much in evidence not only in literature but on Seattle's streets. The shipbuilding industry, vital to Seattle's wartime economy, was directly affected by the Armistice. High wages had been offered to attract workers to the shipyards during the war, but with the war's end, industry management wanted to negotiate a peacetime contract with an anti-inflationary wage scale. On January 21, 1919, thirty-five thousand shipyard workers walked out in protest of the way the contract bargaining was being handled. Several other trade unions followed suit. The result was the Seattle General Strike of February 6, 1919.

The city was perceived as polarized between "reds" and "capitalists," just as it had been divided at the turn of the century between "progressives" and "the interests." The general strike did not result in a takeover of the city government as hoped for by the IWW and radicals like Anna Louise Strong, the daughter of a local Congregational minister who became one of the strike's most vocal and influential leaders. Rather, the strike signaled both the end of the wartime economic boom and of organized radical activity. Because of the university's complicity in suppressing labor agitation, it was rumored that Anna Louise Strong and other Wobblies were going to "flood" certain classes and take possession of the course and teacher. Evidently courses in business administration, English, and philosophy were considered promising targets. One wonders if the English course was one of Parrington's.[19]

Partly as a result of the postwar Red Scare and the fear that the university was a spawning ground for leftist ideas, and partly as a result of Washington's sagging economy, in 1920 the state legislature imposed fiscal restrictions that threatened to undermine the autonomy of all state educational institutions. It put the university on a starvation budget that prevented raising enrollments and already low faculty salaries. Although President Suzzallo's personal austerity had generally alienated him from the faculty, in this instance he joined with them and the newly created American Association of University Professors in protesting the legislature's infringement on academic freedom. Despite Suzzallo's wartime service on behalf of the state, this action, combined with charges of budgetary mismanagement, led to his dismissal by the governor in 1926.[20]

The implications of such events as the general strike, the role of "the interests" in suppressing wartime labor agitation, the success of conservative pressure groups in influencing state interference in university policies, and—earlier—the Everett massacre, were not lost on as interested an observer of democratic theory and process as Parrington. His observations were expressed mainly in his new book and his courses rather than in campus or community involvement. But the issue of whether intellectuals should remain detached from or become active in social and political affairs had been clearly raised. His concern over the role of the intellectual in a changing society became increasingly important as he evaluated the contributions of American writers and thinkers.

In the short run, Parrington handled the issue of detachment in an acceptably academic way. He began to publish book reviews in the *Nation* of works on political, economic, and philosophical topics. The earliest designs for "The Spirit of Radicalism" had included a chapter on founding editor E. L. Godkin. Parrington's interest in the *Nation* was no doubt stimulated when fellow Harvard class of 1893 classmate Oswald Garrison Villard became editor in 1918 and oversaw the journal's energetic renewal. The literary editor was now Carl Van Doren, who may have solicited Parrington's services based on acquaintance with the tenor of the ideas in his *Cambridge History* chapter. Parrington was not well enough known always to rate a signature, for only two of the eleven reviews written for the *Nation* between 1919 and 1921 are signed with his full name.

The best-known works reviewed during this period were George Santayana's *Philosophical Opinion in America* (Parrington stresses the charm of Santayana's prose style and states that the book is most suggestive on the transformation from idealism to realism) and Charles E. Merriam's *American Political Ideas, 1865–1917.* "We have so long been content to be intellectual parasites on Europe that when we assert our sovereign competency to do our own thinking—as in the realm of politics—our sterility is revealed" was the response to this work covering the same period as his own new book. Among others, there was Dartmouth professor J. M. Mecklin's *Introduction to Social Ethics* (Mecklin complained of Parrington's qualifications when he took such views as "It is in Europe and not in America that the most intelligent social speculation is developing and the most suggestive experiments are being made . . . communism, anarchism, guild socialism, syndicalism"); O. F. Boucke's *Limits of Socialism* (on this specialized exposition of Marxianism, he wrote, "To vast numbers of men and women today socialism is a gospel of hope, the single promise of betterment in a world of sordid struggle; and a persuasive battle cry is more potent to stir the blood than all the science of the schools"); and Richard Roberts's *Unfinished Programme of Democracy* ("the Marxian collectivists . . . worshipped a machine regimentation of society, forgetful of the fact that the sole test of a democratic society is the free flowering of individual men and women," he admonished, expressing the nonabsolutist position from which he critiqued systems of thought in *Main Currents*).[21]

These last three reviews help document Parrington's political opinions, whereas three others show him in his role as an educator. He criticized Stella S. Centre's *Worker and His Work,* a high school literary anthology based on "the idea that English courses should serve to awaken interest in present day life" because there was not "interwoven with the pure literature some discussion of elementary economics, sociology, and ethics." Interestingly, he suggests Arturo Giovannitti's, Carl Sandburg's, and Charlotte Perkins Gilman's poetry as alternatives to the author's selections. Parrington also criticized a civics text book, Edgar Dawson's *Organized Self-Government,* for being so colorless and inoffensive it would not disturb a school board. But he advocated the use of Irwin Edman's *Human Traits and Their Social Significance* as a college text to encourage a shift from emphasizing English composition ("write clearly") to social psychology ("Know Thyself").

During 1920–22, Parrington also contributed reviews and an article—"The Incomparable Mr. Cabell," included in the Addenda to Volume 3 of *Main Currents*—to the *Pacific Review,* a short-lived journal published by the University of Washington. On the literary side he warmly greeted Sinclair Lewis's *Main Street,* the first publishing success of the new firm of Harcourt, Brace and Company; Edith Wharton's *Age of Innocence,* which would win a Pulitzer Prize; and Carl Van Doren's critical study *The American Novel,* which Parrington promptly began recommending to his students. On the political/economic side, he reviewed Frank Tannenbaum's *Labor Movement* as well as some farmer-labor books in a combined review of Herbert Gaston's *Nonpartisan League,* Charles Edward Russell's *Story of the Nonpartisan League,* Mary R. Beard's *Short History of the American Labor Movement,* John Graham Brooks's *Labor's Challenge to the Social Order,* and Samuel Gompers's *Labor and the Employer.* Parrington's comments on these last studies carry a special weight because of their proximity in time to the Seattle General Strike. For example, of Mary Beard's condensed work he wrote:

> The labor movement in its diverse phases is so significant, that is worthy of all the time and attention necessary to read its history in abundant detail, to follow the cycles of development and retrogression, to see it being wooed by larger social philosophies, like collectivism and cooperation.... But most readers will not devote the time to understand more adequately, and to them this short history will be useful. It is the only brief statement available, and if one will not read [John R.] Commons, let him read Beard, and if not Beard, then let him sit down quietly in his ignorance and say nothing.

In these early reviews in the *Nation* and the *Pacific Review* the modulated voice of the professor dominates rather than the shriller pitch of the author of "The Democratic Spirit in American Letters." This is an indication of the closer congruence between public and private spheres, between the behaving and observing self, that eased Parrington's future work.

A Washington English Department colleague had remarked that though Parrington might have appeared "wild and wooly" in his political opinions and classroom technique, "he was really a very courtly guy who conducted himself with finesse." The courtliness, rather than the wild and wooly radical, is what was apparent to Washington students if the following sketch from an April 1920 campus paper is any guide. Hyperbolic effects aside, the article reveals a great deal about Parrington's personality, his classroom procedure, and the way students responded to his enthusiastic interest in them:

> You've heard tell of Professor Parrington—his court is worthy of Mr. Bloom's consternation. Not only are the coeds adoring followers, but young men who would swallow their English requirement toute suite are given to lingering at his feet.

Christopher Marlowe isn't Christopher Marlowe in Professor Parrington's class. He is "Kit"—gay, tremendously full of life with a tongue for wine and an eye for women. Queen Elizabeth isn't merely the muchly beruffled lady [who] tripped the light fantastic over Raleigh's radiant raiment—she is the vain woman who let only likenesses of the good side of her face be marketed.

Timid youngsters just arrived from the little red schoolhouse back n' Swamp River with their pigtails hardly cold from their first marcel, creep into his office for the smile and blessed encouragement they know awaits them. The veteran flirt steals to him with all her sins and tells him humbly about the One and Only who has at last jazzed into her heart—and he rejoices—and teases a bit if the flirt deserves it.

Mrs. Parrington doesn't worry about her popular husband. She realizes there is safety in numbers. She's very used to hearing folks say they just love Mr. Parrington. She's very used to them remarking about his wonderful hair and his charming manners. She doesn't need to worry, because she's very charming, too.

If you happen to be walking with your Sunday beau, one of you who adore him, and the beau suggests strolling over the twentieth bridge, you may see your favorite professor just having the time of his life pulling weeds in his garden. There is a skeleton in the Parrington closet, but it isn't coed admirers—it is hoes and potatoes.

This portrait echoes the admiration Parrington earned in his Oklahoma classrooms. It also suggests that he was richly gifted in portraying his own persona, with a mixture of showmanship and workmanlike honesty. Students in areas of the liberal arts besides English were beginning to feel that a course from Parrington was a necessary part of their university experience.[22]

In the "Autobiographical Sketch," Parrington recorded that when he first taught at the College of Emporia, he wrote out his lectures almost in full. When he taught the first American literature sequence at Washington, the requirements included "lectures, reports from assigned reading, and a thesis." Eventually, though, he abandoned the lecture approach. Once in the 1920s a questionnaire was sent out to the English professors asking them to tally the amount of time each spent preparing lectures. Parrington is reported to have seized the form and, eyes twinkling, written down "Not one minute!" commenting that he was spending all his time reading.[23]

As he departed from structured lectures, a process well under way at Oklahoma, he began conducting classes entirely by discussion, following the Socratic method. Sitting on a table in front of the room, Parrington might call on one student to defend the "conservative" position and another the "liberal," a strategy that reflects his successful training in debating. A former Washington student has recalled how,

swinging one foot and smiling blandly, he would suddenly pounce upon a student with a volley of Socratic questions that usually shocked the victim into awed silence. Hardier and less sophisticated students would sally to the aid of the distressed one, and the noise of verbal combat would fill the room, only to subside in private debates that frequently were protracted long after the clanging chimes brought the academic day to an official close. Taking notes in a Parrington class was almost impossible, but it was wholly impossible to leave a single session without carrying away some pithy comment that illuminated a whole section of our national life or letters.[24]

The students were not wholly unaided, for Parrington provided them with remarkably detailed (and continually revised and updated) course syllabi. A not untypical example are the portions from his contemporary course syllabus, titled "The American Novel Since 1890," reprinted in the Addenda to the third volume of Main Currents. Such course guides were provided as well for Parrington's British literature classes, which were well-known campus phenomena. In addition to his classes in poetry and prose styles, which he taught regularly until about 1922, along with an occasional section of composition, in 1915–16 Parrington began offering each year a course called Main Tendencies in English Literature from 1590–1900. Fondly referred to as his eighteenth-century course, here students learned to see "balance, harmony, and proportion" in all areas of English art and culture. Main Tendencies was taught from a perspective analogous to Parrington's multifaceted cultural approach to American literature, and the course title may have been a partial inspiration for the final title of Main Currents.[25]

This approach to English literature was not entirely unique in the department, primarily owing to Parrington's influence. In 1910–11 Professor Allen R. Benham, who was a decade younger than Parrington and his office mate for many years, began teaching a course titled Social Ideals in English Literature, described as "a study of model commonwealths, and of such other literature as illustrates the growth of English social and economic thought." Also, in 1920–21 Parrington's student Kate Gregg, who was hired after receiving her Ph.D. in 1916, began teaching The Growth of the Democratic Ideal in English Literature, which studied "the development of political and religious ideals from the age of Chaucer to the present."[26]

After the establishment of the University of Washington's graduate school, a larger body of undergraduate courses had been developed to support a full-scale graduate program. In 1915–16 the growth of the English Department was graphically illustrated in the university catalog, for the British and American offerings as well as the freshman and graduate courses were listed in separate sections of the department course roster. By the 1916–17 academic year, in addition to Parrington's graduate seminar, six undergraduate courses in American literature were being taught: Professor Milliman's two major figures courses (he now included Poe and Whitman) and Parrington's two year-long sequences.[27]

With the exception of his graduate seminar, after 1916 Parrington increasingly specialized in contemporary literature, a specialization also reflected in his work on "The Spirit of Radicalism in Recent American Literature." For example, in his American Literature from 1870–the Present course, the concluding date of the spring semester (1890 to the present) was changed each successive year so that the 1916 course incorporated works published in 1915, that taught in 1917 incorporated works published in 1916, and so on. Then in 1920–21, Parrington added a third year-long sequence to his teaching load called Present Day Tendencies. This new course covered the period from 1914 to the present, and in it too the concluding year was continually updated. As a result, his original contemporary sequence was redesigned to end with the pre–World War I period.

Parrington's scholarly energy certainly remained in force, although he was aided by readers and assistants such as Kate Gregg team teaching a course the year Present Day Tendencies was incepted. He refused to be fettered by academic literary conventions or by a department that he described as "fossilized" and "medieval" in several letters to his friend W. A. Darby, a former University of Washington colleague. His emphasis on understanding literary sources as cultural documents molded by a complex web of social forces, an emphasis that raised his literature courses to the level of intellectual and cultural history, finally began to be incorporated in his course titles. In 1923–24 the sequence that had its roots in the first semester of the inauspiciously titled American Literature course of 1909–10 was retitled American Culture and described as the "development of American ideals and their expression in literature and other arts" from the beginnings to 1870.[28]

Parrington's *Nation* reviews had, like his 1917 *Cambridge History* chapter, taken him via print beyond Seattle's confines. In 1922, he took a rare break from his usual University of Washington summer session duties and traveled south to teach at the University of California's Berkeley campus. Berkeley itself seemed "messy" and sun-dried brown, but the well-stocked library was "delightful." During his stay he did a little sightseeing in San Francisco (he had not been in the Bay Area since passing through on his way from Norman to marry Julia in Seattle) and in Sacramento, visited his former Oklahoma student Jay Ferguson, who was now California state librarian. His graduate seminar enrolled a manageable 20 students, but the undergraduate class attracted 120. There were too few texts available so Parrington split the class, with a morning session treating American romantic writers and an afternoon one the development of naturalism. Some students attended both sessions and the enrollment shot up to 200.

Parrington was a little surprised by his obvious popularity and by his work load. The students jammed into the lecture hall, but the standing room only situation got on Parrington's nerves, and proctors had to be placed at the doors to ensure seats for the regular students. In the classroom fifteen hours weekly, Parrington found the routine "pretty stiff." Although he objected to the system, he left all the session's five or six hundred papers and exams in the hands of his reader (a young woman) and spent a good portion of his remaining time reading and preparing notes. A small notebook survives with twenty-eight pages of notes on naturalism, and the Addenda to Volume 3 of *Main Currents* reprints Berkeley lecture notes on "naturalism in American fiction," "the problem novel and the diversion from naturalism," and Theodore Dreiser.[29] The environs—so near to Jack London's Oakland and Frank Norris's San Francisco—were conducive to Parrington's literary subject.

"The Darkening Skies of Letters" he would later call this period, with "clouds gathering on the 'gay' horizon of American optimism." It was a subject and a mood that peculiarly suited the postwar years. One suspects the transformation from the bumptious radicalism of "The Democratic Spirit" and 1918 was well under way during that Berkeley summer. Parrington celebrated his fifty-first birthday and twenty-first wedding anniversary alone there before returning by steamer to Seattle. The autobiographical tones ring painfully clear in his description of the "intellectual revolution" of the 1890s:

> Young men born in the early seventies . . . were coming to intellectual maturity in a very different age; a new science and a consolidating economics were creating a somber temper that was eventually to produce *An American Tragedy*. . . .
> It was the conception of determinism that after long denial was at last coming to wide acceptance—a conception that underlay the thinking of such diverse men as Comte and Spencer and Marx . . . and now disencumbered of its teleological wrappings, disillusioned with the doctrine of progress, it was to shape the new intellectual attitude towards life.[30]

Parrington was born in the 1870s, had thrown off his own teleological wrappings, and experienced a revolution in his thinking. All this gave an immediacy to his teaching of such contemporary subjects as naturalism. This personal quality may have added an extra dimension in Berkeley to the magnetic teaching skills that were the hallmark of a Parrington classroom. One student in his seminar, Lucy Lockwood Hazard, went on to write a small scholarly classic, *The Frontier in American Literature*. It appeared the same year as the first volumes of *Main Currents,* with an acknowledgement in the Preface to Professor V. L. Parrington, "who first taught me the economic interpretation of literature."[31]

While in Berkeley Parrington did spend some time making professional contacts, once attending a dinner for nearby Stanford's visiting English faculty (from Harvard, Wisconsin, Delaware, and Cambridge) and promising his wife he would "snoop around" to meet the University of California faculty. Yet a letter to Julia at the summer session's end shows he rated his colleagues unfavorably and his students favorably. The English Department members "were a lovely bunch of medievalists—with an occasional exception. . . . They are pleasant and clean & welldressed & polite and intellectually dead." Yet he felt "reasonably satisfied with the way things have gone here. It's been rather easy picking in one sense—so much bad teaching seems to be done here that ordinarily good teaching makes an appeal."[32]

There is a hint in the same letter that Parrington may have gone to Berkeley thinking about obtaining a new position. After 1920 the situation at Washington became less satisfactory. The university's financial constraints necessitated a virtual open admissions policy that produced lower academic standards. There had been controversy over finding a new English Department chair after Padelford became dean of the Graduate School, following J. Allen Smith's resignation. Although he concluded that he would not want to teach at Berkeley, Parrington's experience was positive enough for him to accept an offer from Columbia University's Frank Frankenthal to teach even farther afield the following summer.[33]

His 1923 New York sojourn duplicated on a smaller scale one of the disappointments of his grand tour. Julia was to have joined him but was prevented from that pleasure by her mother's illness. So Parrington journeyed alone again but made the trek with a Seattle target shooting companion, driving east across the northern tier of states. They stopped in Ann Arbor to visit Parrington's Oklahoma English colleague W. R. Humphreys, who arranged a gathering with a dozen or so Michigan faculty. The sentiments expressed in his 1918 class letter did not dissuade him from visiting Boston and Cambridge for the first time in thirty years, since the 1893 commencement. "The place seemed smaller and less crowded than I remembered—in fact nearly everything I have seen has shrunk in a strange way," he wrote to his wife on the Fourth of July. In an architecturally nostalgic vein, he continued: "I was disappointed with Harvard. The city is crowding up against the yard and the brick and mortar have destroyed the old village. The yard is very much as it was except for a monstrosity of a new library and certain other buildings." Parrington detoured north to Quebec ("a lovely old world city—the most unlike Gopher Prairie of anything I have seen in America") and Montreal, where he was to meet his eldest daughter, Elizabeth, and see her off for a wedding trip to England. Her train was over a day late, causing her father to cancel a stop in New Haven and to miss his first Columbia class.[34]

Parrington's teaching load was lighter than at Berkeley, two graduate courses with fifty and seventy students respectively, filled with "people from everywhere—north, south, and west." One small notebook for English 326T, American Literature, 1870–1896, from that 1923 summer survives;

it contains a hand-copied insertion of Santayana's speech "Genteel Tradition." Also in contrast to Berkeley were Columbia's twelve thousand enrollment ("The very largeness of the place makes for individual freedom") and his initial impressions of the faculty ("I have met a good number of the men of the dept. & they have been pleasant & considerate"). He was introduced to the elderly and frail William Peterfield Trent ("a pleasant, quiet, unpretentious sort, with more degrees than you would think he could carry"), lunched with Percy Holmes Boynton of Chicago ("a pleasant, rather mediocre chap"), and spent an evening on the Harlem and East rivers with a group of New York University professors and their wives ("They are all liberals, know Europe well, and are unusually intelligent, and good talkers").[35]

Much of Parrington's time was spent shopping—he particularly enjoyed Lord & Taylor—and sightseeing. He visited Lillian Wald's Henry Street Settlement in the Lower East Side, finding the lovely house "a different world" from the crowded shops and noisy streets "alive with children & grownups—mostly Jews—who seemed to be healthy and dirty." The subways were "enormously efficient yet noisy & dirty"; the Great White Way was "a bad market to buy in, even if one is out to buy—but a good many seem to be in the market"); it seemed a marvel "why so many people pay such high rents just to be uncomfortable" in fourteen-story apartment buildings; Union Theological Seminary was "the loveliest thing here . . . an entire block done in admirable Gothic . . . crowded with a good deal of feeling in native stone." He was disappointed in the Botanical Gardens; surprised that tenements were only three blocks from Fifth Avenue; and wrote to his nine-year-old son, "I don't think little boys have much fun here . . . I think you would like Alaska better than New York."[36]

About Greenwich Village Parrington was less crotchety and finally interested enough to take along his camera. He hunted up the offices of the *Dial*, on a quiet residential street from which the *New Republic* had just moved. A few doors down was located the *Freeman*, a short-lived (1920–24) experimental journal published by B. W. Huebsch and served by a staff including Van Wyck Brooks. On the *Dial*'s staff was Sam Craig, the husband of a friend of Julia's, a connection that opened the office doors to Parrington. That evening he wrote a long letter to his wife recording his day's outing. In microcosm the letter expresses much of the spirit of intellectual life in the early 1920s. Of the *Dial* visit he related:

> While I was there, I met Robert Morss Lovett, Professor of English at Chicago & a well-known liberal, a director of the Federal Press that provides news to the Union Record, John Macy, literary editor of *The Nation* & author of an excellent little book on American literature—a man of almost 50 who looked as if he had worked in whiskey for years—and Lewis Mumford, author of a book on utopias which Benham uses—a very attractive young fellow of about 30—keen & alert.

Both this roll call of contemporary writers and the nativism apparent in Parrington's comments about Henry Street continue in a passage describing Washington Square:

> The latter is a queer mongrel place, three-fourths slum with tenements lousy with Italians, negroes and the like, and one-fourth very clean looking streets where Americans live. . . . They are supposed to be Bohemians, but may be only writers or near writers. President Wilson's daughter is living in one of them. Theodore Dreiser in another—Willa Cather last winter was in another, Max Eastman in another & so on.

Adventurously, he topped off his evening with a simple but very good dinner in a Bohemian cafe,

> a basement affair with tables in what used to be the backyard, now floored roughly & with a rough covering. Everything in good taste but "artistic"— plates of heavy yellow porcelain like old fashioned pie plates & other dishes sold by the pound & pronounced in color. . . . The proper Americans, well-dressed and intelligent looking, decidedly not from Gopher Prairie but not risque. It is not the Boul Miche . . . but there is just a suggestion of it.[37]

A week later Parrington returned to the area, this time to the *Freeman* offices. There he met Van Wyck Brooks and Albert Jay Nock. The remainder of his New York stay also included the news of President Warren G. Harding's death ("the weakest president we have had in my time and I think Coolidge will be worse. . . . He has been a staple joke among liberals for three years") and visits to such religious landmarks as St. Patrick's, the Cathedral of St. John Divine, and Temple Emanu-El.[38] Among the foremost items on his agenda, prompting the cultivation of contacts at the *Dial* and the *Freeman*, was the fate of yet another book manuscript.

In March 1923, just before his New York trip, Parrington had sent a revised version of "The Democratic Spirit in American Letters, 1620–1870" to the New York University Press. Now titled "The Democratic Spirit in Early American Letters, 1620-1800," the manuscript omitted the third book covering the 1800–1870 period, but Parrington provided new materials that swelled the page count from 284 to 430. An extensive introduction, titled "The Foundations of Democracy" and divided into four parts ("The Philosophical Foundation," "The Economic Foundation," "Democracy and Art," "Democracy and American Letters"), was rather awkwardly attached and could have been published as an autonomous monograph. New figures appeared: Nathaniel Ward, John Eliot, the rest of the Mather dynasty, and, most significantly, Jonathan Edwards. Edwards was lodged between Franklin and the chapter sorely needed in 1916, "The Decay of Dogmatic Calvinism."

Surprising, but in accordance with the change of ending date from 1870 to 1800, were the omissions of individual chapters on Hamilton, Jefferson, and John Adams as well as on the framing of and debates over the Constitution. An earlier outline for this manuscript had included these figures and a new chapter contrasting William Maclay ("Democrat') and Fisher Ames ("Federalist"). Despite these major deletions—which were retrieved for the final section, "Liberalism and the Constitution," of the first volume of *Main Currents*—the 1923 manuscript was thickened with the addition of crucial explanatory chapters, primarily on aspects of the colonial period. These chapters, such as the one on Calvinism and others called "Pilgrim and Puritan," "Theocratic Ideals and Economic Determinism," "Back Country Unrest and the Beginnings of Populism," as well as a new forty-page opening section titled "Old World Backgrounds," supplied much of the social and intellectual fiber lacking in "The Democratic Spirit in American Letters."[39]

The changes met with editorial, but not publishing, success. The New York University Press accepted the manuscript but with the proviso that Parrington subsidize its printing with $500. His pride and financial situation prevented this arrangement so the manuscript was sent to B. W. Huebsch, from which Parrington might expect personal attention. Whatever the fate of Parrington's writing projects, his teaching continued to sway students and he continued to think about leaving Washington. In one letter to Julia he mused, "If I could choose between Harvard and Columbia—and there is a remote possibility of such a choice—I should certainly take Harvard." But neither the faculty, students, nor facilities were what impressed him after his urban forays: "The country is nearer Cambridge & one can go out a little way & be comfortable." In another letter written shortly before his mid-August departure, he commented, "No news about prospects here altho I am pretty sure I am being considered—probably for year after next. For the coming year Van Doren is scheduled for work as usual. The way different members of the dept come up to me is suspicious."[40]

The estimation of Parrington's students happily dovetailed with his suspicions. On the last day of classes, his concluding lecture was greeted with "very hearty" applause. A girl came from the back of the room with a copy of a letter, signed by the rest of the class, to be sent to the English Department requesting Parrington's appointment to the Columbia faculty.

On that note, Parrington returned by train to Seattle. That fall he retrieved the 1800–1870 portions of his first book excised for "The Democratic Spirit in Early American Letters" and "started my winter's work of writing—theme, the 19th Century in American Letters as an expression of middle class development."[41] Thus Volume 2 of *Main Currents* took more concrete shape on his desk; his manuscript in New York more closely resembled Volume 1.

The changes in tissue and tone between "The Democratic Spirit in American Letters" and "The Democratic Spirit in Early American Letters" were also reflected in the differences between Parrington's 1918 and 1923 Harvard class reports. Whereas the *Sixth Report* declared his growing radicalism, the *Seventh Report* expressed the pose of ironic self-caricature found in "A Chapter in American Liberalism" and the attitude of cultural rapprochement in the Introduction to Volume 3 of *Main Currents in American Thought:*

> Very little happens to a teacher after he has achieved his professorship, beyond the routine of his studies and the drama of seeing his children through college. . . . He has not made much stir in the world, but he likes to think of himself as more or less a philosophical spectator of the curious ways of men, and discovers satisfaction in an assumed intellectual superiority. Thank God, at any rate, we teachers are not as the Philistines, who believe whatever the newspapers have them believe. It may be only a defense mechanism against professorial salaries, but I prefer to regard it as a pedagogic form of that romance which the ingenious Mr. Cabell would have us believe is so necessary to human happiness.

Yet he cannot resist the competitive arena, even though he now sides with the Harvard team:

> I never fail to point out to my Yale colleagues that of the younger American intellectuals who are heckling the self-righteous today, more have come out of Harvard than from all the other universities; and I take pleasure in rubbing that fact in. Ninety-three has contributed somewhat conspicuously to the great game through Villard and *The Nation*. He is the only member of our class whom I really envy. What a gorgeous time he must have, laying on at every smug and shoddy respectability that crosses his path! And I get my fun out of it rooting from the bleachers.[42]

Harvard had not changed, but Parrington had. He was not too disillusioned to stop writing, but his writing gained an acerbic edge, and he sounded like the alienated intellectual his temporary allegiances with Populist "farmer cranks" and radical Puritans had masked. He was relaxing into the role of detached observer that he had been creating for himself for years. The difference was that now he could afford to, with his *Nation* reviews, his summers in Berkeley and New York, and his books, even though they were still unpublished. One could never say that he had sold out, but one could conclude that he now understood his own radicalism as an activism of the mind.

10

~

"Three Cheers! A Book at Last"
1924–1927

In the fall of 1923, after Parrington's Columbia summer, the manuscript of "The Democratic Spirit in Early American Letters" remained in New York at the avant-garde firm of B. W. Huebsch. Its stay was shepherded by Sam Craig, Parrington's contact at the *Dial*. In November Craig wrote that "the only thing now standing in the way of publication by Mr Huebsch are financial considerations." This was the same problem Parrington had had with the New York University Press, whose offer he was still holding. But Craig's letter also carried the news that the manuscript had been read by Van Wyck Brooks and Alfred Jay Nock (both of whom Parrington had met at the *Freeman* offices) as well as by a third unknown person, and "the reports were all enthusiastic recommending publication." Huebsch was interested not only in Parrington's colonial volume but in the two potential succeeding volumes. It was the cost of the three and not the single volume that was giving the firm pause.[1]

Although finally accepted by Huebsch, the manuscript was adrift again a few months later, when the firm's financial problems intensified after the failure of its experimental journal, the *Freeman*. Craig, however, had promised that if Huebsch could not undertake publication, he would "take it to Harcourt, Brace, and Company, who have a great deal more money, and where Mr Brooks' and Mr Nock's recommendation will count for fully as much." Just founded in 1919, by the following year Harcourt, Brace and Company had successfully established itself with the publication of Sinclair Lewis's *Main Street*.[2]

At last, on Sunday, September 14, 1924, Parrington could write in his diary:

> Today signed a contract with Harcourt, Brace and Co. to publish a three volume history of American thought. The work to appear in two installments: volumes 1 and 2 together—from 1620–1870; volume 3 when completed—in about three years. The contract was based on Vol. I which has been in New York over a year. . . . Through Van Wyck Brooks, who had read it for Huebsch, it was accepted by Harcourt. A great relief.

The diary entry gives little indication of what a momentous event this was. There are only two prior references to any book manuscript since his diary keeping resumed in 1917: one note on New Year's 1922, about spending the past week rewriting the Paine and Jefferson chapters and another in late March 1923 about sending "The Democratic Spirit in Early American Letters" to New York University Press after revising it all winter. The 1924 entries preceding the Harcourt, Brace contract sketch the proportions of a life not bound by the burden of constructing a professional reputation: the death of J. Allen Smith, the birth of a first grandchild, selling the Ellensburg fruit ranch, buying the family's first car (a used Buick sedan), welcoming home Elizabeth and her husband from England, transplanting evergreens, cleaning the basement, building a retaining wall. After the passage about the contract, there are no more entries for the rest of the year, when he was no doubt busy revising, but they resume in January with their usual preoccupations: gardening, household projects, weather, Camp activities. Yet once Parrington raised his periscope, as it were, the view was possibly more attractive than he had anticipated. The reverse was also true: once Parrington became visible through his teaching and publishing efforts, he became an attractive feature in the scholarly and academic landscape.

Professionalization and Its Rewards

Parrington described the Harcourt, Brace contract as applying to a "history of American thought," not as a study tracing manifestations of democracy in American literature or letters. This demarcation of discipline—or, more exactly, definition of intent—corresponds to the focus Parrington now designed for his American survey course, retitled from American Literature to American Culture in 1923–24. The 1925–26 academic year was the *annus mirabilis*, for Parrington brought the course title into congruence with his methods and content and changed it to History of American Culture.[3]

On a day-to-day basis, of course, Parrington's teaching occupied a good portion of his time. But as his *Cambridge History* chapter and *Nation* reviews had begun promoting connections beyond Seattle, so now did his Columbia summer and New York book contract. Parrington's correspondence files began to fill with letters to and from major figures—Jay Hubbell, Norman Foerster, Ernest E. Leisy, Robert Spiller, Stanley T. Williams, among others—active in the development of American literary study. Much of the story of Parrington's role in the professionalization of this field can be discerned from his correspondence of the 1920s.[4]

Typical of what seems a rebellious, almost cavalier, attitude toward the institutionalized academy, by leaving Columbia posthaste after his last class Parrington missed by hours one of the early meetings of the recently established American Literature Group of the Modern Language Association (MLA). In 1920, when its membership reached fifteen hundred, MLA had been organized into three large sections and eleven discussion groups. American literature was omitted and had to be added by petition as the twelfth group. By 1923 the new American Literature Group had formed committees to compile bibliographies of research sources and of articles being published in the field as well as to keep lists of Ph.D. dissertations so that work would not be duplicated.[5]

This last task fell to Ernest E. Leisy, then of Illinois Wesleyan, who sent a form to Parrington requesting information about Washington students in early 1924. Parrington replied, apologizing for missing the Columbia meeting but also preferring to "make some notes" rather than fill out Leisy's questionnaire. Parrington explained that in the twelve years graduate work at Washington had been carried on, about thirty master's theses in American literature—three to six yearly—had been presented, but the library facilities were still inadequate to sustain doctoral studies. Parrington also drew Leisy's attention to the "difficulty of persuading publishers to reprint texts for classroom purposes." He had discussed this problem with Percy Boynton the previous summer. Its solution led both to correspondence with Stanley T. Williams of Yale and to another book contract for Parrington.[6]

Williams, the first member of an English Department to hold a professorship devoted wholly to American literature, was shortly to become the general editor of a series of selected works by American authors for classroom use, also to be published by Harcourt, Brace. Parrington's supportive response to an inquiry regarding such a project was drawn from long experience:

> Classes in American literature in every field except the conventional New England period suffer seriously from lack of available texts. This is particularly true, of course, of the Colonial period, but it is largely true also of the southern writers like Simms and Kennedy. In my judgment no anthology will serve. What is needed is a series of reprints, each prefaced by an introduction that will set the work against a suitable historical background. The difficulty, of course, is to find competent editors.[7]

Parrington recommended as titles Ward's *Simple Cobbler of Aggawam,* Sewall's *Diary,* a collection of Cotton Mather ("rather difficult to do"), the Hartford Wits, a collection of Federalist and Anti-federalist satires, and Brackenridge's *Modern Chivalry.* By February 1925 Williams secured a competent editor for the fourth suggestion—Parrington himself. By July, Parrington had written a forty-page introduction for his hearty sections from Richard Alsop, Joel Barlow, Timothy Dwight, Lemuel Hopkins, David Humphreys, and John Trumbull. And in May 1926 *The Connecticut Wits* appeared as the second number—Charles Brockden Brown's novel *Wieland* was the first—in Harcourt, Brace's American Authors Series.

"It is odd that we should owe this collection of their works to Vernon Louis Parrington," Kenneth Silverman writes in a 1969 edition of the pudgy volume. The radical of 1918 had not even suggested a collection of Tom Paine. As Silverman comments, "He was a progressive, reform-minded Midwesterner, while the Wits were conservative Connecticut men, among whose deepest fears was the opening of new Western territory. He shared with those 'men of notable ability and striking individuality,' as he calls them, a genteel devotion to verse, great personal energy and learning, but little else." Parrington's introduction immediately corrects the temptation to equate authorial belief with authorial interests. It manifests the concerns of an intellectual historian, not of a literary aesthetician, and previews the viewpoint to be carried out on a larger scale in *Main Currents:*

> We shall probably find their verse stilted and barren, and their robust prejudices hopelessly old-fashioned; but stilted and barren things their couplets may be, and extraordinary though their dogmatisms may seem to us, they throw a clear light on provincial New England in the acrid years of the seventeen-nineties, when America was angrily debating what path to follow in order to arrive at its pre-destined objective. The Hartford Wits may not deserve the high title of poets; they were smaller men than they esteemed each other and their generation rated them; but though they fell short of their ambitious goal, their works remain extraordinarily interesting documents of a critical period.[8]

Teaching led not only to publishing but to offers to teach elsewhere. In late 1924 Parrington received an invitation from Louis Straus to teach in the coming summer session at Ann Arbor. He declined by modestly stating he was "under contract for some work." Meanwhile, Parrington was seriously courted for a full-time position at the University of Wisconsin. The university president, Glenn Frank, had evidently received from Carl Van Doren details regarding Parrington's forthcoming publication and in mid-1926 began urging him to help create a proposed faculty of outstanding scholars in English and American literature. A telegram came in June, proposing a salary of $6,000 yearly. Instead of accepting Frank's offer, Parrington used it as leverage in seeking a raise at Washington, where he was making about $4,200. In March 1927 Parrington received notice from the University of Washington's administration that "in view of your very fine offer to go elsewhere," he had been granted $4,650 for 1927–28 and $5,100 for 1928–29. This latter figure would have advanced him to the highest-ranking salary group, where he argued that he belonged on the basis of seniority, but Parrington was not now content to wait, and the salary dispute continued.[9]

This must have been one of the times, forecast in his "Autobiographical Sketch," when a sporadic rebellion rose in his heart against his lot, spent laboring in the unprofitable profession of teaching and writing. Moreover, although Wisconsin could offer the honor to "captain our investigation," the hoped-for offer from Columbia had not arrived.[10] His New York summer had shown what opportunity resulted from an intense, complex academic and urban environment. But Parrington was deeply rooted by his sense of place, and Seattle held him as securely as the new spring plantings in his beloved garden.

If he were younger—if an offer had come ten years earlier, in 1916, when "The Democratic Spirit in American Letters" was completed—instead of now when his family was nearly grown and he was already a grandfather—perhaps the ties to place would have been easier to loosen. Clearly, the university did not hold him, although after nearly two decades he had an entrenched personal concern for its welfare. But his decision to stay was also related to his appraisal of the state of American literary studies: things were not much better elsewhere. As he wrote to an inquiring Chapel Hill student in January 1927:

> Very frankly, I rarely advise a student to come to Washington for graduate work. Our library facilities are inadequate. Just at present, indeed, there are few places in the country to which one can advise students in American literature to go. Several centers will develop in the next few years, but just at this moment where adequate library facilities are to be had—as, for example, at Harvard, Michigan, Wisconsin, and Chicago—no adequate direction is available. On the whole, I think Columbia is probably the best lot.

Yet being in Seattle, Parrington admitted in a March letter to Ernest Leisy, was not only hampering for graduate students but also for his confidence in his own scholarship. Describing his manuscript, now in press, Parrington wrote, "I have tried to puncture a good many myths and where I have fallen into them I want to be pulled out. . . . I am so far from the center of things that I am little informed."[11]

Since the Harcourt, Brace contract, Parrington's energies had been consumed by completing his second volume. On New Year's Day, 1926, he dated the foreword to his first volume, an act reminiscent of the year-end stocktaking in his Harvard diaries. By February 22, he had polished the foreword to its companion. Over the next months discussion ensued regarding the work's final titles. At last, in April 1927, when Parrington was fifty-five years old, the first two volumes of *Main Currents in American Thought: An Interpretation of American Literature from the Beginnings to 1920* appeared in print.

"Here Is the Shifting Battleground of American Ideas," announced the May Day edition of the *New York Times Book Review*, a leader in the praise that greeted Parrington's long-conceived work. Written by Donald Adams, a former young English Department colleague at Washington now on the *Times* staff, the unsigned third-page review observed:

> In all the writing that has been done to put us truly in possession of our past, nothing will take higher place than this study of our cultural development. . . .

Biographically, it is unquestionably the richest historical study that this country has yet produced. . . . Mr. Parrington has caught the moving drama of the development of American thought as exemplified in the life of the early political and religious leaders, and he has recounted the drama with a fine simplicity and careful discrimination which mark him as a stylist as well as a scholar.

In the *New York Herald Tribune Books*, Carl Van Doren declared that *Main Currents* "supersedes its rivals about as the sun supersedes the moon." In a private rather than a public format, British political scientist Harold J. Laski (whose *Political Thought in England, Locke to Bentham*, is cited several times in *Main Currents*) wrote in late May to his aging friend Justice Oliver Wendell Holmes that he had just read "a remarkable American book . . . by V. L. Parrington . . . which is, I think, pretty nearly a masterpiece. It is learned, well-written, and most stimulating, and it makes America part of the world instead of an independent hemisphere."[12]

There was criticism, too, of course, though most of it was tempered by appreciation. For example, after Holmes (whose father had not escaped scrutiny in *Main Currents*) completed Parrington's two volumes, he opined to Laski:

Now I have read him and if you were here we would jaw a volume. *Imprimis.* His work seems to me solid and probably as just as any man would be likely to be. I felt as if I had seen the movement of New England as I never had seen it before. Yet I was conscious all through of an antagonism that would have reached issues had we both been articulate as to fundamentals. The dogmatic postulate implied in the word "exploitation" occurring on every page, and the sympathy that I infer with the church-descended talk of the transcendentalists as to the infinite value and potentialities of every human soul, got my hair up. I know that we are not at one on these themes—but I don't think politeness requires me to disguise my opinion that the implications are noxious humbug. . . . But in spite of all criticism Parrington has instructed and stimulated me more than anything that I have read for some time.

A sampling of periodical reviews echoes Holmes's tone. In a June 1927 issue of the *Saturday Review*, Henry Seidel Canby first described *Main Currents* as "a work of the first importance, lucid, comprehensive, accurate as sound scholarship should be, and also challenging, original in its thinking, shrewd, and sometimes brilliant" and then went on to charge that Parrington's "chief weakness is esthetic." In a July issue of the *New Republic*, Percy Boynton stated: "The virtues and defects of these volumes are the virtues and defects natural to a work that is the result of freshness of approach, vigor of treatment and vivacity of manner. . . . He throws all professional caution to the winds. . . . He has shown a surprising disregard for the importance of the frontier." And in the January 1928 issue of the *Yale Review*, Kenneth Murdock wrote that although *Main Currents* "should awake historians of American literature to the possibilities in a new method of approach," nevertheless it was "not a history of American culture in any general sense, not a comprehensive treatment of the whole range of American thought or literature. . . . Education, in theory and practice, artistic ideals and criticism, metaphysical philosophizings, scientific writings— these are excluded as off 'the broad path.' "[13]

Most of these critics were not personal strangers to Parrington, and most also had literary backgrounds. From another discipline and a respected mentor came historian Charles Beard's prescient mid-May review in the *Nation*. Beard had attached to his manuscript a penciled sketch, a stick-figure caricature captioned, "Three Cheers! A Book At Last! Parrington Yanks Miss Beautiful Letters Down to Earth!" Mark Van Doren, new *Nation* literary editor, forwarded the cartoon to Parrington, and on the publication day of *Main Currents* Parrington sent a modest reply: "I should have felt a very considerable degree of concern about being reviewed by so militant a political scientist considering the fact that I am only an amateur, but that concern was dissipated by the sketch."[14]

Parrington's concerns about being an amateur were partly produced by the publication, almost simultaneous with the first two volumes of *Main Currents,* by Harper & Row, of Beard and his wife Mary's two-volume work, *The Rise of American Civilization*. In several cases, including that of the *Nation,* the works were reviewed together. Beard's review, titled "Fresh Air in American Letters," was preceded by Carl Becker's review of the Beard volumes, titled "Fresh Air in American History."

These twin reviews mark the only time that these three scholars—born within three years of one another into midwestern farm families (Parrington, 1871, in Illinois; Becker, 1873, in Iowa; Beard, 1874, in Indiana)—appeared together in any contemporary format. Parrington had leaned heavily on *An Economic Interpretation of the Constitution of the United States* and *Economic Origins of Jeffersonian Democracy* in his journey through the avenue of art to the new social thought. He had found Becker's characterization of "the business of history" so arresting that it served as the epigraph to the unpublished predecessor of *Main Currents*. But the titles—"Fresh Air in American History," "Fresh Air in American Letters"—of the reviews reinforce the disciplinary distinctions between *The Rise of American Civilization* and *Main Currents in American Thought,* while their tenor and style underscore the methodological connections.

Beard, whose first contributions to the upheaval in history had appeared some fourteen years earlier, opens his review of *Main Currents* by observing:

> It appears that Mr. Parrington is about to start an upheaval in American literary criticism. He has yanked Miss Beautiful Letters out of the sphere of the higher verbal hokum and fairly set her in the way that leads to contact with pulsating

reality—that source of inspiration of all magnificent literature. No doubt the magpies, busy with . . . the use of the adverb by Emerson, will make a big outcry, but plain citizens . . . will clap their hands with joy and make the hills ring with gladness.[15]

Becker's review of *The Rise of American Civilization* concludes that the Beards' new work satisfies the interdisciplinary perspectives of the "new history." In addition to *The Rise*'s concern "with the sweep of economic forces," it devotes four chapters to the " 'cultural' aspects" (defined as "manners and customs, the intellectual activities, art, science, music, and education") of American life. Moreover,

In these chapters you will find a little of everything which the "newer historian" clamors for—not a "synthesis of society" exactly, but something more than a hodge-podge, an entertaining and intelligible account in fact. Inevitably, in this book which is so free from bunk, in which nothing is too great or too little to be noted (from Immanuel Kant to Will Rogers, from Jacobinism to jazz), it is often difficult to recognize the ancient lady Clio, famous for her spotless flowing robes. She is offstage so much of the time! Her hair is bobbed, and you can see her bare knees if you care to look, for she rolls 'em too, and will in any company as like as not be seen tapping a cigarette or fumbling for a liptsick. It's all right with me. What the lady loses in dignity she gains in appeal—sex maybe.[16]

For Beard and Becker, the older form of each discipline is disconnected from reality: Clio wears "spotless flowing robes," and Miss Beautiful Letters occupies "the sphere of higher verbal hokum." But at one point in Beard's review, Parrington's approach to literature is approvingly described as "down to bedrock," and Becker aptly personifies the New History as a jazz-age flapper. In place of formalization and stylization, the three authors will ensconce a realism based on facts and a more "masculine" (or, in less sexist terms, earthly) attitude toward historical and cultural experience.

Yet Beard's review identifies *Main Currents* as an innovation within literary criticism and not an innovation that might serve to connect literature and history, ideas and culture. And Parrington would probably question Becker's approval of *The Rise of American Civilization*'s devotion of only four chapters (in a work sixteen hundred pages in length) to cultural aspects of the American experience. Because Parrington was working between several traditional academic fields, his fundamental achievement was not immediately perceived by either historians or literary scholars. That he had done something new was obvious to both; just what he actually had done was not as clear.

The Image of the Current

Nowhere has the confusion over Parrington's aims and methods in *Main Currents* been more obvious than in the controversy over its final title. Over the years both literary scholars and historians have anchored their criticisms in the supposed discontinuity between the scope implied by "main currents in American thought" and what Parrington actually, in their view, accomplished. In one well-known instance, in his 1950 essay "Reality in America" (revised and collected in *The Liberal Imagination*), Lionel Trilling argued:

> Parrington's characteristic weakness as a historian is suggested by his title, for the culture of a nation is not truly figured in the image of the current. A culture is not a flow, nor even a confluence; the form of its existence is struggle, or at least debate—it is nothing if not a dialectic. And in any culture there are likely to be certain artists who contain a large part of the dialectic within themselves, their meaning and power lying in their contradictions; they contain within themselves, it may be said, the very essence of the culture, and the sign of this is that they do not submit to serve the ends of any one ideological group or tendency.[17]

Then in their 1962 article, "Vernon Louis Parrington: The Mind and Art of a Historian of Ideas," Robert A. Skotheim and Kermit Vanderbilt claimed that the image of

> the voyage through the "main currents of American thought" was structurally the book's predictable metaphor to insure a dynamic sense of unity to all three volumes. Parrington used it variously and often and always with a sense of its fitness in his epic story of the role of ideas in American history. What is most striking in his "currents" imagery is the insistent way in which "liberal" ideas become *the currents*, while ideas Parrington is unfriendly to are described as "reefs," "barriers," "foundering bark," "barnacled craft," "dragging anchor," or as "moral squalls" or "chill winds."[18]

Some six years later, Richard Hofstadter described reading Parrington's work as being "in the presence of two great historical currents that course through our history, the currents, roughly speaking, of democratic and anti-democratic thought." Hofstadter had had limited access to Parrington's papers and knew that Parrington's working title had not been *Main Currents in American Thought* (although he cited one of Parrington's alternate titles—"The Democratic Spirit in American Literature, 1620–1870"). More recently, in mid-1990, Thomas Bender offered a variant of this view, first citing Trilling's attack on Parrington's title and then reprising the position that *Main Currents* subordinates the aesthetic to the political: "Parrington used a liberal formula that relied too much on the manifest political content of literature. This formula left him unable to accommodate in any adequate way the achievements of Poe, Hawthorne, or James."[19]

Interestingly, the image of the current is explicitly used only five times in *The Colonial Mind*. The first use occurs in an opening chapter, "The Transplanting of Ideas," when the intellectual leaders of Plymouth are described as living "remote from the current of events in England" before their re-moval to America. The image occurs twice in an appropriately titled section, "Social Drifts," that closes Book 1: after 1688, "New England was to swing back into the broad current.of English political development," and Mather Byles's *New England Weekly Journal* brought colonial writing into "the mid-current of the eighteenth century." The only full use is found in Benjamin Franklin's portrait: "Like Samuel Sewall, he swam easily in the main current of colonial life." The final use occurs in the section on the Hartford Wits: "Fresh currents of thought that were stirring the pulpits of eastern Massachusetts—suggestions of an Arianism that was to lead to the Unitarian schism—did not reach so far as New Haven."[20]

In *The Romantic Revolution,* the explicit use of the term *current* in its association with water or flow appears approximately nine times, as when antebellum Northerners and Southerners are pictured as being "borne like corks on the current of the times," and William Ellery Channing is de-scribed as being "influenced slowly by world-currents of thought." But the term *main current* appears only once, in the portrait of Edgar Allan Poe, whose critical evaluation is judged to lie outside "the main current of American thought." In addition to several dozen instances of the term *cur-rent* as an adjective in its senses of "at the present time" or "prevalent," Parrington three times uses the term in the context of electricity, as in de-scribing Margaret Fuller's mind as "an electric current that stimulated other minds to activity." In *The Beginnings of Critical Realism in America, cur-rent* appears less frequently than in Parrington's second volume, but the completed text—excluding the materials in the Addenda, which cannot be considered conceptually a part of *Main Currents*—is nearly 150 pages shorter than the second and 80 pages shorter than his first volume. The term *main current(s)* appears only twice, once simply as a reference to the work's general title and once in an extended example in which currents im-agery is invoked to explain the development of the sociological novel: "The broad movement towards a realistic portrayal of the economic city pro-duced its eddies and minor currents, which at times brought such a com-motion of the waters as to appear like the main current."[21]

The image of the current can be expanded numerically to include the metaphor of a voyage with the attendant imagery of ships, sails, tides, drift, reefs, rocks, and storms. Yet even all these do not form the dominant system of figurative and symbolic language in *Main Currents*. A larger number of images in Volume 1 are drawn from organic sources such as flowers, trees, soil, fields, crops, harvests, the cycles of the days and seasons. In Volume 2, the instances of currents and organic imagery are nearly equal (although there are approximately triple the number of currents and double the num-ber of organic images as in *The Colonial Mind*). In Volume 3, the propor-tion of images found in Volume 1 is reversed, with more currents than organic images appearing.

Moreover, in all three volumes there are significant instances of miscellaneous images drawn from such diverse areas as architecture and construction, battles and warfare, tailoring and fashion, domestic activities, fire, mining, farming, land travel, disease, family relationships, and—most strikingly in the Great Barbecue section in Volume 3—eating and drinking. These instances by far outnumber either the currents or organic images; indeed, they outnumber the currents and organic images when added together in each volume.[22] The general title—*Main Currents in American Thought*—may simply point to an emphasis that is not supported by the text.

In the case of Volume 3, the increase in currents images could be accounted for by *Main Currents in American Thought* being determined early enough in its revision from "The Spirit of Radicalism in Recent American Literature" for Parrington to ensure continuity between his title and his content. The notable increase in all categories of images in Volume 2 may be partly accounted for by sheer length and partly by the number of finished portraits, for Parrington's style tends to the colorful and dramatic when he is painting historical portraits but remains more subdued in analytical sections. There is less imagery of all types in Volume 1 largely because Parrington must devote so much attention to the exposition of theological and political ideas; he becomes more expansive when describing the augmenting number of literary figures in the nineteenth century. In the case of the immense fund of miscellaneous images in all three volumes, a practical approach suggests that Parrington was drawing upon the variety of his interests, as well as echoes of his lifelong reading, in developing figurative language. His teaching habits led him to seek pithy, evocative phrases; his deep interest in poetry, no matter how unsuccessful his own verse may have been, certainly had its effect on his prose style. Perhaps the organic imagery, like the miscellaneous, can be attributed to Parrington's rural background, his avocation of gardening, his attraction to the arts and crafts movement's calls for a return to the natural and simple. But if Parrington's figurative language is indeed central to his portrayal of the role of ideas (as Skotheim and Vanderbilt claimed) and of the form of American culture (as Trilling claimed), then it is possible that the organic imagery is used for different purposes than the currents imagery.

The currents imagery may reflect a linear, teleological interpretation of the past—the interpretation that the Progressive historians, including Parrington, have been judged as promoting. Ideational and cultural development thus might be pictured as a kind of Mississippi Valley drainage system, with each stream of thought and each experience flowing along separate channels until converging into a massive gulf that corresponds to a homogeneous American mind. Indeed, the first fully developed example of currents imagery in *Main Currents*, which occurs fairly early in the section on the southern mind in Volume 2, illustrates such a picture:

In the year 1825 three streams of tendency were flowing through the southern mind, rising from different sources, incompatible in spirit and purpose, strong in their diverse appeals; and in the end the major current was certain to engulf the lesser. The humanitarianism of Virginia, the individualism of the new West, and the imperialism of the Black Belt might seem to mingle their waters for a time, but there would be confusions of thought and diversity of counsels until one or another had worn a deeper channel through which the dominant opinion might run. ... Of these three streams of tendency it was the new imperialism of the Black Belt that wore the deepest channel, gathering its tributaries till it was swollen to an overwhelming flood that drew in every lesser current.

In contrast, the organic imagery may reflect a cyclical, less deterministic, more interactive view of history allowing for changes of course, growth and decay, seasonal variations. Such an implication may be drawn from the Introduction to Volume 2, in which Parrington proposes "considering certain new growths that sprang up in the land thus cleared" of the Old World ideals and institutions discussed in Volume 1:

A cult of romanticism ... laid hold of men's minds, consuming the stubble of eighteenth-century harvests, sweeping away the drab realisms of a cautious past. ...
Such drastic overturnings of the customary and familiar, such swift ruptures with the past, quite evidently do not come from trivial causes. Men do not put off the old before the new is ready; and if in those credulous years they turned romantic and refused to heed the counsels of experience, it was because the soil had been new-plowed for the growing of such crops as their fathers had not known. The grapes from which the wine of romance is vinted, it must not be forgotten, are rooted in the common earth. The loveliest romantic dreams spring from a parentage that is humbly prosaic.[23]

Most important, a cyclical view offers a way to include the role of ambiguity and irony in the formation and evolution of ideas, a role that Gene Wise and Richard Reinitz have deemed crucial for the sophisticated functioning of intellectual history. It is consistent with the depiction in *Main Currents* of alternating cycles of centralization and decentralization—apparent in all three volumes—as characteristic of historical development. It helps explain why Parrington, very unlike a Progressive, criticizes the ideal of progress in Volume 3. It also provides a philosophical foundation for his claim, made in the Foreword to Volume 3, that "after three hundred years' experience we have returned, intellectually, to the point from which we set out. ... Our intellectual history thus conceived falls into three broad phases: Calvinistic pessimism, romantic optimism, and mechanistic pessimism."[24]

The competing systems of imagery may indicate a fundamental inconsistency if not a contradiction in Parrington's view of history, with the realistic Progressive (currents) battling the older romantic Jeffersonian as well as the ironic postwar critic (organic). But the entire issue may be verbal hairsplitting: currents, after all, are part of the natural world in which the organic orginates. And the past—after the certainties of "God in History" almost four decades earlier—had become a mixed matter in which one quietly sought order amid chaos, purpose amid chance, morality amid corruption, hope amid disillusion.

The controversy over the accuracy and significance of Parrington's final title, with its attendant arguments regarding style and historical interpretation, would not bulk so large in commentary on *Main Currents* if more had been known about how it was determined. As it turns out, even in the case of Parrington's most common working title—"The Democratic Spirit in American Letters"—various drafts among his papers yield variants indicative of restiveness with purpose, intention, and disciplinary boundaries. Several titles are closely related, such as "Literature and Democracy: A Study in American Letters." This is also reversed to "Democracy and Literature," suggestive of a changed perception of emphasis. In another case the subtitle "A Study in National Ideals" is added to the general ("Democratic Spirit") title.

Several variants contain the term "Main Currents," although these are titles for what became Volume 2: "Main Currents in Nineteenth Century American Letters," "Main Currents in Nineteenth Century American Literature," "Nineteenth Century American Letters: Main Currents." Parrington was considering the latter as a title for a revised second volume after he separated the first part of his original manuscript into "The Democratic Spirit in Early American Letters." A related variation substitutes "Tendencies" for "Currents," once in "Main Tendencies in American Literature, 1870–1916," clearly a tentative title for Volume 3, and once in a general title, "Main Tendencies in American Letters: Aspects of the American Mind."

A variant that uses the phrase "The American Mind," the title of Henry Steele Commager's 1950 book, as the main title occurs half a dozen times, although with different subtitles. In three cases the subtitles indicate that the work belongs to the realm of literary history: "Studies in Letters and Literature," "Studies in the History of American Literature," and "Studies in the History of American Letters." In other cases, the subtitles indicate that the work belongs to the realm of intellectual history: "A History of Ideas in American Letters from the Beginnings to 1920" occurs once, and once Parrington qualified it to read "A History of the Major Ideas in American Letters" but used the same dates. In yet other instances, "American Mind" appears in the subtitle of a main title which links literary history with intellectual history—"Ideas and Letters in America: A Study of the American Mind." In another main title—"Literature and Ideas in America"—he drops the subtitle.

A general title that again unites both literary and intellectual history and more accurately reflects Parrington's intentions as expressed in the introduction to Volume 1 reads "Social Backgrounds of American Letters: A Study in the Genesis of Ideas (1620–1920)." Related to this are such variants as "Social Forces in American Letters," "Social Tendencies in American Letters," and "Backgrounds of American Letters." Others, though, indicate that Parrington's focus was primarily one that has engaged intellectual historians: "The Growth of Ideas in American Literature," "The Conflict of Ideas in American Literature," "Determining Ideas in American Literature." Finally, a general title employing the 1925–26 title of his American literature sequence, "A History of American Culture," indicates that Parrington had perceived, as many later interdisciplinary scholars would, that the "culture concept" provided a way to link literary and intellectual history with social history.[25]

In addition to these alternate titles, among Parrington's files are several pages on which he had arranged and rearranged such key terms as "social," "ideas," "historical," "backgrounds," "letters," "literature," "main," "tendencies," and "thought" to form still other title variants. Is this jigsaw puzzle procedure simply a characteristic pastime of any author searching for the most euphonious and attractive name for his work? In Parrington's case, it was indicative of something more profound. The literary refugee had carved himself a scholarly niche, but it lacked a recognizable methodological or disciplinary name.

When Parrington sent his revised manuscripts for Volumes 1 and 2 to the Harcourt, Brace editors, he evidently referred to them as "American Letters." One of the manuscript readers suggested, appropriately, that this title was misleading. In April 1926, Harcourt, Brace suggested a variation of Parrington's working title, "Democracy in American Thought," "to which might be added a sub-title like 'As Reflected in American Literature.'" In May Parrington replied that "the title for the entire work has bothered me not a little" and he had no objection to his publisher's suggestion. But he altered the subtitle to "An Interpretation of American Literature from the Beginnings to 1920." And thus the subtitle was fixed.[26]

By December, however, the main title was again bothering Parrington. He wrote to Harcourt, Brace that it must be "somewhat of a misnomer" because "in the fall announcements the work was listed by the *New Republic* under the heading Government, Politics, Current Affairs, and in the *Nation* under the heading, Philosophy, Psychology, etc. In neither case was it listed where it belonged, which might be either history or criticism." Parrington added that he had "never liked the word 'democracy' in the title." Surely this is a striking complaint after a decade of fairly consistently calling his manuscript "The Democratic Spirit in American Letters." Then he stated that he preferred "Main Currents of American Thought," partly because it would help bring the work "to the attention of those who are interested primarily in literary history."²⁷

The reply from Donald Brace makes clear that Parrington himself had suggested "Main Currents of American Thought" sometime before "Democracy in American Thought" was agreed upon. Brace commented that the substitution of "Main Currents" for "Democracy" was "a happy one." He thought that "the word 'Democracy' suggests government or politics rather than history or criticism and might confuse teachers and librarians." The publishers preferred to change the preposition from "of" to "in."²⁸ And thus the work received its final title, as a result of the demands of cataloging and, perhaps, of the political thinking of the late 1920s that desired not to be reminded of "democracy."

The Shape of a Culture, the Shape of a Book

J. Allen Smith died suddenly of heart failure on January 30, 1924, some eight months before Parrington signed his Harcourt, Brace contract. The death of this close friend and influential colleague moved Parrington to dedicate his work to Smith. The "Scholar, Teacher, Democrat, Gentleman," and "friend to all who loved justice" had served with William Morris as Parrington's primary intellectual mentor. In addition to the title change, another clue to the evident shift in political emphasis between "The Democratic Spirit" and *Main Currents* is that Parrington dropped the epigraph from the *Dial*—"The business of history is to arouse an intelligent discontent, to foster a fruitful radicalism"—in favor of the admiring dedication to Smith. Although fostering radicalism had become a dangerous pursuit in the wake of World War I, it is difficult to imagine the radical of 1918 going into print on behalf of the qualities of gentlemen. But we must also remember that the Populist of 1896 wondered what he had in common with "a lot of farmer cranks."

The particular nexus of ideas and attitudes signified by the dedication to Smith seems to mark a return to the Morris ideal, after a period of political intensification corresponding with the upheavals of the previous decade with Parrington's identification as a historian. *Main Currents* manifests a rapprochement between art and politics—between Morris and Smith, between Parrington's aesthetic sensibilities and intellectual allegiances—that is reflected in the volumes' stress on liberalism. For Parrington, liberalism came to mean not only a noble political tradition but also a style of mind, identifiable with free and open thinking. A third clue, then, to the shifting emphasis between "The Democratic Spirit" and *Main Currents* is the substitution of the term "liberal" for "radical."

This change, entailing substantive revision as well as accounting for subsequent difficulty in determining Parrington's point of view, was first commented upon by S. Kahan, a New York City reader of the *Communist*.

Kahan had mailed Parrington a copy of Bertram D. Wolfe's review of the first two volumes of *Main Currents* that appeared in the *Communist*. He enclosed a letter pleading for "radicals within one branch of human knowledge and endeavour" to "be in touch with their fellows in other branches." Kahan dared to write so frankly because he did not find Parrington "inimical to us by temper—the volumes show that. Though you mention the word 'liberal' with approval and call yourself one, it is quite obvious that you mean by it 'un—or 'anti-conservative.' Many passages lead me to believe that you mean by it 'radical.' "[29]

Parrington returned an appreciative and informative letter, first commenting on the *Communist* review:

> Mr. Wolfe's assertion that I am a diluted Marxian is pretty near the truth—at least I was a good deal of a Marxian, and perhaps still am, although a growing sense of the complexity of social forces makes me somewhat distrustful of the sufficiency of the Marxian formulae. You were quite as shrewd as Mr. Wolfe in commenting on my use of the term liberal. That word I used deliberately, and for reasons that will be obvious to you. I could see no harm and some good in using the term, and warping it pretty well to the left. As a matter of fact, in my first draft I used the word radical throughout, and only on revising did I substitute the other. I feel greatly honored that you should have read the volumes with sufficient care to have discovered what none of the orthodox critics seem to have suspected.[30]

Parrington is covering his tracks too hastily here, for "my first draft" refers to "The Democratic Spirit in American Letters," and the period of revision could be anytime between 1916 and 1926.

Kahan passed Parrington's reply on to Wolfe, who in turn wrote to Parrington, inquiring about the appearance of the third volume, "which is awaited with much interest." He closed with an evaluation that could only have pleased Parrington and forecasts the influence of *Main Currents* in the left-leaning 1930s:

> I feel that your two volumes represent a fundamental contribution to the understanding of America. It completely overshadows all the puerile stuff that is now appearing in the guise of an interpretation of America itself. Of course, we Communists are particularly grateful, because we want to understand America thoroughly in order to be better equipped for the job of changing it, but even those who wish to understand it in order to be more intelligent and appreciative spectators and get more out of looking on, should also be grateful for your work.[31]

Parrington's response to Wolfe, who had clarified that one of the gaps criticized in the *Communist*'s review was a more detailed treatment of frontier thought, ends on a note of poignant realism: "After all the job that I have been trying to do is a bit discouraging in its complexity. I am always troubled by the fear that I have overlooked some important factor that would change my p[er]spectives."[32]

The Kahan/Wolfe correspondence may shed light on why Parrington told Donald Brace he "never liked the word 'democracy' in the title." While he may have been willing, for purposes of ever getting published, to make the change from "radical" to "liberal," he may have preferred to omit a reference to political orientation in the title so that readers like Kahan might come away with individual interpretations. This possibility also suggests strongly that the controversy over his final title actually concerned Parrington's interpretation of *which* currents were the main currents in American thought, not his use of the image of the current at all.

The Kahan/Wolfe correspondence again raises the issue of just what type of Marxian Parrington had been and, most importantly, what of Marxism he might now retain. In this connection Alfred Kazin—who cites Parrington's letters to Kahan—has observed in *On Native Grounds:* "Parrington's radicalism is not easy to define. He was more radical than he pretended to be and certainly less radical than he always meant to be." Here Kazin has perceived another manifestation of the public/private dichotomy that continues to characterize Parrington's life. With one major exception, Kazin is also close to the truth in claiming that "the partisanship that holds his book together is . . . an eloquent democratic humanism cheerfully indiscriminate in its allegiance rather than a grim class loyalty. . . . His was not a rigorous or philosophically conceived idea of class struggle; it was the image of a persistent conflict that had sundered American life neatly in half."[33]

Parrington was one of those Wolfe described who "get more out of looking on." *Main Currents* was itself a great exercise in looking on. We can with certainty agree that Parrington expressed "an eloquent democratic humanism" based in a special way on the economic interpretation of history. But neither he nor his book was "cheerfully indiscriminate" in their allegiances. Parrington was soberly committed to discovering and encouraging a particular style of mind and to the history of ideas. This is not the kind of allegiance one expects on the surface from a Marxist.

A fairly loose interpretation of Marx, derived from his Hegelian-influenced early writings instead of from *Capital,* does allow for the interplay of both economic forces and ideas in history. The importance of such an interpretation is that it emphasizes the social basis of history and does not see history idealistically, as the result of abstract absolutes. This viewpoint had been expressed in a work that Parrington was much more likely to have read than *Capital*—Edwin R. A. Seligman's *Economic Interpretation of History,* first published in 1902 and reprinted in 1907. His assessment of the economic interpretation of history was far closer to Seligman's observations in his concluding chapter than it was to classic materialism:

The economic interpretation of history, in emphasizing the historical basis of economic institutions, has done much for economics. On the other hand, it has done even more for history. It has taught us to search below the surface. The great-man theory of history . . . simplified the problem to such an extent that history was in danger of becoming a mere catalogue of dates. . . . The newer spirit in history emphasizes not so much the constitutional as the institutional side in development . . . social growth. . . . History now seeks to gauge the influence of factors some of which turn out to be exceedingly elusive.

Parrington recognized this elusiveness as the "discouraging complexity" he wrote of to Bertram Wolfe. In another passage, Seligman explains how such complexity arises from a broader definition of economics. He states that after Marx's death, Engels "pointed out that economic actions are not only physical actions, but human actions, and that a man acts as an economic agent through the use of his head as well as of his hands. The mental development of man, however, is affected by many conditions; at any given time the economic action of the individual is influenced by his whole social environment." Moreover, Seligman continues, "the actual form of the social organization is often determined by political, legal, philosophical and religious theories and conceptions." While these observations pertain directly to the content of *Main Currents,* a key section in Seligman's second chapter illuminates its structure: "The importance of [the] dialectical method lay in the idea of process—in the realization of the fact that the conclusions of human thought and action are not final. Translated into social and political language, it formed the basis of the aspirations of the liberal and progressive elements in the community.[34]

My suggestion here is that Parrington's Marxism may be most clearly traceable in his sense of the dialectical interplay of ideas in history, which he carried out through his biographical method, with individual thinkers arrayed to highlight the contrasts between their ideas. Democratic—or even radical—ideas may have been defeated at various points in the American past, yet the "idea of process," as Seligman calls it, not only gave Parrington personal social and political hope. It gave his book a dramatic mood and a framework.

There are other possible sources for the structure of *Main Currents* than a Marxist-derived or Marxist-related (or perhaps most precisely, a Populist-inspired) dialectical model. Parrington was a gifted teacher who knew how to dramatize figures and ideas before a classroom, necessarily simplifying the complex to draw patterns and contrasts. Howard Mumford Jones has described the volumes as "a lawyer's brief," and we know Parrington was thoroughly trained in oratory and persuasive writing. E. H. Eby has called the structure of *Main Currents* "archetectonic," attributing its sense of balanced tension to this avocation of Parrington. One may also discern the outlines of a dialectical interpretation of historical development in the nineteen-year-old Parrington's "God in History" oration, which argued: "Take whatever revolution you please, and you will find that each one which has effected a final advance, has been preceded by a distinguishable line of causation. . . . Out of each conflict comes a purer society, from each revolution springs advancement."[35]

Parrington was almost certainly acquainted, however erroneously, with some aspects of Hegelian philosophy by 1892, the spring of his junior year at Harvard. Although he was slated to give the College of Emporia's commencement oration, "The Influence of Edgar Allan Poe on Contemporary Literature," when he did not return to receive his B.A., his close friend Vern Byers delivered the opening oration, titled "The Philosophy of Hegel." Abstracts of Byers's oration were published in *College Life*, which Parrington read avidly while at Harvard. Byers's position was similar to that expressed in his friend's 1891 "God in History" oration:

> Hegelianism destroys personality, freedom and responsibility and thus enables man to indulge his appetites and desires unrestrained. . . . The tendency of Hegelianism to destroy morality, to lessen the heinousness of evil and to overthrow Christianity. Because of the great power of philosophy in moulding our national life, we must be on guard against such a philosophy as Hegel's. Instead of a dialectic evolution we must adopt a philosophy that recognizes the living God as the personal Creator, the immortality of the soul, with a high destiny to be attained by the free agency of man.[36]

Parrington's own description of the structure of the first volume of *Main Currents* does not necessarily implicate a dialectical intention: "The line of liberalism in colonial America runs through Roger Williams, Benjamin Franklin, and Thomas Jefferson. . . . Over against these protagonists of liberalism must be set the complementary figures of John Cotton, Jonathan Edwards, and Alexander Hamilton." Nevertheless, *Main Currents* can be outlined schematically, as if Parrington had carefully selected figures embodying particular political persuasions and set them against each other, following the dialectical pattern of affirmation, negation, and negation of negation—or more popularly, of thesis, antithesis, and synthesis. This dialectical pattern is also carried out between groups of individuals so that each successive synthesis of ideas moves the overall discussion in each volume dynamically forward in time. Gregory Jay has called attention to the tendency of post-1930s American literary historians to simplify Hegel's "dialectical speculation" by constructing binary, oppositional schemes that reify into static contradictions. While Parrington may be criticized for overschematization, his residual Marxism prevents him from "a dehistoricizing of dialectic and a separation of the aesthetic from the psychological, the philosophical, and the political."[37]

Although the dialectical structure of *Main Currents* is modified in the second and third volumes to incorporate more portraits, it illuminates two crucial features of Parrington's analysis. First, characteristically each book in each volume concludes with a discussion of literary figures or movements, emphasizing that Parrington measured the outcome of the synthesis of political, economic, and social ideas by their expression in written or aesthetic forms. Second, neither Volume 1 nor 2 concludes with an ideological synthesis. Parrington's historical hesitation is matched in both cases by a corresponding hiatus in the development of literature. This first feature can be briefly abstracted from the opening books of *The Colonial Mind*, the second from its final book.

The initial portraits are of John Cotton and John Winthrop, both conservative "stewards of theocracy," who are contrasted to the differing "contributions to independency" made by Thomas Hooker and Roger Williams. Related to the latter are two idealistic "dreamers in Israel," Nathaniel Ward and John Eliot. From this conflict emerges the realistic Samuel Sewall, the first representative of the rising middle class and the first secular figure in *Main Currents*.

After Sewall comes a retrospective evaluation of the Mather dynasty's outmoded, absolutistic Puritanism, which is contrasted to John Wise's adaptation of Puritan theology to the emerging village democracy. Then, to illustrate the shift from Old World beliefs to the rise of New World democracy, Book I closes with a discussion of the development of newspapers.[38] The liberalizing influence of the public press is to be contrasted with the dogmatic pronouncements of Puritan sermons, preached by a select minority. Literary expression, through the jeremiad and the press, is Parrington's vehicle to show how ideas may become part of cultural experience, potentially affecting social and political behavior.

A corollary to this focus on literary expression is Parrington's intense concern with all forms of debate. Indeed, the American Revolution, the subject of Book II of *The Colonial Mind*, is fought entirely on the battleground of ideas. No military engagements and few public events are recorded. Book II then closes—ominously—with a discussion of the Whig and Tory satirists. Literature is produced, but it reflects aristocratic biases. The Revolution has been fought, but it has the unanticipated result of consolidating the middle class, ensuring the rise of capitalism and of the "coercive state."[39]

Thus in Book III the opponent of independence and democracy is not imported but native-grown, the Federalism of the new Constitution. Alexander Hamilton and John Adams, subjects of the opening portraits, are influenced by English liberalism, with its undemocratic system of checks and balances. The French Revolution provides a fresh body of philosophy, including the doctrines of majority will and local self-government. Brought to America and purveyed by Tom Paine, it is grafted onto the decentralizing tendencies of American agrarianism by Thomas Jefferson. But Jefferson fails to take into account the economic centralization facilitated by the Industrial Revolution.[40]

The debate between English and French thought is analogously carried in the final section in *The Colonial Mind*. The Federalist group, made up of the conservative Hartford Wits, is highly skilled artistically; but the French group (Philip Freneau, Joel Barlow, Hugh Henry Brackenridge) is more vital, putting its pen in service of the Revolution. These revolutionary writings are the first evidence that a literature responsive to the new culture is taking root in America, but their authors are not committed to being artists alone.[41] Paralleling the defeat of Jefferson's agrarianism, these writings fail to mark the flowering of American letters. *The Colonial Mind* concludes, therefore, with the ideological debate still open, in tragedy rather than triumph, if *Main Currents* is read as a defense of democratic economics. If it is read as a record of the power of ideas, however, the very existence of the debate—in literature and in politics—validates the republic's health.

The Colonial Mind is organized by ideas and the conflict between systems of ideas in America before 1800. In contrast, *The Romantic Revolution* is organized by geographic regions and the conflict between the characteristic ideas within each region from 1800 to 1860.[42] The dialectical model that schematically structured the succession of portraits in *The Colonial Mind* is modified in *The Romantic Revolution* by increasing complexities in the political, economic, and cultural development in the first half of the nineteenth century. R. W. B. Lewis's strategy in *The American Adam: Innocence, Tragedy, and Tradition in the Nineteenth Century* of defining intellectuals according to the three parties of Hope, Memory, and Irony offers an alternative structural model for clarifying Parrington's intentions in Volume 2.

Indeed, Lewis's influential 1955 study seems to have labeled what was implicit in Parrington's first and second volumes. For Lewis's model entails a dialectical sense of the interplay of ideas, with its portrayal of cultural formation as a discourse out of which other "voices" may emerge. In the Prologue, "The Myth and the Dialogue," to *The American Adam*, Lewis writes:

> I want, first, to suggest an analogy between the history of a culture—or of its thought and literature—and the unfolding course of a dialogue: a dialogue more or less philosophic in nature and like Plato's, containing a number of voices. Every culture seems, as it advances toward maturity, to produce its own determining debate over the ideas that preoccupy it. . . . The debate, indeed, may be said to *be* the culture, at least on its loftiest levels; for a culture achieves identity not so much through the ascendancy of one particular set of convictions as through the emergence of its peculiar and distinctive dialogue. . . . The historian looks

not only for the major terms of discourse, but also for major pairs of opposed terms which, by their very opposition, carry discourse forward. And in this respect the parties of Hope and of Memory virtually created each other. The human mind seems by nature to be "contrary," as by nurture it becomes dialectical. . . . Those belonging to the party of Irony . . . inspected the opposed tendencies and then arrived at a fresh understanding of the nature of tradition and America's practical involvement with the past.[43]

A major difference between *The American Adam* and *The Romantic Revolution* is Parrington's inclusion of political, legal, and economic figures— John Taylor, John Marshall, John C. Calhoun, Alexander H. Stephens, Francis Lieber, Andrew Jackson, and Abraham Lincoln in the South; James Kent and Horace Greeley in the Middle East; Fisher Ames, Joseph Story, Daniel Webster, and William Lloyd Garrison in New England—in addition to writers, theologians, and historians, the three voices Lewis listens to. Another difference is that Lewis focuses on New England figures (Holmes, the elder Henry James, Horace Bushnell, Hawthorne, Bancroft, Parkman, and Orestes Brownson) and on representatives from the "Middle East" (Whitman, Charles Brockden Brown, Cooper, Robert Montgomery Bird, and Melville).

Most crucial for Parrington, his discussion of nineteenth-century ideas begins with the southern mind, which Lewis omits. He thought Book I was the "most important part of Volume II," regarding it as "pioneer work—by all odds the most significant of the whole." It was a task that his Harvard experience laid upon him, and it caused some readers to think—despite his New England origins and long years in the Pacific Northwest—he was a southerner.[44]

These differences in breadth of canvas serve to tie Parrington more closely to the aims of the intellectual historian than the literary critic. They also illustrate Parrington's concern with the relations between economic and political factors, a concern that allows us to connect his use of the dialectic with a more overtly ideological—if not exactly Marxist—interest. Lewis's categories, however, affirm the tenor of Parrington's evaluations of the varied participants in the romantic revolution. To the Party of Memory can be assigned most of the figures in the Virginia Renaissance, all of the Carolina imperialists, the old Philadelphia school and the new Knickerbocker romantics, the New England Tie-Wigs and Brahmins. To the Party of Hope belong the frontier romantics and most of the New England Unitarian liberals and Transcendentalists. Finally, the Party of Irony consists of such critics of capitalism as Cooper and Melville from the Middle East and such moral critics as Emerson and Hawthorne from New England.

This party, it must be stressed, is composed of skeptics, brooding intellectuals, detached artists—the very figures Trilling insisted carried on the cultural dialectic within themselves. They are not necessarily the democratic heroes that a Progressive reading of *Main Currents* has stressed. But they are the figures who are closest in spirit to Parrington himself.

In this connection Parrington's intellectual affiliation with another influential postwar critic, whose interests were primarily political and social rather than literary, should be emphasized. In 1944, theologian Reinhold Niebuhr described two of the parties Lewis identifies and the character types belonging to them, although his discussion focused on the twentieth-century debate over the nature and direction of American politics whereas *The American Adam* focused on the nineteenth-century debate over the nature and direction of American literary culture. In *The Children of Light and the Children of Darkness*, Niebuhr defined "the children of light" as believers in the optimism and innocence that characterized the thinking of the Party of Hope and "the children of darkness" as believers in the pessimism and evil that characterized the thinking of the Party of Memory.

By 1952, Niebuhr found these two categories insufficient for explaining the course of American history and politics. In *The Irony of American History* he argued that the whole American experience must be viewed from an ironic perspective.[45] Only such a perspective, Niebuhr felt, could help us now account for the ambiguities of history and politics and the unpredictability of human nature. Parrington did not explicitly detail Niebuhr's description of the transcendent role of the ironic historical observer who sees both good and evil in human nature and both the tragic and comedic aspects of experience. But this description most aptly fits the complex figure Parrington saw striving toward intellectual independence and contributing profoundly to the currents of the cultural debate.

In his essay "Vernon Louis Parrington as Historical Ironist" (1977), Richard Reinitz clarified the use of irony in historical writing:

> Like other literary forms used in the writing of history, Niebuhrian irony is a device for drawing some aspects of the past to the center of our awareness while leaving others on the periphery. It implies a kind of world in which people are free to act but not so free or powerful that they can control the consequences of their action consistently. Historical events are the product of human intentions that have been imperfectly realized. People perceived ironically are complex and contradictory. Their virtues are seen as linked to their faults, and their weaknesses to their strengths. . . .
>
> To write effective ironic history, the historian must assume an attitude toward his subjects that combines criticism of their faults with recognition of their virtues. Neither the traditional pretense to cold objectivity nor a partisanship that judges the past in absolute terms is appropriate.[46]

Although Reinitz does not see Parrington's ironic interpretation of the American past as fully emergent until Volume 3 of *Main Currents*, his observations on the significance of the appearance of the ironic mode in a supposedly Progressive text bear repeating:

It has often been recognized that Parrington stands near the end of a historical tradition. Since progressive modes of perception are most fully realized in his work, he has seemed to be most discredited by the undermining of those modes. But we can also see how in his last volume he stands near the beginning of another historical tradition, one to which many of the most perceptive of our recent historians belong. The ironic vision that shaped Parrington's perception of late 19th-century America continues to govern much of our historical writing, cutting across political and other lines which seem to divide contemporary scholars. Thus his work can be regarded as a link between earlier conceptions of our past and those of our own time.[47]

The underlying structure of *Main Currents* provides a key to understanding Parrington's ironic sense of the role of ideas in shaping history and to his judgment of whether liberal democracy has ever been—or will be—achieved in America. Based on the dialogue between the southern, middle eastern, and New England portraits, the absence of a synthesis at the end of Volume 2 indicates that it has not been by 1860. The southern mind, with its Jeffersonian heritage but also its legacy of slavery, concludes in some ways the most positively, with emphasis on the development of romance in literature and on Lincoln's political acumen and humanitarianism. Yet the destruction of the slave economy by the Civil War also strengthened northern capitalism.

The second book, linking New York and Philadelphia, after a dark look at Cooper, peculiarly reserves its closing pages for transplanted New Englanders (William Cullen Bryant, Horace Greeley, and Herman Melville), pessimistic about the meaning and machinery of democracy. The two middle sections on the "mind of New England," considering "the rise of liberalism" and "the Transcendental mind," depict promising political trends and cultural innovations. But the opening section, "The Twilight of Federalism," resumes the "war of belles lettres" that began during the Revolution and inconclusively ended Volume 1's portrayal of the colonial mind. And the last section, "Other Aspects of the New England Mind," after dispatching the remains of the genteel tradition and examining Hawthorne's skepticism, closes with portraits of Oliver Wendell Holmes, Sr., an eighteenth-century wit turned romantic but still a Brahmin who disliked plutocracy, and of James Russell Lowell, too influenced by heredity and environment to free himself from intellectual confusion, who criticized political corruption but failed to see democracy as its solution.

Whether liberal democracy and cultural evolution will occur in the latter nineteenth century or during Parrington's own generation is the major issue to be addressed by Volume 3, which would not appear for another three and a half years. Parrington's initial readers ended their tour of American ideas with Holmes and Lowell. This seems less a call to action than a bleak denouement and the "romantic revolution" less a political vindication than an oxymoron.

11

∼

Styles of Mind
1927

Whereas a dialectical model provides structural unity to *Main Currents,* Parrington's definition of an intellectual and his or her social role provides thematic unity to its biographical portraits.[1] In these Parrington's touchstone is not democratic radicalism, as it was before "The Democratic Spirit in American Letters" underwent its "liberal" revision. It is not the life of one idea but the life of ideas.

Intellectuals and the Critical Idiom of Main Currents

Many critics have remarked upon the highly personal quality of *Main Currents in American Thought,* observing that it usually is clear whether Parrington likes or dislikes the subjects he discusses and that these likes and dislikes are generally determined by whether or not a subject held liberal ideas.[2] In *The Colonial Mind* Parrington obviously likes Roger Williams, Sam Adams, and Thomas Jefferson and dislikes the Mathers and Governor Hutchinson. In *The Romantic Revolution* he obviously likes William Gilmore Simms, Abraham Lincoln, William Ellery Channing, and Ralph Waldo Emerson and dislikes John Marshall, Fisher Ames, and Henry Wadsworth Longfellow. In *The Beginnings of Critical Realism* he obviously likes Walt Whitman and Henry George and dislikes General Ulysses Grant and Thomas Bailey Aldrich.

There are several figures in each volume, however, whose personality and political or economic philosophy, religious views, or literary work Parrington dislikes but whom he nevertheless admires because they had the ability to think abstractly, astutely supported their convictions in the face of changing circumstances and public criticism, and were genuinely committed to a cause or a system of belief even though that cause or belief was under attack. A simple classification based on evident like or dislike is insufficient for explaining, for example, how Parrington can criticize the failings in both John Adams's and John C. Calhoun's political beliefs but compare the two men favorably and praise them for having a firm grasp on abstract political theory. Nor is it sufficient for explaining how he can call

Jonathan Edwards a theological anachronism but express admiration for the intellectual qualities that enabled him to write *Freedom of the Will;* or for explaining why Edgar Allan Poe deserves to be called "the first of our artists and the first of our critics" but contributed nothing to the development of the democratic tradition in American literature; or for explaining why, despite his conservative prejudices, James Fenimore Cooper was so deeply troubled by the failures of democracy. Nor is it sufficient for explaining how he could oppose Daniel Webster's rigid constitutional legalism yet sympathetically describe him as a broken man whose potentially brilliant career foundered on the issue of slavery, or for explaining how the House of Adams could nurture both the finest flowers of eighteenth-century New England and the most perceptive critics of early twentieth-century society. In more personal terms, it is not even sufficient for explaining how Parrington could be strongly influenced by J. Allen Smith, then later call him the epitome of the naive first phase of Progressivism.[3]

These instances suggest that Parrington was an open-minded critic who could set aside his personal biases to evaluate a figure's life and work. He developed a methodology that allowed him to treat literary artists and political, theological, and economic thinkers similarly by classifying them according to a shared style of mind rather than by vocation or ideological categories.

In his early years, studying under Lewis Gates at Harvard and on into his University of Oklahoma career, Parrington was influenced by French critic Hippolyte Taine. In his *History of English Literature* (translated into English in 1871), Taine applied current evolutionary thinking to explain the origins of writers' ideas, attributing them to heredity and environment. This deterministic scheme of interpreting a writer and his work as keys to "race, surroundings, and epoch" causes one to search for representative men who embody the prevailing spirit of their age. But such a method cannot account for variation from the type or from what is judged the dominant social and political ethos. In *Main Currents* the figures Parrington considered original thinkers, those who made the most outstanding contributions to American cultural life and political theory, were by definition not representative. Nor could they embody the spirit of their age, for such an internalization of prevailing norms would prevent the attainment of a detached, critical perspective on cultural and political development.

The preceding chapter illustrated how the portraits in Volume 2 could be categorized according to the typology that R. W. B. Lewis employs in *The American Adam.* Parrington sometimes likes and admires, sometimes dislikes and castigates, figures who express attitudes that allow them to be placed, albeit hypothetically, wholly within either Lewis's Party of Hope or Party of Memory. But of the figures in *Main Currents* who profoundly labored to reconcile older cultural and political ideals with newer challenges to those ideals, none can be said to belong wholly to either the parties of

Hope or Memory. Rather, their quizzical stance toward the direction of American development or their dismay at finding themselves living in a world their background unsuited them for or, in the case of imaginative authors, their problems in finding the proper form to express the desired content, serve to make them candidates for a Party of Irony.

Parrington did not articulate a system of classification like Lewis's, but he worked with a more varied cultural array and a longer time span. It is more in accord with Parrington's explicit statements about his subjects to classify the scholars, critics, skeptics, and thoughtful authors who might be included in the Party of Irony as intellectuals. A focus on intellectuals not only entails a more sophisticated scheme of classification than the like-dislike approach and allows Parrington to treat, say, a political figure like Franklin, a religious figure like Channing, and a novelist like Howells as significant contributors to American thought. It also elucidates the apparently multiple and shifting connotations Parrington gives to such terms as idealism, romanticism, and realism.

In *The Colonial Mind,* romanticism—which Parrington primarily attributes to the impact of French revolutionary thinking on American political theory and to the impact of the native American environment on nineteenth-century economic practices—is absent as a key term. Absolutism, idealism, and realism are the three key terms that characterize the dominant voices in the political debate issuing in the creation of the republic. Here realism (or, more correctly, the potential for realism) is the synthesis of the conflict between the absolutism inherent in the older theories and past experience of Puritan theocrats, Whigs and Tories, and English-inspired thinkers and the idealism inherent in newer theories and present experience of Congregationalists, revolutionaries, and French-inspired thinkers. As a result, the intellectuals in Volume 1 do not so much transcend these three terms and the ideological attitudes they symbolize as they unify, in their realistic style of thought, both the idealistic and absolutistic positions.

Idealism, romanticism, and realism are the three terms that characterize the dominant voices in the debate that forms the dynamic structural basis of Volume 2. For Parrington, the true intellectual does not adhere to entirely romantic, realistic, or idealistic attitudes toward the nature of man, political and economic institutions, or the fabric of culture. Instead, the true intellectual transcends these three attitudes by tempering his romantic hopes for human betterment with a realistic appraisal of human history and potential in light of an idealistic theory of government that will ensure a just and equalitarian political and economic system.

In Volume 3 Parrington gives this transcendent intellectual blend a name—critical realism. Yet, as indicated by the difference between the titles of the second and third volumes (*The Romantic Revolution in America* and *The Beginnings of Critical Realism in America*), the development of the critical realism position entails a lessening of romantic optimism and an increasing sense of skepticism, pessimism, and irony about human nature, institutions, and culture.[4]

The Colonial Mind, 1620–1800

The first portrait in *The Colonial Mind* illustrates Volume 1's critical idiom as well as the salient characteristics of Parrington's definition of an intellectual. John Cotton is classed with John Winthrop as one of the "chief stewards of theocracy" and the epithet applied to him is "priest." But it is not the priest, the role that subsumed his later years after 1637, in John Cotton that Parrington seeks to explain in his ten-page portrait. Rather, he is attracted by Cotton's intellectual qualities, their sources, and their potential to change him from an open-minded scholar into a blind defender of the theocracy.

In the portrait Parrington first tells why he has chosen to describe Cotton: he was "the most authoritative representative in New England of the ideal of priestly stewardship." The choice is based on Cotton as the representative embodiment of an ideal. Then Parrington undertakes his restorative task as a historian: "It is not easy today to judge fairly the life and work of John Cotton. No adequate biography has been written, and his dreams and aspirations lie forgotten in the grave of lost causes and forgotten faiths. But to the Boston freeman of his own day, Master John Cotton was a very great man."[5]

Next he outlines Cotton's features, first drawing attention to heredity and environment: "Of excellent family and sound university training, he was both a notable theologian and a courteous gentleman." Before describing Cotton's contributions to New England, Parrington devotes two and a half pages to his personality and identity as a scholar, at the outset writing that "from the hour when he entered Trinity College, Cambridge, at the age of thirteen, to his death in 1652, he was a bookman, and in sheer bulk of acquisition probably no man of his time outdid him. In Cotton Mather's judgment he was 'a most *universal scholar,* and a living system of the liberal arts, and a *walking library.*' "[6] Not only did the conservative Cotton Mather respect him, but also the liberal Roger Williams, whose principles Cotton would so roundly refute in *The Way of the Congregational Churches Cleared.* Parrington attributes Cotton's appeal to his character, which was manifested in his visage and bearing:

> Good men were drawn to him by his sweetness of temper, and evil men were overawed by his venerable aspect. He seems to have been an altogether lovable person, with white hair framing a face that must have been nobly chisled, gentle-voiced, courteous, tactful, by nature "a tolerant man" who placidly bore with a dissentient and gladly discovered a friend in an antagonist.

In addition, "however much he loved cloistered scholarship," Cotton's priestly role and eloquent preaching kept him in vital contact with his parishioners and thus "the immediate source of his great influence was the spoken rather than the written word." He was also well-known and esteemed in England, shining "as an intellectual light at the university" and counting as his friends Cromwell and other Puritan gentlemen and political figures.[7]

Yet Cotton had his faults. Ironically, they seem to be an outcome of his strengths, being related to his tolerant, scholarly nature. "His quiet yielding before opposition suggests that he may have been given to opportunism," and "his fondness for intellectual subtleties" prompted his grandson to call him " 'a most excellent casuist.' " Both of these traits were unfortunately reinforced by "his daily contact with narrow-minded and intolerant men" and "gave an unhappy bias to his later career." So Parrington singles out Cotton's Boston environment as the cause of the pitiable process by which "the priest . . . overcame the intellectual."[8]

Clearly, these environmental pressures were strong, for in addition to being a charismatic preacher and a respected English gentleman, he had "an openminded curiosity that made him receptive to new ideas and tempted him to play with doctrines that were intolerable to his bigoted associates. It was possibly this native sympathy with free speculation that drew him into the camp of Mistress Hutchinson with her doctrine of inner light."[9] Interestingly, Parrington gives a psychological explanation for how Cotton's "openminded curiosity" and "native sympathy with free speculation" were hindered by his Boston environment and put into the service of casuistry. Cotton "was not a man to persecute and to harry, nor was he one to stand in isolated opposition to associates whom he respected." He yielded to the judgment of men such as Endicott and Dudley in the Hutchinson case, in the first whippings of the Quakers, and in urging the death penalty for King Philip's son and "the enslavement of the remnant of Philip's tribe." On this point, Parrington approvingly quotes James Truslow Adams's evaluation that although Cotton had "a broader mind and wider vision than any of the other clergy of the colony, he had not the courage to stand alone, beyond a certain point." After citing these explanations and charges, Parrington writes a passage that illuminates much of his own character as well as his empathy with the dilemma Cotton faced as a result of the conflicting claims of his personality, his scholarly predisposition, and his role in the theocracy:

> An apologist—and whoever has felt the charm of John Cotton's personality easily becomes an apologist—will perhaps find some grounds of excuse for his later position. He was in an unhappy position. He was ill at ease in his mind, and his frequent tacking in the face of adverse winds was characteristic of the intellectual who sees all sides of the question.[10]

But Parrington knows that empathy is an insufficient defense of Cotton's acts and looks beyond Cotton's "frequent tacking"—and beyond his admirable personal and intellectual qualities—for another clue to Cotton's change of mind. Switching his own role from sympathetic biographer, Parrington writes that "the historian, however, will seek a more adequate explanation in the roots of his environment." At this point Parrington begins, appropriately, to focus on Cotton's social thought, and the concluding seven pages of the portrait are devoted to describing Cotton's contributions to the theocracy and how they reflect the twin claims of his theological training and his political experience in England before coming to America at age forty-six. Parrington argues:

> The idealism of John Cotton was the fruit of his training, and his theocratic dreams were conditioned by the facts that he was both a Calvinist and a Carolinian gentleman. The fusion of these two influences resulted in the unique political theory of an ethical aristocracy, consecrated to moral stewardship in the state. A lifelong student of Calvin's *Institutes,* he found there a system of social organization that responded to every demand of the theologian and the aristocrat.[11]

Cotton's conception of a "Presbyterian Bible commonwealth" run by elders who were "responsible to God for the spiritual well-being of the people" was antithetical to "the doctrine of unlimited popular sovereignty," which was based on a democratic belief in natural rights. Nevertheless, such a conception had revolutionary social implications, for it "would substitute an aristocracy of the Saints for the landed aristocracy, and refashion society upon ethical rather than economic lines." Although Cotton's primary duty was "to assist the magistrates in checking the dangerous drift towards a democratic organization of church and state, which the new environment encouraged; and to defend the theocratic ideal against all critics," Parrington insists that the ethical basis of a theocracy was a "negation of the principle of hereditary aristocracy" as well as "the negation of democracy." Thus "it must be set down in John Cotton's accounts that he discouraged the transplanting of English aristocracy to the soil of Massachusetts."[12]

It may seem strange to see John Cotton enlisted in the camp of Hamiltonian critics and to see Parrington defend an opponent of democracy. But it is characteristic for him to evaluate whether his subjects contributed anything to the development of liberalism, and in Parrington's view, Cotton did. Yet he did so at great personal cost, for ultimately his defense of theocracy and Presbyterian principles against English critics caused him to close his once open mind to the Congregational principles expressed by Roger Williams and to the Antinomian implications of his own teachings.

In concluding the portrait, Parrington comments on how Cotton reacted to the social upheaval in England that was "threatening to submerge, not only Presbyterianism, but the very social order in which he had been nurtured." Again giving a psychological explanation for Cotton's actions, he writes: "How easy it is for good men, in presence of the new and strange, to draw back in timid reaction; and failing to understand or fearing for their prestige, to charge upon the new and strange a host of evils that exist only in their panic imaginations!" Because he appreciates Cotton's personal qualities, his intellectual capacity and potential, the effects of his aristocratic English background on his political and social sympathies, and his ethical idealism that helped prevent the creation of a landed aristocracy in the New World, Parrington is generous in his final estimation of Cotton's reputation. He cites the prevailing spirit of the age as the causative factor in swaying Cotton toward intolerance of new ideas in his later years:

> For this the age was more to blame than the man. It was no fault of John Cotton's that he was the child of a generation reared under the shadow of absolutism, fearful of underling aggression, unable to comprehend the excellence inhering in democratic faith. He reasoned according to his light; and if he rather too easily persuaded himself that the light which shined to him was the single divine light, he proved himself thereby an orthodox Puritan if not a catholic thinker.[13]

Cotton's portrait has been described at length because it so well illustrates the features of Parrington's definition of an intellectual and his role, providing a model by which nearly all of the other portraits in *Main Currents* can be evaluated. Those features may be summarized as follows:

1. John Cotton was a scholar, a bookman.
2. He did not cloister himself but participated in the life of the community; that is, he was an active scholar.
3. He was open, at least in his earlier years, to new ideas and tolerant of differing opinions.
4. Even in his later years, he was an idealist and astutely defended ethical principles in the face of opposition.
5. He underwent a period of intellectual change necessitated by a crisis that threatened his career.
6. He was a child of his age—in this case, an age of absolutism—yet contributed at least one liberalizing idea that would later serve the development of democracy in America.
7. He was unable to stand apart from his narrow-minded Boston environment, but he knew what it was to challenge the existing order, for he had abandoned his aristocratic background and promising career in England and removed to America.
8. His insight into the course of American development was informed by his knowledge of revolutionary English social and political changes. His Eu-

ropean experience thereby gave him a cosmopolitan perspective on American experience which prevented him from becoming narrowly provincial in his thinking.

9. Because he lived in both England and Massachusetts, he literally lived in both an old world and a new world. Then, in the new world, he witnessed the order he had helped create being challenged by new ideas and shaped by the new environment. Thus, he twice experienced a sense of "dwelling between worlds."

Once these major features are abstracted from Cotton's portrait, Cotton begins to resemble Vernon Parrington, especially the Parrington portrayed in the 1918 "Autobiographical Sketch." Although Parrington does not call himself an intellectual in the sketch, he does apply the term six times to Cotton. The portraits are similar because the painter sees a kindred style of mind in his subject. These similarities may be enumerated point by point:

1. Parrington was certainly a scholar and a bookman. An avid reader since boyhood, he pursued his education in the library stacks, not only at Emporia and Harvard but also at Washington, reading voluminously in preparation for writing *Main Currents.*

2. An inspiring, innovative, and engaging teacher throughout his adult life, he was no armchair philosopher but an active scholar in the Emersonian mold described in the "American Scholar" (1837).

3. In the first thirty-seven years of his life he made the transition—sometimes painfully—from farm life to small town life to Cambridge; from country boy to the Judge's son to college professor; from nominal Republican to political radical; from Protestant pietism to late nineteenth-century aestheticism to early twentieth-century Progressivism.

4. His succession of American literature courses at the University of Washington during the last two decades of his life indicates a remarkable facility for amassing new material and new ideas, yet this process was guided by his idealistic conception of democratic theory and the way art can affect people's lives.

5. His experience of being fired at the University of Oklahoma led directly to his entry into "the field of modern social thought through the avenue of art."

6. This entry, signified most dramatically by the publication of *Main Currents,* was made possible in part because he was born in an age of exploitation and came to intellectual maturity in an age of increasing doubt and uncertainty about the value of progress.

7. Parrington knew well the price and the gain of standing apart, having been an outsider at Harvard because of the socially and intellectually

cramping effects of his Kansas origins. Later, his approach to American literature and to American ideas would set him outside of traditional academic boundaries and methods.

8. His 1903–4 European grand tour convinced him that a cross-cultural perspective was essential to understanding American political, economic, cultural, and institutional development. The tour was supplemented by his cross-disciplinary interest in painting, architecture, modern languages, and the whole Anglo-American literary tradition. Clearly, he was no narrow academic but sought to be an intellectual cosmopolitan.

9. Having lived in the Midwest, in Cambridge, and in the Pacific Northwest, Parrington was sensitive to the differing geographic "worlds" within America. But most important, he felt that he belonged to a transitional intellectual generation, one that came to maturity at the beginning of the Progressive Era and began the work of reforming American society only to have the next generation that came to maturity after World War I criticize their elders' political ideals and cultural values. This sense of dwelling between two worlds of thought, coupled with his experiences of changing allegiances from art to social thought, made him acutely sensitive to other intellectuals throughout American history who had undergone similar experiences.

Parrington's practice of defining the visual images of the figures he discusses in *Main Currents* lends itself to his task as a biographer to personify and revivify his subjects and to his task as a historian to restore and clarify reputations. It is almost as if he is dusting off an old painting, squinting to discover the personality behind the cracked and faded canvas. The visual component in *Main Currents* is the reflection of Parrington's long and lively interest in painting, in architecture, in prose style, and in poetry (where images and symbols are inextricably linked with denotative meaning). Parrington, however, pulls back from "the charm of Cotton's personality" to resume his task of defining Cotton's ideas, as if he were in a gallery and stepped away from a painting to gain another, more objective perspective and to consider it in the context of the rest of the exhibition.

Until Benjamin Franklin's portrait appears, all of the figures in Volume 1 are religious Puritans and/or were born in England. After Franklin, the sphere of an intellectual's activity shifts to the political and cultural life of the colonies and then that of the new nation. As a result, the way in which an intellectual stands apart and challenges or critically surveys American experience changes from a religious to a secular context, as more avenues of career and social identification open, concomitant with American development. In addition, for an intellectual to gain European experience and familiarity with the European origins of American ideas, he could not rely on the accident of birth but must either physically visit Europe, as Franklin did, or be well read in European political theory, as John Adams was. If a person did neither of these things (and the second is the more important), in Parrington's opinion he or she remained intellectually limited and narrowly provincial.

Franklin's and Adams's portraits illustrate, in different ways, the limitations of the realistic style of mind uninformed by idealism about human nature. Franklin is called "an intellectual cosmopolitan" whose "mind from early youth to extreme old age was curiously open and free," but "by temperament he was what we should call today a sociologist. He cared little for abstract reasoning, but much for social betterment." Though Parrington states at the portrait's beginning that "the Calvinism in which he was bred left not the slightest trace upon him; and the middle-class world from which he emerged did not narrow his mind to its petty horizons," in the end he observes that "a man who is less concerned with the golden pavements of the City of God than that the cobblestones on Chestnut Street in Philadelphia should be well and evenly laid . . . does not reveal the full measure of human aspiration." He was not a great thinker, but "he proved himself a great and useful man." In contrast, John Adams "in spite of his dogmatism and inconsistencies . . . remains the most notable political thinker—with the possible exception of John C. Calhoun—among American statesmen." Parrington compares him to Samuel Johnson, stating that he "was an uncompromising realist who refused to be duped by fine dreams or humanitarian panaceas; he was much given to throwing cold water on the hope of social regeneration through political agencies." Yet Parrington also ascribes to Adams's "excellent qualities of mind and heart. . . . A stubborn intellectual independence and a vigorous assertiveness" and praises him for "his refusal to hunt with the pack," a trait resulting in unpopularity.[14]

As in John Winthrop's case, both Franklin and Adams are too involved with affairs of state to be true intellectuals. But neither would suffer the fate of Cotton Mather, who let his once inquisitive mind become circumscribed by the boundaries of old Boston. Unlike his father, Increase, Cotton Mather failed to be enlarged by contact with European political ideas. This failure was not offset by his membership in the Royal Society or his scientific achievements. He did not know what it meant to dwell between worlds but was subsumed by his environment and by the absolutistic spirit of his age. When he closed his study windows to the fresh breezes of current thought (which were liberalizing and realistic), his mind turned inward and, in Parrington's judgment, he became a grotesque caricature of a scholar, a psychological aberration interested only in psychological aberrations.[15]

Between John Cotton's and Cotton Mather's contrasting styles of mind—that is, between those who come close to fulfilling all nine of the features abstracted from Cotton's portrait and those who fail, for various reasons, to fulfill the most critical features (numbers 4, 5, and 6 are variables that are not always significant)—most of the rest of the figures in *Main Currents* can be ranged. There is, however, one crucial exception. In the case of creative writers, Parrington modifies his stipulations that an intellectual be an active scholar involved in the life of the community or in affairs of state and that he be open to European political ideas. Thus there are two categories of intellectuals in *Main Currents:* religious, political, and economic thinkers whose social thought is directed toward the idealistic betterment (in their view, for this category includes conservatives as well as liberals) of American society and government; and artists whose creative work may reflect daily experience and ideas but whose creativity must be nurtured by detachment and whose work must be firmly rooted in native grounds and not in European themes and locales.

If Parrington's requirements for artists seem to indicate a surprising streak of aesthetic formalism, they also echo how he differentiated between literature expressly written as propaganda and literature originating in a love of beauty in his 1917 essay "Economics and Criticism." If Parrington's requirements that religious, political, and economic thinkers be well read in European theory places more weight on the autonomy of ideas than a strict application of an economic interpretation of history seems to allow, they also support his announcement in the Introduction to Volume 1 that "the child of two continents, America can be explained in its significant traits by neither alone."[16]

The first full-fledged portrait of a writer in *Main Currents* is of Philip Freneau. The life and career of this "poet of two revolutions" illustrates how Parrington modifies his general definition of an intellectual in the case of artists. The portrait opens with the statement: "It is fitting that our first outstanding poet should have been a liberal." Then Parrington identifies political liberalism with idealism, observing: "The idealist has always seen deeper into the spirit of America than the realist, and been less complacent with halfway achievement. And it is equally fitting that his idealism should have got him into trouble with the dominant group of his generation."[17] Unlike John Cotton, Freneau was not afraid "to persecute and to harry" the exponents of authority in "the dominant group of his generation," nor was he an aristocrat. Rather, he believed that "if government were truly democratized, if it concerned itself with realities, serving the people in the homely affairs and common needs of everyday life, there would be no need of aristocratic ceremonial." Comparing Freneau to Tom Paine, Parrington identifies idealism with realism, claiming that "Freneau was an idealist, with his head full of ideas which to practical men were only silly French notions; and yet the idealist, in this matter of *res publica,* was the true realist."[18] Thus Freneau unifies the three key terms of Volume 1 by combating the absolutism of the Federalists with an idealistic belief in a democratic, and therefore realistic, conception of the political state. In contrast, John Cotton could be said to have combated the democratic realism of the Congregationalists with his idealistic belief in an aristocratic, and therefore absolutistic, conception of the religious state.

Like Cotton, though, Freneau's life and career were divided into two major phases. In the first, such poems as "The Rising Glory of America" were written which supported the aims of the leaders—Adams, Hamilton, and Washington—of the Revolution of 1776. But after the Revolution of 1793 in France, Freneau parted company with the Federalists and became a Jacobin. This act ruined his reputation, not only because he held ideas antithetical to the dominant group but also because he began to express them in journalistic prose as the editor of the *National Gazette,* the rival liberal alternative to Hamilton's Federalist organ, the *United States Gazette.*[19]

Of this second phase, Parrington comments that Freneau's literary activity "was remarkable. Songs and odes and satires came from his ready pen in unending stream, eager, cutting, vibrant with feeling." The stimulus to this activity came from two sources: the French uprising and a two-year sojourn, begun in 1775, in the West Indies and followed by voyages about the islands and along the American coast. During his removal from New York, he "was free to cultivate the romantic strain of poetry that was strong in him." But a period of stagnation soon followed upon his return, for "the spirit of romantic poetry was deadened by an unsympathetic environment." Then the French uprising occurred, and Freneau decided that "If he could not be a poet to America he would enlist in the army of democracy. . . . So Freneau enthusiastically joined with Paine and Jefferson in the partisan labor of spreading the new faith."[20]

Like John Cotton, Freneau was open to European ideas and achieved a cosmopolitan perspective on American culture. Parrington approvingly writes that "if fresh fuel had not been brought from overseas to kindle anew his social enthusiasms, it is likely that he would have drifted into a stale and unprofitable old age." But no matter how sympathetic Parrington is to Freneau's political beliefs and admiring of his service in conveying French democratic ideals through the *National Gazette* and through poetry dealing with political figures and topics, in his final evaluation he criticizes Freneau for abandoning his role as poet and turning partisan during both phases of his career.

Toward the beginning of the portrait, Parrington had claimed:

The chief desire of Freneau's life was to be a poet, and if the country had not been turmoiled by revolution, doubtless he would have been content to "live unpromoted and write poems." But revolution and not poetry was the serious business of the age, and he chose to have a hand in that business. . . . He had only to stand apart from the turmoil, refusing to soil his hands with politics, and cultivate his faculty for verse, to have made himself the indisputable founder of American poetry. He was endowed with a romantic imagination and love of natural beauty, a generation before the romantic revival, and he might well have become a notable contributor to that revival.

But he refused to stand apart.

As a result, "his place in American letters was fixed by a Federalistic verdict," based on his role as a democratic journalist. Thus Parrington's task as a historian is to restore Freneau's reputation as a poet, a task that had been impossible because "only within recent years has a collected edition of his poems been accessible, and his prose writings still remain buried in newspaper files."[21]

In concluding the portrait, Parrington writes that instead of becoming a notable poet, Freneau can most accurately be judged, like Paine and Jefferson and Franklin, as "a notable American." That is no small achievement, but it was attained at both personal and professional cost.

> After all, the poet in Freneau was deeper than the partisan. Despite his conviction that a sordid America cared nothing for poetry . . . his love of beauty was never killed nor the spring of poetic creation dried up. . . . His life was bitter and turbulent, cast in a bitter and turbulent age; yet he found some grains of comfort in the contemplation of nature and the exercise of the poet's craft. . . . If he was not a great poet whom all the critics praise, he loved beauty and served it in a careless world among an indifferent people, and it ill becomes America to forget his contribution or deny him some portion of the honor that has fallen generously to others no more deserving.[22]

If the scholarly John Cotton had turned liberal journalist, Parrington would have praised him. But when an artist like Freneau enters into public affairs and, under the influence of European ideas, writes upon political topics, Parrington accuses him of abandoning his proper role, for subjugating the call of beauty to a partisan call to ideological arms. As in Cotton's case, the age is more to blame than the man for this shift in roles. Both men dwelt between changing intellectual worlds, but neither one could stand far enough apart from those changes to achieve a transcendent, ironic perspective on them and thus both were subsumed by their environments and the prevailing spirits of their ages.

Of the other two writers considered along with Freneau in the "French Group," Joel Barlow suffers a similar fate. Barlow is praised for being "a thoroughgoing radical in economics and politics" and an intellectual cosmopolitan, but he was "no innovator in polite literature," letting the "heroic note in the vein of a political pamphleteer" play havoc with the poetry of *The Columbiad*. In contrast, Hugh Henry Brackenridge escaped subjugating art to politics in *Modern Chivalry*. Brackenridge had collaborated with Freneau on "The Rising Glory of America," but in his later years he remained "a free-lance critic, independent in thought and act . . . no vociferous party or class advocate given to enlisting God on his side." In addition, unlike Barlow and his stultifying use of the grand style, "he is a refreshing person to come upon after one is satiated with the heroic."[23]

One clue to Brackenridge's success is that, unlike Freneau and Cotton, he refused to howl with the pack. A stout and unrepentant democrat, he was no visionary to shut his eyes to unpleasant facts lest they disturb his faith. As he considered the turbulent confusions of an America in rough process of democratization, he saw the evils as clearly as the hope, and it amused him to satirize those evils after the manner of Don Quixote.[24]

Another clue is that he "had become a thorough Westerner with a fresh point of view." As a judge, traveling "among the stump fields of his Pennsylvania circuit he was equally removed from the cynicism of Hamilton and the romanticism of Barlow." Though he was educated in the East at Princeton, from his western, outsider's vantage point, he was able to aim *Modern Chivalry*'s satire "primarily at backwoods shortcomings, but with an eye that kept turning towards the older settlements to scrutinize their equal shortcomings." In this respect, Brackenridge can be seen as anticipating the work of Cooper and other figures in Volume 2 who were troubled by Jacksonian equalitarianism but were committed to the ideal of democracy. By being able to see clearly both the evils and the hope as America underwent the "rough process of democratization" and by finding a balance between form, style, and content in his creative work,[25] Brackenridge becomes the first artistic candidate for the Party of Irony in *Main Currents*. Fittingly, his portrait is the last to appear in Volume 1.

The Romantic Revolution in America, 1800–1860

Throughout *The Romantic Revolution*, the idealistic figure and romantic spirit of Thomas Jefferson are the criteria by which Parrington evaluates his subjects' political ideas. The central problem in Volume 2, however, is whether that brand of idealism and romanticism can be realistically achieved. Parrington's concern with the intellectual's style of mind colors his portrait of Jefferson as much as his concern with Jefferson's political principles. The techniques by which Parrington evaluated John Cotton are brought into play in this passage:

From the distinguished group of contemporary political thinkers Jefferson emerges as the preeminent intellectual, widely read, familiar with ideas, at home in the field of speculation, a critical observer of men and manners. All his life he was a student, and his devotion to his books, running often to fifteen hours a day, recalls the heroic zeal of the Puritan scholars. He was trained in the law, but he was too much the intellectual, too curious about all sorts of things, to remain a lawyer. For such a man the appeal of political speculation was irresistible, and early in life he began a wide reading in the political classics that far outweighed Coke and Blackstone in creative influence on his mind. He was equally at home with the English liberals of the seventeenth century and the French liberals of the eighteenth. . . . [H]e judged old world theory in the light of its applicability to existing American conditions, and restrained his love of speculation by immediate practical considerations. The man of affairs kept a watchful eye on the philosopher in his study.[26]

Although Jefferson's changes of mind did not have the effect, as Cotton's did, of buttressing an outworn order, he did suffer reversals of reputation and knew what it was to dwell between worlds. Parrington explains that Jefferson was "apparently inconsistent, changing his program with the changing times," seeming

> to his enemies devoid of principle. . . . One of the most bitterly hated and greatly loved men in the day when love and hate were intense, he was the spokesman of the new order at a time of transition from a dependent monarchical state, to an independent republican state. Back of the figure of Jefferson, with his aristocratic head set on a plebian frame, was the philosophy of a new age and a new people.[27]

Concurrent with the changes from volume to volume in the critical idiom of *Main Currents* is a transformed possibility for the intellectual's role. None of the changes in critical terms—from absolutism, idealism, realism to romanticism, idealism, realism to critical realism and pessimism and irony—affects the nine features abstracted from John Cotton's portrait or the two modifications from artists abstracted from Philip Freneau's portrait. Three portraits—one from each of the regions demarcating Volume 2's structural divisions—will illustrate Parrington's consistency in applying his criteria for attaining the status of an intellectual: Poe from the South, Cooper from the Middle East, and Webster from New England.

Particularly since the appearance of *The Liberal Imagination*, Parrington's treatment of Poe has been served up as evidence of his disregard in *Main Currents* for the aesthetic, the belletristic, in favor of the didactic, the realistic. Fortunately, a focus on intellectuals helps to collapse this distinction, to offer a rebuttal to Trilling's estimation of Parrington's sensibility as artistically reductive and politically programmatic.[28]

The portrait of Poe may well have been seized upon as evidence of Parrington's disregard of belles lettres simply because it is shorter (two and a half pages) than the typical portrait (ten to twelve pages) in *Main Currents*. The length is not an indication, however, of Parrington's knowledge of or interest in Poe. He imitated Poe's techniques in his Harvard short story "The House of Memoire." He was slated to give the 1892 commencement address at the College of Emporia on the influence of Edgar Allen Poe on contemporary literature. He incorporated Poe in his literature courses regularly at the University of Washington from at least 1912 onward. And he included a Poe section in "The Democratic Spirit in American Letters" that is close in tone to that in *Main Currents*. The closing paragraph is instructive:

It ill becomes a democrat to censure Poe for the aloofness of his art from the world of reality. If there is one right which every rational society will ultimately regard as sacred, it is the right to free untrammeled expression. If the artist choose to remain aloof from his fellows, we can only accept that choice in the conviction that a free creativeness is nobler than any compulsion—be it even a compulsion to service. . . . In serving the cause of beauty in spite of an unsympathetic age Poe must be accounted a friend to the deeper purpose of democracy, which can be no other than the development of a fine and free individualism.[29]

After such high praise in 1916, why such abrupt treatment a decade later in *The Romantic Revolution?* The Poe section in Parrington's original manuscript is similar in length to that allotted the other figures—Bryant, Irving, Hawthorne, and Longfellow—grouped in a chapter titled "Romanticism and Democracy." All were deployed into separate sections and chapters in *Main Currents,* where the earlier estimations were usually revised. Bryant's poetry is judged as ephemeral in the early work, his journalism and criticism of capitalism judged highly in the later. Irving's class allegiances ensure his low estimation in both works. Hawthorne (whom Parrington had so loved at Harvard) and Poe are treated similarly in both works, with high ratings for their devotion to art; moreover, Hawthorne's epithet, "skeptic," aligns him closely with the intellectual's style of mind. And Longfellow, rated highly in "The Democratic Spirit" as "almost . . . a radical," is reduced in *Main Currents* to an aloof "poet of the library" with "little intellect . . . little creative originality." He receives as brief treatment as Poe, but Parrington's assessments of each contrast markedly.[30]

The reason for Parrington's later treatment of Poe is found not in these portrait changes but in the structural changes between the two manuscripts. Instead of the general "Romanticism and Democracy" chapter contained in the larger division of the proposed third book of "The Democratic Spirit," "Democracy and Individualism: 1800–1870," Poe is grouped in the more specific historical section "The Virginia Renaissance," the first part of the regionally focused "Mind of the South," which also includes sections titled "The Renaissance of Slavery" and "The Romance of the West." (Similarly, these last parts are expansions of "The Democratic Spirit" chapter "Democracy and Slavery: 1830–1860.") Instead of appearing with two New York and two New England writers, Poe appears with economist John Taylor, conservative jurist John Marshall, and fellow southern authors William Wirt, Nathaniel Beverley Tucker, William Alexander Caruthers, and John Pendleton Kennedy. Instead of in the context of literary romanticism, he is considered in light of the "Heritage of Jeffersonianism." Here is another illustration of Parrington's self-definition shifting from that of an English professor grappling with the question of how literature reveals political allegiances to an intellectual historian weighing how a region participates in the formulation and transmission of ideas.

One may still criticize Parrington for a limited, politically driven conception of ideology and culture that lacks a sophisticated, nuanced understanding of the covert ways literature may be a source of cultural experience. But that is to convict him by late twentieth-century standards and to overlook the actual contribution he had made in transforming the study of literature into the study of culture. It is noteworthy that for Poe's portrait in *Main Currents* Parrington expunged the political rhetoric of "The Democratic Spirit" and evaluated him by aesthetic rather than democratic qualities. Moreover, it should be clear that to one valuing detachment as highly as Parrington, finding Poe "outside the main current of American thought" is not a condemnation but a salutation to a fellow traveler. Despite its length—which may partly result from its being perhaps the final section completed before the manuscripts of both *The Colonial Mind* and *The Romantic Revolution* were returned to Harcourt, Brace—the Poe portrait is remarkable for its defense of the very qualities that it has been deemed as denigrating.[31]

Poe is the only writer in "The Virginia Renaissance" as well as the only writer from the entire South whom Parrington does not criticize for abandoning or retreating from the demands of the artist-intellectual definition. Unlike the writers treated in *The Colonial Mind,* Poe did not participate explicitly in the liberal-conservative debate over the nature of American politics, economics, and culture. This is not a detriment but an asset, considered in light of Parrington's insistence that artists eschew involvement in public affairs and that their work spring from beauty and not from the ideological claims of propaganda. Neither heredity, environment, nor the spirit of the age can explain Poe's personality. That is the task of the abnormal psychologist, and "it is for the belletrist to evaluate his theory and practice of art."[32] Parrington here assumes neither role; he does not use his biographical skills to portray Poe's personality as he did with John Cotton nor attempt the restoration of his work's reputation as in the case of Freneau.

Because Poe's work is so clearly autonomous, bearing no explicit connection to the characteristics of the southern mind or to American political experience, Parrington evaluates him briefly, stressing Poe's contributions to the aesthetic component of the nation's cultural life. But these contributions are noteworthy:

> He was an aesthete and a craftsman, the first American writer to be concerned with beauty alone. . . . He was the first of our artists and the first of our critics; and the surprising thing is that such a man should have made his appearance in an America given over to hostile ideals. He suffered much from his aloofness, but he gained much also. In the midst of gross and tawdry romanticisms he refused to be swallowed up, but went his own way, a rebel in the cause of beauty.[33]

Like Melville, whom Parrington singles out as one of the most noteworthy writers of the Middle East, Poe also came "to shipwreck" on American materialism because "the day of the artist had not dawned in America." That day would not truly dawn for Parrington until Volume 3. In the meantime, the Poes and Melvilles would find it difficult to serve the cause of beauty among an indifferent people. Parrington's emphasis on American life as too utilitarian, too materialistic, too busy with everyday affairs to pause and read imaginative works is as characteristic as his emphasis on liberal ideas. The two emphases actually go hand in hand: a liberal nation is open-minded both to political innovations and to cultural experimentation. Therefore, one of the tests that the day of liberalism has not dawned is the fact that the day of the artist has not dawned either.[34]

Poe is the last figure treated in the section on the Virginia Renaissance, and thus his devotion to the ideal of beauty and art can be understood as the extreme expression of the romantic ("romantic" is the epithet Parrington applies to him) strain in Virginia letters. Here is an example where a key term functions with varied meanings in several critical contexts in *Main Currents*.[35] A romantic view of the nature of man assumes man is inherently good and must be treated by equalitarian political principles. Romanticism in literature is a barrier to inclusion of common people and common experience (as well as to the realistic treatment of exceptional persons with exceptional experiences). Yet romanticism in political thought is synonymous with humanitarian idealism and allows the inclusion of all people—including black slaves—in political theory and practice. In Parrington's view, a realistic, liberal, equalitarian politics must include a romantic view of the nature of man; but realistic literature includes only the aspect of romanticism that encourages the role of imagination in creating art.

Poe was a romantic because his work belonged entirely to the realm of imagination. That is, he created his own fictive world instead of using the real world for his short stories' and poems' settings and materials. But Poe is an exception. Several other southern writers are criticized for treating the real world romantically in the tradition of Sir Walter Scott. Romanticism is not an adequate or appropriate form for accurately portraying the varieties of experience comprising the content of their work. As examples, William Wirt forced Patrick Henry into a romantic model despite Henry's flaws, and Nathaniel Beverley Tucker confused art with propaganda, using romanticism to defend Calhoun's successionist policies in *The Partisan Leader*. Other southern writers failed to achieve Poe's artistry and autonomy because they were not committed enough to art as a vocation. Wirt's "excursions into the field of belles lettres were only pleasant outings from the courtroom"; and though John Pendleton Kennedy was one of the first practitioners of local color, his professional life took precedence over his creative ("He was a man of letters rather than a lawyer, and if he had eschewed politics and law and stuck to his pen our literature would have been greatly in his debt").[36]

Poe is the standard by which William Gilmore Simms, the only literary figure in the section "The Renaissance of Slavery" treated seriously or at length, is evaluated. William J. Grayson and William Crafts are quickly dispatched; the other portraits focus on political figures—Calhoun, Alexander Stephens, the academic Francis Lieber—and legal scholar Hugh Swinton Legaré, the only figure in *The Romantic Revolution* specifically labeled "intellectual."[37] Simms, the "Charleston romancer," could not detach himself from his environment and remained a romantic partisan to the southern cause. Simms's portrait includes a passage that reiterates the fundamentals of Parrington's critical theory as well as his charge that America is hostile to art:

> It is a pity that he constructed himself to the shell of an outworn order, instead of realizing that *social orders and institutions are significant to the novelist only as he stands apart from them, observing their ways and considering their interplay in the lives of men and women*. . . . If he had served his art more jealously, *if he had learned from Poe to refuse the demands of inconsequential things*, he would have viewed his beloved Charleston with keener eyes. . . . He struggled as few other Americans have done to further the cause of letters in a desperate environment. . . . Our literature has suffered few greater losses than this wasting of the genius of Gilmore Simms. . . . It was the inevitable outcome of the conflict between the creative artist and the citizen of South Carolina.[38](Emphasis added)

Simms's use of frontier locales and treatment of native Americans, especially in *The Yemassee*, allows Parrington to compare him with James Fenimore Cooper. Thus Simms's portrait provides a bridge to the first artist-intellectual who appears in "The Mind of the Middle East," the second book of *The Romantic Revolution*.

When Parrington turns his attention from the mind of the South to the mind of the Middle East, he also shifts from portraying a variety of figures drawn from the spectrum of intellectual life to a more narrow selection drawn almost entirely from literary life. Only one figure, Horace Greeley, fits the category of social thinker–intellectual. Although Parrington describes the middle eastern mind as a potpourri that lacks the "coalescing unity of spirit and purpose" of a "common culture,"[39] the major features of his definition of artist-intellectuals does provide thematic consistency to Book II as well as continuity with Volume 1 and the two other regional "minds" described in *The Romantic Revolution*.

For example, as in Book I, literary romanticism is evaluated as a distorting tendency, pandering to the popular taste for the melodramatic and picturesque. The work of Charles Brockden Brown, Robert Montgomery Bird, Fitz-Green Halleck, Washington Irving, and James Kirke Paulding all suffers to some degree either because the romantic conventions are the improper form for conveying their desired content or because their use of romantic settings prevents the inclusion of realistic detail.

In the case of Irving, "a boyish wit from the eighteenth century, a genial loiterer in the twilight of the old," Parrington's major criticism is that he was not concerned with the events and ideas that were transforming contemporary America. He detached himself, but from the present, and looked fondly backward, ingratiating himself in a picturesque past undisturbed by progress. Clearly, Irving is a member in good standing of the Party of Memory. Though he gained the reputation of being America's first man of letters, "there was in him nothing of the calm aloofness of the intellectual that stands apart to clarify its critical estimate, and none of the reforming zeal of the Puritan that is at peace only in the thick of a moral crusade."[40]

Parrington does judge the Knickerbocker *History* as a vital and enduring work. But it uses native materials drawn from Irving's New York experience. When Irving's European travels influence his choice of settings and themes, as in *The Alhambra*, or when he attempts to mine the vein of historical romance, as in the Astoria trilogy's recounting of the western fur trade or in *The Life of Washington*, Parrington criticizes him for tiredly pursuing the picturesque. Although he was a "born humorist," Irving lacked the true artist's "brooding intellectuality, and instead of coming upon irony at the bottom of the cup—as the greater humorists have come upon it after life has had its way with them—he found there only sentiment and the dreary poetic."[41]

Cooper is the only genuine product of the Middle East who seriously tries to master his craft, adapting romantic principles to native subjects, and to develop an analytic perspective on American politics and culture. The epithets that Parrington applies to Cooper ("critic") and to Herman Melville ("pessimist"), the last figure treated in Book 2, are indicative of both men's questioning stance toward the course of American development. In Parrington's view, Melville did not achieve an intellectual perspective that transcended idealism, romanticism, and realism; rather, he possessed an idealizing mind that caused him to erect romantic dreams as a defense against reality and, in the end, led him to "Nirvana."[42] As in his discussion of Poe, Parrington does not attempt to unravel the mysteries of Melville's personality. Cooper, Parrington asserts at the outset of his portrait, is also puzzling, and his character appears to embody "a bundle of contradictions." But Parrington does try to resolve Cooper's inconsistencies.

Parrington emphasizes that Cooper was torn between the staid virtues of his hereditary eighteenth-century aristocratic background and the "bumptious leveling" that characterized Jacksonian Democracy. In Cooper's mind, "doubts and uncertainties" about democracy "dwelt side by side with stubborn dogmatisms" regarding the moral values of an older, simpler world. This made him the "barometer of a gusty generation," for "his busy life covered the busy years of the great shift from an aristocratic order to a capitalistic order." Although his temperamental prejudices and loyalties "ran at cross purposes" to his conscience, he endeavored to reconcile the irreconcilable, and establish sure standards amid the wreck of all standards. He could not drift. He must discover some working agreement between the old America and the new, between the reputed excellencies of the traditional aristocratic order, and the reputed justice of the democratic ideal. . . . It is this fond lingering between worlds that sets Cooper apart from his fellows.[43]

Cooper not only fulfills the requirements of standing apart and of dwelling between worlds. He also spent seven crucial years in Europe (from June 1826 to November 1833), beginning in his thirty-seventh year. Parrington writes that "it is impossible to trace the steps of his intellectual development," but he dates Cooper's late shift from "provincial contentment" to a concern with political theory to his European travels, claiming that "no other American was so unsettled by contact with European civilization." Cooper was not, evidently, a scholar or a bookman; Europe was his true university.

It made a critic of him and turned his mind to social and political problems. Europe appealed to his native aristocratic prejudices, but repelled his democratic; Jacksonian America appealed to his democratic prejudices, but rode roughshod over his aristocratic. He found himself nowhere at home. Puzzled and perturbed, he leveled his shaft at both worlds and sought a haven of refuge in vicarious existence.[44]

Torn between the past and the present, between intellectual worlds, and by "the contrast everywhere between the real and the ideal," like Melville Cooper could never be wholly a realist, an idealist, or a romantic. Parrington does not defend the confusion that led Cooper on the one hand to praise a wholesome life lived close to the soil and on the other to a vindictive hatred of the frontier. But he admires Cooper's struggle to abandon the old eighteenth-century principle of gentleman rule and the social stake theory and his attempt to evaluate the merits of the new nineteenth-century middle-class Yankee spirit of acquisitiveness. Parrington summarizes Cooper's post-European outlook by, appropriately, comparing him to John Adams and then specifying how Cooper's point of view was a complex mixture of the three key terms of Volume 2: "A realist in his long brooding over social and political evils, he was at heart an idealist greatly concerned with justice among men, with a romantic fondness for dwelling on the virtues of earlier days." Cooper expressed this mixture most fully in his essays in *The American Democrat* and in *The Monikins,* a satire that criticizes the cant and hypocrisy of both English and American society, institutions, politics, and manners and "conceives of man as a queer mixture of good and evil . . . something nearer to Swift's conception than to William Ellery Channing's . . . prone to error even under a republican system."[45]

Despite Cooper's attempts at objective analysis and his clear rejection of a naive Rousseauistic view of human nature,[46] *The Monikins* is "sadly bungled." As in so many of Cooper's other novels, such as *Home as Found, The Redskins,* and the Anti-Rent trilogy, he could not separate his role as an artist from his role as a critic: "His romantic art suffered from the intrusion of realism; the romancer was constantly impelled to turn critic." But Cooper's most characteristic work, the five Leatherstocking tales and the sea tales, generally suffer the opposite flaw: in them Cooper romanticized the past and, influenced by French thought, idealized the natural man in a state of nature, beyond the bounds of both civilization and the frontier. Only in one novel, *Wyandotté,* was Cooper successful in substituting "a critical for a romantic treatment of materials," avoiding both the romanticization of Indians and of patriotism and probing "skillfully into the motives and impulses that divided honest men" during the revolutionary war.[47]

In the portrait's conclusion Parrington enumerates Cooper's shortcomings as a romancer and critic, but he also praises Cooper—in the same terms that he praised Freneau—as a man and a democrat who "loved justice and decency more than popularity."[48] In other words, he stood apart from current trends and astutely defended his own idealistic vision of the possibilities of democracy. Though Parrington does not call him an intellectual, Cooper fulfills almost all the major features of one. Because his creative work, influenced by his European travels, often mixes art with ideas and lets its political and social ends determine its imaginative means, he does not fulfill the two special requirements for artists. But his work illustrates Cooper's struggle to reconcile the old with the new and, by mirroring changes of mind, offers documentation of the troubling issues that other thoughtful members of his generation confronted. Cooper is significant because he is complex and contradictory; his portrait is significant because it shows Parrington's perception of the often ambiguous processes of intellectual change.

The treatment of intellectuals in "The Mind of New England," the third and last book in Volume 2 of *Main Currents,* is more conventional than in the earlier books for several reasons. The major figures of the New England Renaissance had long been considered important contributors to and shapers of American thought. Indeed, one of Parrington's objectives in *Main Currents* was to show that those figures were not the only contributors and shapers. In addition, the fact that a renaissance took place removed one of the barriers—hostility to artists, men of letters, and idealistic thinkers—that made it so difficult for other writers to pursue their craft and to devote their energies to their work. In short, New England fostered intellectual communities because of the particular historical confluence of a tradition of serious-minded thinking, the rise of liberalizing movements in the Unitarian church, the ethical response to slavery in the South, and the impact of innovative European philosophical, religious, political, and economic ideas, which was partially (and ironically) made possible by increased American contact with Europe through industrialization and commercial growth.[49]

The uniqueness of Parrington's treatment of "the mind of New England" lies primarily in his interpretation and organization of his subjects and in his continued focus on the components of his definition of intellectuals and their roles. In his introduction to Book III, Parrington states that the major significance of the renaissance (1830–50) was that "for a brief time, at least, liberal ideas found a welcome in homes where they had hitherto been strangers; for a brief time the intellectual and not the merchant dominated New England." The confluence of liberalism with intellectualism was facilitated by the "reawakening of the ethical passion of Puritanism," which united "the New England minister, and spiritual heirs of the minister"— specified as the intellectuals and reformers—in a common search for

> freedom for individual righteousness . . . not freedom for intellectual epicureanism, for romance, for aesthetic or pagan beauty. . . . They were too eager for the coming of the kingdom to dawdle over fiction or patronize the playhouse. They had been bred from their youth on printer's ink; they came of a race that had long respected the printed page.[50]

This unification of the minister with intellectuals and reformers in a broadly ethical and not a narrowly religious or artistic movement affects Parrington's treatment of intellectuals in two ways. The minister, at last freed from the dogmatisms of a dead system, now joins the ranks of social thinker–intellectuals. Partly as a result, there will be no artist-intellectuals—like Poe, concerned with beauty alone—in New England. In sum, we might say that the minister and the creative writer are now grouped together as men of letters, a category that unites the social thinker and the artist. What is most crucial is what unites them: a shared view of the nature of man which is fundamentally romantic in its moral stress on the perfectibility of human nature and the political necessity of making institutions responsive to human needs. Thus the renaissance is part and parcel of the romantic revolution that is the great theme of Volume 2; and the emergence of the category of "men of letters" foreshadows the development of critical realism, out of another confluence of liberalism and intellectualism, that is the theme of Volume 3.

Nevertheless, not all of the intellectuals in Book III are liberals. As one prime example, Parrington is not favorably disposed toward Daniel Webster's Whig politics and thinks he displayed "gross shortcomings in character." But he regards Webster as a "sound political scholar" who possessed a solid, if not creative, mind that was "strongly realistic and broadly philosophical, acute in analysis and with great powers of imagination." In his final judgment, Webster was "a great man, built on a great pattern who never quite achieved a great life." Because Parrington is so generous in his praise, the reasons for his criticism are especially illuminating, and they go beyond the obvious fact that Webster's "stately bark foundered in the squall of Abolitionism."[51]

At the outset he explains that "Webster's intellectual development falls into distinct and rather sharply defined periods." Appropriately employing the method used earlier in Lincoln's portrait, Parrington traces Webster's development through his speeches. The first period occurred before 1825, when "his mental processes were still under the dominion of the solid, rationalist eighteenth century," and his intellectual master was the English economic determinist James Harrington. The two speeches that exemplify this period both were delivered in 1820 and elucidate the stake-in-society principle: "Basis of the Senate" and "The First Settlement of New England."[52]

Between 1824 and 1825, however, Webster broke "with the old English tradition," and the realistic philosopher "gave way to the lawyer, the politician, the opportunist of the unhappy later years." His earlier belief in laissez-faire economics and the diminished state "came into collision" with his constituents' demands for "protective tariffs, internal improvements, and a policy of governmental paternalism." The speeches that exemplify this phase are his famous reply to Senator Robert Hayne in 1830, which defended Federalistic policies; his criticism of Calhoun in "The Constitution not a compact between Sovereign States" in 1833; and the "Declaration of Whig Principles and Purposes" in 1840. The third period began in the 1840s when, bitten by presidential ambitions (he ran unsuccessfully in 1836 and 1840), Webster turned his legalism to the issue of slavery. In his defense of the Fugitive Slave Bill of 1850 and in his Seventh of March speech in support of the Compromise of 1850, he made a "futile attempt to stifle the New England conscience by ramming the Constitution down its throat."[53]

Parrington notes that since Webster's death "both earlier and later phases of his career have fallen into the background, and the middle period of constitutional interpretation has stamped itself indelibly upon his fame." Parrington disagrees with this evaluation and sees greater value in Webster's first period, when he exhibited "the solid reasoning of the political philosopher," which placed him in the "distinguished line of political realists, from Harrington through Locke and Burke, to Hamilton, Madison, and John Adams."[54] As a Jeffersonian and a believer in the decentralized state, Parrington was personally opposed to the Federalism of Webster's early period and of his political forebears. But as an intellectual historian he was continually drawn to restore the scholarly reputation of those figures who grappled most soundly and vigorously with ideas.

Placing the foregoing analysis into the context of Parrington's definition of an intellectual, we can conclude that there are two main reasons why

Webster "never achieved a great life." One is that, like so many other think-ers, he dwelt between worlds yet was hindered by environmental factors from reconciling the old with the new. "He was launched on a stormy sea," Parrington explained, "born too late to profit from the old mercantile Fed-eralism to which his affections were always attached, and too early to profit by the industrial federalism that came to greatness after the Civil War." The other is that Webster "foolishly coveted" high civic honors, abandoning his role as a thinker and going beyond the sphere of the active scholar to pursue a career in public life.[55]

Webster's defense of slavery also placed him outside the main current of the New England Renaissance's ethical idealism. Indeed, his two later pe-riods helped bring this renaissance to an end. To substantiate this point, at the beginning of the portrait Parrington contrasts Webster with Emerson, claiming that the two men respectively

> embodied the diverse New England tendencies that derived from the Puritan and the Yankee: the idealistic and the practical; the ethical and the rationalistic; the intellectual revolutionary, ready to turn the world upside down in theory, plant-ing at the base of the established order the dynamite of ideas, and the soberly conservative, understanding the economic springs of political action, inclined to pessimism, neither wishing for Utopian change nor expecting it.

Further to delineate their mental contrasts, Parrington then paints a phys-ical contrast between Emerson—the slender, nervous, unworldly Puritan child of a long line of ministers—and Webster—the massive, stolid yet stately Yankee child who seemed to descend from a line of English squires. Later in the portrait, Parrington approvingly quotes Emerson's judgment of Webster as "a man who lives by his memory, a man of the past, not a man of faith or of hope."[56]

Although, like Webster, Emerson was vitally responsive to contemporary social movements and political events, he "surveyed his world with the de-tachment of posterity" and only reluctantly enjoined as a participant: "To be a critic rather than a fighter, and a critic because he was a poet and a philosopher—this was the duty laid on Emerson." Parrington was fully aware of the pejorative categorization (already a stereotype in the 1920s) of Emerson as the cheerful, sunny, "brilliant dispenser of aphorisms." Thus he takes pains to explain that moralistic pessimism was "thin gruel for the nourishment of a vigorous life" and avers that

> despite the jaunty optimism of which he was often accused, his eyes were never blind to reality. . . . He did not shrink from the ugliest fact, and the unhappy con-dition he discovered men to be in would have discouraged a less robust faith. At times even he doubted. At times he seems half-persuaded, with Cotton Mather, that the potential children of light are strangely and fiercely possessed of the devil.[57]

Parrington does not claim that Emerson attained what Reinhold Neibuhr later called an ironic perspective on the human condition and the nature of institutions. But he does show that Emerson saw evil as well as good, dark as well as light, and sought to explain "the tragic gap between the real and the ideal." This capacity for double vision was facilitated by his trip to Europe in 1835, "where he discovered ways of thinking unknown to Concord and Boston, that effectively liberalized his mind and released him from the narrow Yankee provincialisms." The immediate intellectual result of the year abroad was the three influential essays *Nature* (1836), *The American Scholar* (1837), and *The Divinity School Address* (1838), followed by the second series of *Essays* (1844). These successive works show the elaboration of "the master idea of the Emersonian philosophy . . . the divine sufficiency of the individual." Parrington observes that this idea differed "only in its radiant dress" from the revolutionary conception, drawn from the French romantics, that had inspired Channing, Jefferson, and Rousseau and laid the basis of the nineteenth century's "ebullient democratic faith."[58]

For Emerson, and for many of the other disparate renaissance figures, that utopian ebullience was soon modified by quotidian realities: the Industrial Revolution was submerging the older agrarian simplicity of New England, and the centralizing power of State Street was submerging the doctrine of the minimized state as well as the sacred rights of the individual. These were the very possibilities Jefferson had feared. As Parrington had predicted early in Jefferson's portrait in *The Colonial Mind,*

> There had been created here the psychology and institutions of a decentralized society, with a corresponding exaltation of the individual and the breakdown of caste. In the broad spaces of America the old-world coercive state had dwindled to a mere police arrangement for parochial duties; the free citizen refused to be regimented; the several communities insisted on managing their affairs by their own agents. Such was the natural consequence of free economics; but with the turning of the tide would not the drift towards centralization nullify the results of earlier American experience and repeat here the unhappy history of European experience?[59]

That "turning of the tide" produced the ironic outcome of the romantic revolution.

12

~

Legacies

1927–1929 and After

The publication of *The Colonial Mind* and *The Romantic Revolution* allowed Parrington to join the properly accredited procession of American intellectuals. Like many of the independent figures he admired, he never received his Ph.D. Although nearly everyone at the University of Washington called him "Dr. Parrington," any commencement observer could see that his simple stole belied the honor. Such academic trappings might have supplied a degree of public confidence, but his books now filled that lack. In early 1928, a young Howard Mumford Jones wrote to Parrington from Chapel Hill: "I think you bid fair to become a classic. Looking backward, historians of American literature will . . . date their studies A. P. and B. P."[1] In one sense, Parrington's life continued as it had for so long—writing, teaching, enjoying his family, gardening. But by most of the outward signs by which professional life is measured, the pace increased so rapidly that it looked as if life had begun anew. Jones did not overestimate the effect of *Main Currents* on literary historians, and he was correct about its effect on Parrington's career. It would have had a greater effect had he completed the last volume and allowed himself to become more fully immersed in the streams of scholarly life. But doing so meant giving up his beloved Seattle, his carefully tended sense of detachment, the edge of anger that continued to fuel his attraction to American culture.

"Scholar, Teacher, Democrat, Gentleman"

In May 1928 the first two volumes of *Main Currents in American Thought* won the Pulitzer Prize in History. On this occasion the *Seattle Times* announced that "the eyes of all American scholars are turned toward Seattle today for a glimpse of Vernon Louis Parrington . . . who has been awarded the largest Pulitzer Prize of the year, $2000." In comparison, $1,000 awards went to Edward Arlington Robinson in the poetry category for *Tristram;* to Charles Edward Russell for the best biography, *The American Orchestra and Theodore Thomas;* to Thornton Wilder for the best novel, *The Bridge of San Luis Rey;* and to Eugene O'Neill in the drama category for *Strange*

Interlude. It was a telling contrast to the last contest Parrington had won, the annual oratorical debate back in Emporia thirty-seven years earlier, for "God in History" and $25.

When the University of Washington newspaper, the *Daily,* carried the Pulitzer story, it quoted from a revealing interview with Parrington. "My book is somewhat similar to Prof. Charles A. Beard's," whose *The Rise of American Civilization* had been a contender for the prize. "The viewpoint is somewhat different, though. Beard looks at matters from an economic viewpoint. How is mine different? Well, call it a history of American culture." Although "God in History" had its jejune moments, in retrospect its concern with the shape of American history seems to point forward to his central professional concern. When word of the Pulitzer filtered back to one of Parrington's College of Emporia classmates, Will C. McCarty, he sent with his congratulations an injunction that must have called up many memories: "You are the only one of the three Verns left, consequently your friends all expect you to win many laurels."[2]

The *Daily* also announced that Parrington had received job offers from the universities of Minnesota, Wisconsin, and Michigan as a result of "the fame which the book has brought to him." The book also brought fame to the University of Washington. At an alumni reunion in July 1928, its new president, M. Lyle Spencer, gave a speech that "emphasized the importance of the winning of the Pulitzer award by Professor V. L. Parrington and stated that no single thing had done more to satisfy eastern educators that things are again on a stable basis at the University than the fact that Professor Parrington had turned down tempting offers from big eastern institutions to remain at Washington." Sensitive to its far western location and to the fiscal and political problems that had occurred during President Henry Suzzallo's administration, the university was understandably pleased that Parrington had polished its tarnished image. But the favor was not returned in kind, for the administration continued to refuse Parrington's request for a raise, which he had been seeking since the Wisconsin offer was tendered the summer before publication of *Main Currents.*[3]

Wisconsin vigorously renewed its courtship in early 1927, again offering $6,000 and moving expenses. Parrington officially declined the offer on the grounds that recent changes at Washington (no doubt including the small raise the earlier Wisconsin offer had produced) made the proposition less attractive. Unofficially, he explained to a colleague seeking advice on graduate institutions that the English Department at Wisconsin was "distressingly weak." He declined the Minnesota offer after publication of *Main Currents* in early May. About a week later came the offer from the University of Michigan as professor of American literature, to begin in the fall of 1928 at a $7,000 annual salary. Instead of following in the footsteps of Moses Coit Tyler, Parrington used this offer to justify his request for Washington to raise his salary to $5,500, which was $500 higher than any other senior professor was earning there. Parrington did finally receive $5,000 for the 1927–28 academic year, but in an uncommonly disputatious mood he continued to press for $5,500.[4]

By early 1928 he had adopted a new strategy for obtaining the disputed amount: he requested a sum for increasing the library's American literature holdings. In May he wrote to President Spencer that "the library situation is a heavy handicap on my work—as the Deans have both long known— and the low figure set for my salary seems to me to exact a very high price for the privilege of staying at Washington." Parrington had been paying out of his own pocket for many of the books needed for research on *Main Currents*. This must have been another one of the times, forecast in his "Autobiographical Sketch," when a sporadic rebellion rose in his heart against laboring in the unprofitable profession of teaching and writing. Perhaps the uncharacteristically vitriolic tone in all these financial proceedings can best be understood as a manifestation of his latent, lingering Populism, with the university cast in the role of Emporia's Major Hood.[5]

The salary dispute was not pleasant, but it clearly shows how firmly Parrington clung to Seattle. A fourth offer had come from a bona fide big eastern institution, American University in Washington, D.C., inviting Parrington as its first professor of American literature on a visiting basis for 1928–29. Moreover, Berkeley asked him to return for the summer of 1929, despite Parrington's assumption, as expressed to Lucy Lockwood Hazard, that "I must have been regarded at the University of California as a rather queer animal who preferred common and vulgar things like economics and political theory, instead of feeding on the dainties of literature as all English teachers should do."[6]

Although the part-time American University salary was too low and Berkeley out of the question because Parrington planned to spend much of 1929 abroad, he did venture out once more to teach in summer school when the University of Michigan renewed its offer, initially made in 1925. Parrington's Oklahoma colleague W. R. Humphreys was now assistant dean of arts and letters at Ann Arbor. Ann Arbor seemed not "much of a place to live," but during the summer after the appearance of *Main Currents*, Parrington found it a place to revive an old friendship, to retreat from the curious eyes of Seattle, and to bask in a sense of collegiality also tasted at Columbia. He taught two graduate courses, Beginnings of the Romantic Revolution in New England and Studies in American Realism, and became acquainted with a young colleague who taught the undergraduate American survey, John Brooks Moore.[7]

The Pulitzer, the job offers, and the accompanying praise—Glenn Frank once wrote that "De Tocqueville has found his match"—must have pleased Parrington. But he was just as pleased by the increasing volume of correspondence, much of it from unknown, distant general readers, that now crossed his desk. Parrington's response to one California woman who inquired regarding his motives in writing *Main Currents* is the most illuminating commentary we have from him about his work's origin and viewpoint. That such a commentary should be found in such a form illustrates the antiestablishment stance that characterizes so much of *Main Currents* and his own life. Parrington's letter, quoted here almost in its entirety, is cast in an autobiographical framework that highlights his intellectual development:

> For years I had lived in an atmosphere of what I call "genteel culture". I was educated at Harvard where that culture used to pervade the whole academic world. Later, when I found myself removed to some distance, I could look back on that snug little world of Boston and Cambridge, and the more I contemplated it the less it seemed to me to be the real America.
>
> In a mood of reaction from Cambridge Brahminism I set about inquiring what, after all, has been the development of thought in this country. I had become at that time much more interested in ideas than in political or military facts, and so as a historian I endeavored to trace the relations between groups—chiefly political or theological—as revealed by their intellectual ties.
>
> At the same time I was passing through the great liberal upheaval that took place in the decade preceding the World War. I followed with interest the development of the younger school of American historians under the leadership of Professor Turner, and as a result of these three things, namely, my dislike of the "genteel," my enthusiasm for the scholarship of the liberal revival, and the help that came from the younger historians, I set about the work.
>
> The general plan was conceived in 1910, but with the passing of years and the accumulation of knowledge that plan was modified in a thousand details until one could scarcely recognize it in the light of the two volumes published. I still think, however, that a sober and intelligent Americanism must have put aside the myths that were so abundantly created in the 19th Century and come to an understanding of the creative ideas that lie back of our historical development. In such matters one should be a realist rather than a romanti[ci]st.[8]

Yet however wide the streak of realism was in Parrington's scholarship and general outlook, it never covered the edges of the romantic layer applied so thickly in his youth. He really had fulfilled his wish of age sixteen and become a particular kind of painter. He knew a good deal about portraiture and about the images a camera could capture. What he learned about color and chiaroscuro in fine arts courses at Harvard, he applied in his book and in his own life. Thus he preferred to see himself as a realist, as a Populist, as a misfit at Berkeley, as an isolate in Seattle, as an outsider to the main current of teaching and scholarship.

But the Pulitzer had made his rebelliousness respectable. In 1928 Parrington was listed in *Who's Who* and as an Episcopalian instead of a Methodist. Genteel culture came knocking at his door in 1929, when Kenneth

Murdock sent his personal lawyer to research whether Parrington was eligible for membership in the Colonial Society of Massachusetts. He was, indeed: one of the early James McClellans of Sutton, Massachusetts, had served barely two weeks in the Continental Army before receiving injuries at Bunker Hill.[9]

In the end, despite the confidence his "laurels," as Will McCarty would say, should have given him, Parrington was still the visiting Colombia professor flustered by the applause of grateful students. He would take the time to write an acutely detailed letter to a stranger from California. But he would not change his plans to go to Europe to work on the final volume of *Main Currents* when he was invited to spend the summer of 1929 at the Yaddo writer's colony or to deliver the 1929–30 Turnbull lectures on phases of American poetry at Johns Hopkins.

The Yaddo invitation was patiently extended for the summer of 1930, and Johns Hopkins sweetened the Turnbull offer with a request to accompany the poetry lectures with a course in any phase of American literature.[10] But it was as a writer that Parrington had won recognition, not as a public figure. Although he was a gracious and friendly person, writing was his craft, and there was now more and more writing to do.

A request for a biography of Samuel Adams for a University of Chicago history series came from William E. Dodd. D. C. Heath proposed that he collaborate with Edwin Mims of Vanderbilt, of whom he thought highly after they taught together in the Michigan summer session, on an American literature anthology that (like *Main Currents*) devoted less space to New England and more to the South, Midwest, and West. Neither of these projects came to fruition, but several others of lesser scope did. In 1928 he was asked to contribute articles on abolition, Crèvecoeur, and Brook Farm (the last was the only one published) to the new *Encyclopedia of the Social Sciences*, an attempt to unify recent knowledge and research stimulated by this expanding area under the general editorship of E. R. A. Seligman. In 1929, at the author's request, he wrote an introduction for Harper's edition of O. E. Rölvaag's novel about the hardships of midwestern farming and immigrant life, *Giants in the Earth*. The same year his essays on Nathaniel Hawthorne and on seventeenth-, eighteenth-, and nineteenth-century American literature (Henry Seidel Canby wrote the section on twentieth-century developments) appeared in the new fourteenth edition of the *Encyclopaedia Britannica*.[11]

During the late 1920s, Parrington also continued to write book reviews. In contrast to those written before the appearance of the first two volumes of *Main Currents*, the new reviews were all signed and concerned works of literary, cultural, and historical—but not political—topics by well-known authors. For example, the seven reviews he wrote for the *Nation* between 1926 and 1929 included Kenneth Murdock's *Increase Mather* (published in 1925, its materials were promptly incorporated into Parrington's revision of Volume 1); Mark Van Doren's new edition of *Samuel Sewall's Diary* (one of the best "homespun" pictures of daily life in late seventeenth-century Boston); Howard Mumford Jones's *America and French Culture: 1750–1848* ("For guides he turns to such left-wing students as Simons and Beard, as well as to Turner and Schlesinger and Becker and Alvord and the entire school of economic and social historians," Parrington noted approvingly of this "new evidence that proves how much more widely French influence penetrated America than has been commonly believed"); and *Whither Mankind,* edited by Charles A. Beard, an anthology of essays by contemporary scholars—including Bertrand Russell, Havelock Ellis, James Harvey Robinson, Lewis Mumford, John Dewey, and Stuart Chase—evaluating the impact of science and the machine on modern civilization (Parrington felt that "it waves aside somewhat too blithely the Victorian criticism of the machine order and the Victorian emphasis on the psychology of work"). Almost ironically, his last review for the *Nation* was of Ralph and Louise Boas's new biography of Cotton Mather. Parrington observed in a modern vein: "It is a source of wonder to me that a problem in psychology so fascinating as Cotton Mather should not before this have caught the attention of a Freudian biographer. . . . In these pleasantly written pages psychology is skillfully used to explain the seeming contradictions of Cotton Mather's neurotic character."[12]

Among a dozen or so miscellaneous reviews appearing in a variety of publications, Parrington contributed to *Modern Language Notes* several brief reviews of works by Kenneth Murdock and Stanley T. Williams; for a local newspaper, he reviewed *Trumpets of Jubilee* by Constance Rourke, whose work on American humor marks her as one of the first American Studies scholars; and for the *Bookman* he reviewed Esme Wingfield-Stratford's *History of British Civilization,* which prompted the comment: "History is imagination playing over a handful of facts, seeking their hidden meaning, fusing them into a whole." His final review, of Waldo Frank's *Rediscovery of America,* appeared in the *Bookman* the month of his death. "The problem of America—and of Europe as well—," Parrington observed, "is the problem of how to achieve in the midst of the jungle an intellectual and spiritual reintegration—to learn to live once more in the whole."[13]

The *New York Herald-Tribune Books,* the Sunday book review supplement currently edited by Irita Van Doren, printed a series of reviews that show Parrington had achieved a reputation as a historian after *Main Currents'* publication. For example, of Carl Becker's contribution to *The Spirit of '76 and Other Essays,* Parrington fashioned this acute comment: "In a pleasantly informal way that disarms criticism Mr. Becker has purveyed a surprising amount of Revolutionary history as that history is interpreted today by the younger school of historians. . . . In casual fashion he has written a suggestive story of the long battles of ideas and prejudices that turmoiled the total movement." He also reviewed four volumes from the series

A History of American Life, edited by Dixon Ryan Fox and Arthur M. Schlesinger. Here Parrington made very clear that his own interest was intellectual history and not the social history—how people "lived and worked and played . . . what sort of houses they built, what books they wrote and read, what ways of money getting they followed"—primarily recorded in the series. He stated that although diaries, magazines, and land office records are excellent primary sources that are used tellingly by the authors, they have their limitations, for "ideas are made of little account; manners are of more consequence than systems of thought. The daily life of the past— . . . is spread before us vividly; but the emotional and intellectual life is somewhat less adequately revealed."

Finally, for the *Herald-Tribune* Parrington reviewed ten of the volumes in the series The Pageant of America, published under the general editorship of Ralph H. Gabriel. Overall, Parrington is critical of the volumes, which were directed to a wide, popular audience, commenting that most of the authors—they include Gabriel, Stanley Williams, and John S. Bassett—"have not learned caution and they put their fingers on 'typical American' qualities with an easy assurance that is amusing." Writing as if he were anticipating the criticisms that began to be made of intellectual history in the 1950s, Parrington also observed that "the pursuit of the American spirit is, no doubt, a seductive game, but there are pitfalls in the path of one who plays it. An elusive butterfly, the American spirit flutters out of every net designed to imprison it."[14]

These later reviews were a result of the Pulitzer. The first volumes of *Main Currents* were not reviewed in a single major historical journal and received only brief mention from Edmund S. Meany in the *Washington Historical Quarterly*. Parrington's low profile at Washington ensured that the volumes' appearance took most of the university community by complete surprise. His sense of deference—of being "a literary refugee among the drilled hosts of the historians"—prevented contacts beyond the more superficial in the historical field. As one measure of this, among his correspondence almost the only letters from historians are Beard's sketch of Miss Beautiful Letters and Dodd's request for the Adams's biography.[15]

In contrast to its reception locally and among historians, *Main Currents* seems to have solidified Parrington's reputation among kindred spirits working in American literature. His 1927–29 correspondence files are filled with letters through which we can trace his major activities and scholarly contacts. For example, when Ernest Leisy of the MLA's American Literature Group had inquired about doctoral work at Washington in 1924, Parrington had had to reply that the resources to sustain it were lacking. But by 1928, when seventy-seven dissertations in American literature were in progress and fifty-six had been completed nationally, Parrington was able to report that his university was contributing a handful to the total. "The Political Theory of Roger Williams" by James E. Ernst, who later authored a study of Frank Norris, was acknowledged by Parrington for its shaping of the Williams chapter in *The Colonial Mind*. "American Romantic Criticism, 1815 to 1860" was the title of a dissertation by E. Harold Eby, who was already teaching in Washington's English Department. Eby organized his study regionally, consecutively treating the South, the Middle East, and then New England as Parrington had in *The Romantic Revolution*. Notably, the dissertation devotes a lengthy chapter to Poe, whose "psychopathic personality" is judged as the cause for his behavioral and critical eccentricities. The opening words of the study's first chapter, "Backgrounds," illustrate one way his major professor's viewpoint was interpreted:

> American literature cannot be understood apart from the economic, political, and cultural forces which helped make it. This is particularly true of those early periods when it could hardly be called a literature, for upon literary grounds the scholar cannot justify his study of such writing in place of Milton's, Shakespeare's, or Spenser's. He is forced to turn to it as a literature in the process of birth, and then to consider the heritage and environment which moulded its early life.[16]

Another central *Main Currents* figure was studied by Victor Childs Christianson in "Edwin Lawrence Godkin as a Utilitarian." Christianson, who served as a reader for Parrington during 1926–28, offers an interesting commentary on Parrington's continued wrestling with his own formative influences in a chapter titled "Godkin's View of the Farm Problem." In its conclusion, Godkin is seen as a Coopervian figure, the sort of eighteenth-century troubled elitist who fit Parrington's definition of intellectual:

> But we sense something else under Godkin's arguments not only against the farm movements but against labor agitation. He believed that the working classes were of a distinctly lower social order than the professional class, and he could never quite understand why such people felt they had the right to make such a fuss over their condition. Theoretically he could praise democracy. [But] . . . the farmers and laborers were an ignorant class, and since the Utilitarians believed in a sort of intellectual aristocracy, Godkin could not believe progress possible except through the guiding hand of the superior classes. This sublimated feeling of Godkin's may be the real basis for his dislike for these popular movements of the toiler.[17]

A fourth dissertation, by Russell Blankenship, was originally to analyze Thoreau's social theories but with a switch in major figures was completed as "The Perfectionism of John Humphrey Noyes in Relation to Its Social Background." A history major before coming to Washington for his M.A. and older than most graduate students, Blankenship had already published *American Literature as an Expression of the American Mind* (Henry Holt, 1931), by the time he received his doctorate in 1935. And by that point he was under contract with Scribner's for two high school texts on American literature. Parrington is not mentioned in Blankenship's foreword, possibly because he died before its completion, but Blankenship was certainly among the most prolific of Parrington's students in the American field.[18]

The range of early University of Washington doctoral subjects (and the varying success of their executions) helps support the concerns of the still new American Literature Group. The group saw the need for a book outlining its aims: to differentiate the scholarly study of American literature from "journalistic" treatments and to define, as a pedagogical guide, methods of investigation and areas of focus. The result was *The Reinterpretation of American Literature*, published in 1928 under the editorship of Norman Foerster of Chapel Hill. Foerster had solicited from Parrington a chapter on the development of realism the prior year; it was a foretaste of the materials to be developed in Volume 3 of *Main Currents*. "Back of every changing technique lies a changing philosophy, and back of a changing philosophy lie changing social ideals that in the end determine the national culture," Parrington began, echoing the Introduction to *The Colonial Mind*. Honing in on his subject, he elaborated:

> Realism in America, it would appear, rose out of the ashes of romantic faith. It sprang from social discontent, and it came to maturity when that discontent was clarified in the light of Old World thought. European science and European social philosophy, augmented by European literary technique, completed the realistic revolution begun by the first disillusionment with middle-class economics. There is suggestion in the fact that the progressive phases of realism in America have synchronized closely with the recurrent periods of economic depression that marked the development of an industrial order.

This is the view, "warping it pretty well to the left," that readers of the *Communist* such as S. Kahan would welcome. Parrington's blend of class analysis and attention to European antecedents is applied to four stages of American realism: Howells's "realism of the commonplace"; Garland's "realism of social protest"; Crane's, Norris's, and Dreiser's "realism of naturalism"; and the "realism of impressionism—and perhaps expressionism"— that began with Crane and was continuing with Sherwood Anderson. In the essay's conclusion, however, Parrington expresses no faith in any political creed:

> In the cynical post-war days ... Realism, bitter and disillusioned, was the common mood, and it threw upon men and war and civilization the light of its disillusion. Determinism no longer wore a benevolent Marxian aspect, discovering in every revolution a potential Utopia; it had again become grim, sordid, amoral, pessimistic. ... The last shred of Victorian reticence has been stripped away, and the animal called man stands before us naked and unashamed—in poetry and the drama, as well as in fiction. America, we like to say, is coming of age.[19]

The essay, like the rest of *The Reinterpretation*'s eight others, was as much a manifesto as an academic treatise, as American literary study flexed its wings, brushing aside the "dainties bred in a book" that Parrington had long inveighed against and offering meatier, interdisciplinary fare. The volume contained Fred Lewis Pattee's "Call for a Literary Historian," which memorably retitles Barrett Wendell's *Literary History of America* as "A Literary History of Harvard University, with Incidental Glimpses of the Minor Writers of America," as well as a particularly modern-sounding plea for exploring the relations between American history and American literary history by Arthur M. Schlesinger. Appearing in this context, Parrington came as close as any literature professor ever had in merging his training with the methods of the New Historians.[20]

The American Literature Group had also met in Cambridge and Toronto—Parrington was invited but did not attend—to plan a new journal under the general editorship of Jay B. Hubbell of Duke. Hubbell corresponded frequently with Parrington, asking him to serve on the advisory board ("We had to have you!") and discussing possible contributions to the journal in addition to its approach. At issue was the conflict between aesthetic formalism and cultural interpretation which, when *American Literature* opted for the former, helped lead to the founding of *American Quarterly* (in 1949), the journal of the American Studies Association, whose aims were closer to Parrington's.[21]

The first number of *American Literature* appeared in March 1929, carrying Parrington's review of Albert J. Beveridge's biography of Abraham Lincoln. The next number appeared in May carrying Esther Burch's essay "The Sources of New England Democracy: A Controversial Statement in Parrington's *Main Currents in American Thought*," a foretaste of the treatment he would receive two years later from young Perry Miller in his first published article, "Thomas Hooker and the Democracy of Connecticut," which took issue with Parrington's view of independency and political development, and twelve years later from young Richard Hofstadter in his second publication, "Parrington and the Jeffersonian Tradition," which challenged Parrington's assumption that physiocratic agrarianism had strongly marked Jefferson's thinking.[22] But by then Parrington would be dead, leaving his third volume completed just to the point at which he was beginning to put an intellectual framework on his nineteenth-century midwestern experience and to treat the contributions of the new generation of scholars, liberals, and writers who were refashioning the currents of twentieth-century American thought and culture.

Parrington's burgeoning volume of correspondence, his writing projects (although they were providing a quality of scholarly community he had never experienced), and his involvement with University of Washington doctoral work were inhibiting progress on the last volume of *Main Currents*. His students had had a preview of its literary materials, for in March

1925 the university book store had published his syllabus for English 165 and 166, The American Novel Since 1890, in a forty-six-page pamphlet. In 1927 the university also began a chapbook series, and the first number was taken up by Parrington's essay on another important Volume 3 figure, *Sinclair Lewis: Our Own Diogenes*. Even though Sophus K. Winther and Joseph B. Harrison were teaching sections of his survey courses, *The Beginnings of Critical Realism* was going slowly. "I have persuaded myself that I need a rest," he wrote to Howard Lee McBain of Columbia's Department of Public Law and Jurisprudence, who was suggesting yet another publishing project.[23] Thus Parrington arranged for a leave of absence for the spring quarter of 1929.

In late March, Parrington left Seattle with his wife and son for a six-month European sojourn, intended for study at the British Museum but also for pleasure, now that he could take Julia with him. Their family responsibilities had recently eased. His mother-in-law had died in 1926, so after twenty-five years of marriage Julia and Vernon were alone in their own home. Elizabeth had her own home and family; Louise had just graduated, as an English major, from the University of Washington; Vernon, Jr., was fourteen. Another death in 1926, that of Vernon's brother, Dr. John Parrington in Emporia, further severed old ties. John had remarried after his first wife's early death, fathering another family. But his mother remained in the Parrington family home on Rural Street until his death, when she went to live with his daughter by his first marriage in Dodge City. Although after Judge Parrington's death in 1909, Louise McClellan Parrington visited regularly in Seattle, some time in the mid-1910s the rift that began with her disappointment in Vernon's marriage widened. The subsequent estrangement was so total that, after 1916, Parrington's children were unaware of any communication with her and presumed their paternal grandmother dead. In fact, she would die in Dodge City in November 1930, outliving both of her sons.[24]

At the time of his second European trip, Parrington was fifty-seven. His thick shock of hair, parted in the middle, had never thinned, although it had turned a vivid snowy white during his early Washington years. As an amateur athlete, he had always prized his health. Although he had given up field sports long ago, his arduous gardening and maintenance tasks at home and at Camp helped maintain a physique nearly as youthful as the one described in his early diaries. But he had never ceased smoking the hand-rolled cigarettes of Bull Durham tobacco that had been a point of contention back at the University of Oklahoma.

In one letter dated March 1, 1929, regarding unwritten articles requested by the *Encyclopedia of the Social Sciences*, Parrington confessed, "I have been under the weather for some time." E. H. Eby recalled that his older colleague experienced a few unidentified spells, one in a campus bank lobby, during the months before his departure for Europe. The Atlantic passage was rough, with continuous swells. Julia noticed that her husband looked unwell, walked slowly, and seemed to have lost enthusiasm for the trip, but she knew he was too sensitive to consult a doctor. After debarking in Plymouth in mid-April, he could not carry any bags and was eating very little. Several times he even wondered aloud why they had come.[25]

One of the first spots on their itinerary was Oxford. Parrington seemed to have recovered at least his sense of humor when he wrote to the English Department secretary—altering the image he had taken home on his grand tour so many years before—that Oxford "looks dirtier & more dilapidated than I remember it & I am not so sure now that it is the loveliest spot in the world." Always the academic rebel, he added wryly that "the *American Literature* magazine was a bit too scholarly to suit my present taste as a gentleman traveller."[26]

Following an extended stay in London, in June the Parringtons wound their way through Gloucester to Cheltenham, then on to the George Inn in nearby Winchcombe. The inn dated from 1251, and the present manager had restored the architectural features that William Morris would have admired. It must have felt almost like a homecoming for Stuart Forbes's creator, so reminiscent was the George Inn of the hand-built arts and crafts–style house in Norman. Indeed, he was planning to take Julia to visit Chipping Campden.

On this trip, Parrington customarily wrote each day until two or three o'clock. All morning on Sunday, June 16, he sat at his typewriter, finishing the introduction for J. Allen Smith's *Growth and Decadence of Constitutional Government.* Parrington had been trying to arrange publication and overseeing Smith's daughter's revisions since Smith died five years earlier, leaving the nearly finished manuscript behind. Before Julia went to lunch with their son, she asked Parrington if he felt satisfied with the introduction. Yes, he replied, but he could always improve with rewriting. When they returned, they found him lying on the bed, a victim of a coronary thrombosis. "Father had slipped away from us," Julia wrote a few days later to Elizabeth. "He had finished his work and signed his name."[27]

The notices of her father's death appearing in the American as well as London papers and the Paris edition of the *New York Times* were kept by an understanding captain from Louise, who was en route aboard ship to meet her parents and brother in England. She arrived in Winchcombe shortly after Parrington's burial in the village cemetery. The family sensed that England was a fitting resting place for a disciple of William Morris. A marble gravestone bears the inscription, drawn from the dedication to J. Allen Smith in *Main Currents,* "Scholar, Teacher, Democrat, Gentleman."

It is also fitting that the last scholarly piece Parrington wrote was the introduction to the last book by Smith, who had been one primary guide on Parrington's intellectual journey to modern social thought "through the avenue of art." The year 1930 saw the posthumous publication of both

Growth and Decadence of Constitutional Government, accompanied by Parrington's admiring introduction, and the fragmentary third volume of *Main Currents in American Thought,* dedicated like its companions "to the memory of J. Allen Smith."

In many ways, Parrington's and Smith's deaths marked the end of the Progressive intellectual synthesis that had been characterized by the debate over the role of democracy in shaping a liberal society. More immediately, they brought to a close a remarkable chapter in the history of the University of Washington, although echoes from that chapter could be heard three decades later.

During his absence in England, Parrington's long-fought-for request for $500 to increase the university's American literature holdings had been approved. The task of spending the sum and of editing the incomplete manuscript of *The Beginnings of Critical Realism in America, 1860–1920,* fell to E. H. Eby, then a young instructor in the English Department. Parrington's courses were taken over by Eby, Joseph Harrison, and John Brooks Moore from the University of Michigan.

Close associates in the English Department felt as though someone in their family had died. Students responded by dedicating the 1929 edition of the campus yearbook "To Dr. Vernon L. Parrington, whose study of literature has won him national recognition; whose charm of manner has made him the most beloved of University professors and whose study of the past is infused with the spirit of modernity." The university book store published Joseph B. Harrison's appreciative *Vernon Louis Parrington: American Scholar* in the series of chapbooks that included Parrington's *Sinclair Lewis: Our Own Diogenes.* The dean of the Graduate School, Frederick Morgan Padelford, Parrington's longtime colleague in the English Department, reviewed the chapbook in the December 1929 issue of the alumni magazine and praised Harrison for his portrayal. The same month, the university faculty adopted a resolution presented by David Dudley Griffith, the current chair of the English Department, that read in part: "Not to many may it be given to duplicate his late-achieved success, but to all of us the life of Vernon Louis Parrington will remain as an inspiration to a better devotion to professional ideas, without pondering to the desire for factitious fame."[28]

After Parrington's unexpected death, O. E. Rölvaag wrote to Julia: "American letters needed your husband so much. Sometimes one feels like rebelling against the Ways of Life." In the *Saturday Review,* Norman Foerster lamented, "It was my unhappy privilege to receive one of the last letters written by Vernon Louis Parrington, whose sudden death . . . was a serious blow to scholarship in American literary history." The *Nation* observed, in its editorial pages, that the former reviewer

was that rare thing among university professors of English, a man who was familiar with not only literature but with the things out of which literature is made—politics, economics, sociology, theology, to mention only a few. . . . [H]is most important work, "Main Currents in American Thought," . . . was generally recognized as an extraordinarily significant contribution to American letters. He was a thorough scholar and at the same time completely aware of what was taking place in the world around him. His opinions were radical and none more so than the concept which guided him in his chef d'oeuvre—that literature is not a nun set chastely separate from "life" but an expression of a given culture, part of the pattern of society and governed by the pattern as a whole.[29]

The Beginnings of Critical Realism in America, 1860–1920

When *The Beginnings of Critical Realism in America, 1860–1920,* appeared in November 1930, readers and reviewers were on firmer ground than when Parrington's first two volumes were published. They knew who he was, and they shared more of the mood that had underlain *The Colonial Mind* and *The Romantic Revolution* but was now clearly detectable. It was just a year after the stock market crash; the Great Depression was widening and deepening; many were beginning to question the political and economic realities entailed by the ideal of progress. If the first volumes of *Main Currents* seemed to belong to a world that was passing, its last one seemed to speak directly to the spirit of the world daily taking shape. "Disillusion Is the Keynote of Professor Parrington's Monumental Work" ran the subtitle of the front page *New York Times Book Review* cover article, which reprinted the sober Pulitzer Prize photograph. The *Christian Century* and the *Churchman* reviewed the work with insight and praise, whereas no religious publication had been alert to the earlier volumes' extensive treatment of Puritanism and Unitarianism. "Evidently the course of events in the United States since the Great War (a crusade which debauched all its participants) had eaten into Parrington's old-fashioned Jeffersonian soul. . . . Was the great experiment in Democracy . . . about to founder in the emergent paradox of unmitigated plutocracy?" asked John Chamberlain in the *Forum,* who then answered the question: "Had he lived to complete his book, it is certain that so energetic a man as Parrington would not have rested content with leaving us a rind to chew on."[30]

The loss to American letters owing to Volume 3's incomplete form was a constant theme, prompted by the publisher's title page note: "Completed to 1900 Only." In the *New England Quarterly,* Stanley T. Williams was willing to exclaim, "He is trenchant, still original, still militant against stupidities . . . still ireful against Tory and Harvardensian—what a pity that these shining and decorous targets have lost their sharpest marksman!" Edward Wagenknecht's review in the *Virginia Quarterly Review* was titled "Death and the Scholar." In the *New York Herald Tribune Books,* Carl Van Doren observed: "If he had lived to finish this third volume it would have been the best treatment of these matters ever written. Even as a fragment it is still the best." In *American Literature*, V. L. O. Chittick—who had known Parrington at the University of Washington and could reveal that he "is more at home in the later phases of his inquiry than in the earlier"—went even further, claiming that Volume 3 "is so much the superior of those to which it is the sequel that it is more likely to prove an enduring monument to Professor Parrington's profound consideration and understanding of his country's intellectual and cultural development than they."[31]

After Harold Laski, whom Parrington had planned to visit on his fatal trip, read *The Beginnings of Critical Realism*, he resumed his correspondence with Justice Holmes: "The posthumous volume of Parrington's work . . . even in its fragmentary form seems to me a brilliant performance. I thought him particularly good on the Adams family and on the Knights of Labour people, but overeulogistic of Henry George who to me always seemed rhetorical small beer and incapable of serious analysis." Four months later Holmes responded, echoing his evaluation of the prior volumes: "There is a touch of radical dogmatism in his tone and speech—the catch words catch him—'exploitation'—'acquisition' & c. He cares most for those of his way of thinking . . . but he has a great deal of keen insight." Only one review—interestingly, it was the *Nation*'s—thought Parrington's insight into contemporary American culture was fundamentally flawed. "He is in despair . . . at the great numbers of young men who are enchanted by Mr. Mencken of the facile and irresponsible cynicism. . . . Even more pathetic is Parrington's final bewilderment as he considers the still younger members of the postwar generation," Matthew Josephson complained, on the defensive. In the *New Republic*, Morris R. Cohen pursued a different strategy. The philosophy professor carefully and acutely outlined the third volume's inconsistencies but concluded: "This is a book whose faults must be pointed out with some emphasis precisely because its merits are so obvious on every page that the sympathetic reader is likely to be carried away by enthusiasm and to lose his critical caution."[32]

Parrington's last book did strike nerves, partly because he could not smooth over the differences, audible in his prose style, between the rebellious artist and the detached scholar. It is true that Parrington faced the dilemma which all historians of and commentators on present events have faced: he did not know the conclusion to the story. But as V. L. O. Chittick pointed out, he was a more astute student of the present than his prior publications suggested. Parrington had focused on teaching contemporary American literature since the war years, and he had begun planning the third volume of *Main Currents*—then titled "The Spirit of Radicalism in Recent American Literature"—in 1917. The first decades of the new century were the years he knew most intimately; they were the years of his intellectual maturity.

But little of this preparation found its way between the covers of *The Beginnings of Critical Realism*. The disparity between the completed sections—about 325 pages—and the inclusive sweep of the Table of Contents is enormous; less than a third of the proposed material was written. Like the first two volumes of *Main Currents,* the last is divided into three books— "Changing America," "The Old and the New: Storm Clouds," and "The New America." Only the initial book, treating the 1860 to 1900 period, is substantially complete. But most of its general introduction and several proposed chapters, including one on William James, are missing. In Book II, the sections on the Populistic program, Bryan, and Edward Eggleston, among others, are missing from Part I, "The Middle Border Rises"; only the section on Bellamy is finished in Part II, "Proletarian Hopes"; Part III, "The Hesitant South," is blank. Book III, with such tantalizing subsections as "Liberalism and the Intellectuals" designed to treat Walter Weyl, Thorstein Veblen, Charles Beard, Herbert Croly, Randolph Bourne, Van Wyck Brooks, and Waldo Frank, was never begun.

Publishing Volume 3 was not a mistake. The first book alone is only about 80 pages shorter than *The Colonial Mind,* 150 shorter than *The Romantic Revolution.* Indeed, Parrington had realized that a fourth volume containing the proposed Book III would have to be created. (Similarly, what became *The Romantic Revolution* was originally the latter part of "The Democratic Spirit in American Letters.") But editing Parrington's fragmentary materials was a daunting task. E. H. Eby had very little to work with. There were few, if any, multiple drafts of completed sections as in the case of the earlier volumes. When the decision was made to include an Addenda to help flesh out the missing parts of Books Two and Three, only a few sources were available, and these were all literary: lecture notes on naturalism from Parrington's 1922 summer in Berkeley, the syllabus for Parrington's course The American Novel Since 1890 published by the University of Washington in 1925, an article on Cabell reprinted from a 1921 issue of the *Pacific Review,* the essay on Sinclair Lewis published in the University of Washington chapbook series in 1927, a handful of additional lecture notes, as in the comments on Dreiser.[33]

None of the left-wing activists, none of the muckraking journalists, none of the political Progressives, none of the liberal intellectuals, none of the new postwar philosophies are included. Nothing could better illustrate the difference between a more purely literary history and the richer scope of *Main Currents* than the disjunction between the Addenda and Parrington's detailed Table of Contents. In addition, the items in the Addenda do not follow the order stipulated by the Contents, so that Parrington's sense of historical development is obscured. Moreover, the placement of the essay "A Chapter in American Liberalism" as the last item in the Addenda and thus the last piece in the volume, has produced the impression that Parrington despaired over the course of contemporary American culture and politics. Belying this impression are the title of the volume itself as well as these pronouncements in the Introduction: "literature at last has become the authentic voice of this great shapeless America that means so much to western civilization," and "one may turn hopefully for a revelation of American life" to "the intellectuals, the dreamers, the critics, the historians, the men of letters."[34]

Despite the fragmentary state of *The Beginnings of Critical Realism*, as a whole Volume 3 is arranged dialectically. And the implications of dialectical structure further reinforce the positive claims in the Introduction. The "changing America" characterized by the rising plutocracy's belief in progress, exploitation, and preemption described in Book I is challenged by the plight of the Middle Border and by the development of radical political and economic theories described in Book II. Then from behind the "storm clouds"[35] resulting from the clash of "the old and the new" emerges "the new America" of Book III, characterized by a new wave of liberalism in politics and letters and by a sophisticated criticism of middle-class values.

This is as close to triumph as *Main Currents* ever comes. It is more optimistic than the Jeffersonian defeat at the end of Volume 1 and the regional cultural stalemate at the end of Volume 2. Yet Parrington makes more modest claims for history, and for his theme, in his last volume. He needs only to demonstrate that critical realism is beginning; he is not attempting to define the colonial mind or to trace the course of the romantic revolution. The open-endedness of the contemporary period gave him a sense of freshness, of interpretative freedom that is lacking in the earlier volumes. Some of this may be because Volume 3 was begun just after "The Democratic Spirit in American Letters" was finished; some because of fortuitous lack of revision; some because of Parrington's skill in dramatizing the animating issues of his own lifetime.

This freshness is amply apparent in the following passages caricaturing a gallery of picturesque figures from the 1870s generation:

> Created by a primitive world that knew not the machine, they were marked by the rough homeliness of their origins. Whether wizened or fat they were never insignificant or commonplace. On the whole one prefers them fat, and for solid bulk what generation has outdone them? There was Revivalist Moody, bearded and neckless, with his two hundred and eighty pounds of Adam's flesh, every ounce of which "belonged to God." There was the lyric Sankey, afflicted with two hundred and twenty-five pounds of human frailty, yet looking as smug as a banker and singing "There were ninety and nine" divinely through mutton-chop whiskers. There was Boss Tweed, phlegmatic and mighty, overawing rebellious gangsters at the City Hall with his two hundred and forty pounds of pugnacious rascality. There was John Fiske, a philosophic hippopotamus, warming the chill waters of Spencerian science with his prodigious bulk. There was Ben Butler, oily and puffy and wheezy, like Falstaff larding the lean earth as he walked along, who yearly added more flesh to the scant ninety-seven pounds he carried away from Waterville College. And there was Jim Fisk, dressed like a bartender, huge in nerve as in bulk, driving with the dashing Josie Mansfield down Broadway—

prince of vulgarians, who jovially proclaimed, "I worship in the Synagogue of the Libertines," and who on the failure of the Erie coup announced cheerfully, "Nothing is lost save honor!"

Impressive as are the fat kine of Egypt, the lean kine scarcely suffer by contrast. There were giants of puny physique in those days. There was Uncle Dan'l Drew, thin as a dried herring, yet a builder of churches and founder of Drew Theological Seminary, who pilfered and cheated his way to wealth with tobacco juice drooling from his mouth. There was Jay Gould, a lone-hand gambler, a dynamo in a tubercular body, who openly invested in the devil's tenements as likely to pay better dividends, and went home to potter lovingly amongst his exotic flowers. And there was Oakey Hall, clubman and playwright, small, elegant, and unscrupulous; and Victoria Woodhull who stirred up the Beecher case, a wisp of a woman who enraged all the frumpy blue-stockings by the smartness of her toilet and the perfection of her manners; and little Libby Tilton with her tiny wistful face and great eyes that looked out wonderingly at the world—eyes that were to go blind with weeping before the candle of her life went out. It was such men and women, individual and colorful, that Whitman and Mark Twain mingled with, and that Herman Melville—colossal and dynamic beyond them all—looked out upon sardonically from his tomb in the Custom House where he was consuming his own heart.[36]

In the presence of such a vivifying style and the marshaling of such trenchant detail, the reader no doubt comes close to experiencing a Parrington classroom. The passage also illustrates one of Volume 3's basic organizational problems and its solution: the sheer number of proposed portraits— approximately ninety names are listed in the Contents—augmented by countless auxiliary sketches. Unlike Volume 2 (which contains forty-five portraits), the portraits are not divided neatly between three books corresponding to three geographic regions, although Book II pays particular attention to the Middle Border region and to developments in southern literature. Like Volume 1 (which contains twenty-eight full portraits), the sections more clearly read as a debate between liberalism and conservativism, though now radicalism has a voice, as the section on proletarian hopes demonstrates. Unlike *The Colonial Mind* but similar to the group portrait in the "The Transcendental Mind" section in *The Romantic Revolution*, the portraits are generally organized into thematic units, but a great deal more analytical material is provided to construct a unifying frame.

For example, Benjamin Franklin could be selected as the embodiment of the colonial mind (in Book II of Volume 1) and is introduced by a fourteen-page section covering four literary works concerned with immigration and the frontier, but Parrington finds no one particular individual who embodied the Gilded Age in Book I, "Changing America." After twenty pages of introduction, which includes the "fat and lean" passage quoted earlier and the oft-quoted description of "The Great Barbecue," he selects three folk heroes—General Grant, Jay Cooke, and Charles A. Dana—who reflect differing aspects of the middle-class mind's aspirations.[37] Following this overview of "the American scene," another example occurs when three literary strands that together form the culture of the 1870s are depicted. The aristocratic strand includes five New England figures—Thomas Bailey Aldrich, Elizabeth Stuart Phelps, Harriet Beecher Stowe, Sarah Orne Jewett, and Mary Wilkins Freeman—to whom only fifteen pages are devoted. The romantic strand is typified by Walt Whitman (seventeen pages), who lived in the Middle East, and the frontier strand by Mark Twain (sixteen pages), whose most characteristic work is set in the West and the South of the Mississippi Valley.[38] The section on the culture of the 1870s forms a point-by-point contrast to the three major divisions of Volume 2. Thus the above figures can be seen as measures of the intellectual changes being wrought in the South, Middle East, and New England during the latter nineteenth century. And the section as a whole forms an antithesis to the section on the Gilded Age, with older cultural values being contrasted to the newer.

The third section is largely unfinished but was designed to include six brief portraits of contributors to "changing theory" in the areas of politics, economics, and law. The final section of Part One of Book I, "The Beginnings of Criticism," provides evidence that an intellectual critique of the conflicting conservative, plutocratic, and democratic tendencies of the Gilded Age is developing. Here Parrington inserts three strategic studies—of aging orator Wendell Phillips, "the last survivor of the great age of Puritan conscience," and editor-journalists George William Curtis of *Harper's Weekly* and E. L. Godkin of the *Nation*. As characteristic of the other concluding sections in *Main Currents,* "The Gilded Age" closes with literary reflections of the contemporary theoretical debate. Described here is the emergence of three new genres of novels: the political novel (Twain's and Charles Dudley Warner's *Gilded Age,* Henry Adams's *Democracy),* the economic novel (John Hay's *Breadwinners;* this section is unfinished), and the sociological novel as illustrated by the work of H. H. Boyesen.[39]

Parrington was working with a more thickly textured canvas than in his earlier volumes, isolating key themes and yoking related figures that had not heretofore been covered in the pages of a book. If "The Mind of the South" was pioneer work, *The Beginnings of Critical Realism* is an act of almost visionary prophecy. In addition to the foregoing stylistic and structural differences between Volume 3 and the preceding volumes, there are several differences that have special bearing on Parrington's treatment of intellectuals. In the Introduction to *The Beginnings of Critical Realism,* Parrington writes (in the present tense):

In the welter that is present-day America militant philosophies with their clear-cut programs and assured faiths are wanting, and *many feel,* as Matthew Arnold felt fourscore years ago, *that they are dwelling between worlds, one dead, the other powerless to be born.* The old buoyant psychology is gone and in the

breakdown and disintegration of the traditional individualism no new philosophies are rising. Builders of Utopia are out of a job.[40] (Emphasis added)

Whereas the cultural, economic, and political insights of many of the intellectuals in *The Colonial Mind* and *The Romantic Revolution* were sharpened by the experience of dwelling between worlds—both between the Old
World and the New World and between the worldviews that characterized
successive eras in American development—those in Volume 3 are living in
a world bounded on one side by a closed past but opening on the other on
an uncertain, ominous future.

The distance between the romantic optimism that characterized the main
currents of American thought in the first half of the nineteenth century and
the sense of powerlessness that characterized, for intellectuals, the second
half of the century is reflected in the critical idiom Parrington employs to
describe the intellectual style and the dominant debate in Volume 3. Here,
idealism and realism are together replaced by critical realism, and Volume
2's romantic attitude toward the nature of man is replaced by a sense of
pessimism and skepticism and irony.

This change in key terms is also accompanied by a changed content for
Volume 3's underlying dialectical debate. Volume 1's dynamic basis was
formed primarily by the political debate that issued in the new nation. Volume 2's dynamic basis was formed primarily by the economic debate that
issued in the Civil War. Now Volume 3's dynamic basis is formed primarily
by the cultural debate that issued in the emergence of a group of men of
letters who questioned the very grounds of America's political and economic faith.

Consequently, the role of the intellectual becomes more clearly defined in
Volume 3. The term "critical realism" is synonymous with a detached, analytic, observant stance. The achievement of that stance requires a transcen-
dence of the cultural regionalism symbolized by the structure of Volume 2
and of the two-sided political struggle symbolized by the theme of Volume
1. Moreover, it is also related to what Parrington identifies as the driving
force in history in each of the three volumes of *Main Currents*. In *The Colonial Mind* the driving force of history is the struggle to throw off the yoke
of theological and political absolutism. In *The Romantic Revolution* the
driving force is the doctrines drawn from French revolutionary theory. In
The Beginnings of Critical Realism it is the machine, created by science and
serving industrialism. The intellectual in Volume 3, therefore, must make a
place for himself in a culture dominated by the middle class, whereas in the
earlier volumes, whether he was a liberal or a conservative, he fulfilled an at
least historically sanctioned social role.

Yet the intellectual in Volume 3 must follow some design in cutting his
new role, and the fabric he wears is often of the same weave that clothed the
cultured eighteenth-century gentlemen of the Enlightenment. As a result, he

resembles not only the Henry Adams of *The Education,* who feels rather uncomfortable in the new coat styles of the twentieth century, but also the Vernon Parrington who professed Populism and taught contemporary American literature but was rather dandified in deportment and dress and encouraged his students to see "balance, harmony, and proportion" in all phases of eighteenth-century English culture.

Parrington's plea for a reassertion of the solid, sober virtues of the eighteenth century, coming as it does amid his description of the turbulence of the Gilded Age, might seem anomalous and contradictory if the major features of the portraits in Volumes 1 and 2 have not been observed. The values identified with the eighteenth century are the same ones that guide the definition of intellectuals and their roles throughout *Main Currents,* but the rosy optimism of the Enlightenment is being destroyed by science and the machine—by progress. The Enlightenment may remain an ideal, a golden age when ideas were taken seriously, that intellectuals may turn to as a behavioral model. But they must now make for themselves new ideological models. In Volume 3 a transitional romantic position is epitomized by Walt Whitman; the new skepticism and pessimism by such figures as Henry Adams and the naturalistic writers. The portraits of Weyl, Veblen, Beard, Croly, and the "younger intellectuals" surely would have helped define Parrington's sense of the ways critical realism was experienced in the works of recent social critics, writers, and historians. But of the "new America," *Main Currents* remains silent.

Parrington does not include Whitman's portrait in Volume 3 simply as a lovely epitaph on the lost hopes of the romantic revolution. Whitman is called an "afterglow of the Enlightenment" because he expresses a buoyant optimism in the future of democracy well into the later nineteenth century and because as "a pagan, a romantic, a transcendentalist, a mystic," he exhibits the major features of the Transcendental mind.[41] Yet several significant aspects of Whitman's personality and writings mark him off from the renaissance milieu and emphasize his function as a bridge into the twentieth century.

The first of these is Whitman's sensuousness, virility, and sense of joyful abandon in the full tide of experience. Unlike "Emerson with his serene intelligence almost disencumbered from the flesh, and Hawthorne with his dessicating skepticisms that left him afraid of sex," Whitman was a caresser and lover of life. He was a "childlike pagan" rather than a Puritan, "emotional rather than intellectual," and had more in common with "the modern expressionist" than with prior American poets. In these respects Whitman is similar to Randolph Bourne and other early twentieth-century critics and artists who desired to free the human psyche from Victorian moral restraints and to free poetry from the restraints of traditional forms and genteel content.[42]

Another difference between Whitman and the New Englanders is his view of the West, "where, he believed, a freer and more democratic America was taking shape." Whitman probably traveled as much in Brooklyn and Camden as Thoreau did in Concord, but his journeys west made him as much a poet of the prairies as of the eastern seaboard. Thus Whitman had more in common with Mark Twain, a younger man who was born in Missouri and drew his early inspiration from the western frontier, than with Herman Melville, who was born in the same year (1819) as Whitman and who, like Whitman, was a native New Yorker but who drew his early inspiration from the Pacific frontier. By dint of birth and habitat, Whitman could have been included in "The Mind of the Middle East." Instead, on the basis of his Turnerian insight into the connection between the West and democracy, his portrait immediately precedes Twain's in the section "The Culture of the Seventies." Whitman is the first figure in Volume 3 to transcend the regional bounds of Volume 2 and to express in the context of his poems an awareness of the varieties of national experience that were a product of post–Civil War population growth and territorial expansion. He both personifies and praises the welter of change that was remaking America and would issue in a national culture. Ironically, as Parrington observes, that new culture "was daily betraying" Whitman's romantic idealism and humanitarianism.[43]

Despite his western sympathies, which link him to the realistic tradition of Twain and Garland, and his religious mysticism, which links him to the philosophical position of the Transcendentalists, Whitman was also "deeply impregnated with the spirit of science." Although his romantic optimism about the evolutionary progress of civilization as symbolized by scientific achievements contrasts diametrically with Henry Adams's skepticism regarding the ultimate beneficence of science and the machine, it also contrasts markedly with the agrarian sympathies that lay at the base, in Parrington's view, of most of the political and cultural thinking done during the romantic revolution. In this respect Whitman seems to be less a child of Jean-Jacques Rousseau than a child of the Progressives, who tried to define the machine and the industrial metropolis in organic terms to make them consonant with the traditional agrarian basis of democratic theory.

Although Parrington evidently approves of Whitman's openness to science, as evidenced in "A Passage to India" and "Song of Myself" (which contains the line "Hurrah for positive science!"), he notes that Whitman searches beyond the material manifestations of progress for their spiritual reflections of God's universal design. This oracular faith would not suffice for Mark Twain, who described the horrors of technology in *A Connecticut Yankee* and the demonic creator in *The Mysterious Stranger*. But it has parallels in Henry Adams's spiritual quest for the Medieval Virgin and for the inspiration behind *Mont-Saint-Michel and Chartres*. Parrington also stresses that the inventions Whitman praised—the transcontinental railway, the steam engine, the transcontinental telegraph—in "A Passage to India" would not only bind men together. Fluid communications would hasten the development of the interior and the centralization of the American economy, producing a new urban psychology and new social philosophies.[44]

Whitman was a prophet and critic rather than a political theorist or economist. His vision of a beneficent, unified cosmos seems to bear little relation to the doctrines of theorists like Henry George. Yet Whitman's emphasis on the brotherhood of man, his romantic belief in fraternity, link him in some respects more closely with late nineteenth-century radical political movements than with the individualism that lies at the core of Transcendentalism. As Parrington explains:

> The hermit Thoreau in his cabin at Walden Pond was no symbol of a generous future. In the struggle for liberty and equality the conception of fraternity had been denied and the golden trinity of the Enlightenment dismembered. . . . The conception of solidarity, entering the realm of proletarian thought through the labors of Friedrich Engels and Karl Marx, was his response to the new times. . . . Democracy spiritualized by Channing and Emerson and Parker had suffered limitations from . . . the Puritan passion for righteousness. . . . In Thoreau it had been subjected to caustic skepticisms. . . . But in Whitman all limitations and skepticisms were swept away by the feeling of comradeship.[45]

Toward the conclusion of the portrait Parrington cites the passage from *Democratic Vistas* (1870) in which Whitman expresses the view that democracy has yet to be fully achieved in America:

> I say that our New World democracy, however great a success in uplifting the masses out of their sloughs, in materialistic development, products, and in a certain highly deceptive superficial popular intellectuality, is, so far, an almost complete failure in its social aspects, and in really grand religious, moral, literary, and esthetic results. . . . We sail a dangerous sea of seething currents, cross and undercurrents, vortices—all so dark and untried.

Twenty years later, at the end of his life, Whitman would modify his earlier revolutionary sentiments, call himself an evolutionist, and refuse to become a partisan to the socialist cause. Of course, as an artist, he was required to stand apart, and Parrington praises him as "a great figure, assuredly the greatest in our literature."[46] He may have sometimes been a harsh critic of democracy, but he was too romantic in his belief in human perfectibility and optimistic view of scientific progress to be called a critical realist.

Thus, like two other major writers in the section "The Culture of the Seventies," Thomas Bailey Aldrich and Twain, as well as the rest of the "colossal yet grotesque" figures of the Gilded Age treated in Part I of Book I, Whitman belonged "to an America that was passing."[47] In Part II of Book I, Parrington begins to describe the "new patterns of thought" that will replace the last vestiges of romantic thinking. As in Volumes 1 and 2, the new ideas that will once again contribute to changing the face of America are drawn from Europe. Even more schematically, they are drawn from France and England, the two sources of influence out of whose confluence (symbolized in the conflict between the Federalism of Adams and Hamilton and the Republicanism of Paine and Jefferson) the new nation emerged.

But now the political heritage of the French thinkers has been replaced by the sociological doctrines of Comte and Condorcet; that of the English by the biological determinism of Herbert Spencer. This time Parrington sees nothing noble in this intellectual bequest, for both the theological idealism of Volume 1 and the romantic idealism of Volume 2 have been shouldered aside by the gospel of progress. Necessarily this philosophical change is accompanied by a changed view of human nature; instead of either the ethical Puritan or the romantic Jeffersonian, a standardized being, stripped of his power of will and imagination, now occupies the bleak spaces of a mechanized, deterministic universe.

As Parrington makes clear in his introduction to Part II, although science is remaking the New World,

> Our present concern, however, is not with the contributions of America to abstract science, but rather with the changing mental attitude that resulted from familiarity with scientific methods. . . . To speak exactly, it is not so much science that has taken possession of the mind, as certain postulates of science, certain philosophies, presumably derived from science and justified by science, which we have felt bound to incorporate in our thinking as a hundred years before the conclusions of the Enlightenment had been incorporated.[48]

In the first two volumes those intellectuals who were open to new European ideas were generally praised. Now those who are open to new European ideas are usually criticized, for Parrington has identified science as the coercive agent in the negative shift toward a deterministic universe that denied "all the aspirations of our traditional social philosophy, sundering society to a new regimentation and reducing the individual to an impotent victim of things as they are."[49] Consequently, the intellectual is now always on the defensive. Instead of actively purveying, in public life or through art, a new climate of opinion, the intellectual is now called to inveigh actively against the dominant cultural climate.

As expected, one of the most explicit statements of Parrington's definition of intellectuals occurs in his portrait of Henry Adams, the only other single figure in *Main Currents* in addition to Hugh Legaré to be assigned the epithet "intellectual." In Henry, as in his brothers, Charles Francis Adams, Jr., and Brooks Adams, "the family virtues of independence, intellectual integrity, and disinterested criticism found abundant expression."[50] The scholarly Henry is a "veritable walking library," like John Cotton, of both history and art. Parrington writes that, while Henry Adams was teaching medieval history at Harvard during the 1870s, "the passion of the student was in his blood, and he turned with zest to the scanty records of past generations, trying to arrange the meaningless fragments in some sort of rational pattern, in the hope of discovering an underlying unity in what seemed on the face only a meaningless welter of complexity and irrationality." After quitting Harvard, he turned to political life and began writing on American themes, publishing *Life of Albert Gallatin* (1879), *John Randolph* (1882), and the nine-volume *History of the United States During the Administrations of Jefferson and Madison* (1889–91). Yet even working in this narrower sphere, Adams did not make Cotton Mather's mistake of becoming parochial once he turned away from European experience: "He could not deal with narrow parochial themes; he would not fall into the 'sink of history—antiquarianism,' that satisfied Charles Francis Adams. From the beginnings of his intellectual life he had been concerned with the ideas and ideals that presumably lie behind periods and civilization."[51]

Parrington does not comment on the personal crisis, the suicide of Adams's wife in 1885, that eventually turned him down the introspective road of autobiography, of personal history rather than scholarship, and caused the elision of twenty years (1870–90) in the chronology of *The Education*. Parrington locates the significant turning point in Adams's life as the time during the 1890s when he recognized the importance of economic factors in shaping history and of the physical sciences as a metaphor for explaining the course of historical events. Although Adams felt that he needed to reeducate himself so he could understand the impact of the gospel of progress on his present age, he himself would never subscribe to the new faith. As an intellectual, he remained an observer rather than a participant. "In the welter of change that resulted from the revolutionary transitions of the Gilded Age," Adams is identified as the one man who

> at least stood apart, skeptical about the worth of the current revolutions, unconvinced that all the hurly-burly meant a rational progress. . . . He was not at home in the new world of the Gilded Age; and as he watched the disintegration of the older New England in which he had been brought up, an incurable nostalgia seized upon him and he set about seeking another home.[52]

By the turn of the century, Adams found that other home in the balanced lines of the medieval cathedral and in the mysticism they expressed. Parrington thinks *Mont-Saint-Michel and Chartres* (1904) is a lovely book, but he criticizes Adams for perceiving religion as the core of medieval society instead of the guild, as William Morris had. Like the rest of the Adams family, whom he calls "the most distinguished in our history," Henry remained too much of a Yankee-Puritan to adjust his eighteenth-century mind "to the demands of a sordid capitalistic order," which owed much to the exploitation of the craftsmanship that William Morris loved and valued. All three brothers ultimately "met with failure," even though "they tried to bridge the chasm between the two worlds, though they honestly sought some working compromise that would suffer them to share in the work of their generation."[53]

Along with Henry James and William Dean Howells, Henry Adams belonged to the generation of the 1870s who came to intellectual maturity before the genial optimism of Spencerian evolutionary doctrine was stripped away to reveal the bleak determinism below. As a historian, Adams confronted the issue of realism differently than James or Howells. Whereas his role was to develop a realistic critique of the nature of American culture, as artists they were called to develop a new form and a new content, to begin the work of substituting realism for romanticism. Just as Adams failed to make the transition into the twentieth century, so too would James fail to free his work from romanticism and Howells to free his from the constraints of Victorian moral rectitude.[54]

The varied manifestations of the 1870s generation are the entire focus of Book I of *The Beginnings of Critical Realism*. In Book II Parrington planned to employ a regional structure similar to that used in *The Romantic Revolution* and describe three locales—the Middle Border, the city, and the "hesitant South"—which reflect differing responses to the transition period between the generation of the 1870s and the rise of the Progressive generation. Both the political and artistic figures from the Middle Border and the literary figures from the South would fail to make an intellectual rapprochement with the machine that was destroying the agrarian way of life. They would be shoved off the stage of history as the city with its "proletarian hopes" and its sociological chroniclers came to dominate the center of late nineteenth-century literature and politics.

Until Book III, which was to document the rise of the third phase of liberalism and the emergence of the vital new group of men of letters, the distinction between social thinker–intellectual and artist-intellectual can still be made. The overall tendency, though, in *The Beginnings of Critical Realism* is not only toward a national culture dominated by the middle class that obliterates regional bounds, but also toward a unification of social thought and aesthetics. Indeed, such a unification forms the core of Parrington's sense of liberalism. His hope is finally not in liberal politics, but in the creation of liberal minds. Thus, although new economic and political theories were pivotal in the transition of "an agricultural people changing to an urbanized people,"[55] the development of literary realism was a crucial register of the impact of that transition. Most important, the realistic movement was part of the cultural and political revolt against the ethics of the Gilded Age. Realistic writers understood themselves as contributing in some measure to reforming society. The genre of advocacy fiction was even more sharply delineated as naturalistic writers such as

Frank Norris and Theodore Dreiser subsequently perceived the earlier realism of Howells as portraying inadequately the harsh underside of American life, particularly urban life.

Parrington welcomed the development of realism as a democratizing force in the realms of both politics and culture. On this point he apparently agreed with Howells's opinion that modern realism, drawing its passion for the truthful treatment of material from science, is "the child of democracy because the realist is one who 'feels in every nerve the equality of things and the unity of men.' "[56] Realism not only seeks to overcome the aristocratic and individualistic characteristics of romanticism; it also can be a means of unifying the newly felt impact of science with traditional democratic equalitarianism through a new aesthetic relation between form and content. As a result, in Book II of Volume 3, no matter how much he may be in sympathy with their reformist aims, Parrington will criticize on this aesthetic basis those writers who retain an old-fashioned residuum of romanticism in their art as well as those whose work has been unduly influenced by the mechanistic and deterministic postulates of science.

The former criticism explains Parrington's final judgment on Hamlin Garland, whose portrait comes at the conclusion of Part I ("The Middle Border Rises") of Book II. Garland belongs to the intellectual world of Howells, even though he did not forswear his western origins. Parrington writes that, despite the early bitter protest of *Main Travelled Roads* and *Prairie Folks* and the militant literary creed outlined in *Crumbling Idols,* which would function as the manifesto for the local color school, "in the light of his total work one hesitates to call Garland a realist. Perhaps more justly he might be called a thwarted romantic." The novels *Her Mountain Lover* and *Captain of the Greyhorse Troops* and the autobiographical *Son of the Middle Border* all express his romantic longing for an older and simpler America:

> He was so deeply colored by this earlier native America that he never outgrew it; and when the Populistic revolt had died down, when this last organized agrarian rebellion against the exploiting middle class had become only an episode in our history, he had outlived his day. He was too deeply stirred by Whitman's romantic faith in democracy, too narrowly a disciple of Henry George's Jeffersonian economics, to fit an industrializing America. Despite his discipleship to European realism he refused to go with the group of young left-wing naturalists who were boldly venturing on new ways of fiction.[57]

Parrington's discussion of the rise of naturalism was designed as part of his description of "the darkening skies of letters," the concluding section of Part II ("Proletarian Hopes") of Book II. As the Table of Contents indicates, this discussion was to include only Stephen Crane and Frank Norris. Parrington's analyses of the other writers usually included in the naturalistic movement—Jack London ("revolutionist"), Upton Sinclair ("social detective"), and Theodore Dreiser ("a modern")—were delayed until Part II, "Liberalism and Letters," of Book III. Despite their disparate placement in Volume 3, all five writers are "intellectual children of the nineties" whose work "reflects the shifting winds of scientific doctrine" from the optimism of Spencer's biologically derived social theories to the pessimism of determinism, drawn from the new physical sciences.[58] Although the naturalists ventured further than Garland down new paths of thinking and literary techniques, they did not venture quite far enough from the romantic conception of individual will to fulfill consummately the tenets of naturalistic theory:

> The ferment of social thought, shot through with Marxianism, familiarized American novelists with the one doctrine important for the naturalists—the doctrine of economic determinism. In none of them did it pass over into a larger conception of philosophical determinism, and this sets the limitation to their naturalism. The common zeal for reform or revolution, moreover, kept them from objectivity. *In none is there the calm detachment and amoral presentation of material without which naturalism sinks into propaganda.* Their position presupposes a large confidence in individual initiative—a confidence in the power of men to alter the world they live in. It is admirable, but it is not the way of the naturalists, who do not seek to change what they regard as an essentially unresponsive world that changes only after its own way.[59] (Emphasis added)

Of the five naturalists treated in *The Beginnings of Critical Realism,* Dreiser comes closest to fulfilling the intellectual's proper role, for he "is of this changing world and yet apart from it . . . the most detached and keenly observant of all our writers." Nevertheless, although he possesses "a vast and terrifying imagination," "instead of suffering his portrayal to stand on its own feet he props it up with argument and interminable debate. The artist suffers at the hands of the disputant."[60]

If Parrington were only interested in literature, no matter of what quality, that reflected the economic basis of social structure and experience, he should applaud the naturalists' efforts. If Parrington is viewed primarily as a supporter of Populist and Progressive reform movements, then these examples of aesthetic formalism might appear entirely anomalous in a work supposedly devoted to political thought. After seeing Parrington praise such writers as Poe for serving beauty alone and chastising writers like Freneau, William Gilmore Simms, and Harriet Beecher Stowe for failing to stand apart from social issues, however, we should not be surprised that Parrington similarly evaluates contemporary writers.

Parrington was himself a member of the generation of the 1890s, born after the Civil War and coming to intellectual maturity in the fin de siècle. Writing about his own lifetime sharpened rather than blunted Parrington's perceptions about the possibilities of achieving either a democratic politics or a rich culture as America moved into the third decade of the twentieth century. Like many other creative people of his age, he felt compelled to reconcile his aesthetic taste with the new social theories propounded in the early Progressive period. *Main Currents* as a whole can be read as a document of the period in which it was conceived and written, as a means to place order on the turbulent World War I years and to act as a stay against the loss of faith in culture and politics that characterized the 1920s.

Curiously, in its fragmentary form, *Main Currents* covers nearly the same time period as Parrington's "Autobiographical Sketch." The sketch begins by noting that the Parrington name originated in old Saxon times but that "family tradition runs no further back than my greatgrandfather," who was born near the time of the American Revolution, the period covered in *The Colonial Mind*. Two pages from the end of the sketch, Parrington notes that he voted for William Jennings Bryan and was giving "increasing attention to the agrarian proposals, thereby gaining my first real insight into economics and political science." In Volume 3 Parrington completed the sections on Hamlin Garland and William Dean Howells, the only American authors mentioned in the sketch. But he came just short of writing the sections of Populism and Bryan. Such is the supplementary nature of intellectual history as the history of ideas and intellectual history as the history of intellectuals.

"The Artist Works in Perpetual Contempt of Court"

Following the posthumous publication of *The Beginnings of Critical Realism*, the wider University of Washington community paid "a debt of gratitude" by renaming the old Science Hall, built in 1901, in honor of Parrington. On the recommendation of President M. Lyle Spencer, the Board of Regents also granted a sum for remodeling so that the English Department could be moved there from its neighboring quarters in Denny Hall. Ironically, Parrington had loved Denny Hall's architecture, with its twin Victorian cupolas, and found Science Hall, a more severe structure, far less appealing. The building was officially rededicated, with the help of Parrington's widow, Julia, on August 3, 1931, a day that also marked the sixtieth anniversary of his birth.[61]

Even more ironically for those who remembered the Parrington-Padelford rivalry, after Dean Padelford's death in 1942 the university saw fit to honor this well-known scholar and devoted administrator. Instead of remodeling an old building, a new one was built across campus from Parrington Hall, and in 1967 the English Department was moved into Padelford Hall.[62] The physical relocation of the English Department was the outward symbol of more subtle, but more far-reaching, changes that were occurring in the department curriculum and hiring policies.

When the university catalog was printed in the spring of 1929 while Parrington was on leave, the title History of American Culture was dropped from his sequence that covered American literature from the beginnings to 1870. From then on, it would simply be listed as American Literature, the title Parrington had used when he inaugurated the sequence in 1909.[63] The shift from "culture" back to "literature" was a preview of what took place, not only at the University of Washington, when the New Criticism, advocating the intrinsic study of primary texts and the exclusion of extrinsic (biographical, cultural, political) materials, began to make an impact on English studies in the 1940s. In 1948 a new department chairman, Robert B. Heilman, was appointed. Heilman does not describe himself as a New Critic or see his appointment as primarily reflecting the nationwide trend in critical attitudes, but he had taught at Louisiana State University from 1935 to 1943, where two of his colleagues were Robert Penn Warren and Cleanth Brooks. As co-editors of the *Southern Review* from 1935 to 1942 and co-authors of *Understanding Poetry* (1938), Brooks and Warren had been influential in disseminating the methods and viewpoints of the New Criticism, particularly among college professors.[64]

Whether or not Heilman was perceived as a New Critic, he did represent new blood and was charged with the task of infusing the department with a sense of professional activism. This loss of professionalism, evidenced by poorly prepared graduate students, was not simply a departmental problem. During the years of financial stringency that followed President Henry Suzzallo's dismissal in the 1920s, the university had resorted to hiring professors from the ranks of its graduate students and to recruiting students with lower qualifications. The provincialism that resulted is partly illustrated by the university community's shock at discovering it harbored excellent scholars like Parrington when it read about his Pulitzer Prize award in the *New York Times*. To reverse such trends and embarrassments, between 1945 and 1953 twelve new directors of schools and department heads were appointed in the College of Arts and Sciences alone, when many senior faculty and administration members retired. The 1953 catalog showed that, in twenty-six out of thirty-four schools and departments in the college, at least half the members of the teaching staff had been appointed since World War II. That year another member of the English Department, the poet Theodore Roethke, would win the university's second Pulitzer for his collection *The Waking*.[65]

The administrative change and physical relocation of the English Department were tied closely to the growth and development of the entire university. Yet Heilman was very much aware of the old loyalties that divided that department between the "Old Historicism" as represented by Padelford's emphasis on the historical accuracy of sources and the "New Historicism" represented by Parrington's emphasis on the historical relationships between literature and culture. The real problem, however, was not the continuance of the original clash between the two men and their methods but that a complacent following in the masters' footsteps had replaced the vitality that had animated the masters' scholarship.[66]

Politics soon intervened in this delicate situation, as had happened several decades earlier. In the interest of revitalizing the department, in 1948 Heilman asked Malcolm Cowley to come to the university as a visiting professor. Cowley was interested and agreed to come for the winter quarter of the 1950–51 academic year. The appointment was criticized, however, after Cowley testified against Whittaker Chambers, and when the "local vigilantes" got wind of it, they searched Cowley's works for evidence of Communist ideas. The most damaging evidence they could find was a few scatological terms, and Cowley was finally hired. This incident, unfortunately, was replayed again shortly thereafter when the English Department tried to hire critic Kenneth Burke in 1952 for a Walker-Ames lectureship, funded by a special university endowment. Although Heilman defended Burke as he had defended Cowley, this time the appointment was rescinded by the Board of Regents as McCarthyism increasingly made itself felt on college campuses.[67]

The debate over academic freedom that took place during the Cold War years had actually begun at the University of Washington well before Senator Joseph McCarthy's rise to prominence in the early 1950s. Action taken in December 1946 allowed the Washington legislature to create a Joint Legislative Fact-Finding Committee on Un-American Activities to be chaired by Albert Canwell, a Republican from Spokane who had the support of conservative Democrats as well as of his own party in attempting to curb supposed radical activity and opinion. By 1948 Canwell informed the Board of Regents that his committee was investigating several university faculty members. With the approval of the regents and of President Raymond B. Allen, who thought it would be healthy to bring such matters out in the open, a series of hearings began. Ten faculty members were investigated, including E. H. Eby and Garland Ethel of the English Department, both of whom admitted past Communist party membership, and Melvin Rader of the Philosophy Department, who had not been a party member. In the course of the hearings, personal association with Parrington and William Savery, his friend and colleague from the Philosophy Department, was acknowledged.[68]

At this time Parrington had been dead for nearly twenty years. Savery, who came to Washington just after the turn of the century, had died two years earlier, in 1946. Although one university historian claims that no attempt was made to evaluate their influence on these younger men, he also notes that "academic inbreeding . . . was especially pronounced in the departments of English and philosophy." So perhaps it was no mere coincidence that the English Department gained a new head in the very year of the hearings and that by 1953 six of the seven philosophy faculty were new.

These two departments in addition to political science, where by 1953 ten of the fourteen members were new, had been recognized as bastions of liberal opinion since pre–World War I years. The same historian observes that the memory of J. Allen Smith and Vernon L. Parrington did have "a certain relevance" to the hearings:

> Liberals both, these men had grappled as best they could with problems of responsible government in an age when the forces of political and economic consolidation seemed to be threatening the very foundation of the republic. Both had been vigorous in their analysis and unsparing in their criticism. Yet neither had found answers. Students, now their successors, confronted similar issues in situations that were even more disturbing, but they found no answers, either. . . . So it came about that men who were essentially moderates drifted somewhat farther to the left and through their dalliance with Communism appeared more radical than they were.[69]

The degree of commitment of none of these persons is under question here. What is at issue is how Parrington might have responded to being identified as an influence on his former students' and colleagues' opinions. Although the Board of Regents eventually ruled that there were no grounds for dismissal of the English and Philosophy Department members who were investigated by the Canwell Committee, surely Parrington would have been distressed at the ways their lives were disrupted and their First Amendment rights apparently violated. But were these results primarily effects of changing political climates or of acting upon ideas expressed by Parrington in conversation, in the classroom, or in *Main Currents?*

In retrospect, *Main Currents in American Thought* does not read like a call to arms. Alfred Kazin found that Parrington, too, appeared more radical than he really was. This is not to deny that Parrington's volumes made deep impressions on many who read them when they were first published and that, because of the special characteristics of the Depression years, some of those impressions may have strengthened or even justified left-wing attitudes. But it was primarily in the spirit of free inquiry—which was the real issue in the Canwell Committee hearings and their later counterparts—rather than in the spirit of political radicalism that Parrington launched his long-conceived and carefully redesigned work.[70]

Whatever the degree of Parrington's radicalism, it did not eventuate in political activism, unless his brief encounter with practical Populist politics in Emporia can be termed activism. His most radical political acts took place within the privacy of the ballot box. His votes in 1920 for Debs and in 1924 for LaFollette were followed by one for Norman Thomas in 1928. "I get very little comfort out of the campaign. It is all such a dreary wash of cant and unrealities," he wrote to his former Norman student George B. Parker, now editor in chief of the Scripps-Howard newspapers. "I am against Hoover and all the smug and contented, corrupt managers of the Republican Party. . . . When I get into the voting machine, alone with my conscience and my God, very likely I shall pull down the lever for Norman Thomas."[71]

In respect to this behavior, Parrington's personal intellectual style provides perspective on his political style. Despite the increasing network of professional contacts that ensued after Parrington began circulating his original manuscript and identifying with the "drilled hosts of the historians," they were all carried on at a distance, except for his summers at Berkeley, Columbia, and the University of Michigan. The only evidence that he participated in a scholarly meeting dates from his Emporia years. At Washington one oft-repeated anecdote concerns his preference for transplanting rhododendrons to attending faculty meetings. He belonged to no major professional societies until 1928, when the secretary of the MLA wrote to suggest that he might "wish to abandon [his] present aloof position of 'splendid isolation.' " A bemused Parrington sent in the membership fee with the comments, which may well summarize his career, "I have hitherto clung to my lonesome state outside the pale," because "distinction of any sort is so rare today that I rather pride myself on the small amount I have been able to acquire by playing a lone hand."[72]

Though he was isolated by geography—"Seattle is on the extreme rim of the continent, and we do not know much that is going on elsewhere," he wrote once to a New York acquaintance—Parrington both suffered and gained from his isolation from scholarly interaction. It gave him time to work, although he was hampered by lack of resources. It gave him time to experiment in the classroom, although Washington in the 1920s did not generally draw students of the highest caliber. Isolation enhanced his wariness of academic specialization, for he began wondering if "the teaching of American literature in our graduate schools is going to run into a bog of meticulous scholarship." It produced the feeling that he was an amateur in comparison to Beard as well as the first sentence in *Main Currents:* "It is with a certain feeling of temerity that I offer the present study."[73]

Isolation also informed Parrington's perspective on the experience of alienated artists and detached intellectuals, a perspective that creates the central, tragic theme of *Main Currents.* When Waldo Frank wrote in 1928 that "one gets so accustomed and resigned to working alone in this country of ours," Parrington responded, "One sends out a book over which he has sweat blood with something of a feeling that he is shooting in the dark."[74] Certainly this confession reveals personal discomfort. But Parrington's professional insistence on detachment, on standing apart, had upheld him through his years of lonely writing and of vibrant teaching:

> To understand rather than to enjoy or appraise—that I take it is the function of the historian. To light the candle of the past and throw its beams upon the

present; or rather to fashion a candle out of present materials, and send back its light upon other days, to make out what we can. It is not much that we shall see—so much is gone forever and remains irrecoverable. . . .

Pasting labels on diverse forms, classifying and cataloguing neatly, may serve to fill an idle hour; but it is futile. . . . The critic may lay down the law, he may even threaten to hang and draw and quarter; but. . . . *[t]he artist works in perpetual contempt of court,* and laughs at all critical bailiffs. *He was born a rebel and his art is the product of rebellion.*[75] (Emphasis added)

Rebellious artists, critical of institutionalization and professionalization, do not found schools of academic thought and practice. Parrington saw himself as a boundary breaker rather than as a canon constructor. The scope of his project inevitably revealed the state of American historical and literary studies at the time of its execution. That subsequent scholarship has undertaken to correct features of his interpretation and to build upon areas of inquiry undeveloped in *Main Currents* can be viewed as a tribute to a pioneering task. To write three volumes that allowed him to participate in the ongoing dialogue over the relationship between ideology and aesthetics in American culture exceeded Parrington's hopes, inscribed in his diary as he left for Harvard: "I must—nay, I will—work out a faithful, if not brilliant, work."

Notes

Preface

1. Vernon Louis Parrington, *Main Currents in American Thought: An Interpretation of American Literature from the Beginnings to 1920*, Vol. 1: *The Colonial Mind, 1620–1800* (New York: Harcourt, Brace, 1927), p. i. Vol. 2: *The Romantic Revolution in America, 1800–1860*, was published with Vol. 1. Vol. 3: *The Beginnings of Critical Realism in America, 1860–1920*, was published in 1930 with identical binding. The pagination in all hardbound editions of *MCAT*, including the combined one-volume edition (New York: Harcourt, Brace, 1939) and the three-volume 1987 issue by the University of Oklahoma Press (excluding the brief Forewords by David W. Levy), is identical. The paperbound Harbinger edition of Vol. 3 (New York: Harcourt, Brace, 1958) is paginated the same as the hardbound versions, but the paperbound Harvest editions of Vols. 1 and 2 (New York: Harcourt, Brace, 1954) are paginated somewhat differently.

2. The phrase "a noble ruin" appears in John Higham, "The Rise of American Intellectual History," *American Historical Review* 56 (April 1951): 460. On developments in intellectual history, see Thomas Bender, "Wholes and Parts: The Need for Synthesis in American History," *Journal of American History* 73 (June 1986): 120–36, and its continuation in the special section "A Roundtable: Synthesis in American History," *Journal of American History* 74 (June 1987): 107–30. On developments in literary studies, two sources are Frederick Crews's review essay "Whose American Renaissance?" *New York Review of Books* 35 (October 27, 1988): 68–81, although it contains an erroneous estimation of Parrington, and the symposium "Firing the Canon," *American Literary History* 3 (Winter 1991): 707–52. On developments in American Studies, see Gene Wise, " 'Paradigm Dramas' in American Studies: A Cultural and Institutional History of the Movement," *American Quarterly* 31 (Bibliography Issue, 1979): 293–337. On the New Historicism in literary studies—which may be seen as analogous to the New History and its revivifying effect on historical studies after the mid-1910s as well as to the conceptual thrust of the original American Studies movement in the 1930s—see Lawrence Buell, "The Historicist Explosion in Recent Literary Studies," *Intellectual History Newsletter* 12 (1990): 22–26, and Christopher P. Wilson's review essay "Containing Multitudes: Realism, Historicism, American Studies," *American Quarterly* 41 (September 1989): 466–95.

3. This title is Stevens Parrington Tucker's; Parrington's drafts bear either no title or varying titles, such as "Life Sketch." Richard Hofstadter relied heavily on the "Autobiographical Sketch" in *The Progressive Historians: Turner, Beard, Parrington* (New York: Knopf, 1968; Vintage Books, 1970), 357–74. Perhaps because the sketch was unpublished, he does not list page references, only acknowledging in a footnote that "all reminiscent and self-characterizing statements from Parrington in the following pages, unless otherwise documented, are from this memoir, in the possession of Vernon Parrington, Jr." (p. 358).

The page numbers listed in my notes refer to a copy of the sketch that was typed from Parrington's original manuscript by Professor John Brooks Moore after Parrington's death. I was first loaned a copy of the typescript by Professor E. Harold Eby but have since compared it with several drafts by Parrington as well as with one by Vernon Parrington, Jr., in the 1950s. Unfortunately, this later copy contains many errors and was evidently compiled from Parrington's first draft, which is briefer than his second draft and does not contain several of the most illuminating passages found in the Moore typescript, which was copied from Parrington's second—and, we must assume, final—draft. A copy of the sketch is also in the E. H. Eby Papers, University of Washington Archives and Records Center.

4. Entries were dated and kept in pocket-sized record books. Stevens Parrington Tucker has transcribed and compiled the diaries into a single bound volume. The entries are quite full during Parrington's college years; in the bound volume thirty-two pages, typed on one side, are devoted to 1890, forty-five to 1891, fifty to 1892, and thirty-five to the first ten months of 1893. The entries are resumed in 1896 (seven pages) and kept fairly regularly until the time of his marriage in 1901. Eleven pages are given over to 1897, six to 1898, fourteen to 1899, seven each to 1900 and 1901. There are no entries for 1902 although they may be lost. The diary is resumed on July 7, 1903, the date Parrington sailed for Europe. Nine pages are filled for that year and eight for 1904. Beginning with 1905, the diaries are concerned almost solely with gardening and weather, some bearing the handwritten inscription "Garden Book." There are fifteen pages for 1905, eight for 1906, three for 1907, and a few brief notes for the first four months of 1908, when he was fired from the University of Oklahoma. The diary is not resumed—or possibly volumes were lost or even destroyed—until 1917; that year twenty pages are devoted primarily to gardening. Eleven pages are given over to 1918, seventeen to 1919, twelve to 1920, thirteen each to 1921 and 1922, four to 1924, only two each to 1925 and 1926, and only one to 1927 (the last four years being the period between the signing of the publishing contract with Harcourt, Brace and Co. and the appearance of the first two volumes of *MCAT*). There are no entries for 1928 and less than two pages for 1929, the year of Parrington's death.

5. Eric F. Goldman, "J. Allen Smith: The Reformer and His Dilemma," *Pacific Northwest Quarterly* 35 (July 1944): 195–213, and *Rendezvous with Destiny: A History of Modern American Reform* (New York: Knopf, 1953), pp. 37–38, 106, 309–10, 314, 318, 467. Information about Goldman's teaching is from an interview with W. Stull Holt, Seattle, August 21, 1978. See also Vernon L. Parrington, Jr., "Vernon Louis Parrington: Scholar, Teacher, Democrat—A Biography," and letters from Richard Hofstadter to Vernon L. Parrington, Jr., September 1967–February 1968, regarding the use of Parrington's papers and the composition of the Parrington chapters in *The Progressive Historians*, VLP Papers.

6. Hofstadter, *Progressive Historians*, pp. 488–89 (Bibliographical Essay), 354, 363, 372, 375. Hofstadter also mentions or cites Parrington's papers on pp. 358, 361, 365, 370, 377, 487, 488, and 491. I consulted the papers three times, during two approximately week-long research trips in 1978 and 1982 and for an extended period in 1980 with the aid of a National Endowment for the Humanities summer stipend.

7. Kermit Vanderbilt, *American Literature and the Academy: The Roots, Growth, and Maturity of a Profession* (Philadelphia: University of Pennsylvania Press, 1986), pp. 316, 323–24; pp. 315–32 contain his full and cogent discussion of the issue of Parrington's aesthetic sensibility. My earlier and similarly argued treatment can be found in H. Lark Hall, "Vernon

Louis Parrington: The Genesis and Design of *Main Currents in American Thought"* (Cleveland, Ohio: Case Western Reserve University, 1979), pp. 164–66, 275–90, 351–62.

8. Consult Chapter 12, "Legacies," for information on the editing and compilation of Volume 3, which fell upon the shoulders of E. Harold Eby, Parrington's junior colleague at the University of Washington, whom I interviewed in Seattle, October 3, 1977.

9. This version of Jay's essay appears in the collection *Theorizing American Literature: Hegel, the Sign, and History,* ed. Bernard Cowan and Joseph Kronick (Baton Rouge: Louisiana State University Press, 1991), pp. 83–122. An earlier version that lacked the fuller depiction of the Hegelian aspects of Parrington's writing appeared as "Hegel and Trilling in America," *American Literary History* 1 (Fall 1989): 565–92. See Chapter 10, "Three Cheers! A Book At Last," for specific discussion of Parrington's title and the dialectical structure of *MCAT.*

10. Hofstadter, *Progressive Historians,* p. 378.

11. Ibid., p. 362.

12. Interview with Mrs. W. Stevens Tucker (Louise Wrathal Parrington), San Carlos, Calif., August 17–18, 1980.

13. Matthew Arnold, *The Poetical Works of Matthew Arnold* (New York: Crowell, 1897), p. 428; see pp. 425–32 for the entire poem, first published in 1853, which turns on the questions of doubt and faith raised by the now empty Carthusian Monastery in the French Alps. For reflections in *MCAT,* see 3:xxvi–xxvii, 48, 240.

1 God in History: The Early Years, 1871–1891

1. The text of "God in History" was published in the College of Emporia's campus paper, *College Life* 3 (February 21, 1891): 1, 4, 5. The Kansas State Historical Society in Topeka has a file of *College Life* dating from October 11, 1890, to 1911. The nearly four-page oration was also separately printed; copies remain among Parrington's papers. Subsequent quotations are from this source.

2. Unless otherwise specified, all subsequent biographical information including titles of other orations, descriptions of contests and judging, and Parrington's activities during the summer of 1891, is drawn from Parrington's current diaries.

3. *MCAT,* 3:19.

4. AS, pp. 28–29.

5. Ibid., 29–30.

6. The letters do not remain in Parrington's papers; information is from his current diary.

7. AS, pp. 1, 3; Hugh D. McLellan, *History of Gorham, Me.,* comp. and ed. Katharine B. Lewis (Portland: Smith and Sale, 1903), pp. 358–59.

8. The family plot, in Section L, Lot 210, of Gorham's Eastern Cemetery, contains the graves of Ann Wrathal Parrington (she died at age seventy on September 28, 1861), John Parrington (he died on February 7, 1836), as well as a single, nearly illegible stone marking the grave of two "children of John and Ann Parrington": William's name and birth/death dates are clearly legible; but of the second child's inscription only "Mar. 20" is clearly legible; the year could be 1832, 1836, or 1838. The surviving Gorham town records of births and deaths list William's death but have no entries for this infant.

9. For historical and genealogical information on the McLellans and Warrens, see McLellan, *History of Gorham,* pp. 658–60, 779–800. A fictionalized version of Gorham's founding and of Hugh McLellan's role in it by Reverend Elijah Kellogg, titled "Good Old Times: or, Grandfather's Struggle for a Homestead," was serialized in twelve monthly installments in *Our Young Folks: An Illustrated Magazine for Boys and Girls* 3 (1867); it was also published, with the same title, as a book (Boston: Lothrop, Lee & Shephard Co., 1905). Parrington perused *Good Old Times* when on holiday at James and Mary Parrington Warren's home. A more recent history is *A Pictorial History of Gorham, Maine,* compiled by the Gorham Historical Society (1976).

10. I wish to thank the Minnesota Historical Society for supplying biographical material on Mark Hill Dunnell (1823–1904) and his family, including Steele County 1900 Census Population Schedules (June 2, 1900, 1st Ward of Owatonna, Minnesota), Leaf 98; "Colonel Mark H. Dunnell," an unflattering sixteen-page booklet "by a Republican" on file in the Reference Library, Minnesota Historical Society, Minneapolis; *Who Was Who in America*, Vol. 1, 1897–1942, p. 343. Parrington mentions his aunt Sarah in his "Autobiographical Sketch" twice (pp. 1, 4) and notes her sense of humor, indicating she may have returned to Maine to visit her son during the early 1890s. Warren Dunnell and his bride, Ida, are treated in the July 1892 diary. Another cousin, Mark Boothby Dunnell, remained in Minnesota, also pursuing a legal career. The Dunnell family bears striking resemblance to the John Parringtons, e.g., Republican politics, Civil War service, careers in education and law, moves from Maine to the Midwest.

11. On James Mann, see McLellan, *History of Gorham*, pp. 647–48. Other family information is drawn from AS, pp. 4–6. The future Mrs. Parrington was named at birth Mary Louisa McClellan, but almost all vital records list her as Mary Louise. She was called Louise as an adult and named her second daughter Louise.

12. Caleb A. Wall, *Reminiscences of Worcester, from the Earliest Period, 1657–1877, Historical and Genealogical* (Worcester, Mass: Tyler & Seagrave, 1877), pp. 126–27; Worcester Society of Antiquity Collections, Vol. 12, *Worcester Births, Marriages, and Deaths*, comp. Franklin P. Rice (Worcester, Mass.: The Worcester Society of Antiquity, 1894), pp. 171–72, 383, and Appendix; *Vital Records of Sutton, Massachusetts to the End of the Year 1849* (Worcester, Mass.: Franklin P. Rice, 1907), pp. 110–11, 306–7, 441.

13. Rev. William A. Benedict and Rev. Hiram A. Tracy, comp., *History of the Town of Sutton, Massachusetts, from 1704 to 1876* (Worcester, Mass.: Published for the town by Sanford & Co., 1878), pp. 654–57, 693–97, 771–77; Secretary of the Commonwealth, *Massachusetts Soldiers and Sailors of the Revolutionary War*, Vol. 10 (Boston: Wright & Potter Printing Co., 1902), p. 433.

14. The McClellan genealogy in Benedict and Tracy, comp., *History of Sutton*, 693–97, establishes the family history most securely and lists Parrington himself on p. 695; Harold M. Mayer and Richard C. Wade, *Chicago: Growth of a Metropolis* (Chicago: University of Chicago Press, 1969), pp. 37, 257; Rev. E. W. Hicks, *History of Kendall County, Illinois, from the Earliest Discoveries to the Present Time* (Aurora, Ill.: Knickerbocker & Hodder, 1877), p. 170.

15. *Cook County 1850 Census Population Schedules* (September 21, 1850, Third Ward of Chicago), Leaf 227; AS, pp. 6–7. In the latter, Parrington is uncertain of his mother's family history. I am not certain that Eunice Clark Sherman was Edith Sherman's sister nor have I successfully located Parrington's maternal relatives in the Chautauqua area. To these sources should be added correspondence between Parrington and Kenneth B. Murdock, professor of English at Harvard, that followed the publication of the first two volumes of *MCAT;* see VLP to Kenneth B. Murdock, January 8, 23, 1929, VLP Papers.

I am indebted to Robert A. Cotner of Aurora, Illinois, for sharing his new information regarding James McClellan, Jr.'s, writings for the *Western Citizen*, which substantially enlarge our knowledge of Parrington's maternal heritage; letter and enclosures from Stevens Parrington Tucker to the author, March 9, 1992.

16. AS, p. 7; Daughters of the American Revolution (DAR) genealogical record (Parrington), Kansas State Historical Society, Topeka. The DAR genealogy is the only source for the births and deaths of Louise M. and Florence M. Parrington; neither the "Autobiographical Sketch" nor any Parrington family member or record mentions the twin girls. For information regarding the Parringtons' Aurora home, which is still standing at the northeast corner of Highland and Garfield avenues, I wish to thank Robert A. Cotner (letter and photograph to author, May 2, 1991).

17. AS, pp. 8–9.

18. William Allen White, *Emporia and New York* (Emporia: Gazette Press, 1908), p. 1; Roger Triplett, *1857—Emporia—1957* (Emporia: Emporia Centennial, 1957), pp. 44–46;

U.S. Census Office, *Statistics of Population, Ninth Census of the United States* (Washington, D.C., 1872), p. 145, and *Compendium of the Eleventh Census: 1890,* Vol. 1 (Washington, D.C., 1892), cited in James L. Colwell, "Vernon Louis Parrington" (American Studies Ph.D. seminar paper, Yale University, 1958) and used by permission.

19. AS, pp. 10–13, 24. The old Parrington farm lies in the northeast quarter of Section 26 in Township 17 of Range 10 (26/17/10) and is now owned by the Kayser family, who purchased it from Dr. John Parrington ca. 1918. The original house was torn down in 1950 though some of its timbers were used to build another house on the same location. Copies of the deeds to the homestead and to another quarter-section (36/17/10) bought in 1876 as well as to eighty acres of timberland leased in 1874 are filed with Parrington's papers.

20. Frederick Jackson Turner, "The Significance of the Frontier in American History," in *The Frontier in American History* (New York: Holt, Rinehart and Winston, 1964), p. 1. On Parrington's sensitivity to the immigrant experience, see *MCAT,* 1:131–47.

21. AS, pp. 25–26.

22. Triplett, *1857—Emporia—1957,* p. 37; *Third Annual Catalogue of the Officers and Students of the College of Emporia,* 1885–86, p. 15. Much of the information on Parrington's student years was gathered when I visited the old College of Emporia in September 1980. Since the school was purchased by The Way International in 1974 and renamed The Way College of Emporia, historical records, the remains of the original library, campus memorabilia as well as the early catalogs relevant for this study have been randomly boxed and stored on the second floor of the old Anderson Memorial Library and in the basement of the old Stuart Hall, both now renamed.

23. Triplett, 41–43; Dennis R. Pitts, "The Miracle: History of the College of Emporia," pp. 21–42, 51, 64, typescript, 1973, in The Way College of Emporia Library; College of Emporia Registrar's Office, Enrollment Book, 1883–84 to 1910–11.

24. Copies of *The Semi-Weekly Miniature* and other campus memorabilia mentioned here are from The Way College of Emporia. *Annual Catalogue, College of Emporia, 1884–85,* p. 7, *Third Annual Catalogue, 1885–86,* pp. 5, 10–14.

25. *Fifth Annual Catalogue, 1887–88,* pp. 6, 10.

26. AS, pp. 13.

27. Ibid., pp. 25, 27.

28. For Parrington's three collegiate years, see *Directory of the College of Emporia, Fall Term, 1888–89,* pp. 2, 3, 8 (the regular catalog, published in the spring of 1889, was unobtainable), *Seventh Annual Catalogue, 1890–91,* pp. 5, 9, 12 (printed in 1890), *Eighth Annual Catalogue, 1890–91,* pp. 5, 9, 11, 20.

29. David Riesman, with Nathan Glazer and Reuel Denney, *The Lonely Crowd: A Study of the Changing American Character,* abridged ed. with a new preface (1950; New Haven: Yale University Press, 1961), p. 44; AS, p. 4.

30. AS, p. 31.

31. Information about the literary society is drawn from a large record book, containing club minutes and dated with 1898 and 1899 entries, at The Way College of Emporia. All other information on Parrington's Emporia collegiate years in this section is drawn from his diaries for 1890–91.

32. On Vern Cook, see relevant sections on "Stuart Forbes: Stoic" in Chapter 5; other information in this section and the remainder of the chapter is drawn from Parrington's diaries.

2 Evolution: Harvard, 1891–1893

1. David Riesman, with Nathan Glazer and Reuel Denney, *The Lonely Crowd: A Study of the Changing American Character,* abridged ed. with a new preface (1950; New Haven: Yale University Press, 1961), p. 44. For his Harvard years, Parrington's diaries constitute approximately one hundred pages.

2. *The Harvard University Catalogue, 1891–92* (Cambridge, Mass.: Harvard University Press, 1892), pp. 149, 151, 273, 275, 277, 469; *The Harvard University Catalogue, 1892–93* (Cambridge, Mass.: Harvard University Press, 1893), p. 480; *The Harvard University Catalogue, 1893–94* (Cambridge, Mass.: Harvard University Press, 1894), pp. 515–18.

3. Samuel Eliot Morison, *Development of Harvard University, 1869–1929* (Cambridge, Mass.: Harvard University Press, 1930), pp. xli–xliii, 79, 169. See the 1891–92 catalog for descriptions of Parrington's courses. My copy of his Harvard transcript was loaned by James L. Colwell, who also provided a copy for the Parrington family in the mid-1950s.

4. The "old puritan" is probably John Harvard, as depicted in Daniel Chester French's bronze seated statue, completed in 1884.

5. One classic discussion of identity formation I have found useful for this study is Erik H. Erikson, *Childhood and Society,* 2d ed. (New York: Norton, 1963), pp. 247–74, which contains his description of the "Eight Ages of Man," and pp. 285–325, which focuses on American identity and draws on Parrington's discussion of American thought and of postwar intellectuals.

6. For Wendell's composition pedagogy, see his text, Barrett Wendell, *English Composition* (New York: Scribner's, 1891); Morison, *Development of Harvard University,* p. 75.

7. On changes in Harvard's curriculum, see also E. J. Kahn, *Harvard Through Change and Through Storm* (New York: Norton, 1969), and Richard Norton Smith, *The Harvard Century* (New York: Simon & Schuster, 1986).

8. Howard Mumford Jones, *The Theory of American Literature,* 2d ed., rev. (Ithaca: Cornell University Press, 1965), p. 142.

9. *Harvard University Catalogue, 1891–92,* p. 85. Few notes and no drawings from this class remain among Parrington's papers. He never mentions seeing Norton nor talks about art in his diary, but he does repeatedly mention working in the studio. One study emphasizing Norton's many connections with American and British artists and intellectuals is Kermit Vanderbilt, *Charles Eliot Norton: Apostle of Culture in a Democracy* (Cambridge, Mass.: Belknap Press of Harvard University Press, 1959).

10. *Harvard University Catalogue, 1891–92,* pp. 83, 159; Morison, *Development of Harvard University,* pp. 86, 89, 160.

11. *Harvard University Catalogue, 1891–92,* pp. 78–80. Palmer wrote the chapter on the Philosophy Department in Morison, *Development of Harvard University,* pp. 3–26, except for the pages concerning himself, which were written by Ralph Barton Perry (pp. 20–21, which contain the quotation); George Herbert Palmer, *The Life of Alice Freeman Palmer* (Boston: Houghton Mifflin, 1908).

12. The course outline and content can be deduced from Palmer's study *The Field of Ethics* (Boston: Houghton Mifflin, 1901); Parrington's extant notes run to over fifty pages, covering both sides of each page; AS, p. 35.

13. Adam Storey Farrar, *Critical History of Free Thought in Reference to the Christian Religion* (New York: Appleton, 1863), pp. liii, lvi. Parrington's thesis does not survive.

14. "The House of Memoire" survives among Parrington's papers, despite Wendell's discouraging comments.

15. The Poe theme is quoted in full to illustrate the contrast between Parrington as a young literary critic and as a mature intellectual historian, as in the controversial chapter on Poe in *MCAT,* 2:57–59.

16. Wendell omits Howells in *A Literary History of America* (New York: Scribner's, 1900), which discusses no living authors, while Parrington, following different critical standards, devotes a chapter to him in *MCAT,* 3:241–53.

17. The quote on his health is from his Harvard English 12 autobiography. Although it would be overstating the case to describe Parrington at this point as neurasthenic, like so many other late Victorian American intellectuals (the James family siblings are a case in point), his illness was significant enough to interfere with his studying and of notice because of his concern about physical fitness. It is probably of more psychological than medical interest that

while at Harvard he almost always suffered the day after an evening of dancing or theater, usually a bout of what his diary called "feeling rocky." Neurasthenia is placed in cultural context in Tom Lutz, *American Nervousness, 1903: An Anecdotal History* (Ithaca: Cornell University Press, 1991).

18. *Harvard University Catalogue, 1892–93*, pp. 79, 75, 80.

19. AS, p. 35; Morison, *Development of Harvard University*, pp. 66, 74; *Harvard University Catalogue, 1892–93*, pp. 72–73.

20. Lewis E. Gates, *Studies and Appreciations* (New York: Macmillan, 1900), pp. 192–204, for the Taine essay.

21. In AS, p. 35, Parrington calls Gates, along with Wendell and von Jagemann, "fair second-rate teachers." Parrington's discussion of Norris (*The Beginnings of Critical Realism in America*, pp. 329–34) is unfinished but does mention the Gates dedication, p. 329.

22. Leo Lowenthal's *Literature, Popular Culture, and Society* (1961; rpt. Palo Alto: Pacific Books, 1968) provides a relevant context for these issues and a means to gauge Parrington's struggle with them.

23. 1893 Diary, February 5, May 11, 22, June 8 (on job prospects), VLP Papers.

3 Poetry and Populism: The Return to Emporia, 1893–1897

1. Turner's paper was based on an article, "Problems in American History," University of Wisconsin *Aegis*, November 4, 1892; it was first published in the *Proceedings of the State Historical Society of Wisconsin*, December 14, 1893; it is reprinted in *The Frontier in American History* (1920; New York: Holt, Rinehart and Winston, 1964), pp. 1–38.

2. See Arthur F. Burns, ed., *Wesley Clair Mitchell: The Economic Scientist* (New York: National Bureau of Economic Research, 1952). All other information in this section is from Parrington's 1893 diary.

3. *Tenth Annual Catalogue, College of Emporia, 1892–93*, pp. 9–11, 15; *Eleventh Annual Catalogue, 1893–94*, pp. 6–7, 29.

4. AS, pp. 27, 39–40.

5. On the Printing Committee, see p. 6 of the *Register of the College of Emporia, 1894–1895, 1895–1896*, and *1896–1897*; on the English Department offerings, see *Eleventh Annual Catalogue of the College of Emporia*, pp. 25–27.

6. *Register of the College of Emporia, 1895–96*, pp. 28–29, and the *Register, 1896–1897*, pp. 24, 27–29.

7. MCAT, 1:iii; MCAT, 2:i; MCAT, 3:xx–xxi.

8. The card file of Parrington's extant library was compiled by Mrs. Stevens Parrington (Jeanine) Tucker in 1976.

9. The College of Emporia's library was the first Carnegie Library built west of the Mississippi, its nucleus being the donation by William P. Anderson (a local congressman) of his private library; see pp. 10–11 of the *Registers* for 1894–95, 1895–96, 1896–97.

10. William Allen White, *The Autobiography of William Allen White* (New York: Macmillan, 1946), pp. 287, 302.

11. See the Bibliography for complete citations; the articles are available from the Kansas State Historical Society's file of *College Life*.

12. William Morton Payne, *English in American Universities* (Boston: D. C. Heath, 1895), p. 11; for Wendell's original article, see *Dial* 16 (March 1, 1894): 131–33.

13. Parrington gathered the poems he wished to save in a booklet, "A Plain-Song and Other Poems," in 1906. Three poems appeared in J. H. Powers, ed., *Some Emporia Verse* (Emporia: Privately printed, 1910): "De Profundis," "In Smock and Frock," and "Without the Gates." In the early 1950s Vernon L. Parrington, Jr., compiled a collection of most of his father's poetry, although there are still poems tucked away in various manuscripts and others for which dates and origin cannot now be determined.

14. For an interesting contrast, see Sidney Lanier, *The Poems of Sidney Lanier* (New York: Scribner's, 1915), pp. 53–59.

15. Henry Nash Smith, *Virgin Land: The American West as Symbol and Myth* (1950; rpt. Cambridge, Mass.: Harvard University Press, 1970), pp. 174–83.

16. "Poetry and the Mission of Poetry," holograph, VLP Papers. The commencement was reported in the *Gazette* of June 5, 1895, and is cited in James L. Colwell, "The Populist Image of Vernon Louis Parrington," *Mississippi Valley Historical Review* 49 (June 1962): 61; see also the Souvenir Commencement edition of *College Life* 7 (June 3, 1895): 264, 274 (a photo of the football team). Echoes of Tennyson's poem (the emphasis in the quotation is Parrington's) and the image of Merlin would appear over three decades later in *Main Currents;* see, e.g., 1:vii.

17. On the academy, see *Register of the College of Emporia, 1894–1895*, p. 1, and the Souvenir Commencement edition of *College Life*, p. 276, which prints a list of officers.

18. *Registers of the College of Emporia, 1895–96*, p. 23, and *1896–97*, pp. 23–24.

19. Colwell, "Populist Image," p. 62.

20. See the Bibliography for complete citations. The four "Sketches" are also described in Colwell, " Populist Image," pp. 63–65, and Richard Hofstadter, *The Progressive Historians: Turner, Beard, Parrington* (New York: Knopf, 1968: Vintage Books, 1970), pp. 370–71.

21. *College Life* 9 (April 17, 1897): 205.

22. Colwell, "Populist Image," p. 62.

23. Richard Hofstadter, *The Age of Reform: From Bryan to F.D.R.* (New York: Vintage Books, 1955), chap. 4.

24. AS, pp. 31–32.

25. Ibid., pp. 32–33.

26. See Parrington's current diary for family financial circumstances as well as AS, p. 41; *College Life* 3 (November 8, 1890): 3; *MCAT*, 3:266, 298.

27. Laura French, *History of Emporia and Lyon County* (Emporia: Emporia Gazette Press, 1929), p. 247.

28. Lawrence Goodwyn, *Democratic Promise: The Populist Moment in America* (New York: Oxford University Press, 1976), pp. 95–98, 200; Elizabeth N. Barr, "The Populist Uprising," in Vol. 2 of William E. Connelley, *History of Kansas, State and People*, 5 vols. (Chicago: American Historical Society, 1928), pp. 1137–201; Ray Allen Billington, *Westward Expansion* (New York: Macmillan, 1949), pp. 727–32; French, *History of Emporia and Lyon County*, pp. 55, 190, 229–34; Lucina Jones to James L. Colwell, March 26, 1958, used by permission.

29. On the *Gazette*, see French, pp. 225, 231; on White, see Goodwyn, *Democratic Promise*, pp. 198, 558; on Bryan, see Hofstadter's portrait in *The American Political Tradition* (New York: Vintage Books, 1948), pp. 186–205 and Goodwyn, Chapter 15, "A Cross of Silver," pp. 472–92, 389FF; on the 1896 campaign, see Goodwyn, 497, 511–13, 530.

30. James R. Seales and Danney Goble, *Oklahoma Politics: A History* (Norman: University of Oklahoma Press, 1982), p. 4. While most offices, such as territorial governor and attorney general, were appointed by the president, the territory could elect one voteless congressional delegate. It held presidential preference contests—won by Republicans in 1892, 1900, 1904, and by Bryan in 1896—but had no electoral college votes.

4 Advance and Retreat: First Years at the University of Oklahoma, 1897–1903

1. Erik H. Erikson, *Identity: Youth and Crisis* (New York: Norton, 1968), pp. 128–35.

2. On the 1895 plan to pursue the Ph.D., see J. D. Hewitt to the Dean of the Graduate School of Harvard University, March 22, 1895, holograph copy in VLP's hand, VLP Papers; on his Norman salary, see 1897 Diary, August 18, and AS, p. 40.

3. *College Life* 10 (September 28, 1897): 4.

4. This section and other portions of this chapter are adapted from my article, "V. L. Parrington's Oklahoma Years, 1897–1908: 'Few Highlights and Much Monotone'?" *Pacific Northwest Quarterly* 72 (January 1981): 20–28. Some details have been corrected based on subsequent research. See also William Allen White, "What's the Matter with Kansas?" reprinted in *The Autobiography of William Allen White* (New York: Macmillan, 1946), 280–83, and Carl Becker, "Kansas," reprinted in *Everyman His Own Historian* (New York: F. S. Crofts, 1935), pp. 1–28.

5. The standard, though often unsatisfactory, history of the university is Roy Gittinger, *The University of Oklahoma: A History of Fifty Years, 1892–1942* (Norman: University of Oklahoma Press, 1942); see especially pp. 3–12, 22–24. Another irreplaceable though not entirely reliable source on the university's development and Parrington's role in it is Sardis Roy Hadsell, "Parrington in Oklahoma" (typescript, ca. 1947), Western History Collections, University of Oklahoma Library, Norman. Hadsell took English composition with Parrington, graduated from the university in 1904, the same year began serving as both registrar and instructor of English in the preparatory school, and then joined the English department in 1908. For the charter, see *Bulletin of the State University of Oklahoma, 1892–93*, p. 5.

6. Parrington, "Early Days," in *Mistletoe* (Norman: University of Oklahoma, 1905), pp. 82–83; a version also appears in AS, pp. 41–42.

7. Most information concerning the courses Parrington taught, basic institutional details such as enrollment, and faculty is based on the extant university catalogs, some of which are available only on microfilm. Published each spring beginning in 1892, they list the courses to be taught the following academic year; however, the issue published in 1896 is missing from the archives collection. See *Bulletin of the State University of Oklahoma*, catalog issues (Norman, 1893–1909). My account is subject to error because courses that were announced may have been changed or canceled; however, as at Emporia, Parrington served on the Catalogue Committee, a position that should help ensure the accuracy of the English listings.

8. *Mistletoe* (1905), pp. 11, 37.

9. *Bulletin, 1893–1894*, p. 12; *1896–1897*, p. 18; *1898–1899*, p. 23; *1899–1900, p. 17; 1900–1901*, pp. 21–22.

10. Ben G. Owen to James L. Colwell, March 18, 1958, used by permission; Harold Keith, *Oklahoma Kickoff* (Norman: Privately printed, 1948), pp. 21, 27, 32, 34–38; and George Lynn Cross, *Presidents Can't Punt: The OU Football Tradition* (Norman: University of Oklahoma Press, 1977), provide some information on Parrington's coaching career.

11. Parrington evidently did not keep copies of his *Umpire* editorials; at least none now exist among his papers. Copies of the magazine are in the University of Oklahoma Archives; consult the Bibliography for a complete list of the editorials. For the five editorials discussed in the following pages, see *University Umpire* 2 (December 1, 1898): 4–5 (Thanksgiving); 2 (December 15, 1898): 4–6 (Lafayette Day); 2 (February 1, 1899): 4–5 (on Longfellow); 2 (March 15, 1899): 4–5 (Kipling); 2 (May 1, 1899): 4–5 (on literary fashions). The editorials are unsigned, but it seems unlikely that an undergraduate could have mastered the range of interests reflected in them. During the period he served as editor, his name is listed on the masthead.

12. 1897 Diary, September 11, 16, 26, October 17, 27, VLP Papers; *University Umpire* 3 (March 15, 1900): 1. The poem can be interestingly compared to William Cullen Bryant's 1834 poem "The Prairies."

13. 1897 Diary, November 26, 29, December 31; 1898 Diary, January 30, February 6, VLP Papers. In AS, Parrington states that he suspects his mother had chosen Bertha White as a prospective daughter-in-law. The most explicit diary passage concerning their relationship occurs September 4, 1897, which indicates both emotional and physical intimacy.

14. 1898 Diary, October 29 (on "Amos"), VLP Papers; AS, pp. 42–43. Information on the Williams and Rochester families is drawn from conversations in 1978, 1980, and 1992 with Stevens Parrington Tucker. Eloise later married Roy Howard Dodge and moved to Seattle to be near her sister and mother.

15. 1899 Diary, January 27, July 14, August 28, 31, September 9, VLP Papers. The photograph is reproduced in Hall, "V. L. Parrington's Oklahoma Years," p. 21, and in this book.

16. On Parrington's relationship with Julia, see AS, pp. 43–44, as well as his diaries; a revealing collection of personal letters has been compiled by Stevens Parrington Tucker, including the one quoted.

17. Elizabeth Parrington graduated from the University of Washington in 1923 and was married to Donald Partridge Thomas the same year. They lived in the Seattle area and had three children: Julia Ann Thomas Reynolds, Dorothy Vernon Thomas Todd, and Harlan Parrington Thomas. She died of pneumonia in December 1981 in Seattle.

18. *University Umpire* 4 (October 1, 1901): 1; *Bulletin of the State University of Oklahoma, 1901–02*, p. 45, and *1902–03*, p. 52.

19. "A Layman's View of Isaiah" and the Old Testament notebook remain among Parrington's papers.

20. See *MCAT*, 1:3–128 and 2:124.

21. "On the Lack of Privacy in American Village Homes," *House Beautiful* 13 (January 1903): 109–12. The article is accompanied by two hand-drawn landscape designs.

5 Dwelling Between Worlds: Europe and Norman, 1903–1906

1. VLP to JWP, July 11, 14, 17, 19, 23, 1903; 1903 Diary, July 17, 19, 20, 22, VLP Papers.

2. 1903 Diary, July 26, August 3, VLP to JWP, July 30, 1903, VLP Papers.

3. Stevens Parrington Tucker has transcribed several short but key sections of the novel as well as Parrington's outlines and plans for it, comprising about thirty pages. I have deciphered what I could of the other sections Professor Tucker had collated, based on the composition dates Parrington inscribed on his manuscript and information given in diary entries.

4. 1903 Diary, September 2, 4, 12, 16, 21, 24, October 6, 11, VLP Papers.

5. The arts and crafts movement has received increasing scholarly attention. Two examples are Gillian Naylor, *The Arts and Crafts Movement: A Study of Its Sources, Ideals, and Influence on Design Theory* (Cambridge, Mass: MIT Press, 1971), and Eileen Boris, *Art and Labor: Ruskin, Morris, and the Craftsman Ideal in America* (Philadelphia: Temple University Press, 1985). T. J. Jackson Lears's *No Place of Grace: Antimodernism and the Transformation of American Culture, 1880–1920* (New York: Pantheon, 1981), especially his chapter "The Figure of the Artisan: Arts and Crafts Ideology" (pp. 59–96), offers a complementary discussion within which to evaluate Parrington's attraction to the arts and crafts movement. Parrington could easily be added to Lears's chart of antimodernist figures (pp. 314–23).

6. E. P. Thompson, *William Morris: Romantic to Revolutionary* (1955; rpt. New York: Pantheon, 1976). Part One, "William Morris and the Romantic Revolt," is helpful in setting the general Victorian intellectual scene.

7. Fiona McCarthy, *The Simple Life: C. R. Ashbee in the Cotswolds* (Berkeley: University of California Press, 1981), pp. 19–22; see also Prologue, pp. 9–14, on the arts and crafts context. This is an indispensable source.

8. Ibid., pp. 25, 15, 40–46.

9. Ibid., pp. 78–79, 192–93; 1903 Diary, September 19, VLP to JWP, October 3, 9, 1903, VLP Papers.

10. McCarthy, *Simple Life*, pp. 181, 78 (where Parrington is mentioned); 1903 Diary, October 24, VLP Papers.

11. "The Essex House of Arts and Crafts," written in October or November 1903, typescript by Stevens Parrington Tucker, VLP Papers.

12. VLP to JWP, November 1, 2, 1903, VLP Papers.

13. 1904 Diary, May 1, 5, 8, 14, VLP Papers; AS, p. 44; in the latter the trip and stay in France rate only three sentences.

14. The plaque was willed to Elizabeth, a kind of consolation prize for spending so much of her babyhood without her father. According to the Parrington family, Mme Tollenaar may have asked Parrington to pose for her. VLP to JWP, December 6, 1904, VLP Papers.

15. The quotations and summaries that follow are from Stevens Parrington Tucker's typed version of "Stuart Forbes: Stoic," Book II, "The University," pp. 1-7.

16. The foregoing activities are documented in current diaries; see also VLP to JWP, January 5, 29, February 2, 1904, VLP Papers.

17. See "Stuart Forbes: Stoic," holograph ms., Chapter 2, Part 1, dated January 25, 1904.

18. AS, p. 46.

19. "Stuart Forbes," holograph, Chapter 2, Part 1.

20. "A Chat From Abroad," *University Umpire* 7 (April 1, 1904): 2-4.

21. 1904 Diary, May 12, June 8, 9, VLP to JWP, October 9, 1903, VLP Papers.

22. 1904 Diary, July 16, VLP Papers.

23. March 29, 1904 entry in a notebook entitled "Notes on Architecture and Gardening" (the friend was a Mr. Moorsom), VLP Papers.

24. AS, p. 45.

25. Ibid.

26. *MCAT*, 3:xxvi-xxvii; on Arnold's poem see the conclusion of this biography's Preface (note the change in verbs from Arnold's "wandering" to Parrington's "dwelling"); on Victorian renewal, see Lears, *No Place of Grace*, p. 91.

27. Interestingly, Thomas Jefferson called his horticultural notes "Garden Books," and it is possible Parrington knew this, intentionally modeling upon what might be called the Physiocratic aspects of Jefferson's thought. The earliest mention of Jefferson in Parrington's papers occurs just three years earlier, in the 1902 essay "A Layman's View of Isaiah." For insight into VLP as a horticulturist, I wish to thank Ann Page Stecker.

28. Untitled holograph, of which Stevens Parrington Tucker has made a typescript, VLP Papers. The date is inferred from relevant diary entries. One American source for Parrington's essay is "Loomings," the first chapter of Herman Melville's *Moby-Dick* (1851).

29. *Bulletin of the State University of Oklahoma, 1903-1904*, "Plan of University Grounds," n.p.; V. L. Parrington, *On Recent Developments in American College Architecture, A Report Submitted to the Board of Regents* (Norman: Published by the University, 1908), a twelve-page pamphlet available through Western History Collections, University of Oklahoma Library.

30. David P. Handlin, *The American Home: Architecture and Society, 1815-1915* (Boston: Little, Brown, 1979), pp. 167, 170; the sketches from Parrington's 1903 *House Beautiful* article are reproduced on p. 171; see also chapter 3, pp. 171-231.

31. At least thirteen pages of architectural drawings of various details, both interior and exterior, as well as the actual blueprints for the Norman house remain among Parrington's papers and effects. The Parringtons' bed, now in Stevens Parrington Tucker's home, is Mission Oak style. These drawings closely resemble the interior designs carried in Gustav Stickley's *Craftsman* magazine; see *Collected Works of Gustav Stickley*, ed. Stephen Gray and Robert Edwards (New York: Turn of the Century Editions, 1981; rev. ed. 1989).

32. *Bulletin of the State University of Oklahoma, 1905-1906*, pp. 68, 70, 72.

6 Transitions and Closures, 1906-1909

1. Notebook on "The Novel" (1901), VLP Papers.

2. Wendell's comments on Twain are brief, usually disparaging, and scattered through *A Literary History of America* (New York: Scribner's, 1900), although several can be found in the twelve-page chapter toward the volume's close titled "The West," pp. 500-512.

3. Carl Becker, "Everyman His Own Historian," Presidential Address delivered before the American Historical Association at Minneapolis, December 29, 1931, reprinted in *Everyman His Own Historian* (New York: F. S. Crotts, 1935), pp. 233-55.

4. The Morris quotations and sketch of the London scene are drawn from Philip Henderson, *William Morris: His Life, Work and Friends* (New York: McGraw-Hill, 1967), pp. 241–44.

5. Compare Morris's comment on Marx's economics to that made by Parrington in AS (1918): "My economics must be sugarcoated for me," p. 48.

6. The speech is quoted in Henderson, *William Morris*, pp. 255–58.

7. The Hume and Edwards theses are available in the Bizzell Library, University of Oklahoma.

8. "Western Speech," typescript, VLP Papers. Details about the founding and aims of the American Dialect Society can be located in *Dialect Notes* 1 (1890–96). One concise guide to the development of the study of American speech is Raven I. McDavid, Jr., "American English: A Bibliographic Essay," *American Studies International* 17 (Winter 1979): 3–45; on both the society and development of American speech, see H. L. Mencken, *The American Language*, 4th ed. (New York: Knopf, 1936), particularly chapter 1, "The Two Streams of English."

9. A recent study whose introduction concisely reviews the history of controversies in the realist debate is Amy Kaplan's *The Social Construction of American Realism* (Chicago: University of Chicago Press, 1988); Hamlin Garland, *Crumbling Idols: Twelve Essays on Art Dealing Chiefly With Literature Painting and the Drama*, ed. Jane Johnson (Cambridge, Mass.: Belknap Press of Harvard University Press, 1960), p. 62. While the similarities between Eggleston and Parrington are worth developing in more detail, on Eggleston as a historian, see Robert A. Skotheim, *American Intellectual Histories and Historians* (Princeton, N.J.: Princeton University Press, 1966), pp. 48–65; for Wise's "fault-line" metaphor and analysis, see *American Historical Explanations*, pp. 131, 172, 180, 184–85, 187–88, 192–215, 219, 220, 233–34, 248 (1980 ed.).

10. Parrington, "Thoughts on the Teaching of Literature," holograph, VLP Papers; the essay is undated, but the date can be determined by adding thirteen years (given in the first sentence) to his graduation from Harvard (1893). Subsequent quotations are from this source. Parrington had added some emendations in pencil to the ink original; punctuation, capitalization, and so forth must be regarded as tentative. The quotation, "dainties that are bred in a book," is from Shakespeare's *Love's Labour's Lost*, act 4, scene 2, line 25.

11. For Adams on Arnold's poem, see *The Education of Henry Adams*, ed. Ernest Samuels (Boston: Houghton Mifflin Riverside Editions, 1973), pp. 108, 388, 469, 574, 654, 678; for Parrington on Henry and Brooks Adams, see *MCAT*, 3:214–36.

12. *Bulletin of the State University of Oklahoma*, 1905–1906, p. 70.

13. Howard Mumford Jones, *The Theory of American Literature*, 2d ed., rev. (Ithaca: Cornell University Press, 1965), p. 41; *American Literature in the College Curriculum*, Committee on the College Study of American Literature and Culture, William G. Crane, Chairman (Chicago: National Council of Teachers of English, 1948), pp. 3, 5, 7, 11; see also John Smith Lewis, Jr., "The History of Instruction in American Literature in Colleges and Universities of the United States, 1827–1939" (Ph.D. Thesis, New York University, 1941).

14. On Tyler, see Perry Miller's Foreword to Moses Coit Tyler, *A History of American Literature, 1607–1765* (New York: Collier, 1962), pp. 5–12, and Kermit Vanderbilt's *American Literature and the Academy: The Roots, Growth, and Maturity of a Profession* (Philadelphia: University of Pennsylvania Press, 1986), pp. 81–104.

15. On the *Dial* survey, see Crane, et al., *American Literature in the College Curriculum*, pp. 10–12. Until the publication of Vanderbilt's *American Literature and the Academy*, only Richard Ohmann, *English in America: A Radical View of the Profession* (New York: Oxford University Press, 1976), addressed the professionalization of literary study on a wide scale.

16. Parrington, in collaboration with Wilbur R. Humphreys, *Handbook to English I* (Norman: Privately printed, 1907); English XVIII notes, holograph, VLP Papers.

17. *Bulletin of the State University of Oklahoma*, Quarterly Announcement, 1908–9 (March 1908), p. 16 (the summer session courses do not appear in the regular catalog).

18. S. R. Hadsell, "Parrington in Oklahoma," p. 11, typescript, n.d., Northwest History Collections, University of Oklahoma Library.

19. Ralph H. Gabriel, "Vernon Louis Parrington," in *Pastmasters: Some Essays on American Historians*, ed. Marcus Cunliffe and Robin W. Winks (New York: Harper & Row, 1969), pp. 143, 150–52. I am indebted to Robert A. Skotheim for the succinct summarization of Parrington's conflict as one between high English and low American culture. Vernon L. Parrington, Jr., once stated, but did not provide substantiation for the claim, that his father had started a book "prior to coming to Seattle"; see Don Duncan, "Dr. Parrington's Pulitzer Prize," *Seattle Times Magazine*, April 8, 1973.

20. Hadsell, "Parrington in Oklahoma," pp. 2, 4–5. The same glasses-polishing routine is recorded by another former student, F. A. Balyeat (who became a professor of education at Norman), in a letter to James L. Colwell, March 6, 1958, used by permission.

21. The trial paragraphs, notes, and manuscripts ("The American Literary Spirit" and "The Literary Spirit of the West") described here and in the following paragraphs are filed in various related folders, VLP Papers. They are undated and are best considered as ideas in progress that help chart the development of Parrington's thinking.

22. In *MCAT,* Whitman is treated in 3:69–86 and Hawthorne in 2:442–50.

23. Louise Wrathal Parrington graduated from the University of Washington in 1928 and was married to Wilmon Stevens Tucker in 1929. Their two sons are Stevens Parrington Tucker and Vernon Louis Tucker.

24. Roy Gittinger, *The University of Oklahoma: A History of Fifty Years, 1892–1942* (Norman: University of Oklahoma Press, 1942), pp. 54–56; Richard Hofstadter, *The Progressive Historians: Turner, Beard, Parrington* (New York: Knopf, 1968; Vintage Books, 1970), pp. 271–74. Despite their rather sensational tone and errors in fact, the following *Outlook* columns are worth consulting: "A Serious Educational Blunder," *Outlook* 88 (April 11, 1908): 809–10, "Shall the People Rule—in Oklahoma?" *Outlook* 90 (September 5, 1908): 15–18, "Do the People Rule—in Oklahoma?" *Outlook* 90 (October 3, 1908): 242–44, and "Haskellism in Oklahoma University," *Outlook* 90 (October 17, 1908): 325–26. The institutional changes are passed over in near silence in Gittinger, *University of Oklahoma,* pp. 56–57.

25. Hadsell, "Parrington in Oklahoma," pp. 6, 12.

26. VLP to JWP, June 23, 1904; William Allen White to Board of Regents, May 23, 1908; C. H. Bessent to Lee Cruce, May 21, 1908; Lee Cruce to VLP, June 26, 1908; Morrell Sayre to VLP, July 10, 1908, all in VLP Papers.

27. VLP to W. E. Rowsey, June 14, 1908; VLP to Rev. L. N. Linebaugh, June 16, 1908; W. E. Rowsey to V. L. Carrington, June 30, 1908, VLP Papers.

28. Gittinger, *University of Oklahoma,* pp. 57, 188–89, 196–97.

29. Wesley C. Mitchell to VLP, June 5, 1908, VLP Papers; AS, p. 42.

30. An alternately titled version of "The Teacher" is reprinted in Joseph B. Harrison, *Vernon Louis Parrington: American Scholar* (Seattle: University of Washington Book Store, 1929), prefatory page.

31. VLP to the Secretary of the Graduate School, Cambridge, Mass., June 29, 1908, VLP Papers.

32. VLP to Irving Babbitt, n.d., VLP Papers; Irving Babbitt, *Literature and the American College: Essays in Defense of the Humanities* (Boston: Houghton Mifflin, 1908). On Babbitt, see Richard Ruland, *The Rediscovery of American Literature: Premises of Critical Taste, 1900–1940* (Cambridge, Mass.: Harvard University Press, 1967), pp. 11–56 (Parrington is treated on pp. 186–91). The letter to Babbitt is my only verification of Parrington's Harvard rejection; his 1908 diary stops after the April 23 entry and makes no mention of his employment problems or educational plans, nor is the diary resumed until January 20, 1917, almost a decade later. The Harvard University Archives have no Parrington correspondence.

33. VLP to T. F. Kane, July 28, 1908, VLP Papers.

7 *Retreat and Advance: First Years at the University of Washington, 1908–1914*

1. AS, p. 39.

2. VLP to William Markham (University of Washington Board of Regents), August 11, 1908, VLP Papers. Parrington is first listed in the 1908–9 University of Washington catalog (published in 1909) as an assistant professor of rhetoric (p. 17) teaching in the Department of Rhetoric and Oratory (p. 161).

3. Hofstadter, *The Progressive Historians: Turner, Beard, Parrington* (New York: Knopf, 1968; Vintage Books, 1970), pp. 378–79; Ralph H. Gabriel, in *Pastmasters: Some Essays on American Historians*, ed. Marcus Cunliffe and Robin W. Winks (New York: Harper & Row, 1969), pp. 160, 166; David W. Noble, *Historians Against History: The Frontier Thesis and the National Covenant in American Historical Writing Since 1830* (Minneapolis: University of Minnesota Press, 1965), pp. 98–99.

4. Parrington states in AS, p. 43, that "the last poem I wrote was done in the winter of 1908–1909; an ode to the AYP Exposition, then being prepared for on the University grounds." I have seen no poems written after 1909. Charles M. Gates, *The First Century at the University of Washington, 1861–1961* (Seattle: University of Washington Press, 1961), pp. vii, 49–50, 123–26, 152. This volume, the official centennial history of the university, includes photographs of the old and new campus as well as one of Parrington (p. 119).

5. Norman H. Clark, *Mill Town: A Social History of Everett, Washington* (Seattle: University of Washington Press, 1970), pp. 5, 8, 16; Roger Sale, *Seattle: Past to Present* (Seattle: University of Washington Press, 1976), pp. 51–53.

6. Gates, *The First Century*, p. 133.

7. Ibid., pp. 132–34.

8. Ibid., pp. 77, 88–89, 115, 138.

9. The best edition of Smith's *Spirit of American Government* (New York: Macmillan, 1907) is the John Harvard Library edition, edited with a lengthy introduction by Cushing Strout, which photoreproduces the 1911 reprint of the original 1907 edition. The relationship between Smith and Parrington has been explored in Thomas C. McClintock, "J. Allen Smith and the Progressive Movement: A Study in Intellectual History" (Ph.D. dissertation, University of Washington, 1959), pp. 377–86, 529–30, which credits Parrington with the revival of interest in Smith in the 1930s as well as linking Smith and Beard's mid-1910s thinking. See also Eric F. Goldman, "J. Allen Smith: The Reformer and His Dilemma," *Pacific Northwest Quarterly* 35 (July 1944): 195–213, which quotes a selection of Parrington correspondence.

10. Gates, *First Century*, pp. 114, 134. The existence of an identifiable liberal group with which Parrington was associated has been verified in interviews with Robert E. Burke, E. H. Eby, and Gladys Savage (all in Seattle, October 3–4, 1977) and Egbert O. Oliver (Portland, Oregon, September 28, 1977). There are no documents or any correspondence among Parrington's papers that clearly link him with any such group, however.

11. Roger Sale, *Seattle: Past to Present* (Seattle: University of Washington Press, 1976), pp. 7, 50–93, 136, 157; on Parrington, see pp. 152–58. This brief portrait is of special interest for Sale's defense of Parrington's treatment of Poe and his awareness of the problems caused by the fragmentary nature of Volume 3 of *MCAT*. As a member of the University of Washington's English Department, Sale had undoubtedly heard the standard myths and legends about Parrington, but he writes about him with uncommon sympathy and calls *Main Currents* "the best book to come out of this city." But Sale seems to be under the impression that *Main Currents* was written entirely in the 1920s, and this accounts for his claim that the city was static while the book was being composed. From time to time Parrington had cold frames but never a greenhouse.

12. *Catalogue for 1907–1908 and Announcements for 1908–1909 of the University of Washington*, pp. 106–8, 146–48; *Catalogue for 1908–1909*, pp. 17, 115; *Catalogue for 1910–1911*, pp. 133–34. Because the catalog for each respective year carries the announcements of

the following year's courses, to alleviate confusion between the text and my documentation, remember that if Parrington is described as teaching a course during a specific academic year (e.g., 1910–11), the course description would be found in the 1909–10 Catalogue.

Padelford was slightly younger than Parrington and received his B.A. at Colby College (John Parrington, Sr.'s, alma mater) in 1896 and both his M.A. and Ph.D. from Yale in 1899. He taught at Yale for two years before coming to Washington to chair the English Language and Literature Department in 1901.

13. *Catalogue for 1908–1909*, p. 117.

14. *Catalogue for 1910–1911*, pp. 135–37; *Catalogue for 1908–1909*, p. 16; *Catalogue for 1911–1912*, p. 74.

15. *Catalogue for 1912–1913*, p. 104.

16. *Catalogue for 1912–1913*, pp. 106–7. In light of the criticism Parrington's brief treatment of Henry James in Volume 3 has received, it is significant that James was included so early and so regularly in his courses. For an example of such criticism, see Wesley Morris, *Towards a New Historicism* (Princeton, N.J.: Princeton University Press, 1972), pp. 44–48.

17. This is one of four reading lists, all for contemporary courses, found in the E. Harold Eby Papers, University of Washington Archives and Records Center. The Eby Papers contain syllabi and various drafts of *Main Currents* that were stored in Parrington's office desk when Eby inherited it after Parrington's death in 1929.

18. Barrett Wendell, *A Literary History of America* (New York: Scribner's, 1900), p. 10.

19. John Macy, *The Spirit of American Literature* (Garden City, N.Y.: Doubleday, Page, 1913), pp. vi, 14–15.

20. The syllabi described below are found in the Eby Papers, which had not yet been calendared when I consulted them. Parrington probably kept most course-related materials in his university office, since few syllabi and texts survive among his papers and effects. I reconstructed the original page order as closely as possible by means of dates assigned to various syllabi sections, dates VLP sometimes typed at the foot of pages, and numbers assigned by the catalogs to the sequences.

21. The description of the English Department as divided between traditionalists and nontraditionalists was made by Egbert O. Oliver, interview, September 18, 1977. Although Professor Oliver was a philosophy major (receiving his B.A. in 1927 and M.A. in 1929 from Washington), he returned in the late 1930s to complete a Ph.D. in English, writing his dissertation on "Melville and the Idea of Progress," under the direction of E. H. Eby. Thus he was able to observe the climate in the department both from an insider's and an outsider's perspective. He retains vivid impressions of Parrington, primarily from briefly enrolling in a seminar on Puritanism.

The descriptions of Padelford and Parrington were both made by Gladys Savage, interview, October 4, 1977. She has been an extremely helpful source for insights into Parrington's reputation among students and faculty. She took courses from Parrington, graduated with an English degree in 1926, and served as the English Department secretary from 1927 to 1936. Her husband, George, taught for many years in Washington's drama department.

The description of Parrington as "wild and woolly" was made by Garland O. Ethel, interview, October 4, 1977; he received his Ph.D. at Washington, was involved in left-wing politics in the 1930s, and taught eighteenth-century British literature for many years in the English Department. See also John Brooks Moore, "Vernon Louis Parrington: Aristocrat and Artist," unpublished draft for an introduction to Volume 3 of *MCAT*, Eby Papers; AS, p. 5.

22. Gates, *First Century*, pp. 134–35, 137.

23. Unfortunately the syllabus, from the Eby Papers, is not dated, although the present tense in the last sentence as well as a shorter version dating from 1912–13 that omits a Roosevelt reference help place it chronologically.

24. JWP to VLP, April 7, 1909, VLP Papers. Information on the Outing Club, its members and activities, was obtained from Mrs. W. Stevens Tucker (Louise Wrathal Parrington) in a long and pleasant interview at her home in San Carlos, California, August 17–18, 1980.

Vernon Louis Parrington, Jr., received his B.A. from the University of Washington in 1935 and his Ph.D. from Brown in 1944. His dissertation was published as *American Dreams: A Study of American Utopias* (Providence, R.I.: Brown University Press, 1947), a conscious attempt to complete part of the materials to have appeared in Volume 3 of *MCAT*. He married Margaret E. Neils of Portland, Oregon; their three children are Sarah Parrington, Elsa Louise Desrochers, and Vernon Louis Parrington III. Parrington taught English and history for many years at Seattle's Lakeside School before his death in December 1974.

8 *Democracy, Economics, and Literature, 1914–1918*

1. R. R. Smith to VLP, June 26, 1914, VLP Papers.

2. R. R. Smith to VLP, July 13, 1914, VLP Papers. The identity of the adviser was masked. Hofstadter evidently thought this letter applied to *Main Currents* itself.

3. Perry Miller, *Errand into the Wilderness* (1956); rpt. New York: Harper Torchbook, 1964), pp. viii–ix, and Preface to *The New England Mind: The Seventeenth Century* (Boston: Beacon Press, 1961), pp. xi–xii.

4. R. R. Smith to VLP, August 17, 1916; Houghton Mifflin Company to VLP, September 21, 1916, VLP Papers. Parrington also submitted the manuscript to G. P. Putnam's Sons in 1917 and to Henry Holt in 1918. He received a detailed, five-page rejection letter, dated March 17, 1917, from George H. Putnam, who was intrigued enough to read the manuscript himself and was at pains to correct Parrington's picture of Irving, whom Putnam had known personally. The firm judged "a volume devoted to so special a division of literary history" not potentially renumerative but did offer to sell copies on commission, if Parrington was willing to underwrite production costs. The Holt rejection, dated March 7, 1918, was signed by a Harvard classmate, Ambrose C. Dearborn, who explained that "those in charge of our miscellaneous publications . . . had not the slightest doubt that your manuscript was as good as I had told them it would be. It was simply a case of not adding to our lists at this time."

5. Parrington, "The Democratic Spirit in American Letters, 1620–1870: A Study in National Ideals," ca. 1914–16, p. 9 (hereafter DSAL). Until the summer of 1982, it had been assumed that no copy of DSAL existed. Stevens Parrington Tucker and I were able to reconstitute all but a few pages of the complete manuscript. Among multiple tables of contents, located in 1980, one with consecutive page numbers for individual chapters was found. Using this as a guide, we were able to retrieve the DSAL chapter versions from others for the various figures treated by Parrington in *Main Currents*, for whom Tucker had created separate files. Subsequently, several photocopies of the reconstituted manuscript were made; one is in my possession.

6. DSAL, pp. 9, 8.

7. Ibid., p. 1.

8. Barrett Wendell, *A Literary History of America* (New York: Scribner's, 1900), p. 471.

9. *MCAT,* 1:vi.

10. DSAL, p. 11.

11. *MCAT,* 1:66, 62. See *MCAT,* 1:66–72, on Williams's ideas. Parrington indicates, in a fairly unusual attributive note (1:67, fn. 16), that much of the Williams's material in *MCAT* is drawn from *The Political Philosophy of Roger Williams*, a dissertation by his former University of Washington student, James E. Ernst. A reprint is available, with a variant title, that lists Parrington only in a small footnote; see James E. Ernst, *The Political Thought of Roger Williams* (Port Washington, N.Y.: Kennikat Press, 1966), p. 210.

12. *MCAT,* 1:vi, for *MCAT* organizational quote. Parrington's treatment of Paine in DSAL is worth noting. Paine is the only DSAL figure to bear the unqualified epithet of "Radical": in *MCAT* he becomes a more subdued "Republican Pamphleteer." His placement in both manuscripts is further indicative of Parrington's changing emphases. In DSAL Paine appears in a section titled "The Appeal to Arms: 1760–1785" along with Samuel Adams, John Dickinson, Thomas Hutchinson and the Whig and Tory literary satirists—a section corresponding to

Book 2, Part 2 of Volume 1. Here his place on the political spectrum is stressed, whereas in *MCAT* his ideas are stressed and accordingly he is moved to the section with Jefferson in Book 3, Part 2 of Volume 1. In addition, in DSAL Hamilton is called a Federalist, while his portrait is labeled "The Leviathan State" in *MCAT*, where he is linked with John Adams, who is titled a Realist in both manuscripts. Jefferson changes only from a Democrat in DSAL to an Agrarian Democrat in *MCAT*. Interestingly, the only chapters that can be precisely dated in the reconstituted DSAL are those concerning Hamilton, dated January 2, 1915, and Jefferson, dated January 9, 1915.

13. See *Catalogue for 1908–1909 and Announcements for 1909–1910 of the University of Washington*, p. 117, for the listing for English 24; see the Eby Papers, University of Washington Archives and Records Center for syllabi for this course (although the pages are not in sequence) as well as for English 26, offered in 1910–11, which became English 27 in 1911–12 and English 19 in 1912–13; all versions of the course include Edwards.

14. *MCAT*, 1:102.

15. Richard Hofstadter, *The Progressive Historians: Turner, Beard, Parrington* (New York: Knopf, 1968; Vintage Books, 1970), pp. 398–99.

16. Morton White, *Social Thought in America: The Revolt Against Formalism* (1949; Boston: Beacon Press, 1957), pp. 1, 4, 6–7, 48–49, 28–29.

17. DSAL, pp. 441–42.

18. Ibid., pp. 407–8; *MCAT*, 2:356.

19. DSAL, p. 399.

20. Ibid., pp. 423, 412; *MCAT*, 2:xxi–xxii, 451–72. The Eby Papers contain several DSAL chapter drafts, including those for Lowell, Whittier, Thoreau, and Emerson. A dated revision of the Lowell chapter is also there (January 16, 1916), but it differs from the original DSAL collation and from *MCAT*.

21. DSAL, p. 389.

22. Ibid., pp. 389–90.

23. *MCAT*, 3:xix–xx.

24. See David W. Noble, *The Progressive Mind, 1890–1917* (Chicago: Rand McNally, 1970), pp. 1–22; Gene Wise, *American Historical Explanations: Some Strategies for Grounded Inquiry* (Homewood, Ill.: Dorsey Press, 1973), pp. 179–215; Robert A. Skotheim, *American Intellectual Histories and Historians* (Princeton: Princeton University Press, 1966), pp. 66–172.

25. Wise, *American Historical Explanations*, pp. 249, 259.

26. Robert A. Skotheim and Kermit Vanderbilt, "The Mind and Art of a Historian of Ideas," *Pacific Northwest Quarterly* 53 (July 1962): 105. Also compare Richard Reinitz, "Vernon Louis Parrington as Historical Ironist," *Pacific Northwest Quarterly* 68 (July 1977): 113.

27. *MCAT*, 1:196–97. A lone observer of this passage as indicative of Parrington's early sense of disillusion about the course of liberalism is Arthur A. Ekirch, Jr., in *The Decline of American Liberalism* (New York: Longmans, Green, 1955), pp. 26–27, 37.

28. Carl Van Doren to VLP, March 31, 1915, VLP Papers. Vanderbilt's *American Literature and the Academy* provides a detailed discussion of the development of the *Cambridge History*; see Book One: "Roots," pp. 3–236.

29. William Peterfield Trent, John Erskine, Stuart P. Sherman, and Carl Van Doren, eds., *The Cambridge History of American Literature*, Vol. 1 (New York: Macmillan, 1943), pp. iii, ix–x, 31–56 (for Parrington's "The Puritan Divines"). This is a combined one-volume edition containing the three original volumes published by G. P. Putnam's Sons in 1917, 1918, and 1921.

30. "Professor Turner in the Northwest," *Washington Historical Quarterly* 5 (July 1914): 232; Edmund S. Meany Papers, Box 20, File 90–6, University of Washington Archives.

31. Frederick Jackson Turner, "The West and American Ideals," in *The Frontier in American History* (New York: Holt, Rinehart and Winston, 1964), pp. 290–91, 300, 305–6, 310.

32. DSAL, pp. 51–52.

33. On the IWW and local Washington events, Norman H. Clark, *Mill Town: A Social History of Everett, Washington* (Seattle: University of Washington Press, 1970), pp. 186–231; and Robert Sale, *Seattle, Past to Present* (Seattle: University of Washington Press, 1976), pp. 113–26.

34. This reading list, for English 20a: American Literature from 1890–1915, is in the Eby Papers.

35. There are no extant chapters or notes specifically written for "The Spirit of Radicalism" among Parrington's papers that can be separately identified from those that appeared in Volume 3 of *MCAT*. These may possibly have been misplaced, lost, or destroyed after Parrington's death, during the process of editing and publishing Volume 3. A series of tables of contents for "The Spirit of Radicalism" does exist; they are organizational "works in progress" dated November 10, 1916, January 24, 1917, January 26, 1817 [*sic*], and January 28, 1917 (in the last three the manuscript's inclusive dates are 1870–1900 instead of 1870–1916).

36. The plans for the graduate seminar are taken from notes among Parrington's papers, titled "Graduate Work, Outline of American Literature: Second Semester, 1917." This seminar is listed in the *Catalogue of the University of Washington for 1915–1916* as English 211–212, p. 135.

37. These quotations are from a version of the essay published by Parrington's son long after his father's death; see Vernon Parrington, Jr., ed., "Vernon Parrington's View: 'Economics and Criticism,' " *Pacific Northwest Quarterly* 44 (July 1953): 99. In a preface to the essay, the editor states that the piece was written in 1917 for a proposed series of English Department chapbooks. I have located no information on this series; there are no departmental records for Parrington's years on file at the University of Washington Archives and Records Center. A chapbook series was begun, but not until 1927; the first number contained Parrington's essay "Sinclair Lewis: Our Own Diogenes." The *Pacific Northwest Quarterly* version of "Economics and Criticism" also contains a 1927 photograph of Parrington as well as the cartoon sent by Charles Beard upon the publication of *MCAT*, Volumes 1 and 2; see pp. 100, 103. A draft of the published version exists among Parrington's papers, but so do other partial drafts. One version of the DSAL table of contents (a carbon copy with ink revisions) uses the title "On the Economic Interpretation of Literature" for its introduction, and a version of the contents for *MCAT*, Volume 3 (at this point titled "Main Tendencies in American Literature, 1870–1916") has a detailed, page-length outline for an introduction titled "The Economic Interpretation of Literature." The contents for "The Spirit of Radicalism" indicate the presence of an introduction but supply no title. I think it most likely that the essay, not necessarily in the form in which it was published, was intended as the introduction to "The Spirit of Radicalism" and thus to the forerunners of *MCAT*, Volume 3.

38. This quotation appears in a partial draft titled "Economics and Literature"; a similar but less colorful version that also lacks the confessional final sentence appears in Parrington, Jr., ed., "Economics and Criticism," p. 98. Some of the material in this chapter is drawn from my paper "V. L. Parrington: 'A Literary Refugee Among the Drilled Hosts of the Historians,' " delivered at the Organization of American Historians annual meeting, Philadelphia, April 3, 1982.

39. Carl Becker, review of *The New History: Essays Illustrating the Modern Historical Outlook*, by James Harvey Robinson, *Dial* 53 (July 1, 1912): 19.

9 "I Become More Radical with Every Year," 1918–1924

1. Fifteen pages of architectural drawings, minutely detailed in Parrington's hand, remain among his papers. The blueprints used during construction are stamped "May [2]5 1918" by

the city of Seattle. Ground was broken for 5248 Nineteenth Avenue, N.E., on May 25, and the family moved in on December 17, 1918. Parrington's diary entry for that date states, "Did all the painting myself and a thousand other things." This was the family's fourth residence since coming to Seattle in 1908. The house is still standing although exterior renovations have obscured the original design.

2. *Secretary's Sixth Report, Harvard College Class of 1893* (Cambridge, Mass.: Crimson Printing Co., 1918), pp. 220–21. The report also prints two photographs, one recent and one dating from Parrington's Harvard years.

3. The reports are also summarized in James L. Colwell, "The Populist Image of Vernon Louis Parrington," *Mississippi Valley Historical Review* 49 (June 1962): 59. The class reports appeared at irregular intervals. All of the 1893 class reports issued in his lifetime remain in Parrington's library: *Secretary's First Report* (1898), *Secretary's Second Report* (1899), *Secretary's Third Report* (1903), *Secretary's Fourth Report* (1910), *Secretary's Fifth Report* (1913), *Secretary's Sixth Report* (1918), *Secretary's Seventh Report* (1923).

4. *Secretary's Sixth Report* (1918), p. 338.

5. AS, p. 49–50 (here the variant "Literature" is substituted for "Letters").

6. DSAL, pp. 412–13.

7. AS, pp. 1, 4.

8. Ibid., p. 3.

9. Ibid., p. 16. Garland is one of the two—the other is Howells—American authors mentioned in the sketch; see Hamlin Garland, *A Son of the Middle Border* (New York: Macmillan, 1917), particularly such chapters as "Boy Life on the Prairie."

10. AS, pp. 16–17; the poem "To the Prairie Chicken" was composed in 1896 and is awkwardly exclamatory rather than artfully evocative, as is the prose of the sketch. In *The Progressive Historians: Turner, Beard, Parrington* (New York: Knopf, 1968; Vintage Books, 1970), pp. 359–60, Hofstadter cites passages from MCAT, 3:257–66, 288–300, and the sketch to stress the bitter aspects of Parrington's border recollections, omitting reference to the long passage quoted here, whose rhapsodic qualities nearly offset any discomforts associated with farm life. I thank Kermit Vanderbilt for the observation on Parrington's reawakening artistry and the comparison with *Life on the Mississippi* (1883), which incorporates seven chapters first published in the *Atlantic* in 1875.

11. AS, p. 49; Colwell, "The Populist Image," p. 60; interview with Mrs. W. Stevens Tucker (Louise Wrathal Parrington), August 17–18, 1980, San Carlos, Calif.; letter from Stevens Parrington Tucker to the author, March 9, 1992.

12. AS, p. 48.

13. Christopher Lasch, *The New Radicalism in America, 1889–1963; The Intellectual as a Social Type* (New York: Vintage Books, 1965), pp. ix–xviii.

14. Lasch, *New Radicalism*, chaps. 1, 2, 3, 4, and 8 for case studies of these figures, pp. 147–80 on politics, pp. 286–349 on anti-intellectualism.

15. AS, pp. 49–50.

16. Henry May, *The End of American Innocence: A Study of the First Years of Our Own Time* (1959; Chicago: Quadrangle Books, 1964), pp. 219–332.

17. Information on Parrington's 1920 and 1924 votes is drawn from Vernon L. Parrington, Jr.'s, unpublished biography of his father, Chapter 12, "Democracy and Politics," VLP Papers.

18. The description of the contents of "The Spirit of Radicalism" is based on the last of four tables of contents, dated January 28, 1917.

19. Charles M. Gates, *The First Century at the University of Washington, 1861–1961* (Seattle: University of Washington Press, 1961), pp. 153–56; Roger Sale, *Seattle: Past to Present* (Seattle: University of Washington Press, 1976), pp. 126–36. The standard work on the strike is Robert L. Friedheim, *The Seattle General Strike* (Seattle: University of Washington Press, 1964).

20. Gates, *First Century*, pp. 166–72.

21. Consult the Bibliography for complete citations. Nearly all the reviews are page-length, and the quotes in the text can easily be located. Several letters from J. M. Mecklin, who was upset by Parrington's treatment, are filed among his papers.

22. Interview with Garland O. Ethel, Oct. 4, 1977, Seattle; the anonymous sketch appeared in the April 5, 1920, issue of the *University of Washington Daily;* Joseph B. Harrison, "Vernon Louis Parrington: American Scholar," *Washington Alumnus* 40 (Winter 1950): 10.

23. AS, p. 40; *Catalogue for 1908–1909*, p. 117. Interview with Gladys Savage, October 4, 1977, Seattle.

24. Russell Blankenship, "Vernon Louis Parrington," obituary, *Nation* 129 (August 7, 1929): 142.

25. MCAT, 3:373–86. Parrington's eighteenth-century course was first listed in *Catalogue for 1914–1915*, p. 122, where it is described as "a study in national ideals, with a consideration of significant literary figures and works." One syllabus from the first semester lists as texts Marlowe's *Tamburlaine* and *Dr. Faustus;* Shakespeare's *Henry IV, Part I, Hamlet,* and *The Tempest;* Jonson's *Every Man in His Humour, The Alchemist,* and *Bartholomew Fair;* Bunyan's *Grace Abounding* and *The Pilgrim's Progress;* Cromwell's *Life and Speeches,* edited by Carlyle; Milton's *Areopagitica, Samson Agonistes,* and prose selections; Pepys' *Diary.* The course was divided into three main sections, designed to show that "Literature (is) a reflection of current social forces. A continuous modification of the dominant aristocratic ideal by the emerging democratic ideal": "The Rise of the Courtier Aristocracy and the Literature of Paganism: 1590–1630"; "The Rise of Puritan Democracy, and the Literature of Hebraism: 1630–1660"; and "The Rise of Whiggery, and the Formalization of Literature: 1660–1800."

In this class, Parrington had his students make charts showing the interrelationships between political events, the publication of works by major and minor poets and playwrights, developments in the arts (arts and crafts, painting, sculpture), and so forth. Gladys Savage showed me a chart made by one of her classmates, elaborately drawn on a large sheet of butcher paper rolled into a scroll. "He got you very excited about learning things," she observed. E. H. Eby mentions the eighteenth-century course in his Introduction to MCAT, 3:vi.

26. *Catalogue for 1909–1910*, p. 127 (Benham and Parrington were office mates and shared similar areas of interest, though the line of influence seems to have been from Parrington to the younger man, who received his Ph.D. from Yale in 1905 and came to Washington the same year); *Catalogue for 1919–1920*, pp. 205–6.

27. Lois J. Wentworth, "The Graduate School of the University of Washington, 1911–1912," *Pacific Northwest Quarterly* 34 (April 1943): pp. 147–51; *Catalogue for 1914–1915*, pp. 129–36; *Catalogue for 1915–1916*, pp. 132–33.

28. *Catalogue for 1916–1917*, p. 147; *Catalogue for 1917–1918*, pp. 122–25; *Catalogue for 1919–1920*, p. 206; *Catalogue for 1922–1923*, p. 208; Catalogue for 1924–1925, p. 214; VLP to W. A. Darby, February 1, 1923, VLP Papers. Darby retired because of ill health and became a fruit and vegetable farmer in California. Their correspondence reveals a close friendship in which—perhaps because of the physical distance and format—Parrington could vent some of his frustrations. The two men shared a common love of American ideas and gardening.

29. VLP to JWP, June 27, July 2, 11, 6, 24, 1922, VLP Papers; MCAT, 3:323–33, 346–51, 354–59.

30. MCAT, 3:xxxv, 317.

31. Lucy Lockwood Hazard, *The Frontier in American Literature* (New York: Thomas Y. Crowell, 1927), p. viii.

32. VLP to JWP, July 29, August 2, 1922, VLP Papers.

33. Gates, *First Century,* pp. 156–63; Wentworth, "Graduate School," p. 148.

34. VLP to JWP, July 4, 7, 1923. The trip east and subsequent stay in New York are also recorded in Parrington's 1923 diary, June 20–August 21, VLP Papers.

35. VLP to JWP, July 13, 20, August 8, 1923, VLP Papers.

36. 1923 Diary, July 11, 14, August 5, VLP to VLP, Jr., July 22, 1923, VLP Papers.

37. VLP to JWP, July 19, 1923, VLP Papers.

38. 1923 Diary, July 21, 26, VLP Papers.

39. After compiling DSAL, Stevens Parrington Tucker and I also reconstituted "The Democratic Spirit in Early American Letters, 1620–1800" by matching a table of contents with extant chapter drafts. Parrington spent the winter of 1922–23 revising the manuscript, evidently laying aside plans for "The Spirit of Radicalism" before he began his first period of writing reviews in the early 1920s.

40. 1923 Diary, March 22; Arthur H. Nason to VLP, July 25, August 6, 1923; VLP to JWP, August 1, 11, 1923, VLP Papers.

41. 1923 Diary, August 17, September 10, VLP Papers.

42. *Secretary's Seventh Report, Harvard College Class of 1893*, pp. 218–19, and Robert A. Skotheim, *American Intellectual Histories and Historians* (Princeton: Princeton University Press, 1966), pp. 129–30.

10 *"Three Cheers! A Book at Last,"* 1924–1927

1. Sam Craig to VLP, November 19, 1923, VLP Papers.

2. Ibid.; Ralph H. Gabriel, "Vernon Louis Parrington," in *Pastmasters: Some Essays on American Historians*, ed. Marcus Cunliffe and Robin W. Winks (New York: Harper & Row, 1969), p. 142.

3. *Catalogue for 1922–1923*, p. 208; *Catalogue for 1924–1925*, p. 214.

4. Parrington's correspondence is grouped in several spring binders, including one labeled "Letters to Julia" and one each devoted to 1927, 1928, and 1929. It has not been indexed; I read through the entire collection to make rough tabulations and notes. Parrington kept carbon copies of the typed originals of his letters, usually made by an English Department secretary, so it is often possible to reconstruct an entire epistolary conversation.

5. A brief historical sketch by C. Hugh Holman, "American Literature: The State of the Art," *American Literature* 52 (November 1980): 449–56, covers the information here. See also Gerald Graff, *Professing Literature: An Institutional History* (Chicago: University of Chicago Press, 1987) for a general treatment of the development of academic literary study as well as Vanderbilt's *American Literature and the Academy*, particularly chapters 13–16, pp. 243–99 for more detailed information on the institutionalization and professionalization of American literary study.

6. VLP to Ernest E. Leisy, March 4, 1924, VLP Papers.

7. VLP to Stanley T. Williams, December 1, 1924, VLP Papers.

8. Vernon Louis Parrington, ed., *The Connecticut Wits* (1926; rpt. New York: Thomas Y. Crowell Apollo Editions, 1969), pp. vii (Silverman foreword), xxiii–xxiv (Parrington introduction).

9. Louis Straus to VLP, November 17, 1924; VLP to Louis Straus, December 6, 1924, Glenn Frank to VLP, May 4, 31, June 8, 30, 1926, January 25, 1927, VLP Papers; also Glenn Frank to VLP, June 8, 1926, VLP to Henry Suzzallo, June 9, 1926, VLP to Frederick Morgan Padelford, February 17, 1927, David Thomson to VLP, March 9, 1927, all in President's Office Records, Folder on English Department 1910–30, University of Washington Archives.

10. AS, p. 39.

11. VLP to J. W. McCain, January 7, 1927; VLP to Ernest E. Leisy, March 12, 1927, VLP Papers.

12. J. Donald Adams, "Here is the Shifting Battleground of American Ideas: Professor Parrington Surveys the Cultural History of the United States from Its Beginnings," *New York Times Book Review*, May 1, 1927, p. 3; Carl Van Doren, "Civilization in America," *New York Herald Tribune Books*, May 1, 1927, p. 5; Mark DeWolfe Howe, ed., *Holmes-Laski Letters: The Correspondence of Mr. Justice Holmes and Harold J. Laski, 1916–1935*, vol. 2 (Cambridge: Mass.: Harvard University Press, 1953), pp. 944–45.

13. Howe, ed., *Holmes-Laski Letters*, pp. 1069–70; Henry Seidel Canby, "The American Mind," *Saturday Review* 3 (June 25, 1927): 925; Percy Boynton, "A Turbulent Stream," *New*

Republic 51 (July 6, 1927): 181–82; Kenneth B. Murdock, "New Approach to American Literature," *Yale Review* 17 (January 1928): 382–83.

14. Charles A. Beard, "Fresh Air in American Letters," *Nation* 124 (May 18, 1927): 560, 562; VLP to Mark Van Doren, April 27, 1927, VLP Papers; the sketch is reproduced in Vernon Parrington, Jr., ed., "Vernon Parrington's View: Economics and Criticism," *Pacific Northwest Quarterly* 44 (July 1953): p. 103.

15. Beard, "Fresh Air in American Letters," p. 561.

16. Carl Becker, "Fresh Air in American History," *Nation* 124 (May 18, 1927): 560.

17. Lionel Trilling, *The Liberal Imagination: Essays on Literature and Society* (1950; rpt. Garden City, N.Y.: Doubleday Anchor Books, 1957), p. 7. "Reality in America" is partially a revision of "Parrington, Mr. Smith, and Reality," *Partisan Review* 7 (January-February 1940): 24–40, which is actually a review of Bernard Smith's *Forces in American Criticism* (New York: Harcourt, Brace, 1939). As an illustration of the persistence of Trilling's evaluation of Parrington, in their anthology *Theories of American Literature* (New York: Macmillan, 1972), p. 27, Donald M. Kastiganer and Malcolm A. Griffith cite out of context Trilling's comment on Parrington's title ("A culture is not a flow . . . it is nothing if not a dialectic") as an epigraph to a section called "American Literature as Dialectic."

18. Robert A. Skotheim and Kermit Vanderbilt, "The Mind and Art of a Historian of Ideas," *Pacific Northwest Quarterly* 53 (July 1962): p. 106.

19. Richard Hofstadter, *The Progressive Historians: Turner, Beard, Parrington* (New York: Knopf, 1968; Vintage Books, 1970), pp. 375, 490; Thomas Bender, "Lionel Trilling and American Culture," *American Quarterly* 42 (June 1990): 324–47.

20. *MCAT,* 1:17, 125, 128, 165, 358.

21. Ibid., 2:67, 329, 58, 426; ibid., 3:xix, 186.

22. Kermit Vanderbilt's discussion of Parrington's figurative language in "The Mind and Art of a Historian of Ideas," pp. 105–11, provided a precedent and stimulus for my reevaluation here; see also Robert A. Skotheim's *American Intellectual Histories and Historians* (Princeton: Princeton University Press, 1966), pp. 139–45, which incorporates the imagery analysis from his and Vanderbilt's earlier article. In that article, the term "physiocratic imagery" is used because the authors see it supporting Parrington's environmental interpretation of ideas. I have used a different term, "organic imagery," to underscore my view that Parrington's imagery did not necessarily reflect this political thesis. A precise analysis and count of these categories of images made by a computer instead of a note-taking reader would have to be perfomed in order to enhance the accuracy of my argument. An image has been determined either as a constellation of related figurative terms occurring in proximity (as in the example quoted above on antebellum thinking, which contains four individual currents images) or as a single use of figurative language. There are numerous such constellations of both currents and organic imagery while the miscellaneous images generally occur singly.

23. *MCAT,* 2:67–68, iii–iv.

24. Gene Wise, *American Historical Explanations: Some Strategies for Grounded Inquiry* (Homewood, Ill.: Dorsey Press, 1973), p. 120; Richard Reinitz, *Irony and Consciousness: American Historiography and Reinhold Niebuhr's Vision* (Lewisburg, Pa.: Bucknell University Press, 1980), pp. 19–35. The concept of oscillating cycles of centralization and decentralization is a central feature of Brooks Adams, *The Law of Civilization and Decay* (New York: Macmillan, 1896), as well as J. Allen Smith's posthumous *Growth and Decadence of Constitutional Government* (New York: Holt, 1930), two works Parrington knew intimately.

25. I was first made aware of the title variants in a letter from Stevens Parrington Tucker, May 10, 1978, and have since seen the files containing Parrington's many alternate plans for work, outlines, and trial titles. I do not claim that Parrington was aware of the developments in cultural anthropology that have enlarged the definition of culture from the highest expressions of civilized minds and talents to the characteristic products of a given society. Here he gives a less conservative flavor to the term than in his pre–William Morris, Arnoldian phase or even than his contemporary Van Wyck Brooks, whose thinking was not—as Parrington might

say—as leavened by economics and politics. Parrington's sense of culture is closer to interdisciplinary, as revealed in his class reading lists and pleas in his book reviews for authors to be informed of scholarship outside their own area.

26. Donald Brace to VLP, April 8, 1926 (© 1993 Harcourt Brace Jovanovich, Inc., and published with their permission); VLP to Harcourt, Brace, and Co., May 16, 1926, VLP Papers.

27. VLP to Harcourt, Brace and Co., December 5, 1926, VLP Papers.

28. Donald Brace to VLP, December 16, 1926 (© 1993 by Harcourt Brace Jovanovich, Inc., and published with their permission). Only the general title was settled at this time, however. A bibliography Parrington prepared between May and October 1926 lists these titles and dates for *MCAT*'s three volumes: Volume 1, *The Genesis of American Letters: 1620–1800;* Volume 2, *The Romantic Revolution in America: 1800–1850;* Volume 3, *The Rise of Critical Realism in America: 1850–1920.*

29. S. Kahan to VLP, January 31, 1928, VLP Papers. These letters and the radical/liberal changes are also cited in Eric Goldman, *Rendezvous with Destiny: A History of Modern American Reform* (New York: Knopf, 1953), p. 318, and Alfred Kazin, *On Native Grounds: An Interpretation of Modern American Prose Literature* (1942; rpt. New York: Harcourt Brace Jovanovich Harvest Books, 1970), p. 159. I assume that Kazin saw Parrington's February 24, 1928, letter to S. Kahan in the files of the *Communist* or through personal connections in New York in the early 1940s; Goldman evidently saw these letters as well as other materials during the summer of 1942.

30. VLP to S. Kahan, February 24, 1928, VLP Papers.

31. Bertram D. Wolfe to VLP, March 2, 1928, VLP Papers.

32. VLP to Bertram D. Wolfe, March 7, 1928, VLP Papers.

33. Kazin, *On Native Grounds,* pp. 158–59.

34. Helmut Fleisher, *Marxism and History,* trans. Eric Mosbacher (New York: Harper & Row, 1973); Edwin R. A. Seligman, *The Economic Interpretation of History,* rev. ed. (New York: Columbia University Press, 1917), pp. 163–64, 62–63, 19.

35. Howard Mumford Jones, *The Theory of American Literature,* 2d ed., rev. (Ithaca: Cornell University Press, 1965), p. 142 (the specific reference is only to Volume 3); E. H. Eby, "Vernon Louis Parrington," *MCAT,* 3:v.

36. *College Life* 4 (June 1, 1892): 3; see also 1892 Commencement Program, VLP Papers. The only other reference to Hegel I have located in the VLP Papers occurs in a draft for the ca. 1917 essay published in 1953 as "Economics and Criticism": "Find the master idea of any generation, the idea that makes or breaks social orders, and you find an economic motive tucked away behind it, grinning at the unsophisticated. The idea may exalt the master group, as Hegel's did, endowing with divine sanction the ambitions of the great; or it may prove rebel, as Luther's did, and strike at enthroned mastery. The idea that conforms and the idea that rebels—do not these comprise the significant whole of intellectual militancy?" While Parrington is closer in sympathy to Luther's idea here, the passage as a whole illustrates the dialectical schema linked with Hegel as well as the economic determinism linked with Marx. On the Hegelian aspects of Parrington's thinking, see also Gregory S. Jay's essay "Hegel and Trilling in America," *American Literary Scholarship* 3 (Fall 1989): 565–69, 572–76, where Parrington is viewed as portraying "American literary history as the dialectic of liberal and conservative."

37. *MCAT,* 1:vi; Jay, "Hegel and Trilling," pp. 566–68.

38. *MCAT,* 1:27–84, 88–97, 99–128, 121. It is easier to follow my argument here if the reader consults the Table of Contents, 1:ix–xvii.

39. For Parrington's view of the outcome of the Revolution, see *MCAT,* 1:192–93, and Arthur A. Ekirch, Jr., *The Decline of American Liberalism* (New York: Longmans, Green, 1959), pp. 26–27, 37.

40. *MCAT,* 1:279–91, 292–320, 327–56; Ekirch, *Decline of American Liberalism,* p. 58.

41. *MCAT,* 1:357–95.

42. Parrington's use of regionalism is discussed in John L. Thomas, "The Uses of Catastrophism: Lewis Mumford, Vernon L. Parrington, Van Wyck Brooks, and the End of American Regionalism," *American Quarterly* 42 (June 1990): 223–51.

43. R. W. B. Lewis, *The American Adam: Innocence, Tragedy, and Tradition in the Nineteenth Century* (Chicago: University of Chicago Press, 1955), pp. 1–2, 8.

44. *MCAT*, 2:v; VLP to Victor Lovett Oakes Chittick, July 26, 1927, V. L. O. Chittick Papers, University of Washington Archives. The letter with the southern mind passage was written in response to Chittick's review of Volumes 1 and 2 in the *Portland Oregonian*. Chittick was a former Washington English Department member then teaching at Reed College in Portland, Oregon.

45. See also Wise, *American Historical Explanations*, 2d ed., rev., Chapter 8, "A Paradigm Revolution in the Making: Parrington and the 'Moments' of Lionel Trilling and Reinhold Niebuhr," pp. 223–95.

46. Richard Reinitz, "Vernon Louis Parrington as Historical Ironist," *Pacific Northwest Quarterly* 68 (July 1977): pp. 114–15. My emphasis on the unity of structure of *Main Currents* is partly designed to counter the view that Parrington's fundamental historical outlook changed between the first two and the final volumes. Rather, the crucial change was between DSAL and *MCAT*.

47. Ibid., p. 119.

11 *Styles of Mind, 1927*

1. The extensive literature bearing on the formation of the argument in this chapter is drawn from general studies of American intellectual life, specific studies of periods of intellectual experience, individual studies of intellectuals, and autobiographies by intellectuals. Among the works that have influenced my perception of the features of intellectuals and their roles are H. Stuart Hughes, *Consciousness and Society: The Reorientation of European Social Thought, 1890–1930* (1958; rpt. New York: Vintage, 1961); Christopher Lasch, *The New Radicalism in America, 1889–1963: The Intellectual as a Social Type* (New York: Vintage, 1965); Robert A. Skotheim, *Totalitarianism and American Social Thought* (New York: Holt, Rinehart, and Winston, 1971); David A. Hollinger, *In the American Province: Studies in the History and Historiography of Ideas* (Bloomington: Indiana University Press, 1985), especially the 1975 essay "Ethnic Diversity, Cosmopolitanism, and the Emergence of the American Intellectual Intelligentsia"; Daniel Aaron, *Writers on the Left* (1961; rpt. New York: Avon Books, 1969); Henry May, *The End of American Innocence: A Study of the First Years of Our Own Time, 1912–1917* (1959; rpt. Chicago: Quadrangle Books, 1964).

2. See, for example, Robert A. Skotheim and Kermit Vanderbilt, "Vernon Louis Parrington: The Mind and Art of a Historian of Ideas," *Pacific Northwest Quarterly* 53 (July 1962): pp. 102–6, and Ralph H. Gabriel, "Vernon Louis Parrington" in *Pastmasters: Some Essays of American Historians*, ed. Marcus Cunliffe and Robin W. Winks (New York: Harper & Row, 1969), pp. 143–44.

3. A few figures from Volumes 1 and 2 are selected for closer analysis in this chapter: John Cotton, Phillip Freneau, Poe, Cooper, Daniel Webster, Emerson. From Volume 3, discussed in Chapter 12, are selected Whitman and Henry Adams. Related figures are also briefly treated. This array is drawn from both literature and social thought to demonstrate the consistency of Parrington's treatment of intellectuals. For Parrington's criticism of Smith, see *MCAT*, 3:409. Skotheim and Vanderbilt, "The Mind and Art of a Historian of Ideas" (pp. 110–11) also recognize Parrington's admiration for various of his conservative-minded antagonists.

4. Although the terms *liberal, conservative, radical, aristocratic, democratic*, and *plutocratic* are highly significant and occur frequently in Parrington's lexicon, they are primarily political in application. Since a major quest in this chapter is to show that Parrington's evaluations of the importance of individual thinkers are made independently of their political persuasions, I have focused on those terms that apply to historical periods, philosophical

traditions, and literary movements—three areas often distinguished by the contributions of intellectuals, whereas intellectuals' contributions to politics are more problematic to determine. I have used the term *unify* instead of synthesize in order to avoid confusion, since Chapter 10 claimed that no ideological synthesis was reached at the end of Volume 1. If a figure is primarily realistic—like John Adams, who is labeled *Realist*—and does not have a redeeming dose of idealism to raise his sights sufficiently above practical matters, then Parrington will not consider him an intellectual. Thus, the use of *realism* as a term describing an intellectual position at a stage beyond both absolutism and idealism should be distinguished from its use to describe purely political attitudes. The relation between Parrington's critical idiom and the intellectual's role is taken up again in Chapter 12.

5. *MCAT,* 1:27. While Roger Williams may typify the portraits in *The Democratic Spirit in American Letters* (see Chapter 8, Part 1), Parrington's more mature skills and concerns as an intellectual historian in *Main Currents* are typified by John Cotton's portrait. In Volume 1, Williams is certainly an intellectual ("an original thinker.... He lived in the realm of ideas, of inquiry and discussion; and his actions were creatively determined by principles the bases of which he examined with critical insight," *MCAT,* 1:63–64), but his portrait is the exception rather than the rule—the most rhapsodic, more marked by personal biases, and ultimately one of the least historical of all of the portraits in *Main Currents.* The first full study of Cotton was Larzer Ziff's *The Career of John Cotton: Puritanism and the American Experience* (Princeton, N.J.: Princeton University Press, 1962).

6. *MCAT,* 1:27–28 (the emphasis is Cotton Mather's).

7. Ibid., pp. 28–29.

8. Ibid., pp. 28, 37.

9. Ibid., p. 29. Parrington's use of the verb "to play" in this passage is particularly interesting, for definitions of intellectuals have noted the trait of playing with ideas; see, for example, Lewis Coser, *Men of Ideas: A Sociologist's View* (New York: Free Press, 1965), pp. viii–x, and Richard Hofstadter, *Anti-Intellectualism in American Life* (New York: Vintage, 1963), pp. 29–33.

10. *MCAT,* 1:29–30.

11. Ibid., p. 30.

12. Ibid., pp. 31, 34. On the revolutionary implications of Puritanism for traditional class and political structure, see Michael Walzer, *The Revolution of the Saints: A Study in the Origins of Radical Politics* (1965; rpt. New York: Atheneum, 1972).

13. *MCAT,* 1:37. Note the use of the term *absolutism* here. Parrington often refers to the "formalism" and "rigidity" of Hebrew law in Volume 1 and to the closed-minded, "deterministic" traits of colonials who turned their backs on the democratic future. "Absolutism" best summarizes the senses of these near synonyms and is more inclusive.

14. *MCAT,* 1:165, 170, 178, 320, 307–8.

15. See *MCAT,* 1:106–17, for Mather's portrait. The entire section "The Mather Dynasty" (pp. 98–117) can be read as a critical response to Barrett Wendell's *Cotton Mather, Puritan Priest* (1891; Cambridge, Mass.: Harvard University Press, 1925) and Kenneth B. Murdock's *Increase Mather* (Cambridge, Mass.: Harvard University Press, 1925), both part of "two generations of Harvard scholarship" (p. 98) on the Mathers.

16. *MCAT,* 1:x.

17. Ibid., p. 368.

18. Ibid., p. 378.

19. Ibid., pp. 368, 378–79.

20. Ibid., p. 374.

21. Ibid., p. 370. Parrington, too, made the choice between writing poetry and more thorough involvement in revolutionary times.

22. Ibid., pp. 380–81. Parrington's estimation was echoed by Lewis Leary in *Literary History of the United States,* 4th ed. (New York: Macmillan, 1974), pp. 169–75.

23. Ibid., pp. 387, 393, 390.

24. Ibid., p. 390. Refusing to howl with the pack is analogous to detachment.

25. Ibid., pp. 393, 390.

26. Ibid., p. 343.

27. Ibid. Merrill D. Peterson's *The Jefferson Image in the American Mind* (New York: Oxford University Press, 1960) includes a chapter on Jefferson's appeal to VLP (pp. 321–29).

28. On these points, consult also Russell Reising, "Reconstructing Parrington," *American Quarterly* 41 (March 1989): 157–61, and Kermit Vanderbilt, *American Literature and the Academy: The Roots, Growth, and Maturity of a Profession* (Philadelphia: University of Pennsylvania Press, 1986), pp. 315–28.

29. DSAL, p. 304.

30. The "Romanticism and Democracy" chapter in DSAL occupies pp. 296–308, VLP Papers.

31. *MCAT*, 2:58 (Parrington is actually most concerned with Poe's psychology here); VLP to V. L. O. Chittick, July 26, 1927, V. L. O. Chittick Papers, University of Washington Archives.

32. *MCAT*, 2:58.

33. Ibid., pp. 57, 59.

34. An early reassessment stressing Poe's connections to the American environment was Ernest Marchand's "Poe as Social Critic" (1934), rpt. in *On Poe: The Best from American Literature*, ed. Louis J. Budd and Edwin H. Cady (Durham, N.C.: Duke University Press, 1993).

35. Parrington does not explicitly discuss the romantic characteristics of nineteenth-century American writing; the section "Adventures in Romance" (*MCAT*, 2:41–59) contains no introductory information. He does broadly invoke romance as the general spirit—shifting, restless, youthfully optimistic, acquisitive, progressive, individualistic, at once humanitarian and democratic and imperialistic and aristocratic—of the first half of the century in the Introduction to Volume 2, pp. iii–v. But he does not define literary romance. As early as 1924, A. O. Lovejoy wrote that "the word 'romantic' has come to mean so many things that, by itself, it means nothing. It has ceased to have the function of a verbal sign"; quoted in Lillian R. Furst, *Romanticism* (London: Methuen, 1969), p. 1, a work which reviews the history of the term. Parrington, however, probably helped modernize the study of nineteenth-century American literature by titling his volume *The Romantic Revolution*, no matter how problematic the key term, for at the time of *MCAT*'s publication American literature was usually treated regionally instead of by literary movements. He may also have chosen the title as a rebuttal to the point of view expressed in Irving Babbitt's *Rousseau and Romanticism*, published in 1922. Although Parrington favors French romantic political doctrines, his conception of literary romanticism seems based on the gothic tradition and on the vein of historical romance and adventure tales. See Richard Hofstadter's observations on Parrington's critical idiom in *The Progressive Historians: Turner, Beard, Parrington* (New York: Knopf, 1968; Vintage Books, 1970), pp. 401–2, which note that Parrington often puts his key terms in the plural—possibly an indication he had read Lovejoy's essay.

36. *MCAT*, 2:33–34, 36–38, 51, 56. Only two southern writers are not similarly criticized: William Alexander Caruthers is praised for seeing both good and evil in both the northern and southern positions (ibid., pp. 41–46), and William J. Grayson discusses slavery with candor (ibid., p. 104).

37. Legaré's portrait is particularly interesting because Parrington praises so highly his scholarly qualities despite his conservative politics; see ibid., pp. 114–25. Legaré is treated more fully in Michael O'Brien, *A Character of Hugh Legaré* (Knoxville: University of Tennessee Press, 1985), which notes Parrington's attempt at reassessment (p. xi).

38. *MCAT*, 2:126–27.

39. Ibid., p. 183.

40. Ibid., p. 204.

41. Ibid., pp. 205, 208, 212.

42. Ibid., pp. 259, 267. Melville's portrait is perhaps most significant, not for what it indicates about his pessimistic style of mind that bleakly questioned the basis of democracy and capitalism and marks him as a clear candidate for the Party of Irony, but for its illustration of Parrington's anticipation of contemporary literary scholarship. Volume 2 of *MCAT* was published just as the Melville revival was beginning, stimulated by the publications of Raymond Weaver's psychological biography, *Herman Melville, Mariner and Mystic*, in 1921; D. H. Lawrence's chapter on Melville in *Studies in Classic American Literature* in 1923; and Melville's own almost stillborn *Billy Budd* in 1924. The portrait is curiously deficient in not discussing *Moby-Dick*.

43. *MCAT*, 2:222. There are probably more drafts for various Cooper chapters in Parrington's papers than for any other figure. Cooper rated a separate chapter, "James Fenimore Cooper—Social Critic," in DSAL, pp. 309-21. A provocative study also emphasizing Cooper's relation to a changing social order is Philip Fisher, *Hard Facts: Setting and Form in the American Novel* (New York: Oxford University Press, 1987), pp. 22–86.

44. *MCAT*, 2:225–26.

45. Ibid., pp. 229, 227, 226, 228.

46. Ibid., p. 230. Cooper is compared here to Emerson.

47. Ibid., pp. 225, 234, 232, 235.

48. Ibid., p. 237.

49. Parrington touches upon these factors in ibid., pp. 318–19, 296.

50. Ibid., 273–74. The emphasis on economics in Parrington's analysis of the New England mind is developed more fully and precisely in such recent works as Michael T. Gilmore's *American Romanticism and the Marketplace* (Chicago: University of Chicago Press, 1985) and David S. Reynolds's *Beneath the American Renaissance* (New York: Knopf, 1987), which also explore the influence of the conditions of authorship and of mass culture on various writers.

51. *MCAT*, 2:304–5, 316. A more contemporary study of Webster that similarly explores the "Black Dan-Godlike Man Paradox" is Irving H. Bartlett, *Daniel Webster* (New York: Norton, 1978).

52. *MCAT*, 2:305, 306–7.

53. Ibid., pp. 305, 310, 312, 313.

54. Ibid., p. 305.

55. Ibid., p. 316.

56. Ibid., pp. 304, 315.

57. Ibid., pp. 399, 387–89, 391. A recent study of Emerson's early thinking that similarly treats his dual career as public intellectual and Lyceum lecturer as a way to define a new social role is Mary Krupiec Cayton, *Emerson's Emergence: Self and Society in the Transformation of New England, 1800–1845* (Chapel Hill: University of North Carolina Press, 1989); see "The Calling," pp. 137–60.

58. *MCAT*, 2:391, 389, 390.

59. Ibid., 1:345.

12 *Legacies, 1927–1929 and After*

1. Howard Mumford Jones to VLP, March 2, 1928, VLP Papers.

2. "U. W. Professor Awarded $2,000 Pulitzer Prize," *Seattle Times*, May 8, 1928; "Pulitzer Prize of $2000 Given for Best Book," *University of Washington Daily*, May 8, 1928, both in Faculty Clipping File, University of Washington Library; Will C. McCarty to VLP, October 6, 1928, VLP Papers. Vern Cook had died during Parrington's first year at the University of Oklahoma, and Vern Byers had died in 1927.

3. "Pulitzer Prize of $2000 Given for Best Book"; Sylvia Finlay Kerrigan, "Pulitzer Prize for Parrington," *Washington Alumnus* 19 (June 1928): 4.

4. On the Wisconsin offer, see Dean of the College of Arts and Sciences, University of Wisconsin, to VLP, January 25, 1927; Glenn Frank, President of the University of Wisconsin, to VLP, March 20 (telegram), April 6, May 16, 1927; VLP to Glenn Frank, March 21, 1927; VLP to Dr. Clare Green (of Lehigh University English Department), June 2, 1927; VLP to Professor Joseph M. Thomas (of University of Minnesota English Department), May 2, 1927; John R. Effinger (Dean of the University of Michigan) to VLP, May 11, 1927, all in VLP Papers; also see VLP to Frederick Morgan Padelford ("My dear Paddy"), Dean of the Graduate School, August 7, 1927; Frederick Morgan Padelford to VLP ("My dear Parrington"), August 9, 1927; two memos from conferences between M. Lyle Spencer, President of the University, and F. M. Padelford, July 29 and August 9, 1927, all in President's Office Records, English Department File, 1920–30, University of Washington Archives and Records Center.

5. VLP to President Lyle Spencer, October 12, 1927, May 31, 1928; AS, p. 39.

6. Paul Kaufman (American University) to VLP, April 13, December 8, 1928; VLP to Paul Kaufman, May 19, 20, 1928; T. M. Putnam, Dean of the University of California, to VLP, September 20, 1928; VLP to Lucy Lockwood Hazard, June 7, 1928, all in VLP Papers.

7. VLP to Paul Kaufman, May 10, 1928; VLP to T. M. Putnam, October 11, 1928; author unknown, University of Michigan summer school offer letter, to VLP, February 16, 1927; VLP to Frederick Morgan Padelford, August 7, 1927, all in VLP Papers. Parrington's summer in Ann Arbor exacerbated rather than relieved the difficulty of turning down Michigan's offer, which was clearly far more tempting than Wisconsin's; see, for example, his letter of October 15, 1928, to J. Holly Hanford, VLP Papers, who had just left Michigan to become dean of the Graduate School at Western Reserve University in Cleveland: "I am not yet certain in my own mind whether I acted wisely or foolishly. There is no place in the United States pleasanter to live than the Pacific Coast, but in living here one perforce cuts oneself off from many contacts and advantages that are to be had elsewhere. If Ann Arbor had been on the Atlantic Coast I think I wouldn't have hesitated, in spite of the fact that I have taken pretty deep root here in the Northwest." I thank the Graduate Library of the University of Michigan for supplying a copy of the 1927 summer session catalog; see pp. 65–66.

8. Glenn Frank to VLP, April 29, 1927; VLP to Mrs. H. A. Walton, November 20, 1928, VLP Papers.

9. *Who's Who in America, 1928–1929*, 15:1628; VLP to Kenneth B. Murdock, January 8, 23, 1929; Robert Dickson Weston to Kenneth B. Murdock, January 23, 1929, VLP Papers. Although it is possible to read Parrington's responses to Murdock's inquiries as tongue-in-cheek ("in the event that I should be able to qualify I should regard it as an honor to belong to the Society"), I think that this longing for Harvardian respectability rather overtook him in this interesting exchange.

10. On the Yaddo invitation, see Elizabeth Ames to VLP, January 17, February 5, 1929, and VLP to Elizabeth Ames, January 30, 1929 (he does say that he would accept with "the greatest pleasure" if he were not going to England); on the Turnbull offer, see H. C. Lancaster to VLP, February 3, 1929, Edwin Greenlaw to VLP, February 16, 1929; Frank J. Goodwood to VLP, March 2, 1929; and VLP to H. C. Lancaster, March 11, 1929, all in VLP Papers.

11. VLP to William E. Dodd, October 18, 1927; Frank W. Scott, editor-in-chief of D. C. Heath, to VLP, January 21, 1929; VLP to Frank W. Scott, January 26, 1929; on the *Encyclopedia of the Social Sciences*, Alvin Johnson to VLP, December 23, 1927, June 20, 1928, March 1, 1929; VLP to Alvin Johnson, March 1, 1929; Frank L. MacGregor (of Harper & Brothers) to VLP, March 1, 1929; on the *Encyclopaedia Britannica*, Henry Seidel Canby to VLP, January 13, December 7, 1927; VLP to H. S. Canby, November 30, 1927, all in VLP Papers. Parrington was also contacted by Allen Johnson, December 8, 1927, to write the James Russell Lowell entry for the *Dictionary of American Biography*. The Rölvaag introduction is reprinted in the Addenda to *MCAT*, 3:387–96. The *Britannica* article is worth consulting as a contrast to *Main Currents*, for Parrington was working as a literary scholar and not as an intellectual historian. The *Encyclopedia of the Social Sciences* also contains a sketch of Parrington, written by E. H. Eby.

12. Consult the Bibliography for complete citations for these last *Nation* reviews. Nearly all are page-length, and the quotes in the text can easily be located.

13. For a complete listing of Parrington's miscellaneous reviews as well as the complete citations of those mentioned, consult the Bibliography. Parrington planned to treat Frank in the section on "The Younger Intellectuals" in Volume 3 of *MCAT*, p. xxxvii.

14. VLP, "Revolution and Adam Smith," *New York Herald-Tribune Books,* December 4, 1927, pp. 1–2 (this is the only explicit comment on Becker by VLP of which I am aware); VLP, "The Culture Americans Have Created," ibid., January 29, 1928, pp. 1–2 (he reviewed Vol. 2 by Thomas Jefferson Wertenbaker, Vol. 3 by James Truslow Adams, Vol. 6 by C. R. Fish, and Vol. 8 by Allen Nevins); VLP, "Sight-Seeing American History," ibid., November 13, 1927, p. 2 (several volumes in the series use the phrase "The American Spirit" in their titles, but Parrington seems most disturbed by Stanley T. Williams's contribution, vol. 11, *The American Spirit in Letters,* 1926).

15. Edmund S. Meany, review of *MCAT,* vols. 1 and 2 (jointly with the Beards' *Rise of American Civilization*), *Washington Historical Quarterly* 18 (July 1927): 233–35.

16. VLP to Ernest E. Leisy, December 6, 1927; C. Hugh Holman, "American Literature: The State of the Art," *American Literature* 52 (December 1980): E. H. Eby, "American Romantic Criticism, 1815–1860" (Ph.D. dissertation, University of Washington, 1927), pp. 4 (acknowledging Parrington's "suggestions" as "invaluable"), 77–127 (the Poe chapter), 5 (for quote).

17. Victor Childs Christianson, "Edwin Lawrence Godkin as a Utilitarian" (Ph.D. dissertation, University of Washington, 1929), p. 89 vita (n.p., appended after bibliography).

18. William Russell Blankenship, "The Perfectionism of John Humphrey Noyes in Relation to Its Social Background" (Ph.D. dissertation, University of Washington, 1935), p. 344 (according to his vita, Blankenship—who wrote the *Nation*'s obituary of Parrington—received his M.A. at Washington in 1929, with a thesis also on Noyes).

19. Vernon Louis Parrington, "The Development of Realism," in *The Reinterpretation of American Literature: Some Contributions Toward the Understanding of Its Historical Development,* ed. Norman Foerster (New York: Harcourt, Brace, 1928), pp. 139–59; quotations from pp. 139, 140, 143, 158–59; Norman Foerster to VLP, July 20, November 11, 1927, VLP Papers.

20. *The Reinterpretation of American Literature,* ed. Foerster, p. 5 (for Pattee quote); in addition to Foerster, Pattee, Parrington, and Schlesinger the contributors were Jay B. Hubbell ("The Frontier"), Howard Mumford Jones ("The European Background"), Kenneth B. Murdock ("The Puritan Tradition"), Paul Kaufman ("The Romantic Movement"), Harry Hayden Clark ("American Literary History and American Literature"), Gregory Paine ("Select Bibliography"), and Ernest E. Leisy ("List of Dissertations and Articles, and of Americana in Libraries").

21. Jay B. Hubbell to VLP, July 26, 1927, November 8, December 1, 1928, January 17, 1929; VLP to Jay B. Hubbell, October 10, 1928 ("The new magazine, I suppose, will be more liberal in its attitude toward social interpretations than the M.L.A. publications. We can't very well go in for philology or Sherlock Holmes source work in the American field and survive; I am hoping and expecting, therefore, that the magazine will be broadly humanistic." Parrington's response of January 11, 1929, ran in part to Hubbell's request for manuscripts for *American Literature*); all correspondence is in VLP Papers. Richard Ruland, *The Rediscovery of American Literature: Premises of Critical Taste, 1900–1940* (Cambridge, Mass.: Harvard University Press, 1967), pp. 275–87; Gene Wise, "Paradigm Dramas in American Studies: A Cultural and Institutional History of the Movement," *American Quarterly* 31 (Bibliography Issue 1979): 293–337.

22. For full citations of these pieces, consult the Bibliography.

23. This syllabus is reprinted in part and the Lewis chapbook in full in the Addenda to *MCAT,* Vol. 3; see pp. xxxix (most of the entries are from the syllabus, although they have been rearranged to correspond somewhat to Volume 3's Table of Contents), 360–69; a bound

volume of the syllabus is available in the Northwest Collections, University of Washington Libraries, and another survives among Parrington's papers; VLP to Howard Lee McBain (also author of a chapter in *Whither Mankind,* reviewed by VLP for the *Nation*), February 7, 1929, VLP Papers.

24. Dr. John Parrington's second wife was Frances Overstreet; their children, Martha and Jack, grew up in Emporia. His daughter, Mary Louise Parrington, by Mary Wright, married Shadford Reynolds. Vernon and John's mother is buried beside the Judge in Maplewood Cemetery, Emporia; Frances and John are buried next to them; a dark gray granite monument inscribed only "Parrington" stands just west of the graves. Most information about "Mama Parrington" is drawn from my interview with Louise Parrington Tucker, August 17–18, 1980; on the estrangement, see Louise Parrington Tucker to Stevens Parrington Tucker, October 21, 1980, copy in author's possession.

25. VLP to Alvin Johnson, March 1, 1929; interview with E. H. Eby, October 3, 1977; JWP to Elizabeth Parrington Thomas, June 20, 1929, letters in VLP Papers.

26. VLP to Gladys Savage, May 17, 1929, VLP Papers.

27. JWP to Elizabeth Parrington Thomas, June 20, 1929, VLP Papers; interview with Louise Parrington Tucker, August 17–18, 1980; J. Allen Smith, *Growth and Decadence of Constitutional Government* (New York: Henry Holt, 1930), pp. ix–xvii for Parrington's Introduction; also "Dr. Parrington Dies Suddenly While on Tour," *University of Washington Daily,* June 19, 1929, and VLP to Elfreda Smith, May 16, 1927, J. Allen Smith Papers, University of Washington Archives. Julia's letter to Elizabeth records the attending physician's notation on Parrington's death certificate as "thrombosis of the left coronary artery and fatty degeneration and dilation of the heart."

28. Interview with Gladys Savage, October 4, 1977; the yearbook is available in the University of Washington Library; Joseph B. Harrison, *Vernon Louise Parrington: American Scholar* (Seattle: University of Washington Book Store, 1929); Frederick Morgan Padelford, "An Appreciation of Professor Parrington," *Washington Alumnus* 21 (December 1929): 7, 18; "Faculty Pays Tribute to Professor Parrington," *University of Washington Daily,* December 19, 1929 ("pondering" appears to be a misprint for "pandering"); interview with E. H. Eby, October 3, 1977; see also *Catalogue for 1929–1930,* pp. 260–67.

29. O. E. Rölvaag to JWP, September 25, 1929, VLP Papers; Norman Foerster, "American Letters, 1860—," *Saturday Review of Literature,* April 4, 1931, pp. 705–6 (this is actually a review of *MCAT,* Vol. 3); *Nation* 129 (July 10, 1929): 29 (note the similarity to the images used in the twin reviews of *Main Currents* and *The Rise of American Civilization*).

30. J. Donald Adams, "American Ideas in the Making," *New York Times Book Review,* No. 9, 1930, p. 1; Winfred Ernest Garrison, "A History of American Culture," *Christian Century* 48 (January 21, 1931): 90; Dudley D. Zuver, "Some Books of the Day," *Churchman* 143 (January 3, 1931): 17; John Chamberlain, "Looking Backwards," *Forum* 84 (November 1930): xiv.

31. Stanley T. Williams, review of *MCAT,* Vol. 3, *New England Quarterly* 4 (April 1931): 354; Edward Wagenknecht, "Death and the Scholar," *Virginia Quarterly Review* 7 (April 1931): 301–4; Carl Van Doren, "A Creative Syllabus," *New York Herald-Tribune Books,* November 30, 1930, p. 4; V. L. O. Chittick, review of *The Beginnings of Critical Realism in America, American Literature* 2 (January 1931): 442.

32. Mark A. DeWolfe Howe, ed., *The Holmes-Laski Letters: The Correspondence of Mr. Justice Holmes and Harold J. Laski, 1916–1935,* 2 vols. (Cambridge, Mass.: Harvard University Press, 1953), pp. 1298, 1313; Matthew Josephson, "American Culture Since the Sixties," *Nation* 131 (December 3, 1930): 616; Morris R. Cohen, "Parrington's America," *New Republic* 65 (January 28, 1931): 303–4.

33. Interview with E. H. Eby, October 3, 1977. I am indebted to Professor Eby for confirming many of my hunches regarding Parrington's opinions and working procedures. Although editing *MCAT,* Volume 3, could only have been a disheartening and difficult task, in light of Parrington's unexpected death and inveterate revising, more coherence between

Parrington's intentions in *MCAT* as a whole and the third volume's published form would have been desirable. Eby's role as editor is not evident; he generously wanted all royalties to go to Parrington's widow and requested that his name be omitted from the title page. The publishers should have made clearer how much of Volume 3 was incomplete; the unfamiliar reader is not sufficiently alerted by the brackets around unfinished sections placed in the Table of Contents. Most important, most of the materials collected at the end of Volume 3, pp. 323–413, were drawn from Parrington's syllabus for English 165 and 166, the last two quarters in his sequence American Literature Since 1870, which was mistitled as *The American Novel Since 1890* when published in pamphlet form in 1925 by the University of Washington Book Store. The first part of the 46-page syllabus covers the 1890–1917 period and is divided into four sections, including one on sociology and the problem novel and material on the muckraking movement, that are inexplicably excluded from the Addenda. The second part, covering the 1917–24 portion, contained six sections and not five, as indicated in Volume 3, p. xxxix. Much of this second part is reprinted, but not in the order stipulated by either the syllabus or the Contents. The introduction to Rölvaag's *Giants in the Earth* does not, of course, appear in the published syllabus, nor does the material on the development of the short story, Volume 3, pp. 387–400. It would have illuminated the differences between Parrington's aims as a literature professor and his aims as an intellectual historian if the syllabus had been reprinted in its entirety.

34. The essay titled "A Chapter in American Liberalism," which now appears as the very last item in Volume 3, was probably not intended, as the publisher's note (3:401) indicates, as the introduction to Part I of Book Three, "but covers much of the ground indicated there." The essay is similar to Parrington's introduction to Smith's *Growth and Decadence of Constitutional Government.* Although Parrington's eighteenth-century strain may have been ruffled by the style of the 1920s, he certainly kept himself well informed about artistic and intellectual developments. One should recall, for example, that Sherwood Anderson had only just received wide recognition in 1919 with *Winesburg, Ohio*, and Sinclair Lewis in 1920 with *Main Street.* Parrington might be faulted for not taking F. Scott Fitzgerald more seriously, but *The Great Gatsby* was not published until 1925. He did not plan to discuss Hemingway, but *The Sun Also Rises* did not appear until 1926. Nor did he plan to discuss Faulkner, but *The Sound and the Fury* did not appear until 1929, the same year as Wolfe's *Look Homeward, Angel*, the inauguration of Herbert Hoover, the stock market crash, and his own death. It is also important to keep in mind that Volume 3's original title was "The Spirit of Radicalism in Recent American Literature," a title that helps define the point of view in the quotation here, from Volume 3, xxvii.

35. This title was probably drawn from Ruskin's two lectures, "The Storm Cloud of the Nineteenth Century," delivered in London in 1884 and later collected in *Sesame and Lilies.*

36. *MCAT,* 3:13–14.

37. Ibid., pp. 7–47 (for entire chapter), 23–26 (for Great Barbecue section, one of Parrington's prose tours-de-force).

38. Ibid., pp. 49–50, 54–101. Stowe is dealt with briefly because her full portrait appears in Volume 2. Her reappearance here suggests that this section was partially unrevised, as does Henry Clay's reappearance in Volume 3, p. 22, after his prior treatment in Volume 2.

39. Ibid., pp. 140–68, 169–88.

40. Ibid., pp. xxvi–xxvii. Parrington is paraphrasing Arnold's poem "Stanzas from the Grand Chartreuse."

41. Richard Hofstadter, *The Progressive Historians: Turner, Beard, Parrington* (New York: Knopf, 1968; Vintage Books, 1970), p. 434; *MCAT,* 3:70. For a suggestive discussion of Whitman's portrait, see Wesley Morris, *Towards a New Historicism* (Princeton: Princeton University Press, 1972), pp. 42–44.

42. *MCAT,* 3:70, 69.

43. Ibid., pp. 71, 69.

44. Ibid., pp. 80, 97–101, 102–3.

45. Ibid., p. 76. Among Whitman studies, Betsy Erkkila's *Whitman the Political Poet* (New York: Oxford University Press, 1989) particularly supports this part of Parrington's argument.

46. *MCAT,* 3:82 (note Whitman's currents imagery), 86.

47. Ibid., p. 189.

48. Ibid., pp. 191–92.

49. Parrington's omission of scientists and scientific ideas, owing partly to not completing his proposed text, was emphasized in the reviews by Charles A. Beard, "Fresh Air in American Letters," *Nation* 124 (May 18, 1927): 562; Cohen, "Parrington's America"; and Kenneth Murdock, "New Approach to American Literature," *Yale Review* 17 (January 1928): 382–83.

50. *MCAT,* 3:212.

51. Ibid., pp. 215, 218.

52. Ibid., pp. 218–19, 212.

53. Ibid., pp. 224, 212–13. Parrington was also clearly attracted to Brooks Adams's theory of social cycles; it seems to parallel his view of American history following patterns of centralization and decentralization.

54. On James and Howells, ibid., pp. 239–53. James's portrait seems unfinished; it has met with criticism similar to Poe's. But note that Parrington aptly calls James "a forerunner of modern expressionism" (3:241) and concludes that as an artist, Howells "mistook his calling" and was not "an original genius" (3:252). While he may not admire James, he certainly does not praise Howells, as an insistent supporter of literary realism might.

55. Ibid., p. xxxii.

56. Ibid., pp. 248–49.

57. Ibid., pp. 291–93, 299. This criticism is particularly notable in light of Parrington's personal feelings about the accuracy of Garland's writings, as expressed in AS, p. 16.

58. *MCAT,* 3:xxxv, xxvii, 317.

59. Ibid., pp. 350–51.

60. Ibid., pp. 355, 354. Parrington's judgments on the other naturalists are similar: Jack London is a "potential naturalist" who is "carried away by zeal of revolution" (p. 352); Upton Sinclair "began as a novelist, but his art [is] submerged by propaganda" (p. 353); Frank Norris "never quite attained the scientific detachment" but "yielded to romantic tendencies" even in *McTeague* (pp. 329, 331). Only Stephen Crane, with his painterly techniques, is exempted from criticism (pp. 328–29).

61. "Old Hall Is Named After Parrington," *University of Washington Daily,* February 2, 1931; "Parrington Hall Will Be Officially Opened" (no source or date); "Parrington Hall Now Newest Campus Building," *University of Washington Daily,* August 6, 1931 (with a photograph of Mrs. Parrington helping seal the new cornerstone), all from Northwest Collections Faculty File, University of Washington Libraries; architectural anecdote from interview with Gladys Savage, October 4, 1977.

62. The Philosophy Department was subsequently moved into Parrington Hall. Appropriately, next to the hall are several greenhouses, called Parrington Annex. Parrington Hall underwent extensive remodeling in the late 1980s.

63. *Catalogue for 1927–1928,* p. 272 (last use of History of American Culture for English 161-162-163); *Catalogue for 1928–1929,* p. 269 (last catalog in which Parrington is listed, printed just before his death); *Catalogue for 1929–1930,* p. 264, 1939–1940, p. 262, 1949–1950, p. 231 (for continued use of American Literature).

64. Robert B. Heilman to the author, October 21, 1977, and interview with Professor Heilman, August 16, 1978, Seattle. Much of the portrait of the English Department in 1948 and after are drawn from our cordial interview. A very gracious person, Heilman's long-time tenure as department chairman (1948–79) during some extremely trying years indicates considerable skills in academic diplomacy. Only in the last decades, with the dessemination of French-inspired deconstruction, and the impact of feminist and African-American critics on the presuppositions of the literary canon, have the methods of the new critics been successfully

challenged. See also Walter Sutton, *Modern American Criticism* (Englewood Cliffs, N.J.: Prentice-Hall, 1963); Alexander Karanikas, *Tillers of a Myth: Southern Agrarians as Social and Literary Critics* (Madison: University of Wisconsin Press, 1969); Ruland, *The Rediscovery of American Literature;* Vanderbilt, *American Literature and the Academy.*

65. In our interview, Heilman stressed that the problem in the department he was hired to redesign was not political but one of not turning out high-quality Ph.D.s. See Harold J. Laski, *The American Democracy* (New York: Viking, 1948), p. 351 (on the effect of Parrington's Pulitzer); Charles M. Gates, *The First Century at the University of Washington, 1861–1961* (Seattle: University of Washington Press, 1961), pp. 219–20 (on administrative and faculty changes and Roethke's Pulitzer).

66. Robert B. Heilman to the author, October 21, 1977 (on the terms "Old Historicism" and "New Historicism"); see also Robert B. Heilman, "Historian and Critic: Notes on Attitudes," *Sewanee Review* 73 (July-September 1965): 426–44, and "History and Criticism: Psychological and Pedagogical Notes," *College English* 27 (October 1965): 32–38.

67. Interview with Robert B. Heilman, August 16, 1978; Jane Sanders, *Cold War on the Campus: Academic Freedom at the University of Washington, 1946–64* (Seattle: University of Washington Press, 1979), pp. 86–90, 104–14. Kenneth Burke finally received a Walker-Ames appointment in the fall of 1975.

68. Gates, *First Century,* pp. 167–98; 204–5; Sanders, *Cold War on the Campus,* pp. 3–46 (on Allen and the Canwell Committee), 47–72 (on the committee hearings and figures involved). According to Sanders, Angelo Pelligrini and Maude Beal of the English Department also admitted Party membership but, as did Eby and Ethel, refused to testify against others. In addition, according to Melvin Rader's own account in *False Witness* (Seattle: University of Washington Press, 1969), Joseph Butterworth of the English Department admitted past Party membership; Sophus K. Winter of the English Department admitted past Party membership; and Herbert Phillips of the Philosophy Department, who had always freely told his students of his Marxism, admitted Party membership. Rader also lists Ralph Grundlach of Psychology and Melville Jacobs of Anthropology among those investigated, as well as two members of the Seattle Reperatory Theatre; see *False Witness,* pp. 48–53, 108–11. I am indebted to Kermit Vanderbilt, formerly of the University of Washington and now of San Diego State University, for bringing both the appointment of Heilman and the Canwell Committee to my attention; letter to author, October 23, 1975.

69. Rader, *False Witness,* p. 110; Gates, *First Century,* p. 205. In my interviews with Eby and Ethel, October 3 and 4, 1977, we discussed Parrington's effect on his students as well as his evident political attitudes, and though both affirmed his power in the classroom, neither characterized him as a ringleader or ideologue.

70. Alfred Kazin, *On Native Grounds: An Interpretation of Modern American Prose Literature* (1942; rpt. New York: Harcourt Brace Jovanovich Harvest Books, 1970), p. 158; George R. Cerveny, "A Study of Vernon Louis Parrington's Method of Literary Criticism: Its Origin, Its Content, Its Influence" (Ph.D. dissertation, New York University, 1938), p. 132 (for questionable evidence that Parrington produced radical students); Mary Norie Banks to the author, June 30, 1978. Other former Parrington students with whom I have corresponded—Egbert Oliver, Dorothy U'Renn, and Lawrence Zillman—have also indicated that it was in the realm of ideas that Parrington most influenced them, inspiring them in some cases to enter the teaching profession. One interesting source illustrating contemporary concern over faculty members is a letter from VLP to Lyle Spencer, President of the University, October 9, 1928: "Replying to your circular note sent out pursuant to the instructions of the Board of Regents in regard to the outside interests of members of the faculty, I desire to state that I have not now any outside interests that would bring criticism on the University, nor have I had any in the past. The only engagements outside of my regular University work are in the field or writing, chiefly in the form of book reviews and miscellaneous articles that are in every sense legitimate" (carbon copy in VLP Papers).

71. VLP to George B. Parker, October 26, 1928, VLP Papers.

72. Mrs. Frank Gilson Scrapbooks, Lyon County Historical Museum, Emporia, Kansas (he read his poem "The Sonnet" at the Twelfth Annual Meeting of the Kansas Academy of Language and Literature, April 1895); interview with E. H. Eby, October 3, 1977 (sometimes pansies are mentioned as the object of his attention); Carlton Brown to VLP, February 15, 1928, and VLP to Carlton Brown, February 21, 1928, VLP Papers.

73. VLP to Adwin Burlow Evans, March 22, 1928; VLP to James Ernst, January 12, 1929; VLP to Mark Van Doren, April 27, 1927; *MCAT,* 1:i, in VLP Papers.

74. Waldo Frank to VLP, April 13, 1928; VLP to Waldo Frank, April 19, 1928; cf. VLP to J. Holly Hanford, November 1, 1928: "One of the penalties of the academic life it its isolation from the world of civic and social endeavor. I am sometimes scandalized at my own aloofness. I seem to let the world go by with no very great concern, and I salve my conscience by thinking that I have my own job to do and that if I fail to conserve my time and energy I shan't get it done" (all letters in VLP Papers).

75. This passage follows the opening paragraph of a draft of "Economics and Criticism" (ca. 1917). Here Parrington invokes his assumed role as a historian and effectively echoes the epigraph of DSAL ("The business of history is to arouse an intelligent discontent, to foster a fruitful radicalism").

Bibliography

The Bibliography is divided in two parts. The first contains a checklist of Parrington's known published and unpublished writings. Unpublished items are located in the Papers of Vernon Louis Parrington. The entries are arranged chronologically to illustrate the development of Parrington's intellectual and creative interests. The second part is a selection of sources central to Parrington scholarship. It does not list most primary works of literary history, criticism, intellectual history, or treatments of persons such as William Morris and Charles Beard, who figure prominently in this study; the many genealogical and biographical sources consulted; or reviews of *Main Currents*, all of which appear in the relevant notes.

A Parrington Checklist

BOOKS, ARTICLES, OTHER WRITINGS

"God in History." Text of prize-winning oration delivered at the College of Emporia Oratorical Contest, January 20, 1891, and at the Kansas Inter-Collegiate Contest, Emporia, February 20, 1891, reprinted in *College Life* 3 (February 21, 1891): 1, 4, 5.

"At Harvard." *College Life* 5 (April 17, 1893): 1.

"The Position of English in College Curricula." *College Life* 6 (October 30, 1983): 1.

"Poetry and the Mission of Poetry." Holograph, 1895 Commencement Address, College of Emporia.

"Sonnet—A Dewdrop." *College Life* 7 (January 26, 1895): 1.

"On Novel Reading." *College Life* 8 (November 18, 1895): 73–74.

"Plain English vs. Pedantry." *College Life* 8 (January 13, 1896): 121–22.

"Knowing—Is What?" *College Life* 8 (June 3, 1896): 270.

"The Sunflower." *Topeka Capital*, August 30, 1896, p. 9, col. 5; *College Life* 9 (October 24, 1896): 1.

"Naughty Falling Star." *College Life* 9 (November 28, 1896): 11.

"Some Political Sketches." *College Life* 9 (April 17, 1897): 205, 212 ("Introduction"); *College Life* 9 (April 24, 1897): 228 ("The Business Ideal"); *College Life* 9 (May 1, 1897): 233 (Cont.); *College Life* 9 (May 15, 1897): 243–45 ("The University Ideal"); *College Life* 9 (May 25, 1897): 251–52 ("The Humanitarian Ideal").

"The Fight of the New and the Old." *College Life* 9 (March 27, 1897): 1.

"A Little Homily." *University Umpire* 1 (November 1, 1897): 6–7.

"Comradeship." *University Umpire* 1 (Christmas 1897): n.p.

"My Star." *University Umpire* 2 (December 1, 1898): 5.

Editorials (unsigned). *University Umpire* 2 (November 1, 1898): 4–6; 2 (November 15, 1898): 2–3; 2 (December 1, 1898): 4–5; 2 (December 15, 1898): 4–6; 2 (January 15, 1899): 4–5; 2 (February 1, 1899): 4–5; 2 (February 15, 1899): 4; 2 (March 15, 1899): 4–5; 2 (April 1, 1899): 4–5; 2 (April 15, 1899): 4; 2 (May 1, 1899): 4–5; 2 (May 15, 1899): 4–5; 2 (June 1, 1899): 4–5; 2 (June 15, 1899): 4; 3 (February 1, 1900): 4–5; 3 (April 2, 1900): 4–7; 3 (May 1, 1900): 2–3.

"The Princess Mini, an Egyptian Fragment." *University Umpire* 3 (March 1, 1900): 1.

"To the Canadian River." *University Umpire* 3 (March 15, 1900): 1.

"Jehovah, Father, Unto Thee." *University Umpire* 4 (October 1, 1900): 1.

"A Layman's View of Isaiah." Typescript, 1902.

"On the Lack of Privacy in American Village Homes." *House Beautiful* 13 (January 1903): 109–12.

"A Chat from Abroad." *University Umpire* 7 (April 1, 1904): 2–4.

"Stuart Forbes: Stoic." Unfinished novel, ca. 1903–5.

"Early Days." In *Mistletoe* (Norman: University of Oklahoma, 1905), pp. 82–85.

Handbook to English I. In collaboration with Wilbur R. Humphreys. Norman: University of Oklahoma Press, 1906.

"A Plain-Song and Other Poems." Selected poems, 1906.

On Recent Developments in American College Architecture. A report with drawings submitted to the Regents of the University of Oklahoma. Norman: University of Oklahoma Press, 1908.

"An Ode Dedicated to the Alaska-Yukon-Pacific Exposition, Seattle 1909." Typescript, 1909.

"Without the Gates," "Behold! I Have Lived," and "De Profundis." Three poems contributed to *Some Emporia Verse.* Edited by J. H. Powers, Emporia: Gazette Press, 1910.

"The Democratic Spirit in American Letters." Typescript, ca. 1916.

"The Puritan Divines, 1620–1720." In *The Cambridge History of American Literature,* Vol. 1, pp. 31–56. Edited by William Trent, John Erskine, Stuart P. Sherman, and Carl Van Doren. New York: G. P. Putnam's Sons, 1917.

"The Incomparable Mr. Cabell." *Pacific Review* 2 (December 1921): 353–66.

"Washington—The Far Northwest." Typescript, ca. 1922. (Rejected by Ernest Gruening for inclusion in *These United States: A Symposium,* 1922–23.)

"The Democratic Spirit in Early American Letters." Typescript, 1923.

"Albert Heald Van Vleet as I Knew Him." *University of Oklahoma Bulletin,* n.s. no. 328 (March 1, 1926): 20–22.

Ed. and Introduction. *The Connecticut Wits.* New York: Harcourt Brace, 1926.

Main Currents in American Thought. Vol. 1: *The Colonial Mind, 1620–1800;* Vol. 2: *The Romantic Revolution in America, 1800–1860.* New York: Harcourt, Brace, 1927.

Sinclair Lewis: Our Own Diogenes. Seattle: University of Washington Bookstore, 1927.

"The Development of Realism." In *The Reinterpretation of American Literature: Some Contributions Toward the Understanding of Its Historical Development,* pp. 139–59. Edited by Norman Foerster. New York: Harcourt, Brace, 1928.

Encyclopaedia Britannica, 14th ed. (1929). S.v. "American Literature." Seventeenth-, eighteenth-, and nineteenth-century portions of the article.

Encyclopaedia Brittanica, 14th ed. S.v. "Hawthorne, Nathaniel."

Introduction to *Giants in the Earth,* by O. E. Rölvaag. New York: Harper & Brothers, 1929.

Main Currents in American Thought. Vol. 3: *The Beginnings of Critical Realism in America, 1860–1920.* Completed to 1900 only. New York: Harcourt, Brace, 1930.

Encyclopedia of the Social Sciences, New York: Macmillan and Co., 1930–35. S.v. "Brook Farm."

Introduction to *Growth and Decadence of Constitutional Government,* by J. Allen Smith. New York: Henry Holt, 1930.

"Apologia Pro Vita Mea." Reprinted in Joseph B. Harrison, *Vernon Louis Parrington: American Scholar* (Seattle: University of Washington Book Store, 1929). Also reprinted in Alexander P. Cappon, "Parrington: A Liberal of the Northwest," *The New Humanist* 5 (January–February 1932): 8–9.

"Vernon Parrington's View: Economics and Criticism." Edited by Vernon L. Parrington, Jr. *Pacific Northwest Quarterly* 44 (July 1953): 97–105.

"William Allen White and the Kansas Idea." Typescript, n.d.

REVIEWS

The Nation

Review of *Philosophical Opinion in America,* by George Santayana. 109 (November 8, 1919): 614. (Unsigned.)

Review of *The Unsolved Riddle of Social Justice,* by Stephen Leacock. 110 (June 5, 1920): 772–73. (Unsigned.)

Review of *Socialism and Civilization,* by Boris Brasol. 110 (June 26, 1920): 860. (Unsigned.)

Review of *Economic Democracy,* by C. H. Douglas. 111 (July 3, 1920): 19. (Signed with the initial "P.")

Review of *The Worker and His Work,* by Stella S. Centre. 111 (July 10, 1920): 50–51. (Unsigned.)

Review of *The Limits of Socialism,* by O. Fred Boucke. 111 (September 11, 1920): 304. (Unsigned.)

Review of *The Unfinished Programme of Democracy,* by Richard Roberts. 111 (September 18, 1920): 330. (Unsigned.)

Review of *An Introduction to Social Ethics,* by J. M. Mecklin. 111 (October 6, 1920): 381. (Unsigned.)

"For Certain Complacent Persons." Review of *American Political Ideas, 1865–1917,* by Charles E. Merriam. 112 (March 2, 1921): 342–43.

"What Every Freshman Should Know." Review of *Human Traits and Their Social Significance,* by Irwin Edman. 112 (April 13, 1921): 558–59.

Review of *Organized Self-Government,* by Edgar Dawson. 112 (June 1, 1921): 796. (Unsigned.)

"The Mather-Baiters Baited." Review of *Increase Mather: Foremost American Puritan,* by Kenneth B. Murdock. 122 (21 April 1926): 453–54.

"Our Puritan Artist." Review of *Hawthorne: A Study in Solitude,* by Herbert Gorman. 125 (November 2, 1927): 482–83.

"The Diary of Puritan Boston." Review of *Samuel Sewall's Diary,* ed. Mark Van Doren. 126 (January 4, 1928): 22.

"Old Fences and New Surveys." Review of *America and French Culture: 1750–1848,* by Howard Mumford Jones. 126 (April 18, 1928): 454, 456.

"At the Clinic." Review of *Whither Mankind,* ed. Charles A. Beard. 127 (December 5, 1928): 621–22.

"A Note on the Journey to the Land of Eden." Review of *Nick of the Woods,* by Robert Montgomery Bird, and *A Journey to the Land of Eden,* by William Byrd. 128 (January 9, 1929): 50–51.

"A Puritan Priest." Review of *Cotton Mather: Keeper of the Puritan Conscience,* by Ralph and Louise Boas. 128 (January 30, 1929): 137–38.

Pacific Review

"Some Farmer-Labor Books." Review of *The Nonpartisan League* by Herbert Gaston, *The Story of the Nonpartisan League* by Charles Edward Russell, *A Short History of the Labor Movement* by Mary R. Beard, *Labor's Challenge to the Social Order* by John Graham Brooks, and *Labor and the Employer* by Samuel Gompers. 1 (December 1920): 434–37.

Review of *Main Street,* by Sinclair Lewis. 1 (March 1921): 607–10.

"Our Literary Aristocrat." Review of *The Age of Innocence,* by Edith Wharton. 2 (June 1921): 157–60.

"Even Mr. Mencken Likes It." Review of *The American Novel,* by Carl Van Doren. 2 (December 1921): 516–18.

Brief review of *The Line of Love* and *Chivalry,* by James Branch Cabell. 2 (December 1921): 533–34. (Unsigned.)

"Labor and the Social Transformation." Review of *The Labor Movement,* by Frank Tannenbaum. 2 (March 1922): 694–95.

New York Herald-Tribune Books

"Roadbuilders." Review of *The History of Socialist Thought,* by Harry W. Laidler. July 10, 1927, p. 2.

"Sight-Seeing American History." Review of *The Pageant of America,* Vols. 8 and 11, gen. ed. Ralph H. Gabriel. November 13, 1927, pp. 1–2.

"The Pageant of America." Review of *The Pageant of America,* Vols. 5, 12, and 13, gen. ed. Ralph H. Gabriel. November 20, 1927, p. 2.

"Revolution and Adam Smith," Review of *The Spirit of '76 and Other Essays,* by Carl Becker, J. M. Clark, and William E. Dodd. December 4, 1927, p. 41.

"The Culture Americans Have Created." Review of Vols. 2, 3, 6, and 8 of *A History of American Life,* by Dixon Ryan Fox and Arthur M. Schlesinger. January 29, 1928, pp. 1–2.

"Growing America." Review of *The Pageant of America*, Vols. 4 and 6, gen. ed. Ralph H. Gabriel. September 9, 1928, p. 20.
"The American Pageant Again." Review of *The Pageant of America*, Vols. 7, 9, and 10, gen. ed. Ralph H. Gabriel. January 20, 1929, pp. 3–4.

Miscellaneous Reviews—Various Sources

Review of *The Christian*, by Hall Caine. *College Life* 10 (October 30, 1897): 1–2.
Review of *The Trumpets of Jubilee*, by Constance Rourke. *Seattle Post-Intelligencer*, June 19, 1927.
"An American Schoolmaster." Review of *The Father of Little Women*, by Honoré Willsie Morrow. *Saturday Review of Literature* 4 (January 14, 1928): 519.
"The Last of the Elizabethans in Virginia." Review of *John Smith* by John Gould Fletcher. *The Book League Monthly* 2 (January 1929): 275–77.
"A Frontier Lincoln." Review of *Life of Lincoln*, by A. J. Beveridge. *American Literature* 1 (March 1929): 101–3.
Review of *The History of British Civilization*, by Esmé Wingfield-Stratford. *Bookman* 69 (April 1929): 217–18.
Review of *The Rediscovery of America*, by Waldo Frank. *Bookman* 69 (June 1929): 441–42.
Review of Kenneth B. Murdock, ed., *A Leaf of Grass from Shady Hill* by Charles Eliot Norton; Kenneth B. Murdock, ed., *Handkerchiefs from Paul*, an anthology of Puritan poetry; and Stanley T. Williams, ed., *Letters from Sunnyside and Spain* by Washington Irving. *Modern Language Notes* 44 (June 1929): 408–10.

Selected Sources on Main Currents

Manuscript and Other Collections

E. Harold Eby Papers. University Archives and Records Center, University of Washington Libraries, Seattle, Washington.
Northwest Collection. Suzzallo Library, University of Washington, Seattle, Washington.
The Papers of Vernon Louis Parrington. In the possession of Stevens Parrington Tucker and the Parrington Family, Pacific Grove, California.
President's Office Records, English Department File, 1910–30. University Archives and Records Center, University of Washington Libraries, Seattle, Washington.
The Way College of Emporia Library. Emporia, Kansas.
University of Oklahoma Archives. Norman, Oklahoma.
Western History Collections. University of Oklahoma Library, Norman, Oklahoma.

Unpublished Works

Cerveny, George R. "A Study of Vernon Louis Parrington's Method of Literary Criticism: Its Origin, Its Content, Its Influence." Ph.D. dissertation, New York University, 1938.

Colwell, James L. "Vernon Louis Parrington." American Studies Ph.D. seminar paper, Yale University, 1958.

Hadsell, S. R. "Parrington in Oklahoma." Typescript, n.d. Northwest History Collections, University of Oklahoma Library.

Hall, H. Lark. "Vernon Louis Parrington: The Genesis and Design of *Main Currents in American Thought.*" Ph.D. dissertation, Case Western Reserve University, 1979.

McClintock, Thomas C. "J. Allen Smith and the Progressive Movement: A Study in Intellectual History." Ph.D. dissertation, University of Washington, 1959.

Merikangas, Robert J. "Vernon L. Parrington's Method of Intellectual History." Ph.D. dissertation, Catholic University of America, 1966.

Pitts, Dennis R. "The Miracle: History of the College of Emporia." Unpublished Ms., 1973. The Way College of Emporia Library.

Pressly, Thomas J. "Vernon L. Parrington and the History of American Literature." Ms., 1946 Prize Essay. Widener Library, Harvard University.

Wirth, Elizabeth. "The Political Philosophy of Vernon Louis Parrington." M.A. thesis, University of Chicago, 1946.

COMMENTARY AND CRITICISM

Bellis, Peter. "Vernon L. Parrington." In *Modern American Critics, 1920–1955,* edited by Gregory S. Jay, pp. 210–20. *Dictionary of Literary Biography.* Vol. 63. Detroit: Gale Research Press, 1988.

Burch, Esther E. "The Sources of New England Democracy: A Controversial Statement in Parrington's *Main Currents in American Thought.*" *American Literature* 1 (May 1929): 115–30.

Caughey, John W. "Historians' Choice: Results of a Poll on Recently Published History and Biography." *Mississippi Valley Historical Review* 39 (September 1952): 289–302.

Colwell, James L. "The Populist Image of Vernon Louis Parrington." *Mississippi Valley Historical Review* 49 (June 1962): 52–66.

Commager, Henry Steele. *The American Mind: An Interpretation of American Thought and Character Since the 1880s.* New Haven: Yale University Press, 1950.

Ekirch, Arthur A., Jr. *The Decline of American Liberalism.* New York: Longmans, Green, 1955.

———. "Parrington and the Decline of American Liberalism." *American Quarterly* 3 (Winter 1951): 295–308.

Filler, Louis. "Parrington and Carlyle: Cross-Currents in History and Belles-Lettres." *Antioch Review* 12 (Summer 1952): 203–16.

Gabriel, Ralph H. "Vernon Louis Parrington." In *Pastmasters: Some Essays on American Historians,* pp. 142–66. Edited by Marcus Cunliffe and Robin W. Winks. New York: Harper & Row, 1969.

Gates, Charles M. *The First Century at the University of Washington, 1861–1961.* Seattle: University of Washington Press, 1961.

Gittinger, Roy. *The University of Oklahoma, 1892–1942.* Norman: University of Oklahoma Press, 1942.

Goldman, Eric R. "J. Allen Smith: The Reformer and His Dilemma." *Pacific Northwest Quarterly* 35 (July 1944): 195–213.

————. *Rendezvous With Destiny: A History of Modern American Reform*. New York: Knopf, 1953.

Hall, Lark. "V. L. Parrington's Oklahoma Years, 1897–1908: 'Few Highlights and Much Monotone'?" *Pacific Northwest Quarterly* 72 (January 1981): 20–28.

Handlin, David P. *The American Home: Architecture and Society, 1815–1915*. Boston: Little, Brown, 1979.

Harrison, Joseph B. *Vernon Louis Parrington: American Scholar*. Seattle: University of Washington Book Store, 1929.

Hicks, Granville. "The Critical Principles of V. L. Parrington." *Science and Society* 3 (Fall 1929): 443–60.

Higham, John. *History: Professional Scholarship in America*. New York: Harper & Row, 1965; Harper Torchbooks, 1973.

————. "The Rise of American Intellectual History." *American Historical Review* 56 (April 1951): 453–71.

————. *Writing American History: Essays on Modern Scholarship*. Indianapolis: Indiana University Press, 1970; Midland Books, 1972.

Hofstadter, Richard. "Parrington and the Jeffersonian Tradition." *Journal of the History of Ideas* 2 (October 1941): 391–400.

————. *The Progressive Historians: Turner, Beard, Parrington*. New York: Knopf, 1968; Vintage Books, 1970.

Howe, Mark A. DeWolfe, ed. *The Holmes-Laski Letters: The Correspondence of Mr. Justice Holmes and Harold J. Laski, 1916–1935*. 2 vols. Cambridge: Harvard University Press, 1953.

Jay, Gregory S. "Hegel and the Dialectics of American Literary Historiography: From Parrington to Trilling and Beyond." In Bernard Cowan and Joseph Kronick, eds., *Theorizing American Literature: Hegel, the Sign, and History*, pp. 83–122. Baton Rouge: Louisiana State University Press, 1991.

————. "Hegel and Trilling in America." *American Literary Scholarship* 3 (Fall 1989): 565–92.

Jones, Howard Mumford. *The Theory of American Literature*, 2d ed., 1948; rev. Ithaca: Cornell University Press, 1965.

Kazin, Alfred. *On Native Grounds: An Interpretation of Modern American Prose Literature*. 1942. Reprint. New York: Harcourt Brace Jovanovich Harvest Books, 1970.

Laski, Harold J. *The American Democracy: A Commentary and an Interpretation*. New York: Viking Press, 1948.

Miller, Perry. "Thomas Hooker and the Democracy of Connecticut." *New England Quarterly* 4 (1931): 663–712; rpt. *Errand Into the Wilderness* (Cambridge, Mass.: Belknap Press, 1956), 16–47.

Morris, Wesley. *Towards a New Historicism*. Princeton: Princeton University Press, 1972.

Noble, David W. *Historians Against History: The Frontier Thesis and the National Covenant in American Historical Writing Since 1830*. Minneapolis: University of Minnesota Press, 1965.

Peterson, Merrill D. "Parrington and American Liberalism." *Virginia Quarterly Review* 30 (Winter 1954): 35–49.

Reinitz, Richard. *Irony and Consciousness: American Historiography and Reinhold Niebuhr's Vision*. Lewisburg: Bucknell University Press, 1980.

———. "Vernon Louis Parrington as Historical Ironist." *Pacific Northwest Quarterly* 68 (July 1977): 113–19.

Reising, Russell J. "Reconstructing Parrington." *American Quarterly* 41 (March 1989): 155–64.

Ruland, Richard. *The Rediscovery of American Literature: Premises of Critical Taste, 1900–1940.* Cambridge, Mass.: Harvard University Press, 1967.

Sale, Roger. *Seattle, Past to Present.* Seattle: University of Washington Press, 1976.

Skotheim, Robert A. *American Intellectual Histories and Historians.* Princeton: Princeton University Press, 1966.

———. "Environmental Interpretations of Ideas in Beard, Parrington, Curti." *Pacific Historical Review* 33 (February 1964): 35–44.

Skotheim, Robert A., and Kermit Vanderbilt. "Vernon Louis Parrington: The Mind and Art of a Historian of Ideas." *Pacific Northwest Quarterly* 53 (July 1962): 100–113.

Smith, Bernard. "Parrington's *Main Currents in American Thought.*" In *Books That Changed Our Minds,* pp. 179–91. Edited by Malcolm Cowley and Bernard Smith. New York: Doubleday, Doran, 1939.

Thomas, John L. "The Uses of Catastrophism: Lewis Mumford, Vernon L. Parrington, Van Wyck Brooks, and the End of American Regionalism." *American Quarterly* 42 (June 1990): 223–51.

Trilling, Lionel. *The Liberal Imagination.* New York: Viking Press, 1950; Doubleday Anchor Books, 1953.

———. "Parrington, Mr. Smith, and Reality." *Partisan Review* 8 (January-February 1940): 24–40.

Utter, William T. "Vernon Louis Parrington." In *The Marcus W. Jernegan Essays in American Historiography,* pp. 394–408. Edited by William T. Hutchinson. Chicago: University of Chicago Press, 1937.

Vanderbilt, Kermit. *American Literature and the Academy: The Roots, Growth, and Maturity of a Profession.* Philadelphia: University of Pennsylvania Press, 1986.

Weimann, Robert. *Structure and Society in Literary History: Studies in the History and Theory of Historical Criticism.* Charlottesville: University Press of Virginia; expanded ed. Baltimore: Johns Hopkins University Press, 1984.

Winters, Yvor. *In Defense of Reason.* London: Routledge & Kegan Paul, 1960.

Wise, Gene. *American Historical Explanations: Some Strategies for Grounded Inquiry.* Homewood, Ill.: Dorsey Press, 1973; 2d ed. Minneapolis: University of Minnesota Press, 1980.

———. " 'Paradigm Dramas' in American Studies: A Cultural and Institutional History of the Movement." *American Quarterly* 31 (Bibliography Issue 1979): 293–337.

Index

V. L. Parrington

was composed in 10/12 Sabon
on a Xyvision System with Linotronic output
by BookMasters, Inc.;
printed by sheet-fed offset and
notch bound onto 88′ binder boards
in Holliston Roxite Vellum cloth,
wrapped with dustjackets printed in 2 colors
by Braun-Brumfield, Inc.;
designed by Diana Gordy;
and published by
THE KENT STATE UNIVERSITY PRESS
Kent, Ohio 44242